DATE DUE			
GAYLORD M-2			PRINTED IN U.S.A.

The Southern Tradition at Bay

RICHARD M. WEAVER

❧❧❧

THE

Southern Tradition

at Bay

A HISTORY
OF POSTBELLUM THOUGHT

❧❧❧

Edited by George Core and M. E. Bradford

ARLINGTON HOUSE   NEW ROCHELLE, N.Y.

Contents

Preface

Two of the most representative voices of the American South in the first two-thirds of this century are now silent. It is fitting that what might be taken as their respective valedictions should appear together in this volume. Richard Weaver died on April 3rd, 1963; Donald Davidson, the old friend who was once his teacher, outlived him by five years. Professor Davidson completed the Foreword to *The Southern Tradition At Bay* less than a year before his death. About the latter's identification with the homeland—the place of the hearth and the heart—there has never been any question. And, as Davidson suggests, the same subject will be settled so far as Weaver is concerned with the publication of this book.

Despite the fact that many of his admirers, both from within and without the region, have been unable to recognize what is an obvious truth, Richard Weaver of Weaverville, North Carolina, was, in all his works and days, first and last a Southerner. That the commitment was not one of sentiment alone is demonstrated in the pages which follow. Nor was that absolute commitment made in a vacuum. Few sons of the old Confederacy have known so well what this particular piety entails—what its personal cost or how fruitless its enactment might be. Almost no one has understood so clearly that he could in no way better serve that delicate balance of conflicting impulses we now call the nation than by *belonging* privily to and serving the singular interests of its least national region. Yet in the face of difficulty Weaver behaved thus—in his every gesture, public and private, with characteristic modesty, even humility. His long tenure with the foremost university in the Midwest—the University of Chicago—does not belie this Southernness. Richard Weaver perceived early where, for those of his profession and persuasion, the battle could be joined; and having finished the original version of *The Southern Tradition At Bay*, he "rode to the sound of the guns."

The career of this *rhetor*, literary critic, social philosopher, intellectual historian, and diagnostician of contemporary civilization follows the example he shrewdly described in "Agrarian-ism in Exile," an essay which concerns certain of his friends and teachers—especially John Crowe Ransom, to whom this book is dedicated. As Weaver observed time and again, the essential South has remained, even after one hundred years of bitter experience, still too satisfied with narrowly defensive strategies. Its problem is and ever has been locating and enlisting its natural allies by exposing the gnostic posture of its enemies and by discovering the non-Promethean character and roots of its own position. Recognizing the paralyzing (and near total) hegemony already achieved by positivists and Jacobins at most Southern schools and the inescapable handicaps which frustrate any Southern traditionalist reaching for a national audience from his own region, Weaver turned north once his apprentice-ship was over. He was keenly aware that for a Southern scholar to have genuine influence on the future of his native region—and through it, the nation—he must have a position above the Ohio or the Potomac, or in the far West. This was even more important in 1944 than it is today. Accordingly, Weaver's "flight" to the North was, as he said of the Agrarians, "a strategic with-drawal where the contest can be better carried on."

In Chicago this Southerner made his way, following the dis-cipline of rhetoric (in the old and true sense) while availing himself as moralist and metaphysician of the advantages afforded by isolation and distance. The vision he had both inherited and earned in the South—especially at Vanderbilt and Louisiana State University—he divested of its strictly fortuitous regional overtones in idiom and preoccupation. (This was evident in 1948 when *Ideas Have Consequences* was published.) And he also made the contacts and friends that opened to him oppor-tunities for striking a powerful blow in the cause of reason and order. For this he had exiled himself. All the while, as Donald Davidson has said, Weaver kept his original scholarly work close at hand—the project in which he first found and knew himself—and consequently the loyalties nearest his heart. It was Weaver's testimony, even in his last years (as "Up From Liberal-ism" implies), that his transregional and transnational reflections were prepared, in considerable measure, to earn this book and his other papers on Southern life and letters the kind of respect-ful hearing that they richly deserve. The publication of this book at this time confirms the wisdom of his strategy.

As Davidson has cogently argued, *The Southern Tradition At Bay* is a remarkably far-ranging study, and it illustrates the breadth and profundity of its author's thought while pointing towards the work that was to follow it. Richard Weaver was brilliant as both a synthetic and an analytic thinker, and his work is original in a way that is often astonishing. Moreover, he seldom repeated himself. This is shown by the fact that only four articles are derived in part from this book: "The Older Religiousness in the South," "Scholars or Gentlemen?," "Albert Taylor Bledsoe," and "Southern Chivalry and Total War." In "The South and the Revolution of Nihilism" (1944), Weaver writes of the deep and instinctive distrust by the South of modern fascist regimes despite the surface similarities between the Southern mythology and the myth of the Third Reich; and this essay may be considered an extension of his remarks on the same subject in the epilogue to *The Southern Tradition At Bay*. During the twenty years of his career in Chicago, Weaver often wrote about the South, and "Agrarianism in Exile," "Aspects of the Southern Philosophy," "The South and the American Union," and "The Southern Phoenix" are among his finest essays. It is interesting too that at the time of his death Weaver was working on what he called, with typical understatement, "a somewhat original study of American literature and culture." This study is a comparison of the New England and Southern cultures, through juxtaposition of representative figures; the only published chapter is "Two Types of American Individualism," a contrast of Thoreau and John Randolph. Work in progress includes similar contrasts: "Two Diarists" (William Byrd and Cotton Mather) and "Two Orators" (Webster and Hayne) as well as a detailed analysis of *Uncle Tom's Cabin*. Other unfinished papers are devoted to Hawthorne and Puritanism, Puritanism and determinism, Brooks Adams and Henry Adams, and Agrarianism. Still another essay concerns the American as a new man—a regenerate being—and the way this conception of man has shaped American culture. Therefore, one can see that shortly before his death Richard Weaver was coming full circle in his thinking—that he had turned away from his more philosophical and speculative thought to a consideration of American life that would have culminated in a study closely akin to *The Southern Tradition At Bay*. But we must be content with the single volume.

It remains a curious phenomenon that Weaver's most ambitious (and in some ways his best) book should remain so long unpublished, and a further word of explanation is therefore in order. Davidson reports something of the manuscript's fortune while Weaver lived. Since his death the record has been much complicated. Before coming into the hands of the present editors, the manuscript was the occasion of quiet agitation among those who knew of its existence. Use of its dissertation version had become commonplace by 1960 among students of the Southern mind; and many of them urged Weaver (and later his family) to have the manuscript published, while others argued against its publication. Some of those anxious about the future of the document after Weaver's death did not know of its whereabouts, and others labored under the false impression that it was in the process of publication. The interest cut across ideological and disciplinary lines. For instance, Clement Eaton, a distinguished historian who needs no introduction, wrote an essay entitled "The 'Disappearing' South" which in large part was devoted to a critical summary of *The Southern Tradition At Bay* that is wholly laudatory. This was a deliberate and successful effort to stimulate even greater curiosity about the manuscript. Similar efforts came from other quarters.

Weaver's literary executor, Kendall Beaton, a practical and compassionate man who thoroughly understood his brother-in-law, took counsel at all hands, surveyed the author's private papers, recollected his words, deliberated, and wisely decided to issue exactly what had been left in his keeping. Unfortunately he lived only to place the manuscript with the publisher and to receive the Davidson Foreword which he had commissioned. The editors were then given the trust and privilege of seeing both documents into print by Mrs. Polly Weaver Beaton. Her extraordinary kindness and patient help they acknowledge with deep gratitude.

The quotations in *The Southern Tradition at Bay* have been checked for accuracy, and the final text has been carefully collated with the original manuscript. The editors have followed the scriptural injunction: nothing has been added or taken away.

	George Core	*M. E. Bradford*
July, 1968	UNIVERSITY OF GEORGIA	UNIVERSITY OF DALLAS

The Vision of Richard Weaver

From every book written by the late Richard Weaver surges a tide of intellectual force that critics, even the friendliest, have had difficulty in describing. No wonder—the force is light. And it is never easy to describe light, especially when it shines in times and places where it is disturbing and where darkness, or only a shadowed light, is preferred. To an unaccustomed reader Weaver's light may at first seem only exploratory and instructive. He may be tempted to think that it is merely picking out a devious way among heaps of ancient rubbish. But that reader may not realize how deeply his own thought is being engaged —how he is being persuaded to look and look again at what he may have taken for granted or ignored or assumed, in some vain way, that he understood. Presently he is "seeing" (in the sense of understanding or knowing) as never before. He may also feel that he is in the company of a vision that is high and generous and very brave, and that this vision—the vision of Richard Weaver—is making irresistible claims upon his attention, indeed upon his life. So was it with the poet Rilke when he gazed upon the mutilated "Archaic Torso" of Apollo in the Louvre:

. . . da ist keine Stelle
die dich nicht sieht. Du musst dein Leben . . . ändern.
[. . . here is no place
That does not see you. You must change your life.]

The present book, the work of Weaver at age thirty-three, is in scope and theme very far-reaching, as its title and subtitle suggest. But *The Southern Tradition at Bay,* covering both the Reconstruction and the New South through an exploration of persons and ideas rather than events, is in the end about a good deal more than the South or the Southern tradition or the hundred or more writers, speakers, generals, politicians, nurses, diarists whom Weaver examines in his study of the half-century after Appomattox. As in indirect fire by artillery, his "aiming point" is indeed the South, but the "target," just over the hump, is the modern regime, both North and South, that has emerged in the mid-twentieth century and brought the Republic of the United States of America into its time of troubles. It is a book whose substance fills out the summary statements of the remarkable last paragraph of an article, "Aspects of the Southern Philosophy," that Weaver wrote for the *Hopkins Review* in the summer of 1952:

> If the world continues its present drift toward tension and violence, it is probable that the characteristic Southern qualities will command an increasing premium. While this country was amassing its great wealth, those qualities were in comparative eclipse; but virtues needed to amass wealth are not the virtues needed to defend it. . . . Belief in tragedy is essentially un-American; it is in fact one of the heresies against Americanism; but in the world as a whole this heresy is more widely received than the dogma and is more regularly taught by experience. Just as certainly as the United States grows older, it will have to find accommodation for this ineluctable notion; it is even now embarked upon policies with tremendous possibilities if not promises of tragedy. If we are in for a time of darkness and trouble, the Southern philosophy, because it is not based upon optimism, will have better power to console than the national dogmas.
>
> It will do good to heart and head
> When your soul is in my soul's stead.[1]

"A rhetor doing the work of a philosopher, he tackled problems for which he was not equipped," said his good friend and admirer, Eliseo Vivas, in reviewing Weaver's posthumous *Visions of Order*. "But," Vivas adds, "he nearly always returned from his adventures with something worthwhile to show for them." [2] Elsewhere Vivas describes Weaver as "an intellectually bold man, capable of audacity behind or above the deliberate reflective thinker." [3] I do not think Weaver would have fretted against these honest and realistic observations.

But no philosopher, no philosophical-minded historian even, had tackled his subject. To be sure, there was the psychologist

Dollard's appallingly naive *Caste and Class in a Southern Town,* and W. J. Cash's piece of Menckenesque journalism, *The Mind of the South,* and Howard Odum's laboriously statistical, facing-many-ways *Southern Regions,* and Vann Woodward's exclusively political-economic historical *Origins of the New South, 1877-1913* (which discreetly passed over Reconstruction), and other books of these types. None filled the gap that Weaver saw.

If Weaver had waited to add, to his equipment as a teacher of literature and rhetoric, the perfected equipment of a philosopher, of a historian, a sociologist, a psychologist, and economist, a jurist, a journalist, and so on, he would never have written the present book or any of the books we have from his hand. *Time would not have waited on him.* If challenged as to his competence, he might have had to say that the teaching of literature had already required him to be a "generalist" rather than a "specialist." He did not care to escape the battle by enlisting in philology. The times needed men who could and would think as well as annotate. There were large subjects that could not be handled as pure literature, pure philosophy, pure history, or by any symposium of specialists in those and other fields. *And the times would not wait!* Then Richard Weaver, after long tribulation of heart and mind, saw a task must be undertaken that called for one hand. And the hand might be his. And in the darkness of the modern night he said like Samuel of old, "Lord, here I am . . . Thy servant heareth."

Such was the nature of Richard Weaver's audacity.

Another word for it might be *devotion,* taken in its oldest, most literal sense. Surely Richard Weaver made a vow—whether or not in a formal religious way, a vow that could not have been a merely secular resolve. It came from a certain experience not altogether different from that of Bunyan's Pilgrim when he decided to turn his face away from the City of Destruction. To his dying day Richard Weaver would study, as he long had studied, to better his imperfect equipment. But the experience in part made up for the inevitable lack of the special training for which his life allowed no time. It was the experience of a change of heart, of mind, of life. With it came a period of intense study and thought—above all, of self-searching. One immediate result was the present book.

In its first form it was the dissertation that he presented for the degree of Doctor of Philosophy in English, at Louisiana

State University, in 1943. His "Major Professor and Chairman of the Examining Committee" was Cleanth Brooks, not long back from Oxford, Professor of English and, with Robert Penn Warren, an editor of *The Southern Review*. In his acknowledgements, Weaver expresses his thanks to John Crowe Ransom and to Arlin Turner, as well as to Brooks and Warren.[4]

In his revision of his manuscript for publication Weaver substituted the present title for his cumbrous original one—*The Confederate South, 1865-1910: A Study in the Survival of a Mind and a Culture*. He added an introduction and an epilogue, but otherwise did little more than tighten the prose where he found it loose. It was already a book to begin with—a work in a genuinely literary and historical vein, though it had had to conform to the regular graduate school pattern. He offered it for publication. It was rejected. He laid it aside. One chapter, "The Older Religiousness in the South," appeared in a periodical—his first published article. By this time Weaver was in Northern surroundings, a teacher of English in the College of the University of Chicago, among new friends, busy on a new project. In 1948 it appeared, from the University of Chicago Press, his first published book, *Ideas Have Consequences*. The other one, unpublished, he obviously did not forget. It was found among his papers after his death in 1963. That Weaver kept it for twenty years, all the while virtually ready for the printer, suggests that he may have intended, at some opportune moment, to resurrect it for publication.

Well might he cherish it and wish to have it close at hand. For it marks the turning point of his career—the moment when he renounced the facile radicalism of the Roosevelt period for something more truly radical—the kind of "radicalism" that the current term "conservative" does not always suggest. John Crowe Ransom, commenting on *Ideas Have Consequences*, spoke of Weaver's radical-conservatism as "thoroughgoing, and philosophically articulate." *The Southern Tradition at Bay* can be considered a groundwork for *Ideas Have Consequences* and much of Weaver's subsequent work. For though the South-North issue does not arise in *Ideas Have Consequences*, and even the words "South" and "North" hardly appear, the book could well be entitled "The Northern Tradition at Bay" or "The Tradition of Western Civilization at Bay." For to "Northern" or "American" society in general Weaver puts the same fundamental questions and applies the same searching tests that he had used for the defeated but not reconciled South of 1865 to 1910. In *Ideas Have Consequences* and in later books and essays Weaver gives a broader development of views that had a preliminary exposition and illustration in *The Southern Tradition at Bay*. The chapters entitled "Distinction and Hierarchy" and "Piety and Justice," for example, in *Ideas Have Consequences*, owe much to the analysis that Weaver makes in his earlier work of postbellum Southern society under such headings as "The Code of Chivalry," "The Attack upon Secular Democracy," "The Christian Warrior," "The Class System." In his posthumous book, *Visions of Order* (1964), the remarkable chapters on "Status and Function," "The Attack upon Memory," and "A Dialectic on Total War," bring into a broad, contemporary setting problems that he had already treated briefly in his survey of the South's long effort, during the sequel of Appomattox, to declare what it had been fighting for and what it had been fighting against—what it still was reluctant to accept as right and proper, however materially rewarding or pleasantly idealistic the victor's program might be.

To understand fully the unique quality of Weaver's first book and the momentum that it imparted to his later enterprises, one must go back to the experience that came to him at the crossing of the ways. The story is told by Weaver himself in his autobiographical essay that he called "Up from Liberalism," first published in *Modern Age* (Winter, 1958-1959).[5] Nowhere in that essay, however, does he mention the unpublished manuscript that was at the heart of his experience and that lay close at hand.

Weaver was born in North Carolina, but brought up in Lexington, in the fine "bluegrass" country of Kentucky, and he got his undergraduate education at the University of Kentucky. His professors, he relates, "were mostly earnest souls from the Middle Western universities, and many of them . . . were, without knowing it, social democrats. . . . I had no defenses whatever against their doctrines." By his junior year Weaver was a young socialist in thought. Socialism had for him, he said, "an intellectual attraction." In 1932, after his graduation, he formally joined the American Socialist Party. "My disillusionment with the Left," he writes, "began with this first practical step." The academic people of the group were wildly, comically innocent of politics. Others were nondescripts, eccentrics. Most were "hopelessly confused about the nature and purpose of socialism." Despite the boredom he felt and his rising doubt about socialism, Weaver kept his membership for two years and even served as secretary of the "local."

His discontent with socialism was greatly increased by the years that he spent in graduate work at Vanderbilt University, where he studied under John Crowe Ransom and came in touch with the lively intellectual and literary activity that he found in the company of the "Agrarians." [6] Weaver was particularly taken with the idea that "an unorthodox defense of orthodoxy" was feasible. Ransom, indeed, had demonstrated as much by the defense of religion against science and modernism that he developed in his *God Without Thunder*. Weaver was suddenly troubled by his realization that "many traditional positions in our world had suffered not so much because of inherent defect as because of the stupidity, ineptness, and intellectual sloth of those who . . . are presumed to have their defense in charge."

When Weaver left Vanderbilt he had still not decided which road to take. At this stage, when he had not met the "mass man" face to face or seen the actual workings of socialism and centralism, he did not find it easy to reverse his course, although he felt the strong pull upon him of "the Agrarian ideal." What Weaver calls "my conversion to the poetic and ethical vision of life" did not come until he had taught for some time in Texas in close contact with "its sterile opposite," the rampant and complacent Philistinism that he met around him. One afternoon when he was driving across the prairies of Texas to begin his third year of teaching, the moment came, abruptly: "It came to me like a revelation that I did not *have* to go back to this job, which had become distasteful, and that I did not *have* to go on professing the clichés of liberalism, which were becoming meaningless to me . . . It is a great experience to wake up . . . to the fact that one does have a free will, and that giving up the worship of false idols is quite a practicable procedure." At the end of the year he gave up his Texas job "and went off to start my education over at the age of thirty."

Officially, he recommenced his education at the Graduate

School of the Louisiana State University, and in the summers at the Sorbonne, Harvard, and University of Virginia. Unofficially, he had already begun it by giving himself a course in extensive reading in the history of the American Civil War, "preferring first-hand accounts by those who had actually borne the brunt of it as soldiers and civilians." It was a kind of education that "had been almost entirely omitted from my program." Among other things, he could perhaps learn from it the point at which reason tells men that "reason is of no more avail." They must resort to force. The Civil War, which had "an elaborate ideology on both sides," was a fruitful field for this kind of inquiry. He soon discovered that it had other values —for example, the value of studying "a lost cause":

> I cannot think [writes Weaver] of a better way to counteract the stultifying "Whig" theory of history, with its bland assumption that every cause which has won deserved to win, a kind of pragmatic debasement of the older providential theory. The study and appreciation of a lost cause have some effect of turning history into philosophy. In sufficient number of cases to make us humble, we discover good points in the cause which time has erased, just as one often learns more from the slain hero of a tragedy than from some brassy Fortinbras who comes in at the end to announce the victory and proclaim the future disposition of affairs.

With such thoughts stirring his mind, Weaver spent three years, he says, in reading "the history and literature of the Civil War, with special attention to that of the losing side." He could not claim to have grasped the whole mystery of "the encompassing passion which held them [the Southern people, 1861-1865, and later] together. But . . . I came to recognize myself in the past." This recognition was something more definite than the so-called "search for identity" on which many frustrated moderns are said to be engaged. Weaver did not need to ask: "Who am I?" He knew that. But it braced him in that self-knowledge and enabled him more consciously to relate himself to those all-too-human Southerners—and unquestionably many Northerners too—whose history and memoirs he had been studying. He knew now what path to take. Instead of the tortured, egocentric question "Who am I?" he could proceed to the larger, more philosophical questions "Who are we?" and "What are we doing?" and "What ought we to do?" in the books and articles that soon followed this first-written but last-printed of his works. In somewhat the same way Henry Adams fled the contemporary American scene to study the meaning of Chartres Cathedral and the Virgin. Weaver, not fleeing, but dwelling in the very center of the modern American tumult at Chicago, thought that a devoted and rigorous study of some past experience of disaster—the fall of Rome, the overthrow of Napoleon, the destruction of the Old South—"will compel any honest seeker to see that the lines of social and political force are far more secret than the modern world has any mind to recognize, and that if it does not lead him to some kind of faith, it will lead him away from the easy constructions of those who do not wish to understand, beyond grasping what can be seized for a practical purpose."

That is it! Richard Weaver's book leads away from "easy constructions" and toward faith. It is not about the *events* of Civil War—Reconstruction, and the long aftermath of Populism, farm and labor trouble, the new industrialism. "Things reveal themselves passing away," Weaver writes, quoting Yeats. He is intent to discover what the postbellum Southerners, defeated, all but ruined, yet not really convinced, may consciously or unconsciously reveal about the great American experiment, from Jamestown and Plymouth to date. Events are "the text of a lesson, but not the lesson itself." The lesson must go beyond "the waywardness of events."

> In this research, therefore [he writes], I have attempted to find those things in the struggle of the South which speak for something more than a particular people in a special situation. The result, it may be allowed, is not pure history, but a picture of values and sentiments coping with the forces of a revolutionary age, and though failing, hardly expiring.

The last four words—*though failing, hardly expiring*—declare the center of Richard Weaver's historical and philosophical interest in the amazingly varied material that he explores. What deep-lying beliefs and principles enabled the South so long to be "conspicuous for its resistance to the spiritual disintegration of the modern world?" From what sources of strength did the South derive its immunity to the subversive romanticism of Rousseau and the French Revolution and so hold out to become, as Weaver expresses it, *"the last non-materialist civilization in the Western world"?*

It is a subject that in one way or another has recently attracted other serious writers. I believe it is particularly useful to think of Weaver's book in comparison with William R. Taylor's *Cavalier and Yankee: The Old South and American National Character* (1961), a book that has drawn praise from Edmund Wilson and Vann Woodward. Mr. Taylor's book also started its career as a doctoral dissertation, but at a Northern institution—Harvard. For his academic guides and directors Mr. Taylor had Oscar Handlin, Kenneth Murdock, and the late Perry Miller. Furthermore, he says, "A stimulating discussion of Southern thought in Louis Hartz's seminar in the Fall of 1951 probably determined me to write about the South." Although Mr. Taylor's Ph.D. degree was in history (and he is now a Professor of History), the sources on which he focuses are, as he says, "chiefly literary."

> There are many things [writes Mr. Taylor] about the history of an era that cannot be learned from literature, but historians, it seems to me, have been too timid about searching out the things that can. Stories and novels, even bad and unskillful ones, possess an element of fantasy which is sometimes very revealing. . . .

Now Mr. Taylor, in his highly interesting and often instructive book, seems to take the position that the sectional differences between North and South, so far as they represent divergent ideas, are pretty much "historical rationalization." His book aims to show how the idea of two different "civilizations" developed in the first half of the nineteenth century: "what social problems produced the need for this kind of historical rationalization, what kind of men and women contributed to its growth and dissemination—what sort of mentality, in other words, created this legendary past and this fictional sociology, and what sort of needs it satisfied."

Mr. Taylor then dwells on a relatively few figures, whom he

places in a historical context and subjects to extensive critical
analysis—mainly William Wirt's biography of Patrick Henry;
Cooper's *The Spy;* the writings of Sarah Josepha Hale, the
Northern "Lady Editor" of *Godey's Lady's Book,* especially her
didactic novel, *Norwood,* which is largely about the South; Daniel Hundley's *The Valley of the Shenandoah;* John Pendleton
Kennedy's *Swallow Barn* and *Horseshoe Robinson;* the novels
of William A. Caruthers; the writings of James Kirke Paulding
("The Northern Man of Southern Principles"); and the writings, especially the seven Revolutionary War novels, of William
Gilmore Simms.

Many other figures are touched in passing, but Mr. Taylor's
large and highly speculative thesis rests upon this quite narrow
base. And though it is attractively presented, the upshot of his
study is that "myth" and "legend" have dominated over reality;
the idea of "Southern nationality," based on the notion that
"Southerners and Northerners were distinct and different peoples" was just "popular supposition," which was exploited by
fiction writers and used by politicians. The line drawn by the
English astronomers Mason and Dixon to settle a boundary dispute "possessed no geographical definition. It was a psychological, not a physical division, which often cut like a cleaver through
the mentality of individual men and women everywhere in the
country." With the collapse of the Confederacy "the Old South
as a concrete entity passed beyond history and into legend."
Accordingly, in Mr. Taylor's view there is no "lesson" to draw.
But he admits that the vitality of the "legend" continues "to
startle those unfamiliar with our culture, with our collective
anxieties about the kind of civilization we have created, and
with our reservations concerning the kind of social conformity
which, it appears, it has been our destiny to exemplify before
the world."

Richard Weaver's book, surveying the half-century after Appomattox, but not excluding the conditioning features of the
half-century or more that preceded it, presents evidence for a
philosophical, not merely a *psychological,* division. He, too, deals
with fiction writers and their "myths," all the way from Cooke's
highly romantic *Surry of Eagle's-Nest* (1866) to Thomas Nelson
Page, Walter Hines Page, flamboyant Thomas Dixon, and
"realist" Ellen Glasgow of the later Southern generation; and

like Taylor he believes that the works of fiction should be viewed in the context of intellectual history. But Weaver's treatment of Southern fiction is only a part—and not the major part—of his broad-based study. Where Taylor finds "myth" Weaver finds "the older religiousness" and with it a tradition of "piety" that pervades everyday manners, in fact the entire secular life, and deeply affects the conduct of war itself. He is no sentimentalist. His eyes are open to Southern failings, and in castigation of Southern sins he is a Jeremiah. The numerous works that Weaver examines are, in fact, a long procession of witnesses that testify, each after his own fashion, to the reality beneath and within the "myth" or "legend" that Mr. Taylor hypostasizes. Weaver deals, for example, in "The Case at Law," with the writings of that hard-headed, stubborn advocate, Albert Taylor Bledsoe, who, before the War, practiced law in Springfield, Illinois, and knew Lincoln, and coached Lincoln on the use of broadswords for the duel with Shields that never came off. Bledsoe's *Is Davis a Traitor?* would have been the brief for Jefferson Davis' defense in court if Davis had been tried for treason, as was planned, in the Federal court at Richmond. There is nothing mythical or legendary about Bledsoe, or about the arguments of the various generals—Early, Hood, Longstreet, for example—that sought to vindicate their strategy; or in that remarkable book, *Destruction and Reconstruction,* by Richard Taylor, son of Zachary Taylor and brother-in-law of Jefferson Davis. Of the Confederate political leaders at the beginning of the war Richard Taylor remarked that they seemed "as unconscious as scene-shifters in some awful tragedy."

In these and many other writers, striving earnestly in one way or another to review their past and deal with their present, Weaver found evidence enough for the existence of a tradition that differentiated the South from the North. Its greatest fault in the end was its failure, after all, to give its latent "philosophy" an articulate form. "It [the South] is in the curious position," he concludes, "of having been right without realizing the grounds of its rightness. I am conscious that this reverses the common judgment; but it may yet appear that the North, by its ready embrace of science and rationalism, impoverished itself, and that the South, by clinging more or less unashamedly to the primitive way of life prepared itself for the longer run."

But the South failed "to study its position until it arrived at metaphysical foundations." This book, with much of Weaver's subsequent writing, is a large step toward supplying foundations.

It comes late. But the accidents of time evade our understanding. There seems after all to be a symbolic, even a practical rightness that Weaver's "Study in the Survival of a Mind and a Culture" should appear in the nineteen-sixties rather than in the nineteen-forties as he once hoped. A book like this would hardly have been noticed in the uproar that followed the explosion over Hiroshima and that attended other noisy events in our recent history. It was not quite the appropriate book, either, for the centenary of the Civil War, which we observed a little awkwardly in some few ceremonial occasions but with a great show of expertness in our vast lavishment of ink upon book and periodical paper.

Now the centenary of the Reconstruction is upon us, but where are the celebrations? Where are the books and magazine articles? June 13, 1966, was the centenary of the adoption by Congress of the Fourteenth Amendment. With averted faces we seem to have tiptoed past that and other anniversaries akin to it. All the same, the Fourteenth Amendment, which immediately preceded a decade of non-legendary military rule over the Southern States, is grimly there. Still there, as the song says our flag is. Raised up by a virtual *coup d'état,* a century ago, the Fourteenth Amendment has become "a proud tower," like Edgar Allan Poe's, from which the Supreme Court "gigantically looks down" upon our frantic little scurryings. And the South, yes, is still there. The North too, disguised as the Nation. And the Freedmen—or the descendants of the Freedmen—of a century past, having been freed over and over, are still there, still querulous. With suitable modern variations, history is being repeated.

If, in such a time, questions about the nature of American society are to be bruited about or forced upon our attention, ceremoniously or not, it is exactly the right time to take counsel with Richard Weaver in his wise, good-tempered book.

Donald Davidson
(1893-1968)

Notes

1. Reprinted in *Southern Renascence,* ed. Louis D. Rubin, Jr., and Robert D. Jacobs (Baltimore, 1953), pp. 29-30.

2. *Modern Age,* VIII (1964), p. 309.

3. Richard Weaver, *Life Without Prejudice and Other Essays.* With an Introduction by Eliseo Vivas (Chicago, 1965), pp. xii-xiii.

4. The names of the examining committee who accepted this most unusual thesis should also be recorded. They are, with Brooks: William O. Scroggs, Dean of the Graduate School, Earl L. Bradshaw, T. A. Kirby, W. J. Oliver, Robert B. Heilman.

5. Reprinted in *Life Without Prejudice,* pp. 129-155. The quoted passages are from this source.

6. He entered Vanderbilt in September, 1933, and in the spring of 1934 received his M.A. degree in English. His thesis subject was "The Revolt against Humanism." He continued graduate studies at Vanderbilt for two more years as a candidate for the Ph.D., and also taught in the English department, but left in 1936 without completing requirements for his doctor's degree.

The Southern Tradition at Bay

Introduction

ALL STUDIES OF AMERICAN CIVILIZATION MUST RECOGNIZE THE strong polarity existing since early times between North and South. The government of the United States was founded on abstract propositions: the facts of varying topography, climate, and race made regional development inevitable; the regions arriving at their own interpretations of the propositions produced, on the political level, sectionalism. These circumstances have posed a problem for writers who sought to characterize the United States, and the problem has been solved in the only way possible: that is, by taking the mentality and the institutions of the majority section as best entitled to the name American. I expect to speak of the South therefore as a minority within the nation, whose claim to attention lies not in its success in impressing its ideals upon the nation or the world, but in something I shall insist is higher—an ethical claim which can be described only in terms of the mandate of civilization. In its battle for survival the South has lost ground, but it has kept from extinction some things whose value is emphasized by the disintegration of the modern world.

This work concerns itself with a tradition, which means a recognizable pattern of belief and behavior transmitted from one generation to the next. Traditions must have, of course, a sufficient coherence to be distinguishable as integers; yet in characterizing a tradition as "Southern" one encounters the same difficulties as in characterizing another "American." Within each there will be dissidence and minority reports. It is plain that there were things done in the South which were not "Southern," and things done in the North that were not

"Northern," as we are compelled to understand these terms. Really we are faced with a problem in logic; and it is enough, I think, to be aware of the fallacies of composition and division. The first is an assumption that what is true of a part, or even of a number of parts—the proportion being incapable of determination—is necessarily true of the whole. The second is an assumption that what is true of the whole is also true of every single part. To say that Southerners have differed in point of view from Yankees does not speak for every single Southerner, but it does express a substantial truth.[1]

However much it may offend our sense of fairness, it is a demonstrable fact that the group in power speaks for the country, that the element which controls the government, the education, the means of publication is the nation in so far as its collective action goes. There is truth in the saying that the state is that part of the population which knows what it wants, or better, has a moral ambition. In assaying the Southern tradition, therefore, I have taken the spirit which dominated, and I shall no more apologize for speaking of it than others have for speaking of the New England mind or the American character. It is not the province of this work to discuss early Southern abolition societies or the spread of French infidelity in Southern educational centers save to the extent that they called forth, or served to illuminate by contrast, that unified and preponderating mind which produced the Confederate South.

If asked to tell why in these days Southern history is entitled to thoughtful consideration, I should list first of all the fact that the South, alone among the sections, has persisted in

---

[1] It is useless to argue against generalization; a world without generalization would be a world without knowledge. The chaotic and fragmentary thinking of the modern age is due largely to an apprehensiveness, inspired by empirical methods, over images, wholes, general truths, so that we are intimidated from reaching the conclusions we must live by. The exception neither proves nor disproves the rule; in the original sense of the maxim it tests the rule: *exceptio probat regulam.*

regarding science as a false messiah. This by itself indicates that the Southern tradition has a center of resistance to the most powerful force of corruption in our age. While the Western world has gone after false gods it has clung, often at the cost of scorn and insult, to its lares of the field. More concretely, it has not, in the same measure as "progressive" sections of the country, become engrossed in means to the exclusion of ends.

The precarious state of our civilization has grown with our control over nature, though we were promised an opposite result. We have assembled a vast warehouse of machinery which would, it was hoped, if not minister directly to the civilizing spirit, at least free other forces for that ministration. Yet this spirit shows signs of failing—the signs were in evidence before the World Wars—and everywhere crassness, moral obtuseness, and degradation are on the increase. We have been led to believe that man's chief task is the conquest of nature, including of course space and time. Mere advances in mechanical power, and especially superior mobility, have been greeted as steps in an automatic progress. The thought was plausible enough to find wide acceptance, so that now it is a dogma with which the clever can exploit the unthinking; perhaps indeed its great attraction lay in the emancipation from thinking. Science was hypostatized: a great machine appeared to have been set in motion which needed only operation to produce a civilization beyond present conception. It is easy, while occupied with technics and under the influence of robot-like labor, to forget that the most difficult task is to train and govern men for their own good.

The painful truth is now beginning to emerge that a flourishing technology may make civilization more rather than less difficult of attainment. It leads to mobilization of external forces; it creates enormous concentrations of irresponsible power; through an inexorable standardization it destroys re-

finement and individuality.[2] Other things it does too, and
now with the greatest of all wars behind us, which we fought
with the least enthusiasm and settled amid the greatest moral
confusion, it behooves us to examine some alternatives.

We must see first of all that the kingdom of civilization is
within. We must confess that the highest sources of value in
life are the ethical and aesthetic conceptions with which our
imagination invests the world. We must admit that man is to
be judged by the quality of his actions rather than by the
extent of his dominion. Civilization is a discipline, an
achievement in self-culture and self-control, and the only
civilizing agent is a spirit manifesting itself through reason,
imagination, and religious inspiration, and giving a sort of
mintage to acts which would otherwise be without meaning.

A civilized tradition implies a center, from which control is
exerted, and it is through this control that we give quality to
actions. Civilized man carries a sense of restraint into his
behavior both toward nature and his fellow beings. The first
of these is piety; the second ethics.

Piety comes to us as a warning voice that we must think as
mortals, that it is not for us either to know all or to control
all. It is a recognition of our own limitations and a cheerful
acceptance of the contingency of nature, which gives us the
protective virtue of humility. The attitude of science, on the
other extreme, has become impious to the fullest degree. It
has encouraged a warfare between man and nature, a fanatical warfare, in which without clearly defined war aims, we
seek the total overthrow of an opponent. But nature is not an
opponent, as ancient systems of belief could have instructed
us; it is the matrix of our being, and as such scientists we are
parricides. Piety is a realization that beyond a certain point
victories over nature are pyrrhic. The thought is implicit in

2 Of great consequence is the fact that scientific advance has led to a breakdown of communication between the generations, and thereby has helped to
destroy tradition.

the legend of Prometheus, and I have no doubt that the deep suspicion with which medieval theologians viewed early explorations of the physical world was intuition.[3] They sensed, apparently, the peril in these conquests, a *hubris* leading to vainglory, egotism, impatience, a feeling that man can dispense with all restraints. Every legend of man's fall is a caution against presuming to know everything, and an indirect exhortation to piety; and the disappearance of belief in original sin has done more than anything else to prepare the way for sophistical theories of human nature and society. Man has lost piety toward nature in proportion as he has left her and shut himself up in cities with rationalism for his philosophy.

And here enters one of the alarming facts of our cultural condition. It is the "spoiled child" psychology which appears in all urban populations. This malady, described by Ortega y Gasset in *The Revolt of the Masses,* afflicts any people who have lived so long in an artificial environment that they have lost a sense of the difficulty of things. Their institutionalized world is a product of toil and discipline: of this they are no longer aware. Like the children of rich parents, they have been pampered by the labor and self-denial of those who went before; they begin to think that luxuries, though unearned, are rightfully theirs. They fret when their wishes are not gratified; they turn to cursing and abusing; they look for scapegoats. If the world does not conform to our heart's desire, some *person* is guilty! So runs their tune. Liberals of the type who think for *The Nation* and *The New Republic* are in a constant state of vexation over the unmalleability of the world.

[3] Now comes David Lilienthal, Chairman of the Tennessee Valley Authority, saying that "Research must have a 'soul.' Intelligence is not enough without a spiritual and humane purpose. Research that is only 'enormously developed intelligence' . . . can lead only to one catastrophe after another, one war after another, each more horrible and mechanically perfect than its predecessor, to the exploitation and devastation of natural resources, and finally to the most terrible catastrophe of all, a non-moral rather than a moral world."

The agrarian South, close to the soil and disciplined in expectation, has never behaved as the spoiled child. It has suffered more afflictions than Job but has continued to call God and nature good. It accepts the unchangeable and hopes that it is providential. As a result, the backwoods Southern farmer does not feel as sorry for himself as the better heeled, better padded, and more expensively tutored Northern city cousin. This acceptance of nature, with an awareness of the persistence of tragedy, is the first element of spirituality, and a first lesson for the poor bewildered modern who, amid the wreckage of systems, confesses inability to understand the world.

If asked whether the South has any genuine claim to be considered aristocratic, I would say yes, and this is it. The South has kept something of the attitude of the soldier: aware of the battle, he has only contempt for the tender, querulous, agitated creature of modern artifice, sighing for the comforts he is "entitled to," and protesting that the world cannot really be like this. I am sure that Lee, so reserved in expression, so wise in thought, had this in mind when he called self-denial the greatest lesson to be learned. If part of our happiness comes through transformation of the outward world, another part comes through the pruning of desire, and we return to the original proposition that civilization is a matter of inner conditioning and adaptation.

As piety respects the mystery of nature, so ethics, the restraining sentiment which we carry into the world of our fellow beings, respects the reality of personality. It is well if our code of ethics has a religious origin, so that its power to impress derives from some myth or some noble parable. Its purpose, in any case, is to lead everyone to a relatively selfless point of view, and to make him realize the plurality of personalities in the world. Above all, it must insist upon the rightness of right and keep in abeyance the crude standard of what will pay. A Southern writer, thinking to reflect upon the Yankee Benjamin Franklin, asserted that honesty is not a policy at all, but a principle. The gibe was perhaps unmerited, but there is peril in promising temporal rewards for the things we must do out of profound ethical belief.

It will seem to many anomalous that a slaveholding society like the South should be presented as ethically superior. Yet the endeavor to grade men by their moral and intellectual worth may suggest a more sensitive conscience than proscription of individual differences. I do not claim that the South did this successfully, but the great intellectual effort which went into the defense of slavery indicates an ethical awareness and established some conclusions not yet entirely refuted. More important than this, however, was the astonishing resistance to the insidious doctrines of relativism and empiricism which the Southerner carried about with him. It was manifest in his religion, it showed in his deportment, and it became conspicuous in his conduct of war, as I shall illustrate in the text. Many Northerners had similar conceptions, but I believe fair-minded students of America will admit that in the North conditions were arising which made maintenance of these difficult. They were precisely the conditions which had drawn from Burke the cry: "The age of chivalry is gone—that of sophisters, economists, and calculators has succeeded." It is a remark whose truth has increased with the years. The North was in the first stages of commercialism, and no way has been found to reconcile this with ancient ideals of honor.

Personality can develop only in a humane environment, and nowhere in America has this distillation of life flourished as in the South. Its love of heroes, its affection for eccentric leaders, its interest in personal anecdote, in the colorful and the dramatic, discounted elsewhere as charming weaknesses, are signs that it reveres the spiritual part of man. It has in-

stinctively disliked, though it has by now partially succumbed to, the dehumanizing influence of governments and
factories. Individualism and personality are making a stand—
perhaps a Custer's last stand—in the South.

Civilization is measured by its power to create and enforce
distinctions. Consequently there must be some source of discrimination, from which we bring ideas of order to bear on a
fortuitous world. Knowledge and virtue constitute this
source, and these two things, it must be said to the vexation
of the sentimental optimists, are in their nature aristocracies.
Participation in them is open to all: this much of the doctrine of equality is sound; but the participation will never
occur in equal manner or degree, so that however we allow
men to start in the world, we may be sure that as long as
standards of quality exist, there will be a sorting out. Indeed,
we are entitled to say categorically that unless such standards
are operative, civilization does not exist, or that it has fallen
into decay. That no man was ever born free and no two men
ever born equal is a more sensible saying than its contrary.
To the extent that the South has preserved social structure
and avoided the creation of masses, it has maintained the
only kind of world in which values can long survive.

A society in the true sense must have exclusive minorities
of the wise and good who will bear responsibility and enjoy
prestige. Otherwise either it will be leaderless, or its leadership will rest on forces of darkness; for there is little difference between the tribal chieftain who wins his place by brute
force and the demagogue of the mass state who wins his by
appeal to mass appetite. The man of a civilized tradition,
therefore, will find nothing strange in the idea of hierarchy.
Out of the natural reverence for intellect and virtue there
arises an impulse to segregation, which broadly results in
coarser natures, that is, those of duller mental and moral
sensibility, being lodged at the bottom and those of more

refined at the top. Schemes to control this process, or to expedite it, such as Plato's system of education, testify to our sense of its wisdom. The terms "society" and "mass" are really antonyms. One implies an intelligible order, with the best elements where decisions are to be made, whatever the mechanism of selection may be. "Mass" is shapeless, impotent, really unintelligible. Because it depends upon an ordering of qualities and places, civilization is in fact a protest against this featureless condition.

The notion that all ideas of rank are inimical to liberty is found only among those who have not analyzed the relationship between freedom and organization. It is the process of levelling which distorts reality and leaves us with a situation that is, literally, impossible to conceive. The most assured way to undermine civilization is to surrender to criteria of uniformity and objectivity, losing sight of the fact that the objective cannot be prescriptive and failing to make those distinctions which have their basis in human ambition. True, it requires a degree of tough-mindedness to accept the fact of civilization, just as it requires sternness to execute moral laws, for both are discriminatory; and many forces which would destroy it have been abetted by men of good will, and have come creeping in among us, appealing to blind appetite, to special interest, and capitalizing on a partial awareness of what is at stake. We cannot do better in this connection than ponder the wonderful speech of Ulysses in *Troilus and Cressida.* Just as the deep mind of Goethe grasped the true significance of the French Revolution while the jejune and the half educated were being misled, so the marvelous understanding of Shakespeare saw in an instant the consequences of a classless society:

> O, when degree is shak'd,
> Which is the ladder to all high designs,
> The enterprise is sick! How could communities,

Degrees in school and brotherhoods in cities,
Peaceful commerce from dividable shores,
The primogenitive and due of birth,
Prerogative of age, crowns, sceptres, laurels,
But by degree stand in authentic place?
Take but degree away, untune that string,
And hark, what discord follows! each thing meets
In mere oppugnancy; the bounded waters
Should lift their bosoms higher than the shores,
And make a sop of all this solid globe;
Strength should be lord of imbecility,
And the rude son should strike his father dead:
Force should be right; or rather, right and wrong,
Between whose endless jar justice resides,
Should lose their names, and so should justice too.
Then everything includes itself in power,
Power into will, will into appetite;
And appetite, an universal wolf,
So doubly seconded with will and power,
Must make perforce an universal prey,
And last eat up itself.

This is Shakespeare on nihilism. Milton too, it would seem, though a fierce republican and a foe of absolute authority, believed that

orders and degrees
Jar not with liberty, but well consist.

It was a denial of such propositions that shocked Southern political thinkers. They could not understand how anyone, looking at the face of society and cherishing values, which must always appear tyrannous in the divisions they enforce among men, could preach equality and ridicule the veneration of age and eminence. Such views tended to break down the organization of the world and to substitute a lawless competition of unequals.

Those who seek to evade this dilemma by declaring that ability alone should count, a natural plea in our age of specialization, are often disingenuous, for they narrow down "ability" to mean some special skill, aptitude, or ingenuity at an isolated task. But in the political community ability must take account of the whole man: his special competences plus his personality and his moral disposition, even his history. It is well that people are not ranked for measurable efficiency as engines are for horsepower, but rather for the total idea we have of them. Thus again we face the topic of the whole man and the evil of reducing him to an abstraction to insure his political qualification.

Southern political theory was a *rationale* of society: the Northern theory it was designed to confute was largely a set of aspirations unrealizable even logically.[4] It was a political romanticism, not then subject to severe testing because the Northern world was fluid and expanding. Every old and settled society comes to terms with the physical world and the psychic world, and it forms a judgment that efforts to change either beyond a certain point will cost more than they will yield. The South was in the position of Europe or even Asia; it felt that it had discerned some necessary limitations of existence; the North felt that the South was compounding with ancient evils. Hence the epithets were "fool" and "villain." The North had Tom Paine and his postulates assuming the virtuous inclinations of man; the South had Burke and his doctrine of human fallibility and of the organic nature of society. A difference so wide is not easily composed in any country, and in the United States there were aggravations.

It is a wonder that the South did not draw more freely from Burke, who understood clearly the power of sentiment in civilized communities. A culture defines itself by crystalliz-

4 It could be pointed out here that political machines have been the working arrangement behind what was ostensibly "democracy."

ing around what I should call "unsentimental sentiments."
These are feelings which determine a common attitude
toward large phases of experience; they impel us, on critical
occasions of life, to sense more than we would sense and do
more than we would do if we were only economic man.
There is no demonstrable connection between them and our
physical survival; and therefore from the standpoint of materialism or nihilism they are excessive in the same way as any
sentimental display. They originate in our world view, in our
ultimate vision of what is proper for men as higher beings;
and they are kept from being sentimental in fact by a metaphysic or a theology which assigns them a function understandable through imagination. The propriety of any given
sentiment will rest on our profoundest view of life: our attitude toward the dead, toward traditional institutions, toward
the symbols of community life—all come from a metaphysical
dream of the world which we have created, or have been
taught. It is the loss of this view, and the determination of
matters in a narrow context of material interest—let us recall
the horror with which the direct, practical judgments of a
successful moneymaker are greeted in a family of inherited
refinement—which mark the subsidence of our power to support civilization against the will of outward being continually pressing upon us. Burke saw the French Revolution as an
assault upon just such conceptions:

> All of the pleasing illusions, which made power gentle, and
> obedience liberal, which harmonized the different shades of
> life, and which, by a bland assimilation, incorporated into
> politics the sentiments which beautify and soften private soci-
> ety, are to be dissolved by this new conquering empire of light
> and reason. All of the decent drapery of life is to be rudely
> torn off. All the superadded ideas, furnished from the ward-
> robe of a moral imagination, which the heart owns and the
> imagination ratifies, as necessary to cover the defects of our

naked and shivering nature, and to raise it to dignity in our own estimation, are to be exploded as ridiculous, absurd, and antiquated fashion.

Speaking for a century which had valued men for their "correct sentiments," Burke contended thus for the spiritual character of society against sansculottism. And looking at our own "second American Revolution," we find the South charging the North with lack of sentiment. A Northern professor resident in the South has written that Southerners apply the term "Yankee" as the Greeks did "barbarian." The kinship of ideas cannot be overlooked. The Greek knew that the barbarian could not participate in his luminous world of myth and actuality. The sentiments of a culture may indeed be "delicate arabesques of convention," the appreciation of which demands a state of grace. Their value will lie in their non-utility, in their remoteness from practical concerns, which keeps us from immersion in the material world. So the Southerners who belonged to the tradition thought they saw in the levelling spirit of the North, in its criteria of utility, in its plebian distrust of forms, in its spirit of irreverence—and all of these must be mentioned with apologies to Northern people whom they do not characterize—a kind of barbarian destructiveness, not willed perhaps, but certain in its effect.

There is a point of view from which the sentiments and formalities of civilization will appear absurd, and many Americans, especially those close to the frontier, have fancied a virtue in taking it. But a frontier is by definition not civilization, and the unbought grace of life thrives in a different environment. The destruction of sentiment leaves us not animals, who have their own nobility, but ruined men. Considerable importance must therefore be attached to the Southern fondness for pleasing illusions.

The Southern mind has been sufficiently conscious to recognize subversive influences, by which I mean anything tending to undermine that moral or "sentimental" order constituting civilization. We can explain thus its reaction to French rationalism, and in a more limited field to German "higher criticism."

The instance of Jefferson has led to a supposition that French radicalism found hospitality in the South. To the extent that it was linked with the cause of American independence, this was true; but when that cause had been won, and the South began to consider its necessities and the more permanent arrangements of peace, libertarian and equalitarian doctrines languished. It has consistently exhibited a distrust of social programs initiated on the basis of hypothesis. One could go further and say that the South has a deep suspicion of all theory, perhaps of intellect. It has always been on the side of blood and soil, of instinct, of vitalism. Something in its climate, in its social life predisposes it to feel that "gray is all theory, and green is life's golden tree."

To say that the South had a *rationale* of society is not to say that it favored what has come to be known as "rational planning." On the contrary, it has held that society, though of intelligible structure, is a product of organic growth, and that a tested *modus vivendi* is to be preferred to the most attractive experiment. George Fitzhugh expressed the belief in an epigram when he wrote, "Philosophy will blow up any government that is founded on it." And today, when the South pleads to be allowed "to work out its own problems in its own way," it more often than not has no plans for working them out. Its "way" is not to work them out, but to let some mechanism of adjustment achieve a balance. It is this which has clashed with the North's impulse to toil, "to help the world go around," to have a rational accounting of everything. Undoubtedly it has relation to the attitude of piety, which would respect the course of things and frowns on a busy human interference with what nature seems to have planned or providence ordained.

The German mentality was only a little less suspect than the French, and "German neologism," as it was termed, was viewed as the most dangerous solvent of religion. Learned investigations into the historicity of a religion are not, as time has proved, a means of encouraging reverence for that religion. A religion may be indifferent both to history and to reality of the plebeian sort, which is the reality of correspondence to the visible world. Its origin may embrace things fabulous, and its doctrines may incorporate paradoxes. It would be easy to show, indeed, that the power of Christianity over long periods and in varying intellectual climates lies in its candid acceptance of the paradoxes of existence. This means that its appeal will be to the moral imagination and its endorsement through our experience of life. Literalism is the materialism of religion, and this materialism too, except in the crudest exhibitions of Fundamentalism, the South has shunned.

At the same time it looked with disfavor upon New England's voyages into seas of Transcendentalism and Unitarianism. And if it is asked which course has best conserved religion as an active principle in life, we must admit that here again the South chose right. It viewed these as England viewed continental skepticism, and the fact that modern decadence, political, social, and moral, began in continental Europe, indicates where the instinct of survival lay. Despite sins which are as scarlet, the South has remained a Christian country in that it has persisted in describing the relationship of man to the universe in religious symbols.

Naturally the South did not see these trends as we can see them today, but I think that Southern churchmen of the educated group came close to seeing them. These men were intensely conservative; therefore they had a point of view. In times of profound revolutionary change, it is not the liberals, the "progressives," the social democrats who discern what is at issue, as I shall invoke Leon Trotsky to witness. It is the men of the old order who see most clearly the implications of the new. The failure of values, the dissolution of traditional bonds, the fragmentation of life, which were but as signs then, were nevertheless pointed out. No full diagnosis of the disorder was made, and probably there was none capable of making it. A growing sense for the last fifty years that civilization is at a crossroads, deepened by collapses of astounding violence and consequence, has inspired a greater study of the condition of man.

In presenting evidence that this is the traditional mind of the South, I am letting contemporaries speak. They will seldom offer whole philosophies, and sometimes the trend of thought is clear only in the light of context; yet together they express the mind of a religious agrarian order in struggle against the forces of modernism.

A final word about what is included. Since this work is the history of an articulate tradition, it is concerned almost wholly with published materials. The first chapter describes dominant forces in the tradition; and here the task was chiefly to outline. The Southern apologia is important as showing the reasoned case behind the vague but diffused and persisting sense of injustice felt by people of the section. Military history and autobiography bulk very large in Southern "literature," and no one acquainted with the history of the South will omit the influence of the soldier. Indeed, an inventory of the mind of the soldier is very nearly an inventory of the Southern mind. It was principally through fiction that the postbellum South secured a hearing from the country and the world; trends in this field therefore reflect much. The last chapter relates the South's entrance into the twentieth century, and explains the point of view of forces opposing the tradition. In the epilogue I have sought to draw the moral.

*The simple process of preserving our present
civilization is supremely complex, and demands
incalculably subtle powers.*

—Ortega y Gasset

CHAPTER ONE

The Heritage

THE MIND OF THE SOUTH, WHICH HAS BEEN CONSPICUOUS FOR its resistance to the spiritual disintegration of the modern world, is traditional in the sense that it exhibits important connections with European civilization. The habit of contemporary publicity has been to treat it in terms of superficial contrasts and to ignore the fact that it rests upon conceptions more fundamental in human nature than those envisaged by certain modern philosophies. Like the being contemplated by Aristotle, the Southern tradition has a fourfold root.

The most obvious of these is the feudal theory of society which, although a transplantation from the Old World, appeared in the South so natural a principle of organization that the Southern people have not to this day been persuaded to abandon it.

Another is the code of chivalry, a romantic idealism closely related to Christianity, which makes honor the guiding principle of conduct.

Connected with this is the ancient concept of the gentleman. First presented by Aristotle, and passed down through

Castiglione, Sir Thomas Elyot and others, it significantly pre-supposes a stable social order and a system of class education.

Finally there is a religiousness, difficult of explication be-cause, having little relation to creeds, it stands close to the historic religiousness of humanity. It is briefly a sense of the inscrutable, which leaves man convinced of the existence of supernatural intelligence and power, and leads him to the acceptance of life as a mystery.

All of these existed as determining forces in the antebel-lum South and are discernible in the peculiar complex of Southern culture today.

1. The Feudal System

The South developed as an agricultural region through the institution of a feudal system. The type of society which it created was patterned on an order then declining in Europe, but in the New World it grew to notable proportions, modi-fied by features of land and climate, and especially by the presence of Negro slavery. The impulse behind it was both economic and political; a large estate under central manage-ment and worked by laborers who were bound to their sta-tion proved the best means of acquiring wealth from the soil of Virginia, and settlers here, as in the other Southern colo-nies, had come primarily to make their fortunes. From the incorrigible gentlemen idlers of whom Captain John Smith complained in his dispatches to England, to the host of in-dentured servants who poured into the settlements in the eighteenth century, dwellers in the South aspired to acquire estates and become masters, and though many did not progress beyond the status of yeomen or small farmers, the plantation ideal was dominant in the general ordering of Southern life.[1] Politically the feudal structure was desirable

[1] For a full discussion see F. P. Gaines, *The Southern Plantation* (New York, 1924). A curious piece of blindness has led some writers to assert that

because by making the owner of broad acres true lord of the domain it simplified administration. Lord Baltimore recognized this when in Maryland he offered manorial powers to those able to take up large holdings. Some three score estates were granted on such terms and were run more or less in the fashion of an English medieval manor until in the course of time they turned into its American counterpart, the Southern plantation.[2] The number of truly baronial estates was indeed never great; in many inland districts and especially toward the mountains they were lacking, but in Tidewater Virginia, in the coastal regions of the Carolinas, in the lower Mississippi Valley, and in the Blue Grass region of Kentucky they were numerous enough to be thought of as the characteristic economic organization and to support a society which produced the first Americans popularly identified as "gentlemen."

The structure of the plantation mirrored the structure of the entire Southern social world. Its organization demanded stations, and the stations which men held in their local community bred in them a peculiar pride and dignity, which came to be associated, not always favorably, with Southern character. The method of its operation, moreover, enables one to understand why anything other than a class society was unthinkable to the Southerner of the old regime. In the social order which was overthrown by the Civil War there existed a feature of feudalism incomprehensible to the modern mind with its egotism and enlightened selfishness, subordination without envy, and superiority without fear. This was made possible, as is always true, by an articulation. The typi-

---

the antebellum South was not a true aristocracy because the aristocrats were few in number. It is never the number alone of the dominant element which makes its presence decisive; it is rather the economic, the political, and especially the moral influence it is able to exert. An oligarchy always tends to communicate its attitude and habits to the lower groups, just as in a monarchy the court sets the fashions for the nation.

2 U. B. Phillips, *Life and Labor in the Old South* (Boston, 1929), p. 43.

cal plantation was a little cosmos in which things were arranged by a well understood principle giving coherence to the whole.

Even those estates which grew a single staple for the export trade and depended on foreign sources for their manufactured goods had slaves and servants trained in special occupations. Large estates had a great representation of trades and skills. When "King" Carter of Corotoman devised his will in 1726, he listed seventeen indentured servants among the personnel of the homestead, including "sailors, tailors and carpenters, a glazier, a bricklayer, and a blacksmith." [3] A later member of the Carter clan, Robert, the master of Nomini Hall, counted among his slaves eleven carpenters, two joiners, two postilions, a bricklayer, a blacksmith, a miller, a tanner, a shoemaker, a hatter, a sailor, a carter, a butcher, a cook, a waiter, and a scullion from the men; and from the women three housemaids, two seamstresses, two spinners, a laundress, a nursemaid, and a midwife.[4]

Mount Vernon under the administration of George Washington displayed a comparable diversity of occupations. When he received title to the estate, it amounted to 2500 acres, which he, as a land-loving Virginian, eventually increased to more than 8000. In his operations the owner availed himself of the labor of both free and indentured whites in addition to that of a considerable number of slaves. From the indentured whites he usually expected some form of specialized service. In 1760 he wrote to Philadelphia for a joiner, a bricklayer, and a gardener; in 1786 he purchased the services of a Dutchman, who was to serve as ditcher and mower, and in the same year he got "from on board the brig Anna, from Ireland, two servant men . . . Thomas Ryan, a shoemaker, and Cavan Bower, a Tayler Redemptioners for

3 *Ibid.*, p. 220.
4 *Ibid.*, p. 225.

three years service by indenture." [5] His slaves included waiters, cooks, drivers and stablers, smiths, waggoners, carpenters, spinners, knitters, a carter, and a stockkeeper.[6] With his hired laborers he commonly drew up a contract which allowed them a house, a stated amount of provisions, and which sometimes placed restrictions on their moral conduct.[7]

General John Mason, son of George Mason of Gunston Hall, has testified regarding that division of labor which made each plantation a relatively self-sufficient community: "It was much the practice with gentlemen of slave and landed estates . . . so to organize them as to have considerable resources within themselves; and to employ and pay but few tradesmen, and to buy little or none of the coarse stuffs used by them . . . thus my father had among his slaves carpenters, coopers, sawyers, blacksmiths, tanners, curriers, shoemakers, spinners, weavers, and knitters, and even a distiller." [8]

A fine glimpse of a feudal paradise which survived until 1865 is given by Mrs. Virginia Clay in *A Belle of the Fifties.* During the closing months of the Civil War she spent some time at Redcliffe, the magnificent estate of James H. Hammond, of South Carolina, who had contributed the chapter "Slavery in the Light of Political Science" to the Southern symposium, *Cotton is King, and Pro-Slavery Arguments.* On this spacious property, tilled by the labor of 400 slaves, were a gristmill, a forge, a wheelwright's shop, a hospital and a church, to which there was summoned once a month a white preacher to give the Negroes a somewhat more decorous introduction to Christianity than could be expected from one of their own emotional exhorters. Redcliffe grew not only

5 Paul Haworth, *George Washington: Country Gentlemen* (Indianapolis, 1925), p. 168.

6 *Ibid.,* p. 193.

7 *Ibid.,* p. 169.

8 Quoted in T. J. Wertenbaker, *Patrician and Plebeian in Virginia* (Charlottesville, 1910), p. 50.

cotton, but also corn, wool, vegetables, and grapes.[9] In the palatial residence were marbles, statuary, and paintings, so that this plantation measures up even to the romancer's conception of the antebellum slaveholder's estate.

With such diversity of occupation, there was a task adapted to everyone, and when a worker grew too old for a certain kind of employment, he would be shifted, in paternalistic fashion, to another better suited to his condition. The strong sense of particularism which developed in these communities derived principally from the circumstance that everyone had his place. The feeling of being bound to a locality, which has been almost wholly lost by the deracinated population of the modern metropolis, was a part of the plantation dweller's daily consciousness and an important factor in his self-respect. In the midst of traffic in human beings there was, paradoxically, less evidence of the cash nexus than in the marts of free labor, and even the humble could have the deep human satisfaction that comes of being cherished for what one is. Between the expression "our people," euphemistic though it may have been, and the modern abstraction "man-power" lies a measure of our decline in humanity.

As the plantation freed its members in large part from dependence on institutions outside its bounds, it encouraged an intense provincialism. The lords of these agrarian strongholds regarded foreign influences—and the expression must be taken in its most provincial sense—as undesirable. John Pendleton Kennedy's *Swallow Barn,* which presents the most complete plantation setting in early American literature, gives a good notion of this distrust. Here Frank Meriwether is the benevolent despot. A portly Virginia gentleman of forty-five, he had studied law at Richmond more to learn how to defend his own rights than to represent clients before the bar, and then had retired to his estate to enjoy as a birthright

9 Virginia Clay-Clopton, *A Belle of the Fifties* (New York, 1904), p. 214.

the finest existence a man could conceive. He managed accounts, dispensed hospitality in traditional open-handed style, made himself court of high appeal to override the decisions of overseers, and took a distant interest in politics, exploding now and then over some novelty of invention which threatened to disturb the calm of his Eden. He saw in the steamboat a menace to isolated communities and a forward step toward that "consolidationism" at which Southern statesmen were to point for the next fifty years. "This annihilation of space, sir, is not to be desired," he told his visitor from the North. "Our protection against the evils of consolidation consists in the very obstacles to an intercourse." He felt that "the home material of Virginia was never so good as when the roads were at their worst." [10] Swallow Barn is little dependent on the outside world even for amusements; its wholesome fun comes from annual celebrations, droll incidents, and the kind of interest which humane people naturally take in one another.

With the protection of this seclusion, the hierarchy stood firm. From the owner of the estate at the top, down to field workers, bond or indentured, who, if not bound to the soil, were at least under some constraint to work it, the ranks were plain.[11] The master, as justice of the peace, preserved order and settled disputes. In actual practice he usually possessed more authority than the title or office he held would imply, for his power extended beyond the sphere of business and legal relationships. Though sometimes in practice an autocrat, as John R. Thompson of the *Southern Literary Messen-*

10 John Pendleton Kennedy, *Swallow Barn* (New York, 1906), p. 73.
11 James Roberts Gilmore (*Life In Dixie's Land,* London, 1863, p. 164) found the congregation of a country church in South Carolina seated according to social rank. "All classes were there; the black serving-man off by the door-way, the poor white a little higher up, the small turpentine-farmer a little higher still, and the wealthy planter, or the class to which the planter belonged, on 'the highest seats of the synagogue,' and in close proximity to the preacher."

ger described him,[12] he usually took pride in exercising his power with justice; and he ordinarily acknowledged a responsibility for the welfare of his dependents which proceeded from moral obligation.

Under the owner was the overseer, a sort of lieutenant, who for his subsistence and a moderate wage assumed the direction of planting and harvesting, made the innumerable decisions which wind and weather force upon an agriculturist, and most difficult of all, disciplined the slaves. The overseer was assisted by a "driver," who was often chosen from among the more capable and reliable Negroes. He generally worked as foreman, but sometimes he was given the responsibility of assigning tasks to the other slaves, and even of administering punishment.[13]

The upper-class Southerner developed a notion that only gentlemen were entitled to stand at the head of this hierarchy. Only those habituated to self-restraint and brought up in the "proper sentiments" could wield a degree of authority so terrifying in the abstract. Perhaps experience with overseers from the North encouraged the idea that Yankees lacked the requisite qualities; at any rate a writer in the *Southern Literary Messenger* contended that Northerners were unfit to be masters. "In obedience to isothermal laws," he said, "slavery has already made its exodus from the inhospitable shores of New England, *never to return;* there is no climate there; there is no soil there, and there is no *master* there." [14] Years later Ellen Glasgow was to make Major Lightfoot in *The Battle-Ground* say contemptuously of the low-caste Rainy-day Jones: "There's no man alive that shall question the divine right of slavery in my presence; but—but it is an institution for gentlemen." [15] Although some slave-

---

12 *Southern Literary Messenger,* XX (June, 1854), p. 332.
13 John Spencer Bassett, *The Southern Plantation Overseer* (Northampton, Mass., 1925), p. 2.
14 *Southern Literary Messenger,* X (November, 1860), p. 349.
15 *The Battle-Ground* (Garden City, N. Y., 1922), p. 89.

owners were not gentlemen, there was moral truth in the observation that only under the rule of gentlemen was the peculiar institution tolerable.

The *noblesse oblige* of the plantation owner has been made so prominent a part of the romantic tradition that it might be regarded with suspicion were it not well supported by the records. Washington, for example, who was far from a sentimentalist on the subject of slavery, was accustomed to visit his sick slaves and on occasion to take over personal supervision of their treatment.[16] The spectacle of this typical landowner riding daily about Mount Vernon, which he had divided into five farms, each under the management of an overseer and all under the authority of a single steward, keeping a sharp eye on operations and often reprimanding underlings somewhat impatiently, furnishes a striking picture of this paternalistic social structure.[17]

The sense of trusteeship thus developed has been one of the enduring legacies of the plantation system. The landholder, if he belonged to the tradition, would not concede that his servants meant nothing more to him than the value of their labor, nor did the servant ordinarily envisage the master as nothing more than a source of employment. The master expected of his servants loyalty; the servants of the master interest and protection.[18] Each working in his sphere went to make up a whole, through which there ran a common bond of feeling. It was a type of the corporative society, held together by sentiments which do not survive a money-economy. At this date it seems a condition of primal inno-

16 Haworth, *op. cit.*, p. 196.

17 Washington was, as a matter of fact, regarded as an ideal product of the Southern social system. A writer in the *Southern Literary Messenger* (New Series, I, June, 1856, p. 437) thought that "In the perfect symmetry of the character of Washington may be traced the influence of the Southern family, and an eulogium may be found on the tendencies of her organic influences."

18 One of the routine obligations of the Southern plantation owner today, so many years after emancipation, is to defray the medical bills of his Negroes, and to get them out of jail when they have been committed for minor offenses.

cence, before the disintegration of society into competitive
and envious groups, kept at peace by a state which must grow
more and more powerful to intimidate them.

This is the spirit of feudalism in its optative aspect; some
abuses were inevitable, and in the South lordship over an
alien and primitive race had less favorable effects upon the
character of the slaveowners. It made them arrogant and impatient, and it filled them with boundless self-assurance.
Even the children, noting the deference paid to their elders
by the servants, began at an early age to take on airs of command. After an extensive tour through the Southern states J.
S. Buckingham expressed the opinion that slavery

> trains the free child in the constant exercise of arbitrary power
> over his little slave-companions; it makes him impatient of
> contradiction from any source, as he is always accustomed to
> command; and it engenders such a habit of quick resentment
> and instant retaliation for an injury, real or supposed, by the
> frequent opportunities of its indulgence on unresisting and
> helpless slaves, that at length it forms a part of the individ-
> ual's nature, and can neither be conquered nor restrained.[19]

From this came "the universal irritability of temper, impatience of contradiction, and constant readiness to avenge
every imaginary insult with instant and deadly punishment
of the offender." [20] Horace Fulkerson, who had studied the
life of the lower Mississippi Valley, described the planters as
"arbitrary, self-willed, and dictatorial," so that even from
their equals "they could illy brook contradiction and opposition." [21] These traits, which were almost invariably noted by
Northerners and by visiting Englishmen, gave Southerners a

---

[19] *The Slave States of America* (London, 1842), p. 553.
[20] *Ibid.*, p. 557.
[21] *Random Recollections of Early Days in Mississippi* (Vicksburg, 1885),
pp. 14, 16, 144. Similarly George Mason (*Papers of James Madison,* Washington, 1840, III, p. 1391) declared in the Federal Constitutional Convention
that "every master of slaves is born a petty tyrant."

reputation away from home which they thought baseless and inspired by malice.

Another factor, present in agrarian psychology everywhere, and especially strong in the Southern planter, was the desire for a lasting identification of the family name with a piece of land. He had a profound conviction that a family is not established until it belongs to a place, that a local habitation and a name go together; and it can scarcely be doubted that this coupling of the name with the property was an attempt to regain that connection between the land and its possessor by which the owners become, politically as well as economically, "the estates of the realm." John S. Wise mentions no fewer than seventeen Virginia families of the upper James River Valley whose names were thus identified with estates.[22] In this way the American patrician sought to gain some of the prestige enjoyed by the county families of England. He liked to be alluded to as the proprietor of such and such a hall, for in the South generally, freeholding of itself conferred some kind of superiority in the quality of citizenship.[23] Landless men lacked dignity, and commercial pursuits were traditionally discountenanced. Thomas Nelson Page makes Mr. Gray, on riding off to the war from which he knows he may not return, leave a parting injunction with his son: "And Jacquelin," he said, "keep the old place. Make any sacrifice to do that. Landholding is one of the safeguards of a gentry. Our people, for six generations, have never sold an acre, and I never knew a man who sold land that throve." [24] And in George W. Cable's *John March, Southerner,* the old Judge

[22] *The End of an Era* (Boston, 1900), p. 139. Constance Cary, in *Recollections Grave and Gay* (New York, 1911), p. 3, introduced her father, Archibald Cary of Carysbrooke, with the remark that "all old-time Virginians loved to write themselves down as part of their parental estates."

[23] Grace King (*Balcony Stories,* New York, 1925, p. 179) recalled that in antebellum Louisiana it was considered disgraceful to board out or to live in a rented house.

[24] *Red Rock* (New York, 1925), p. 47.

says to his son proudly: "We neveh sole an acre, but we neveh hel' one back in a spirit o' lan' speculation, you understan'?"[25]

Together with the land hunger of the Southern planter, the desire to retain and augment the patrimony, well illustrated in the careers of Colonel William Byrd, of George Washington, and of many others, there was a vague but ever-present sense of personal relationship to the land. The Virginia or Carolina aristocrat wanted not merely another piece of soil as good as his own, or a sum of money equal to its fair purchase price; he wanted *his* land in the same way that a patriot wants his country. To call this mystical would perhaps explain little, but it may safely be said that this sense of local attachment, of loyalty to the land, is a sentiment to which all people are susceptible, and that it is sure to be found in landholders, small or great, of long establishment. An understanding of this bond goes far to explain why the Southerner chose to battle for his acre, which more often than not was only a poor red acre, rather than for some abstract concept of "Union" about which warm sympathies could not cluster.[26] Nathaniel Hawthorne, who understood better than any other writer of his time the contrary workings of the human heart, took note of this in his pertinent essay, "Chiefly About War Matters," when he remarked that a state was as large a territory as anyone could be expected to love, and that love for an invisible hypothesis like the American Union was something few people had the imagination to achieve.[27]

The relative self-sufficiency of the plantation; the *noblesse oblige* of its proprietor; the social distinctions among those

25 *John March, Southerner* (New York, 1894), p. 63.

26 D. S. Freeman (*R. E. Lee*, New York, 1934-35, I, p. 404) contends that an important factor in Lee's decision not to fight against Virginia was this feeling of kinship with the soil. "Having plowed her fields, he had a new sense of oneness with her."

27 *The Works of Nathaniel Hawthorne* (Boston, 1883), XII, p. 315.

who dwelled upon it, which had the effect of creating respect and loyalty instead of envy and hatred; the sense of kinship with the soil, present too in its humbler inhabitants, who felt pangs on leaving "the old place"—these were the supports of Southern feudalism, which outlasted every feudal system of Europe except the Russian, until it was destroyed by war and revolution. It possessed stability, an indispensable condition for positive values: it maintained society in the only true sense of the term, for it had structure and articulation, and it made possible a personal world in which people were known by their names and their histories. It was a rooted culture which viewed with dismay the anonymity and the social indifference of urban man.

2. *The Code of Chivalry*

A part of the Southern heritage which deserves more attention of the serious kind than it has received is expressed by the term chivalry. Modern spite against all assumptions of superiority has assigned it a comic role; actually it was an institution of strong and, on the whole, good influence. Since chivalry has been one of the main traditions of European civilization, it was not strange that a chivalric code should develop in the South, which was disposed to accept rather than to reject European institutions.

In Europe during the Middle Ages it had existed as a body of forms and sentiments of enormous power in elevating and refining civilization. It appears to have had its origin in the dark years following the dissolution of Charlemagne's empire, when cruelty, rapine, and brutal anarchy so distressed men that there came a passionate reaction which enlisted men in the service of an ideal good, and later found a sanction in the Christian religion. The people recognized a class of knights as representatives of right and defenders of order, idealized them, crowned them with all virtues, both real and imaginary, and for five hundred years respected them as the ruling caste. Although in its later period chivalry became associated with other things, including the worship of woman, it commenced thus as an order of men of good will, pledged to make might serve right; and although it developed forms, ceremonials, and shows, it was first and foremost a spirit. Of this spirit the Knights of the Round Table are perfect if legendary exemplars, engaged in asserting a rule of justice and humanity against naked strength. Candidates for the order of knighthood were given an initiation which made these duties explicit. An early specimen of the vow required of them was: "To speak the truth, to succour the helpless, and never to turn back from an enemy." [28]

The ethical importance of chivalry lay in the fact that where this spirit made itself felt, there it alleviated, even though it could not entirely overcome, the natural brutishness of man. It furnished a standard by which iniquity could be condemned, however dazzling the success of its perpetrators, and in the darkest times stood as an aspiration and a promise that justice would return and lawful relations obtain among men.

In the New World, even more than in Europe, it existed as a spirit, little seen in rituals and ceremonies, but often of surprising influence in determining conduct. It is difficult to say in precisely what company it crossed the Atlantic. That a certain portion of Virginia's first settlers were gentlemen is acknowledged. Captain John Smith's struggles with his indolent colonists, who were "ten times more fit to spoyle a Commonwealth, then either to begin one, or but help to maintaine one," [29] form a striking episode of early American

28 G. P. R. James, *History of Chivalry and the Crusades* (New York, 1857), pp. 26-27.
29 *Travels and Works of Captain John Smith* (Edinburgh, 1910), II, p. 487.

history, and there can be little doubt that these misplaced men-about-town would have been happier deciding points of honor than digging stumps. Like some other European institutions, chivalry came over a seedling, but having struck root in the American soil, achieved a lush growth, though modified, sometimes grotesquely, by the rudeness of the American environment. Its recruits were from a well-established middle class, and it is probably true that the spirit of chivalry was stronger in the Southern states after two hundred years of settlement than when the Virginia and Carolina landholders were first clearing their acres.

Of the characteristic ideas of chivalry, none came to a more exaggerated flowering in the South than that of personal honor. In the Old World chivalry supported a caste, the distinguishing mark of which was an honor that was to be preserved at all costs. In the South, as soon as the gentleman caste had established itself on property ownership and slave labor, this concept was invoked to set it apart from the commonalty. The gentleman was surrounded with prerogatives. He could not be injured with impunity; his motives could not be impugned; and above all, his word could not be questioned. A highly touchy sense of personal pride was built on these premises, and its vindication often called for the duel, a recognized institution in America from colonial days. In the Revolutionary period duelling was fairly common in the North, but it began to disappear there after 1800. In the South on the contrary it continued to flourish, and the toll of life exacted by this rigid convention was so great that in 1858 Governor John Lyde Wilson of South Carolina published a pamphlet: *The Code of Honor: or Rules for the Government of Principals and Seconds in Duelling.* The purpose of this manual was not to encourage the practice, as could be supposed, but rather to diminish it by defining rather narrowly the grounds on which one gentleman might "demand

satisfaction" of another. The author announced it his desire
to save lives which might be lost as a result of challenges
made on insufficient grounds. It is easy to see, however, that
he retained pride in the institution. "Tennessee, Kentucky,
Georgia, and South Carolina," he observed, "would bear away
the palm for gentility among the states of the Union" if the
prevalence of duelling should be admitted as a criterion.[30]
At the same time, Northern criticism of the practice piqued
him. He contrasted the "urbanity" of Southerners with the
"uncouth civility of the people of Massachusetts," and he
intimated that the kind of personal abuse which found its
way into Northern journals would in the South bring challenges to mortal combat.[31] Elsewhere opposition to duelling
was attributed to "the materialistic puritan skeptics of this
country," and anti-duelling laws were described as "transplanted from the pernicious hotbed of puritan skepticism." [32]

Curious memorials of this once widespread custom survive
today: Tennessee requires of all those admitted to the bar an
oath that they will not engage in duelling; and governors of
Kentucky must swear upon induction into office that they
have never fought a duel with a deadly weapon.[33]

Another aspect of the *code duello,* which removes further
question of its origin in the spirit of chivalry, was the empha-

[30] *The Code of Honor: or Rules for the Government of Principals and
Seconds in Duelling* (Charleston, 1858), p. 46. Louisiana, especially New
Orleans, was not far behind. Bishop Henry B. Whipple (*Southern Diary,*
Minneapolis, 1937, p. 155) wrote from this city in 1844: "Perhaps on no
other subject of public morals is there so great an apathy as upon the sin
of duelling. In the Southwest especially duels are of very frequent occurrence.
Seldom do you take up a newspaper here without finding some a/c of 'an
affair of honor' as these fashionable murders are termed." The Englishman
Edward Sullivan (*Rambles and Scrambles in North and South America,*
London, 1852, p. 224), visiting the same city in 1850, was appalled by the
number of personal encounters. He found that "the Southern men are
naturally hot blooded, and duelling is part of their creed."

[31] *Ibid.,* p. 36.

[32] *The Code of Honor. Its Rationale and Uses, By the Tests of Common
Sense and Good Morals, with the Effects of its Preventive Remedies* (New
Orleans, 1883), pp. 19-24.

[33] Don C. Seitz, *Famous American Duels* (New York, 1929), p. 40.

sis placed upon the social rank of the combatants. A gentleman might chastise a low fellow with whip or cane for offering him an insult, but he could not according to the code meet him on the field of honor, because honor was the exclusive possession of the gentleman caste.[34] Governor Wilson noted in his "Code" that if a man received a challenge from a person with whom he was unacquainted, he might demand a reasonable length of time "to ascertain his standing in society, unless he is fully vouched for by his friend." [35] In the days of European chivalry knights jousted only with knights, and sometimes this privilege was insisted upon even on the field of battle. It is recorded that at Bouvier a body of Flemish knights refused to charge a force of infantry because they were not gentlemen, and so lost the battle.[36]

Because the object of a knight's career was that honor which proceeds from feats of arms, it naturally followed that

[34] In this connection it is instructive to learn that Congressman Brooks of South Carolina deliberated for two days over whether to use the horsewhip, the cowhide, or the cane for his assault upon Senator Sumner because a different degree of insult was implied by each. (Charles S. Sydnor, "The Southerner and the Laws," *Journal of Southern History*, VI, February, 1940, p. 22.)

[35] John Lyde Wilson, *op. cit.*, p. 19. Similarly John Augustin ("The Oaks," *The Louisiana Book*, New Orleans, 1884, p. 87) recalled that "you could not fight a man whom you could not ask to your house."

[36] F. Warre-Cornish, *History of European Chivalry* (London, 1901), p. 75. Theodore Spencer (*Death and Elizabethan Tragedy*, Cambridge, Mass., 1936, pp. 136-138) has collected a number of citations showing that the chivalrous orders considered it ignominious to engage in combat with the low-born, and especially to die at their hands: Francisco in Massinger's *Duke of Milan* says (V, i, 185-188):

> And but that
> I scorn a slave's best blood should rust that sword
> That from a prince expects a scarlet dye,
> Thou now wert dead.

The Duke of Suffolk in Part 2 of Shakespeare's *Henry VI* declares (IV, i, 50-52):

> Obscure and lowly swain, King Henry's blood,
> The honorable blood of Lancaster
> Must not be shed by such a jaded groom.

And in Marlowe's *Massacre at Paris* the Duke of Guise exclaims (i, 1021):

> To die by peasants, what a grief is this.

he was expected to be indifferent toward material rewards, and there seems little doubt that the contempt directed at money-getting, as well as the belief that money itself is somehow contaminating, originated with this high and solemn ideal, colored as it was with Christian self-denial. Though the attitude was not, of course, carried over unaltered into the American South, there were unmistakable reflections of it. Here the people had come to the New World for the purpose of gathering fortunes, a fact which could not be denied, but which was kept out of sight in various ways. Southern landholders exhibited an aversion to the handling of money, except perhaps at the gaming table; it seemed more in keeping with the *haut monde* for them to have their business transacted through a factor. To this agent the planter consigned his crop, together with a list of his plantation's requirements, including articles of luxury. The factor sold the produce, forwarded the supplies and so left his client free from all business duties except a periodical settlement.[37] In this way many contrived to live as if they had no ties whatever with the world of money-economy.[38] Reference was often made to the point that money was a topic which men of good breeding never mentioned at the table.[39]

Such views, combined with the inveterate Southern habit of extravagance, created a type not far removed from the aristocratic wastrels of Europe, incapable of making money

[37] Charles S. Sydnor (*op. cit.*, p. 8) has recorded his impression that "the reading of extant plantation records and communications between planters and factors makes one wonder whether any other business of equal size has been run with as few precise records and as little commercial and legal paper as was the Southern plantation."

[38] Opie Read (*The American Cavalier*, Chicago, 1904, p. 209) wrote in a characterization of the Southern planter: "He used to say, 'A gentleman can't buy and sell—unless it's cotton.' He had more respect for a pauper lawyer than for a rich grocer."

[39] An example occurs in Thomas Nelson Page's *Gordon Keith* (New York, 1912, II, p. 52) when the old general remarks: "My son, there are some things that gentlemen never discuss at the table. Money is one of them."

by personal effort, but unable to see why it should not be forthcoming to support their elegant mode of life.[40]

Like the knight of old, the gentleman was required to speak the truth, and it could be said that the Southern code made a fetish of the pledged word. Falsehood, like an act of cowardice, was supposed to lose one his standing in society, and the convention was enforced with considerable rigor by public opinion.[41] If a gentleman's word was questioned, he demanded an explanation, and then, if the matter could not be adjusted, he proved that honorable status was dearer to him than life by going through the ritual of the duel. Only if he met this supreme test was he judged worthy of the companionship of gentlemen, or, in the language of knighthood, was he deserving of a place in the chivalric order.[42]

In antebellum days there was much vague allusion to chivalry,[43] but it remained for the Civil War to provide an interesting commentary on the extent to which this spirit distinguished the Southern people from their Northern adversaries. The difference came out very sharp in the respective attitudes towards war. The Southern people as a whole possessed a highly romanticized picture of the ordeal, which the business-like methods of Grant and Sherman only partly effaced. They regarded it as an elaborate ceremonial, to be conducted strictly according to rules, and with maximum dis-

40 Tyrone Power (*Impressions of America; During the Years 1833, 1834, and 1835*, Philadelphia, 1836, II, p. 136) observed that the Southern planters "are fond of money without having a tittle of avarice."

41 Edward Sullivan (*op. cit.*, p. 225) was told that no New Orleans jury would convict a man who killed another for calling him a liar, and that in general there was strong feeling in favor of justifiable homicide.

42 The "Code of Honor" re-issued in New Orleans in 1883 (*op. cit.*, p. 6) made the point that "among the refined, virtue with women and honor with men are more valuable than life—are more worthy of the last defense."

43 A good example is the statement by Bishop Whipple in his *Southern Diary* (*op. cit.*, p. 43): "The Southerner himself is different from the Northerner in many striking particulars. He is more chivalrous, that is to say he has more of that old English feeling common to the days of the feudal system and the crusades."

play, color, and daring—in other words, as a gigantic tournament with the Lord of Hosts for umpire and judge.[44] Some Southerners actually expressed the opinion after First Manassas that the war would promptly cease because this battle had decided the question of manhood between the two sections and there was nothing else to be settled.

If the people of the North ever subscribed to this notion, they changed it after the removal of the colorful McClellan, and thereafter the task of conquering the South became a business, an "official transaction," which cost a great deal more in dollars and men than had been anticipated, but which was at length accomplished by the systematic marshalling of equipment and numbers. John Pope's Virginia campaign gave the South its first intimation that the North was committed to a "total war." The Southern people became dismayed by this, for it seemed an infraction of that tacit agreement obtaining among all civilized belligerents. Perhaps it is not too fanciful to read in Lee's terse statement, "Pope must be suppressed," a feeling that he was fighting not so much against a particular enemy as against an outlawed mode of warfare. And when Sherman, Sheridan, and Hunter began their systematic ravaging and punishing of civilians, it seemed to the South that one of the fundamental supports of civilization was being knocked out, and that warfare was

[44] There is no better description of this attitude than the one furnished by F. E. Daniel in *Recollections of a Rebel Surgeon* (Austin, Texas, 1899, p. 14): "To give you an idea of my conception of war—notwithstanding I had read a great deal of history, of course,—I took along a sole leather valise with me, full of broadcloth suits, patent leather shoes, linen shirts, fancy shirts and ties. I had an idea (what a fool I was), that both armies would march out in an open place and meet by a kind of understanding, and after a few selections by the band, go to fighting; and at sunset, or sooner, the one that whipped would have some more music by the band, and then we'd retire."

An eyewitness thus described the Virginia troops assembled at Harper's Ferry after the John Brown raid (James B. Avirett, *The Memoirs of General Turner Ashby and His Compeers*, Baltimore, 1867, p. 62): "They talked of war as a pastime, and seemed to think it was a glorious thing."

being thrown back to the naked savagery from which religion and the spirit of chivalry had painfully raised it in the Middle Ages.[45] The courtly conduct of Lee and his fellow officers to the farmwives of Pennsylvania has perhaps been sentimentalized, but the fact remains that these men felt they were obeying a code which is never more needful than in war, when fear and anger are likely to blind men and to destroy their self-control. The material loss in farms and dwellings has been forgotten, nor does the South today appear greatly to resent its economic inferiority, but the memory of how the "Great March" was conducted lingers on in bitterness. It is not unreasonable to suppose that the Southerner, a prodigal by temperament, has been able to accept the material loss without being able to accept the affront to the tradition by which he was brought up. In any case, the South has persisted in making a distinction among McClellan, Hancock, and Grant,[46] who adhered rather strictly to the code; and such "fighting prophets" as Sherman, who inaugurated the war of unlimited aggression. The former, it was generally held, had fought honestly according to the rules of warfare, eschewing vandalism and terrorism. Naturally the thought of being beaten came hard to a people priding themselves on their martial traditions, but the memory which rankled in the South for generations was that the enemy, while masking himself under pretensions of moral superiority, had dropped

---

45 An interesting parallel to this is found in the sixteenth-century *Mirror for Magistrates* (ed. Lily B. Campbell, Cambridge, Mass., 1938, p. 88) where Roger Mortimer complains that the barbarous Irish by whom he has been slain do not recognize the rules of war:

> They know no lawe of armes nor none will lerne:
> They make not warre (as others do) a playe,
> . . . .
> Theyre end of warre to see theyr enmye deade. . . .

46 Robert Stiles (*Four Years Under Marse Robert*, New York, 1903, p. 239), one of the most devoted of Lee's followers, expressed admiration for Grant's "rough chivalry."

the code of civilization and won in a dishonorable manner.[47] Today we have gone so far in the direction of nihilism that this attitude seems difficult to credit, but one has only to read the literature of Reconstruction to find it expressed frequently and with conviction. Against Meade, who fatally dashed Southern hopes at Gettysburg, against Grant, who won decisive victories at Vicksburg and at Chattanooga, or against Thomas, who at Nashville gave the Confederacy its most humiliating defeat of the war, one finds little or no complaint. But against Sherman, who admitted that of the one hundred million dollars of destruction his armies wrought in Georgia only twenty million were of military advantage, words could not contain the measure of Southern indignation.[48] Likewise in New Orleans, resentment against the alleged peculations of Benjamin Butler was as nothing compared with the outrage felt over his famous edict to the ladies, which according to the Southern code of the time was beyond the pale.

A vehement Southern partisan was to declare after the war that the Southern people pride themselves so on their reputation for chivalry they were willing to sacrifice everything in preference to it, including the hope of victory. Such feeling characterized the aristocratic class, and in this case the exceptions would seem to sustain the rule. Those Southern commanders who advocated the other style of warfare, and who, if they had got into the North with independent commands,

[47] A contemporary elaboration of the doctrine that civilization consists in just such adherence to a code, or a body of forms set up between the individual and his impulses, occurs in W. B. Yeats' *A Vision* (New York, 1930, p. 180): "A civilization is a struggle to keep self control"; and one of the first signs of its decay is "a sinking in upon the moral being."

[48] It would be unfair to create an impression that all of the atrocities were committed by one side. John S. Mosby's men indulged in savage acts of retaliation, and Basil Duke apologized for the conduct of some of his soldiers on Morgan's wild dash across southern Indiana and Ohio. In general the fighting done in the West by frontier elements displayed little regard for the code.

might have followed policies analogous to those of Sherman and Sheridan, were not members of the gentleman caste, but were hard, self-made men, who believed simply that "war means fighting and fighting means killing." Of this group were Stonewall Jackson and Nathan Bedford Forrest, both men of the people, and both men in whom there ran a streak of ruthlessness. Those who more completely abjured the chivalric rules of warfare won; the military ritual which had come down from the Middle Ages was dealt a fatal blow, and the way was cleared for modernism, with its stringency, its abstractionism, and its impatience with sentimental restraints.[49] It scarcely needs pointing out that from the military policies of Sherman and Sheridan there lies but an easy step to the modern conception of total war, the greatest threat to our civilization since its founding.[50]

Even if the Southern feeling of superiority in this matter rested upon facts supposed rather than real, it would have to be taken into account as one of the points of sectional friction. More than one observer viewed the Civil War as ultimately a clash of character, and the South naturally preferred to see itself clothed in the armor of chivalry. We may note, for example, a significant interview which took place between Captain Fitzgerald Ross of the Austrian Hussars and Judah P. Benjamin, Confederate Secretary of War. Captain Ross mentioned that on his journey to Richmond he had seen

49 Chivalry was construed as a support of civilization because by keeping their impulses in check, it preserved the humanity of men. Emanuel de la Moriniere in a postbellum essay on the topic ("Chivalry," *The Louisiana Book, op. cit.,* p. 177) described it thus: "The sense of honor in its widest meaning, includes the faculty of forming some ideal standard superior to the lower nature of man and recognizing in ourselves some power of approximating to it."

50 At a banquet given by Bismarck in 1870, General Sheridan, who had been with the Prussian staff in the capacity of unofficial observer, said that he favored treating noncombatants with the utmost rigor. He declared (Moritz Busch, *Bismarck: Some Secret Pages of his History,* New York, 1898, I, p. 128), "The people must be left nothing but their eyes to weep with over the war."

many evidences of depredation by the enemy, whereupon the
Secretary replied:

> If they had behaved differently; if they had come against us
> observing strict discipline, protecting women and children, re-
> specting private property and proclaiming as their only object
> the putting down of armed resistance to the Federal Govern-
> ment, we should have found it perhaps more difficult to pre-
> vail against them. But they could not help showing their
> cruelty and rapacity, they could not dissemble their true na-
> ture, which is the real cause of this war. If they had been
> capable of acting otherwise, they would not have been Yan-
> kees, and we should never have quarrelled with them.[51]

Benjamin was expressing the predominant Southern view.

Perhaps the tradition of chivalry led to excesses of its own,
but they were not of the grosser sort, and it performed the
inestimable service of keeping an ideal of nobility before the
people. Few would wish to see the duel restored, or the pre-
cious sense of pride which made issues of small misunder-
standings; on the other hand our civilization has suffered no
more grievous loss than the disappearance of generosity
toward the weak and the vanquished. With the claim to exclusive right by an individual or a nation, expressing itself in
the arrogant formula of unconditional surrender, the spiritual community of men dissolves, and we are at the threshold
where "everything is swallowed up in power."

The pattern of chivalry, however, had other effects on
Southern culture which must be pointed out. It definitely
tended to discourage art and letters. The barrier which it
raised against persons from "lower" social levels was less serious than that which it set up against the scholar and the
creative thinker, and even the Southern conception of education was influenced by its ideals.

[51] *A Visit to the Cities and Camps of the Confederate States* (London,
1865), p. 29.

Knights are performers of the *gestes;* only rarely are they singers of them. The poets and troubadours of Europe, who made them live in story, had an uncertain position; they enjoyed some license, and they were valued for their special contributions, but the attitude of society toward them was one of tolerance rather than serious respect. And in that transplanted chivalry which grew up on American shores one finds a comparable attitude, even somewhat accentuated by the rawness and philistinism of a new country. For although it is true that only a fraction of the populace belonged to that class, all aspiration was in its direction. There were no centers of commercial or intellectual activity in which competing ideals could emerge, and no other pattern was consciously followed.

The situation of Southern men of letters points to the broader truth that in every aristocracy the artist tends to be *déclassé.* He has often been patronized and supported by the aristocrats; but the patronage and support have only symbolized the gulf between him, a supernumerary, a hireling, and those who have laid title to estates by deeds or by inheritance. This truth is not weakened by the fact that members of the aristocracy have themselves dabbled in art and letters. In instances they have done so to the extent of winning more illustrious names by these than by their rank, but it will be found virtually without exception that they have regarded such employments as elegant exercises, to be pursued for diversion, or to be exhibited as evidence of versatility.[52]

The notion of following letters as a profession was quite as foreign to the Southern gentleman as it was to the English nobleman, and his position was, if anything, less favorable for it. His career was that of a man of the world; his education was devised to meet its demands, and if he developed some

___

[52] It will be recalled that the Restoration wits were gentlemen first, and authors only by way of *divertissement;* and Byron's desire to be regarded as a lord is, of course, one of the commonplaces of literary history.

special skill at authorship, that was a matter for congratulation, but seldom was there a suggestion that he capitalize it
by making it his means of support or his claim to recognition
by society. This aristocratic prejudice, which had its foundation in the institution of chivalry, determined the content of
Southern education and made inevitable the slightness and
sterility of the Southern contribution to *belles-lettres*.

3. The Education of the Gentleman

When in 1828 John Randolph of Roanoke, answering Edward Everett in the House of Representatives, called the
ability to lead men, whether in the field or in the Senate
chamber, the highest of the gifts of heaven, he was expressing
the prevailing belief of his Southern compatriots. "There is,"
he said, with the bitter implication of which he was a master,
"a class of men who possess great learning, combined with inveterate professional habits, and who are (*ipso facto,* or perhaps I should say *ipsis factis,* for I must speak accurately as I
speak before a Professor) disqualified for any but secondary
parts anywhere—even in the Cabinet." [53] It was natural that a
people whose talent lay almost wholly in the direction of
statecraft should consider eminence in war and eloquence in
council the marks of illustrious manhood. The Southerner of
good class was Aristotle's political animal; his antecedents
were auspicious for leadership; his education prepared him
for it, and before the nineteenth century was in its second
quarter the exigencies of his situation created a continuous
demand for its exertion.

Many explanations have been offered to account for the
poor showing of the Old South in literature, but not enough

[53] *Register of Debates,* Twentieth Congress, First session, IV (Washington,
1828), p. 1327.

has been said of the section's actual achievements in terms of its animating ideals. The climate, the lack of cities, the institution of slavery—all have been mentioned as militating against authorship, but inspection will reveal that the Old South wrote fairly prolifically, and that in the field which it had marked out for its own, it held preeminence for close to a century. The Old South was an aristocracy whose hero was the warrior statesman, and because it was intensely interested in the battle for political supremacy, its literature was the literature of the forum.

It is a maxim that in every society education will ultimately serve the needs of the dominant class, and in the South this consisted of gentlemen planters, who contemplated lives of ease and independence. The plantation system, with its patriarchal administration, and the presence of slavery, which drove a wedge between the leisure class and those compelled to toil for a living, kept at the top of society a small group whose immediate tasks called for duties of a political nature. The Southern planter, although his ancestors might have been tradesmen or yeomen, became, once he had perfected his material establishment in America, an aristocrat by calling, upon whom there devolved the work of keeping harmonious the efforts of a stratified and fairly complex community.[54] The question of noble lineage, which usually gets much attention, becomes largely irrelevant when it is understood that once in the New World these settlers created and maintained a class society.[55] By the beginning of the eighteenth century the populace was effectually divided into a lower class of slaves and tenants, a middle class of yeomen, or small independent farmers, and an upper class of

[54]Wertenbaker, *op. cit.*, pp. 105-107. For a good estimate of the influence of such duty on character, see H. S. Fulkerson, *loc. cit.*

[55] Wertenbaker, *The First Americans* (New York, 1927), pp. 1-21. It is not without significance that of all the colonies Virginia stood longest for the Stuarts (Robert Beverley, *The History of Virginia*, Richmond, 1855, pp. 232-233).

planters.[56] The aristocracy of the Old South was small in number, and it was found in restricted areas, but such is the nature of aristocracy that if it is genuine—and that means if it earns and receives respect—its relative number is of little importance. It will set the tone of society, and those who aspire to rise in the world will seek to identify themselves with it. Though the number of antebellum mansions may soon be counted, it is none the less true that those who dwelled in them put their stamp upon the whole of Southern society, not excluding the turbulent frontier.[57]

Virginia, where this system lay in happiest balance, became the spearhead of the American Revolution and gave to the infant republic a wealth of leadership such as might have graced the golden age of another nation. The names of her sons comprise a veritable Plutarchian list of heroes. Patrick Henry, one of the most eloquent of Americans, and a man of prophetic vision; Washington, whose firm and sagacious mind prevented the collapse of the colonial rebellion; Jefferson, cosmopolitan and bold political thinker; Madison, political journalist and learned student of constitutional history;

[56] Louis B. Wright, *The First Gentlemen of Virginia* (San Marino, Calif., 1940), p. 48.

[57] In the Blue Grass region of Kentucky and in the Natchez region of Mississippi, frontier conditions gave way to a fairly settled, aristocratic society in the space of two or three decades. The amazing proliferation of military titles in the South (see Thomas D. Clark, "Gentlemen of Rank," *The Rampaging Frontier*, Indianapolis, 1939, pp. 183-204) which impressed all foreign travellers suggests that Americans were trying to "ennoble" themselves within their political framework. Thus Colonel A. J. L. Fremantle of the Coldstream Guards reports General J. E. Johnston as remarking (*Three Months in the Southern States*, New York, 1864, p. 121): "You must be astonished to find how fond all Americans are of titles, although they are republicans; and as they can't get any other sort, they all take military ones." According to F. E. Daniel (*op. cit.*, p. 157) these titles were broadly proportionate to local importance. "In the South in those days, everybody who was anybody in particular had a military title, and the titles were graded according to one's importance in the vicinity, and ranged all the way from 'Cap' bestowed on the postmaster and city marshall, through 'Major,' the title of the editor, 'Colonel,' the title of the town lawyer and politician, to 'General' for the fat, old rich fellows."

John Marshall, the "legislative judge," who carried far the fateful impulse toward consolidation; and John Taylor of Caroline, farmer-philosopher, whose searching critique of economic society anticipated the assumptions of Marxism— these were the chief figures in that constellation of genius which emerged from the agrarian, feudal society of colonial Virginia, and who, joined with a few from other states, confirmed the South in the habit of governing. Their comparative superiority invites attention to the system of education which prepared them.

The Southern ideal of education rested on those traditional principles which may be traced to Aristotle by way of the Elizabethans. Because it was designed to produce the well-rounded gentleman, its basic features are fairly easy to distinguish. Education beyond the most elementary, it was believed, is adapted only to those whose minds are previously disposed to the virtuous and the honorable—in other words, to an aristocracy.[58] It is not adapted to the masses, who appreciate only the utilitarian, and who are condemned to lead lives of service.[59] According to a writer discussing public education in the *Southern Literary Messenger*, "To enlighten all classes most effectively we should begin with the upper one first. Light should be set on a high place so that it may dispel the darkness that surrounds us, and a few men truly and thoroughly educated would shed more light around them and awaken a desire for improvement in a greater

[58] Jefferson, who led the popular party against the large landowners, projected his system of general education to free the state from a leadership confined to wealth and family (Roy J. Honeywell, *The Educational Work of Thomas Jefferson*, Cambridge, Mass., 1931, p. 25). The failure of his comprehensive program has been attributed to the feudal nature of antebellum Virginia (Charles W. Dabney, *Universal Education in the South*, Chapel Hill, 1936, I, p. 20.)

[59] In the seventeenth century the guardian of one Virginia orphan was obligated by the courts to have him taught "honestly according to his degree" (Philip A. Bruce, *Institutional History of Virginia*, New York, 1910, I, p. 310).

number, than in any other single way in which we could diffuse it." [60] This diffusion, however, did not mean that equality was to be sought. "There are many things in which the attempt to introduce the principles of equality must end in the complete deterioration of all parties concerned. God made the greater light to rule the day, and the lesser to rule the night; and this principle was through the whole of creation, and all attempts of man to subvert it must end, as they always have, in the manifest injury to all parties." [61] In the same vein a writer in *De Bow's Review* had the following to say about common schools and universities: "There are those, I am aware, whose chosen theme it is to declaim upon the *democracy* of science and literature in this favored age, and to undervalue all education and acquirements unless they be of a *popular* character. To such I make no reply further than to say, I believe it is self-evident that it is impossible, in the nature of things, for the multitude to attain more than a very superficial acquaintance with the various departments of learning and knowledge." [62]

Not a few thus wished the Southern system of education to be devised in frank recognition of the section's caste system. William H. Trescott of South Carolina expressed this desire in the baldest fashion:

In establishing, then, a system of education for a slave state, there are two principles which may be placed as a foundation on which to build.

1. That the state is not required to provide education for the great bulk of the laboring classes.

2. That it is required to afford that degree of education to everyone of its white citizens which will enable him intelligently and actively to control and direct the slave labor of the state.[63]

60 *Southern Literary Messenger*, XIII (November, 1847), p. 686.
61 *Ibid.*
62 *De Bow's Review*, XVIII (April, 1855), p. 553.
63 *De Bow's Review*, XX (January, 1856), p. 148.

Though the planters of Virginia occasionally made provision for the common school education of the lower orders in their community, it was thus generally thought that higher education was for those whose position in life carried a mandate for public leadership.[64] This led the antebellum South to an anomalous situation in which the facilities for university training were more widespread and better developed than those for secondary school training. Archibald Roane, writing in *De Bow's Review*, affirmed the Southern choice in this matter:

> If, then, one of the two systems of education—the common school or the university system—must prevail exclusively or even generally (and we have already shown that where the former is of the greatest excellence it does not necessarily follow the latter too must be so, and that even one may exist without the other), I repeat, if a choice between the two must be made, it seems to me that no man who has regard to the honor, reputation, and glory of his country, abroad and in future time, can hesitate to give preference to the university system. We, in the south, at least, who have not been so much carried away by the crude and radical theories of the times, can have no such hesitation.[65]

The education which the South envisaged for its upper class was humanistic, and it was so framed as to instill the classic qualities of magnificence, magnanimity, and liberality. The virtues of a ruling caste depend upon the kind of training which molds character. Discussing the proposal to organize a "Central Southern University" at which the sons of the South would be taught the principles of their society, a writer in *De Bow's Review* set down the following as first consideration: "In the organization of the university, this maxim

---

[64] The circumstance that in early Virginia even primary education was largely dependent on family provision made its possession a sign of one's position in the economic hierarchy (Philip A. Bruce, *op. cit.*, I, pp. 293-307).

[65] *De Bow's Review*, XVIII (April, 1855), p. 554.

should be borne in mind: 'nothing is improper to be taught which is proper for a gentleman to learn.' " [66] While proponents of education talked in general about enlarging the sentiments and developing the powers of the mind, the intimation remained plain that institutions of higher learning were expected to turn out a type, and that the basic aim of instruction was to teach propriety, rather than to cultivate cleverness and ingenuity. This is significant as showing a tendency, for in proportion as a social system is rigid, it will set premium upon conformity to the accepted type and ignore those whose only birthright is ability.

Such education was moral in the sense that it would give the youth a sound set of values. In accordance with the theory of the Greek thinker, it would teach one to approve and disapprove of the right objects in the right manner; or to display a set of correct sentiments determined by the code of the gentleman. In defense of the education of the planter class a writer in *Russell's Magazine* maintained that "apart from professional exactness and professional details, they have the general scholarly training which so well becomes the gentleman, and is so necessary to the perfect development of his character." This was praised as liberal because it resulted in "a catholicity of taste as well as of feeling, and an elevated view of all subjects, particularly public affairs." [67] The student, declared a writer in *De Bow's Review*, "must be regarded as a moral, as an intellectual, and as a physical being; and any system that does not provide for the proper development of each one of these departments (if the term be permitted) falls short of the requirements of his nature." [68]

[66] *De Bow's Review*, XXIII (December, 1857), p. 579.

[67] *Russell's Magazine*, I (May, 1857), p. 100. In a characterization of Jeb Stuart, John Esten Cooke (*Wearing of the Gray*, New York, 1867, p. 30) wrote: "His education was that of the gentleman rather than the scholar. 'Napoleon's Maxims,' a translation of Jomini's Treatise on War, and one or two similar works, were all in which he appeared to take pleasure."

[68] *De Bow's Review*, XXIII (December, 1857), p. 580.

This presumed a well-rounded regimen which would leave him prepared, like Milton's scholar, to perform all general duties, both public and private, of peace and of war.

The significant feature of this training was its avoidance of specialization. That this avoidance was deliberate, and that it derived from the premises there can be no question. Since specialization is illiberal in a freeman, his acquaintance with the arts and sciences must remain that of the amateur. He must learn enough to be a judge of proficiency in others, but proficiency in himself is a sign of vulgarity. Nothing can be clearer than that the men who drew up the program of the Southern universities desired to produce neither bookish minds nor clever specialists. They were training young men for the Southern world, where scholarship was politely admired and then largely ignored. The students were fully alive to these purposes, and thus we find a youthful orator at the College of William and Mary in 1699 warning his institution against turning out the scholar type:

> For in such a retired corner of the world, far from business and action, if we make scholars, they are in danger of proving mere scholars, which make a very ridiculous figure, made up of pedantry, disputatiousness, positiveness, and a great many other ill qualities which render them not fit for action and conversation.[69]

In 1839, nearly a century and a half later, an article in the *Southern Literary Messenger* reflected an identical point of view. The writer declared:

> Men who are endowed in any extraordinary manner with one talent, are generally unfit for any other pursuit in life. They take no interest in the ordinary affairs of society—are lost to all notions of prudence, or considerations of the useful—everything is sacrificed to the indulgence of the one ruling pas-

[69] Louis B. Wright, *op. cit.*, p. 109.

sion. It is well, we say, that society is not made up of such men—but that it consists of those who have no very great capacity for one pursuit more than another—and who possess all the faculties in a moderate degree.[70]

King Philip's famous taunt to his son Alexander, who had performed skillfully upon the flute, "Are you not ashamed, son, to play so well?" [71] would have been understood in the antebellum South. The thought of devoting oneself to learning for its own sake did not appeal to the ruling class.[72] Allowing for the great attention paid to the study of law, one may say that Southerners, like the English whom they imitated, wanted at the head of affairs not professionals, but competent amateurs. Training for leadership there was, of course, as has been noted, but when the training has been scrutinized, it turns out to be such as in another age would have produced the courtier, with special attention given to rhetoric. So great was the value set upon the spoken word that at the University of Georgia "forensic disputation" was a required course, and the testimonials proving the Southern college youth's anticipation of a future in politics are numberless.[73]

The attitude of the Old South toward education, and in a parallel way toward the arts, cannot be understood until it is realized that the propertied classes regarded their roles in life as fixed, and that academic training was expected to prepare

[70] Southern Literary Messenger, V (July, 1839), p. 443.

[71] Plutarch's Lives of Illustrious Men (Chicago, n.d.), I, p. 235. This view, universal among the ancients, was based on the principle that "He who busies himself with mean occupations produces, in the very pains he takes about things of little or no use, an evidence against himself of his negligence and indisposition to what is really good". (ibid.)

[72] Thus a writer in the Southern Literary Messenger (XXVIII, April, 1859, p. 310) could say: "All education should be conducted with reference to the mind. We should not seek knowledge for its own sake."

[73] E. Merton Coulter, College Life in the Old South (New York, 1928), p. 63. See also Virginia Fitsgerald, "A Southern College Boy Eighty Years Ago," South Atlantic Quarterly, XV (July, 1921), pp. 236-246.

their sons to play their parts as leaders in the little plantation world, or perhaps in the state or national legislature, with skill and credit. That many who entered life without possessions received this training does not diminish the force of the assertion, for they were regarded as in a sense probationers, who in the course of a career of the approved type, would be assimilated into this class. Professionalism and specialization, except in the law, were for those unlucky enough to have to make their living by them.

It is axiomatic that in any society self-made men will imitate those for whom greatness is a birthright. This explains the tremendous pressure to conform to the gentleman type. The sons of yeomen who passed by way of education and success at law into the upper ranks of society—and there were many such [74]—must have felt doubly obligated to accept the point of view of the group in which they were parvenus. The gentleman's ideal of behavior has been in all periods the same; he is a self-justifying type, who feels that he does not have to earn his position by special exertions. That is to say, his importance lies not in what he can do, but in what he is. The gentleman expresses an end in himself, and the display of skills, powers, and cleverness alone does not gain one admission to his circle. These are things needed by those who have not yet arrived in the world, their exhibition a sign that the possessor is still in process of becoming. The gentleman, on the other hand, is heir to the aristocratic knowledge that he owes his place to the structure of society, and not to anything that he can do especially well. There is a persisting belief that to make a man a specialist is somehow to interfere with his performance as a whole man. The career of a gentleman is being a gentleman. The social and educational regimen of the Old South was accordingly such as to prepare

[74] See Joshua W. Caldwell, "The Lawyers and the Aristocracy," *The South in the Building of the Nation* (Richmond, 1909), VII, pp. 347-352.

the fortunate for public life, to produce men of integrity and decision, who could talk well and wear the graces—not quill-drivers or "career men" of letters, or explorers of the scientific world.[75]

The comparative absence of imaginative literature in the South must be largely explained by the traditional aristocratic contempt for the artist as specialist. The classic expression of this attitude comes from Hotspur, the *beau sabreur* of a society not unlike that of the antebellum South:

> I'd rather be a kitten and cry mew
> Than one of these same metre ballad mongers.

In such a milieu literature is looked upon as an elegant indulgence, pardonable in those who use it as an entertainment for their leisure, reprehensible in those who pursue it to the extent of neglecting personal or public cares. Where war and statecraft are held the chief offices of man, preoccupation with an art will be regarded as a sentimental weakness.

The talent which went into the orations of Patrick Henry, the journalism of Madison, the state papers of Jefferson, and the political economy of John Taylor was unquestionably of a high order, but it was confined to one field. The endeavors which elsewhere produced imaginative treatments of the human scene, or as in New England, theocratic disputes and transcendentalist philosophies, in the South flowered in political classics. Jefferson, the apostle of liberty, after stating the grounds for American independence, wrote a series of state papers and political speculations which may well be regarded as the most seminal in our history; Henry, political seer, predicted in his three most celebrated orations the division of church and state, the separation of the colonies from the

---

[75] The French traveller Michael Chevalier (*Society, Manners and Politics in the United States,* Boston, 1839, p. 115) noted that the Virginian "is better able to command men, than to conquer nature, and subdue the soil."

mother country, and the then far-off War Between the States; Madison, erudite student of history, joined with Alexander Hamilton and John Jay to write the authoritative exposition of the nature of the union; and John Taylor of Caroline, an unpretending country gentleman, turned like Cincinnatus from the plow to the concerns of his country and presented the case for agrarian civilization in his formidable *An Inquiry into the Principles and Policies of the Government of the United States,* a work which one qualified student has described as worthy "to rank with the two or three really historic contributions to political science which have been produced in this country." [76]

While the South continued to enjoy the political and social leadership which these denote, while her institutions were yet unchallenged, her literary sterility, though often admitted, was not seriously deplored. In 1820, however, the Missouri Compromise sharply dramatized the growing sectional hostility, and thereafter the South considered it a reproach to herself to remain the literary pupil of the North. Sectionalism in politics had now fully emerged, and it was to be followed by a Southern effort to express a regional culture. From this time on repeated attempts were made to establish journals which should be vehicles of Southern learning and present the Southern point of view on topics of general interest. *The Southern Review* of Charleston was the first solid achievement in this direction, and although it attained a standard of real excellence and appears today the most characteristically Southern of all that were attempted, it endured only from 1828 to 1832. Two years after its cessation, however, a Richmond printer, Thomas Willys White, founded the *Southern Literary Messenger,* which, despite faltering first steps, was destined to be a mouthpiece of Southern cul-

---

[76] Charles A. Beard, *Economic Origins of Jeffersonian Democracy* (New York, 1927), p. 323.

ture for thirty years and to come nearer than any other medium to giving the Southland that literary independence which was being sought. The first issue of this distinguished journal, appearing in August, 1834, carried an editorial which is a summing-up of much that has been here pointed out:

> It is folly to boast of political ascendancy, of moral influence, of professional eminence, or unrivalled oratory, when in all the Corinthian graces which adorn the structure of the mind, we are lamentably deficient. It is worse than folly to talk of "this ancient and unterrified commonwealth"—if we suffer ourselves to be terrified at the idea of supporting one poor periodical, devoted to letters and mental improvement.[77]

The issue carried also a list of letters from correspondents saluting its appearance. Their general tone reflects a resentment of Northern intellectual hegemony and a hope that the South would accept the opportunity to express itself on topics other than politics. Said one correspondent:

> With these sentiments, you may be assured that I wish success to your endeavor to rouse the spirit of the South in the cause of literature; to draw its intellectual energies from the everlasting and monotonous discussion of politics, which has run the same round of arguments and topics for forty years, and allure her favored sons and daughters to the kinder and brighter fields of science and letters.[78]

Another wrote:

> I look with much anxiety to your *Launch,* (which I wish had been the title of your work)—the first of any promise in Virginia, heartily desiring it God-speed—yet fearing that you may meet with some inaptitude or distaste to mere literary contribution from the educated of our citizens. This, however,

[77] *Southern Literary Messenger,* I (August, 1834), p. 2.
[78] *Ibid.,* p. 127.

cannot last long; you may feel it at the outset, but it will soon
end; for I doubt not that the *Messenger*, as one of its best
effects, will draw into literary exercise the talents which now
lie fallow throughout the community, or which have long ex-
travasated in politics or professions.[79]

A third likewise found reason to hope that it would create an
appetite for literary fame and thus diminish the obsession
with politics:

We have been too long tributary to the north; it is time, high
time, to awake from our lethargy—to rise to the majesty of our
intellectual strength, put on the panoply of talents and
genius, and *strike* for the "prize of our high calling." If the
object of your labors be attained, of which there can be no
reasonable doubt, posterity will be more grateful to you than
to thousands of political *exquisites* of the day, whose memory
will last only so long as their ephemeral production.[80]

Despite a degree of outward success, however, it is plain
that the *Messenger* had to contend with much apathy and
indifference in its regional constituency. Thus in 1853, nine
years after the hopeful beginning just described, one finds
the editor exclaiming: "How glad to us will be the day, when
an ardent love of liberal learning shall have supplanted some
of the hobbies of Southern intellect, have roused its slumber-
ing energies and imparted a taste for purest joys and sweetest
solaces." [81] By 1857 it appeared that some progress had been
made against the universal preoccupation with politics, and
the editor could exult in the new-found glory of authors:

The literary men are regarded with greater consideration than
formerly, and are not now compelled to walk under the huge
legs of politicians and peep about to find themselves dishon-

[79] *Ibid.*
[80] *Ibid.*
[81] *Ibid.*, IX (September, 1843), p. 575.

orable graves. It is getting to be thought that a man may, perhaps, accomplish as much for the South by writing a good book as by making a successful stump speech; that he who contributes to the enjoyment of his fellow-citizens by a lofty poem or shapes their convictions by a powerful essay is not an idle dreamer merely and that the pen devoted to the treatment of subjects out of the range of political and commercial activities is as usefully employed as the tongue which is exercised in the wearisome declamation of legislative halls.[82]

Such spells of enthusiasm were usually short-lived, for expectations were dashed. Two years later, in connection with a pointless debate then going on in Charleston over whether William Gilmore Simms could write good English prose, there appeared this characteristic note of exasperation: "When will the people of the South learn to know and honour their worthiest literary men?" [83]

The last of such ventures was *Russell's Magazine,* which commenced in 1857 under the sponsorship of Timrod, Hayne, and others. An editorial in the second issue reflected the sense of cultural isolation:

> Year after year, under the influence of foreign pressure and outrage, the Southern states have been drawing closer the bonds of a common brotherhood, and developing in self-reliance, energy, courage, and all the resources of independent nationality, they are rapidly aspiring to the station which God designed that they should occupy and adorn.[84]

Ironically, at the very time when the South declared its literary independence of the North, Southern authors found it imperative to give a larger share of their intellectual energies to the political struggle. The quarrel over the tariff, the nullification movement, and the beginning of incendiary attacks on slavery put the section squarely on the defensive,

82 *Ibid.,* XXV (December, 1857), p. 471.
83 *Ibid.,* XXIX (October, 1859), p. 315.
84 *Russell's Magazine,* I (May, 1857), p. 178.

with the result that in the period 1829-1835 the abler leaders of the South definitely abandoned democracy. From this time on mounting political zeal deflected creative spirits from complete dedication to literature and also altered for the worse the South's contribution to political thought, heretofore its chief claim to intellectual distinction. The speculations of Henry, Jefferson, Mason, Madison, R. H. Lee, and Taylor may be called philosophic in a real sense of the word: resting on assumptions furnished by the French Enlightenment, they deal with the broad topic of man in society and discuss principles certain to assert themselves wherever there is free political organization. After the South had been warned to look for destructive attacks on her institutions, both temper and point of view shifted. Her writings became devoted, on the one hand, to an exposition of propositions already crystallized in law; and on the other, to a demonstration of the humanitarian aspects of slavery. The real question was begged; it was now not how might the South best define the legal status of the African for the benefit of the general polity, but what would be the most effective propaganda to counter the stream flowing down from the North. The first question had been uppermost in many minds before hatred clouded the picture, but in the four decades preceding the war dispassionate opinion practically vanished. One is able to appreciate the intensity of the feeling which was generated when he learns that it drove into sectional consciousness such detached and cosmopolitan intelligences as Thomas Jefferson and Edgar A. Poe.[85]

[85] Gloomy over the Missouri Compromise, Jefferson wrote to John Holmes in April, 1820 (*Works*, Federal Edition, XXI, New York, 1904, p. 159): "But as it is, we have the wolf by the ears, and we can neither hold him safely or let him go. Justice is in one scale, and self-preservation in the other."

Reviewing J. K. Paulding's *Slavery in the United States*, Poe expressed the following opinion of abolitionists (*Southern Literary Messenger*, II, April, 1836, p. 336: "They superinduce a something like despair of success in any attempt that may be made to resist the attack on all our rights, of which that on Domestic Slavery (the basis of all our institutions) is but the precursor."

In this connection John C. Calhoun may be studied as a bridge between the old and the new schools of Southern political thought. Born of up-country yeoman stock, he was of undistinguished origin, but through law and marriage into a family of position he took the sure road to the top of the social hierarchy. Unlike the typical Southerner in his ascetic habits and humorless disposition, Calhoun made a lasting contribution to the political literature of his section, if not indeed to the science of politics, with his doctrine of the concurrent majority, an attempt to fix a procedure whereby in any commonwealth the minority may check the tyranny of the majority. The intellectual resourcefulness indicated by this ingenious theory must place him among the foremost American political thinkers, but at the same time it was so plainly a rationalization of sectional needs that he appears the forerunner of the Southern apologists, and his "dream of Greek democracy" [86] part of the Southern defensive reaction.

This reaction was twofold: it comprised in part an attack on the libertarian dogmas of the French Revolution, and in part a new theory of "social articulation." The leading exponents of this theory, who became quite vocal after 1830, reveal a noteworthy unity of belief. Among them was Thomas R. Dew, a Virginian, who studied in Germany during the era of Fichte and Hegel and returned home to teach at William and Mary, filled with the notion that duties are more important than rights. Called upon to testify before a legislative committee, he dismissed Jefferson's theories as "glittering generalities," stated in substance the iron law of wages, and maintained that all great civilizations are built on the toil of subject peoples.[87]

Another was Chancellor William Harper of South Carolina, who in 1837 published *A Memoir on Slavery*. He took

[86] See V. L. Parrington, *Main Currents in American Thought* (New York, 1927), II, pp. 99-108.

[87] Thomas R. Dew, "Professor Dew on Slavery," *Pro-Slavery Arguments* (Charleston, 1852?), pp. 324 ff.

the position that those who control property will always rule, that society has a variety of offices which must be performed by human beings of different castes, and that education should be given in accordance with the recipient's role in life. "Is it not palpably nearer the truth," he asked in an examination of the axiom that all men are created free and equal, "to say that no man was ever born free and that no two men were ever born equal?" [88] Man is born to subjection, he reasoned, just as he is born in sin and ignorance.

The most striking contribution to this body of thought, however, was George Fitzhugh's *Sociology for the South*, published in 1854. This work is unique in the boldness of its attack on the theory of free society and in its remarkable foreshadowing of the modern corporate state. Fitzhugh argued that competitive society throws the burden on the weak and the ignorant, whose toil goes to swell "the vulgar pomp and pageantry of ignorant millionaires," [89] and that therefore the entire world should return to slavery, for "slavery is a form, and the very best form of socialism." [90] Private property should be preserved, because its possession tends "to beget learning, skill, and high moral qualifications," [91] but liberty is a delusion, since all virtue lies in the performance of duty. Though not without misstatements and exaggerations, the book is an outline of the totalitarian state, which substitutes for individual liberty and free competition a fixed hierarchy and state provision for all classes; and it shows how far out of the main current of nineteenth-century thought the Southern apologists had moved in order to defend their inherited system.

An impulse capable of driving political philosophers so far to the right could not fail to be reflected in general literature. The desire of the South for literary fame, never of hardy

---

[88] Chancellor Harper, "Harper on Slavery," *ibid.*, p. 6.
[89] George Fitzhugh, *Sociology for the South* (Richmond, 1854), p. 92.
[90] *Ibid.*, p. 27.
[91] *Ibid.*, p. 191.

growth, thrusting up in spite of tendencies of education and social pressure, now had to encounter a gathering political hurricane. We have seen that at the time when the South embarked upon literary independence, it embarked also upon militant sectionalism. If previously the pursuit of *belles-lettres* had been viewed as an amiable frivolity, it might, after the South had commenced its bitter ideological struggle with the North, be regarded as nothing less than remissness in duty. The prevailing notion had always been that a man of parts should serve the state, even in times of peace. Opposed to the effort of a few progressive spirits to win the Southern intellectual away from politics there must be noted the tendency, strong and pervasive especially among the popular element, to demand of him some form of public service. Thus the gallant Philip Pendleton Cooke, circumstanced as few were in his time to cultivate the muse, had the following illuminating incident to report: "What do you think of a good friend of mine, a most valuable and worthy, and hard-riding one, saying gravely to me a short time ago: 'I wouldn't waste time on a damned thing like poetry; you might make yourself, with all your sense and judgment, a useful man in settling neighborhood disputes and difficulties.' " [92] Cooke himself was to some extent tinctured with the same attitude. Literature he regarded as an occupation for the middle years; thereafter age and gravity called for statecraft. "My literary life opens now," he wrote to a friend. "If the world manifest any disposition to hear my 'utterances,' it will be abundantly gratified. I am thirty: until I am forty literature shall be my calling—avoiding however to rely on it pecuniarily—then (after forty) politics will be a sequitur." [93]

Richard Henry Wilde, whose delicate faculty gave the world "My life is like the summer rose," drew censure for choosing to spend years studying the legend and romance of

[92] *Southern Literary Messenger,* XVII (October-November, 1851), p. 670.
[93] *Ibid.,* p. 672.

medieval Italy. "The mission to which Mr. Wilde addressed his faculties and gave years to toil in Europe," wrote a chronicler of the bench and bar of Georgia, "was not in harmony with his relative duties to mankind and with that position which his eminent talents and finished cultivation had secured from the world. He was qualified for extensive practical usefulness as a jurist, scholar and statesman. . . . In Europe there was delight to the senses, but mildew to the heart. The voluptuary, the man of fashion, the idler were gratified; but the moral hero, the public benefactor, the man of enterprise, and the scholar of a just ambition, desirous to leave a record of popular utility, would turn with generous self-denial from such enchantments." [94]

This critic could not understand how Wilde could devote years of study to Tasso, "to the sentimental details, to the fantasies of insanity, and that, too, not for the benefit of medical jurisprudence." [95] In short, "The task, with whatever success performed by Mr. Wilde, was below the merit which should have sustained itself in a better field—at the forum, in the walks of political economy, in commerce, in constitutional law, or in the analysis of government, all of which admitted the classic beauties of style." [96]

The "scholar of a just ambition" is an especially meaningful phrase. By it the writer was pointing to the student of public affairs, whose research and meditation may be counted on to promote the interest of society, not to add to self-culture, or to further art for art's sake. As John Donald Wade has remarked, antebellum Georgia considered all activity of the latter kind dilettantism.[97]

Occasionally this attitude took the form of direct patriotic

---

[94] Stephen F. Miller, *Bench and Bar of Georgia* (Philadelphia, 1858), II, p. 360.

[95] *Ibid.*, p. 361.

[96] *Ibid.*

[97] John Donald Wade, *Augustus Baldwin Longstreet* (New York, 1924), p. 190.

appeal to Southerners of a reflective cast of mind to produce a Southern philosophy. "From the Bible and Aristotle," stated a writer in *De Bow's Review*, "we can deduce (added to our own successful experiment) quite enough to build a new philosophy on the ruins of the present false and vicious system." [98] The urgency of the time required a Southern transvaluation of values. "Hence it follows that all books in the whole range of moral science, if not written by Southern authors, within the last twenty or thirty years, inculcate abolition either directly or indirectly. If written before that time, even by Southern authors, they are likely to be as absurd and dangerous as the Declaration of Independence, or the Virginia Bill of Rights." [99]

In an environment where insistent denigration of artistic interest was reinforced by overmastering temptation to enter the political debate, there was no room for *belles-lettres* as a profession. Rewards waited upon other forms of activity, and most of those who in the heat and imagination of youth tried poetry and fiction gave them up for good, or for long intervals, either to take up political journalism, or to become men of affairs.

The gifted man of letters swallowed up in the lawyer is one of the common figures of the Old South. William Wirt, whose *Letters of a British Spy* and *The Old Bachelor* reveal a talent for the genial essay, became Attorney General for the United States and gave to office that energy which might have made him conspicuous in literature, as was noted by a contemporary biographer. [100] John Pendleton Kennedy, the friend and benefactor of Poe, after producing in *Swallow Barn* one of the idylls of American literature, a work which for charm and deftness is not surpassed by the best of Irving,

---

98 *De Bow's Review*, XXIII (October, 1857), p. 339.
99 *Ibid.*, p. 341.
100 F. W. Thomas, *John Randolph of Roanoke and Other Sketches of Character, Including William Wirt* (Philadelphia, 1853), p. 46.

closed a long period of dilettante activity by sinking into the complacent functionary and business man. The career of Nathaniel Beverley Tucker, however, provides perhaps the best example of how Southern men of literary endowment were won from pure literature by the challenge of the sectional political contest. Born at "Matoax" to a family rich in traditions of service to the state, Tucker graduated from the College of William and Mary, spent a period practising law in Missouri, and then returned to his alma mater as professor. In 1834 he published *George Balcombe,* a novel described by Poe as the best America had to that time produced.[101] Two years later appeared *The Partisan Leader,* a remarkable forecast of sectional conflict, issued under the date "1856" in the hope that it would prove a warning to Virginians. *The Partisan Leader* is a prime instance of a novel with a specific political purpose. One beholds in this story, with its long disputes over tariffs and other topics of sectional rivalry, the absorbing political strife which was soon to engulf its author completely. A vehement advocate of state rights and the agrarian order, Tucker accepted the gage which he felt had been thrown down by the North and poured forth a stream of political treatises, but in doing so he silenced one more literary voice for the South.

The career of William Gilmore Simms demands special appraisal, for it is peculiarly instructive in the fascination which the Southern social order exercised upon men of strong and independent mind, even while it tormented them with frustration. Simms was the nearest approach to the professional man of letters to be found in the antebellum South, with the possible exceptions of Poe and Mason Locke Weems. Born outside the aristocratic class, he made a determined effort to gain entry into it by means of his pen; and if an indefatigable industry and allegiance to the principles of

[101] *The Works of Edgar Allan Poe* (New York, 1903), VII, p. 303.

his society had been a measure of success, he would have reached the top. For several years he deserted romance, in which his achievement had been best recognized, to attempt biography, history, and oratory, securing with his "The Morals of Slavery" a place alongside Chancellor Harper and Governor J. H. Hammond in *Pro-Slavery Arguments*. In 1849 he assumed the unrewarding editorship of the *Southern Quarterly Review* with the object of giving the South an organ comparable to New England's *North American Review*. But it was not to be; his considerable exertions in defense of the Southern feudal order did not get him admitted to the magic circle; he discovered that in this milieu proficiency in letters, even loyal service to the regime, was no substitute for property holding or family connections.[102] In Charleston, if anywhere, aristocratic disdain for the mere *littérateur* was decisive, and no conceivable fame in the field of his choice would have been weighed in the scale with the successes of others in camp and senate. Although by some miracle of affection Simms remained a loyal Charlestonian to the end, he could not refrain in moments of despondency from recognizing that celebrated city's indifference to his work. On October 30, 1858, he wrote in a personal memorandum:

Thirty odd years have passed, and I can now mournfully say that the old man [his father] was right. All that I have done has been poured to waste in Charleston, which has never smiled on any of my labors, which has steadily ignored my claims, which has disparaged me to the last, has been the last place to give me its adhesion, to which I owe no favor, having

102 The terms employed by a writer in the *Southern Literary Messenger* (XXVIII, May, 1859, p. 370) to pay tribute to Simms suggest that he was appreciated on two counts: his conformity to the gentleman ideal, and his labor in defense of Southern institutions. It was declared that "Mr. Simms occupies a position in the eyes of the Southern people which is most honorable. The chivalric gentleman—the accomplished scholar—the untiring defender of the South, and all its rights and interests, he is everywhere recognized as one of our most worthy citizens, and distinguished ornaments."

never received an office, or a compliment, or a dollar at her hands; and, with the exception of some dozen of her citizens, who have been kind to me, and some scores of her young men, who have honored me with loving sympathy and something like reverence, which has always treated me like a public enemy to be sneered at than a dutiful son doing her honor.[103]

A passage in his poem "The Western Emigrants" has been taken as reflecting the same feeling:

        Simple change of place
Is seldom exile, as it hath been call'd,
But idly. There's a truer banishment
To which such faith were gentle. 'Tis to be
An exile on the spot where you were born;—
A stranger to the hearth which saw your youth,—
Banish'd from hearts to which your heart is turned.[104]

This, together with his famous self-composed epitaph, "Here lies one who, after a reasonably long life, distinguished chiefly by unceasing labors, has left all his better work undone," [105] is a poignant testimony of defeat. The tragedy of Simms' entire career was that he expected something which this society was not prepared to give, and that in the struggle he sacrificed too much. As compromises are usually fatal, lit-

[103] Quoted by W. P. Trent, *William Gilmore Simms* (Boston, 1892), p. 238. It is not unusual, of course, to find an author railing against the indifference of the local community; thus Hawthorne, Simms' contemporary, had a somewhat analogous opinion of his native Salem. The Southern writer, however, appears to have felt that the social system was confronting him with what Paul Hamilton Hayne described as "a species of ignorance . . . invincibly blind and presumptuous." (*ibid.*) Again Hayne in a letter to Margaret J. Preston (quoted in *The Last Years of Henry Timrod*, edited by Jay B. Hubbell, Durham, 1941, p. 66) spoke bitterly of the local attitude: "Touching the *Southern Public*, and those who from places of practical trust & toil lead,—generally its opinions,—we *artists*—may as well make up our minds to receive nothing—unless it be contumely, and a thinly-veiled contempt."

[104] *Poems Descriptive, Dramatic, Legendary, and Contemplative* (New York, 1853), II, p. 165.

[105] Quoted by W. P. Trent, *op. cit.*, p. 323.

tle doubt exists that the concessions he was compelled to make to be effective as a man account for his relative mediocrity as poet and romancer.

The antebellum Southern humorists, who will be remembered as the creators of an indigenous American literature, exhibit the same drift from art to politics. Augustus Baldwin Longstreet, who with *Georgia Scenes* began the rich tradition of frontier humor, spoke apologetically of his volume as a mere *bagatelle* and soothed his conscience by hoping that the sketches would one day be valuable as history.[106] Later in life, having gained place and respectability, he plunged into the pro-slavery argument with *Letters on the Epistle of Paul to Philemon, or the Connection of Apostolic Christianity with Slavery,* and *A Voice from the South.* Joseph Glover Baldwin, a genius at the comic, followed up his entertaining *The Flush Times of Alabama and Mississippi* not with more writing of the imaginative kind, which the popularity of this work should have encouraged, but with *Party Leaders,* a series of political portraits of such men as Hamilton, Jefferson, and Clay.

An aristocracy, if it is rich and secure, will foster the arts by means of patronage and largesse; but it does not assimilate the artist; it continues to regard him *qua* artist. He is, after all, an entertainer. If on the other hand the aristocracy is menaced, it will gird itself for battle, and the artist, who in calmer times was its charge, will suffer neglect and perhaps contumely. The dominant society of the Old South was an aristocracy, imperfect but in process of perfecting itself. Its position, however, was remarkably precarious. It was threatened flank and rear; from the North came attack on its labor system, which, as everyone recognized, was the kingpin of the whole Southern economy. From the West came the incessant pressure of the frontier, with its natural equalitarianism. De-

---

106 O. P. Fitzgerald, *Judge Longstreet* (Nashville, 1891), p. 88.

fense against these powerful forces demanded that things be kept in battle order. Ranks had to be closed, allegiance made firm. In the light of these circumstances, one understands why the young Southerner was educated to be a political soldier. He was the heir apparent of a civilization which rested on principles antedating the French Revolution. While New England in her golden day was softening down Calvinism into Unitarianism, the Southern intellectuals were busy building up a rigid theology to defend a social order with which their fortunes stood or fell. The concentration upon this task, which began with academic education, continued with maturity, and flowered, as often it did, in a manifesto bearing the fruits of conscientious research and meditation, left little room for the more disinterested kind of creativeness. To many of them literary aspiration appeared a thing of guilt.[107] Pleasure was there; duty was here. They cultivated literature in odd hours and then left it for sterner employments.

Since every system of education is ultimately a tool of the state, the controlling point of view will be that which the state visualizes as its chief source of welfare. In one society it may be commercial skill; in another science and invention. In the Old South it was an *ad hoc* humanism which produced the gentleman scholar and the political soldier. When one considers this education and this temperament, it comes as no surprise that in the era following Appomattox many Southerners felt impelled to re-enter the forum. Nearly all of them believed that the various Northern statements of the origin of the war rested not only upon misinterpretations of the "constitutional compact"—a phrase dear to Southerners of legal training—but also upon shallow and sophistical theories

107 John Pendleton Kennedy in a letter to Washington Irving, dated May 1, 1835 (*Horse-Shoe Robinson*, New York, 1937, p. 3), said: "You have convinced our wise ones that a man may sometimes write a volume without losing his character."

of society. It was a matter of proclaiming justice among the ruins, but the powerful polemic vein which had run from Patrick Henry to Calhoun and Yancey continued in appreciable volume for more than fifteen years after the collapse of the Confederacy. A later chapter will discuss the pivotal ideas with which the apologists of the lost cause sought at least the consolation of a forensic victory.

4. The Older Religiousness

Just as there was much in the economic and social structure of the Old South to suggest Europe before the disintegration of the medieval synthesis, so there was much in its religious attitude to recall the period preceding the Age of Reason. For although the South was heavily Protestant, its attitude toward religion was essentially the attitude of orthodoxy: it was a simple acceptance of a body of belief, an innocence of protest and heresy which left religion one of the unquestioned and unquestionable supports of the general settlement under which men live. One might press the matter further and say that it was a doctrinal innocence, for the average Southerner knew little and appears to have cared less about casuistical theology or the metaphysics underlying all religion; what he recognized was the acknowledgment, the submissiveness of the will, and that general respect for order, natural and institutional, which is piety. A religious solid South preceded the political solid South. Such disputes as occurred among churchmen were ecclesiastical rather than theological, and the laymen themselves preferred not to regard religion as a matter for discussion. Religion was a matter for profession, and after one had professed belief he became a member of a religious brotherhood, but this did not encourage him to examine the foundations of his creed, or to assail the professions of others. There were quarrels over small points of orthodoxy by the clergy, but a prevailing tendency to take the Gospel as handed down prevented the bold speculative flights which gave New England its Golden Day. The Southerner did not want a reasoned belief, but a satisfying dogma, and the innumerable divisions which occurred on the Western frontiers are ascribable to a religious intensity together with an absence of discipline rather than to a desire to effect a philosophic synthesis, as was elsewhere the case. As early as 1817 *The Western Gazetteer; or Emigrants' Directory* made the following report on the condition of religion in Kentucky: "Baptists, Methodists, Presbyterians, and Seceders are the prevailing sects; they manifest a spirit of harmony and liberality toward each other, and whatever may be said to the contrary, it is a solemn truth, that religion is nowhere more respected than in Kentucky." [108] Throughout the South and West there occurred the anomalous condition of an incredible flowering of sects accompanied by the more primitive type of response to religion.[109]   New England, on the other hand, was settled in the early years by people who had been embroiled in religious feuds, which they found occasion for renewing after they had set themselves up in the New World. The doctrinal differences which resulted in the exiling of Anne Hutchinson and Roger Williams, in the withdrawal of Thomas Hooker from the Bay Colony, and

[108] Samuel R. Brown, *The Western Gazetteer; or Emigrant's Directory* (Auburn, N.Y., 1817), p. 114. The observant Francis J. Grund (*The Americans in their Moral, Social, and Political Relations,* Boston, 1837, p. 158) noted that Americans generally were wonderfully tolerant of schism and difference while expecting everyone to admit some religious belief: "Although the most perfect tolerance exists with regard to particular creeds, yet it is absolutely necessary that a man should belong to some persuasion or other, lest his fellow citizens should consider him an outcast from society. The Jews are tolerated in America with the same liberality as any denomination of Christians; but if a person were to call himself a Deist or an Atheist, it would exercise universal execration."

[109] For a good account of the multiplicity of sects in the West see Frances Trollope, *Domestic Manners of the Americans* (Boston, 1832), pp. 139-145.

which later cost Jonathan Edwards and Ralph Waldo Emerson their pulpits are instructive cases in point. Such troubles ensue only when doctrinaires arise to make assent a matter of intellectual conviction. In New England the forces of dissent finally won the day. The right to criticize and even to reject the dogmas of Christianity became at length more important than the will to believe them, so greatly did the tide run against the conformists, and in the nineteenth century Emerson, Channing, and Transcendentalism killed the insistence on uniformity. A conclusion to be drawn from these trends, if one takes the point of view of the older religionists, is that New England, acting out of that intellectual pride which has always characterized her people, allowed religion to become primarily a matter for analysis and debate.[110] Instead of insisting upon a simple grammar of assent, which a proper regard for the mysteries would dictate, they conceived it their duty to explore principles, and when the exploration was complete they came out, not with a secured faith, but with an ethical philosophy, which illuminated much but which had none of the binding power of the older creeds. There followed as characteristic results Unitarianism and Christian Science, two intellectual substitutes for a more rigorous religious faith.

[110] The Presbyterian *Danville* (Ky.) *Quarterly Review* (I, September, 1861, pp. 367-368) attacked the liberal movements as "The New Gospel of Rationalism." It declared: "But during the last three quarters of a century, the Christian world has contemplated the strange spectacle of men holding the highest positions of honor and emolument in the bosom of the Church, eating as a canker into the very vitals of the body they were sworn to protect, and shamelessly sucking the breasts of that mother which nurtured them, while endeavoring with parricidal hand to deal her a death blow. We have seen this exhibited in the great defection of Rationalism in Germany, Broad Church liberalism in Britain, and Arian heresy in New England. The movement is characterized by a denial of all that is essential in Christian faith, veiled under the specious garb of appeal to human reason as a criterion. It is an ingenious species of tumbling in the domain of mysticism, from the basis of a narrow philosophy. As it has none of the lineaments of that system of faith once delivered by the saints, it may not inaptly be termed *The New Gospel of Rationalism*." It was further contended by the same organ (II, March, 1862, p. 17) that when man uses reason to test the Scripture "the inevitable logical result is Atheism."

The consequences of this divergence did not appear at once, for originally both Virginia and the New England colonies conceived religion as a part of the general program of government. The instructions drawn up for the Virginia Company in 1606 required that "the true word and service of God be preached, planted, and used." [111] The first General Assembly, moreover, passed a law ordaining universal church attendance. This, together with various laws against profanation and the sins of the flesh, was enforced with regularity and some severity. Virginia Episcopalians and New England Dissenters thus began *pari passu* in suppressing what they considered alien and subversive views. As time went on, however, their paths separated; the religiousness which in Virginia had originally been supported by laws remained as a crystallized popular sentiment; in New England, always more responsive to impulses from abroad, it gave way to rational inquiry. New Englanders cultivated metaphysics and sharp speculation; Southerners generally, having saved their faith, as they thought, from the whole group of pryers, reformers, and troublesome messiahs, settled back and regarded it as a part of their inheritance which they did not propose to have disturbed.

Such religious persecution as occurred in Virginia found its victims not so often among heretics in theology as among actual or potential disturbers of the peace. The Quakers, who were considered the foremost of these, were treated with extreme hostility throughout the seventeenth century. The charge levelled against these zealots was not that of doctrinal heresy; it was that their principles tended to undermine the whole institutional character of religion, and the state as well. They would not contribute to the support of the established church; they did not hold public assemblies; and they would not bear arms in defense of the commonwealth. It is

---

[111] Philip A. Bruce, *Institutional History of Virginia* (New York, 1910), I, p. 216.

little wonder that to colonial administrators these evidences savored of disaffection to the point of disloyalty, and that Quakers were commonly described as "a pestilential sect," and "an unreasonable and turbulent sort of people." [112] The General Assembly of Virginia in the winter of 1659-60 declared that their beliefs tended to "destroy religion, laws, communities, and all bonds of civil society," and passed measures which forbade the immigration of Quakers and banished those already in the colony.[113] They were being punished not for the sin of theological schism, but for the crime of political noncooperation.[114]

The history of Unitarianism in the South provides a further commentary on the Southern conception of the role of religion. While the Puritan was attempting to make his religion conform to the canons of logic, conscience, or ethical propriety, the Southerner clung stubbornly to the belief that a certain portion of life must remain inscrutable, and that religion offers the only means of meeting it, since reason cannot here be a standard of interpretation. Unitarianism, as a conspicuously speculative kind of divinity, was agreeable to those who test belief by reason,[115] but unattractive to those who long for a sustaining creed, and a means of emotional fulfillment.[116] There were few congregations in the South of sufficiently intellectual disposition to welcome it. Bishop Francis J. Grund explained the situation by saying:

112 *Ibid.*, p. 230.

113 *Ibid.*

114 Clement Eaton (*Freedom of Thought in the Old South,* Durham, 1940, p. 302) found the antebellum South more tolerant than the North toward Catholics.

115 Captain Basil Hall (*Travels in North America in the Years 1827 and 1828,* Philadelphia, 1829, p. 276) gives an amusing account of a Unitarian preacher whom he heard in Boston: "He then embarked on the great ocean of religious controversy, but with such consummate skill, that we scarcely knew we were at sea till we discovered that no land was in sight."

116 Peter Cartwright (*Autobiography,* New York, 1857, p. 48) rejoiced that in the Great Revival "Universalism was almost driven from the land."

The inhabitants of the South are principally Episcopalians, and as much attached to authority in religion as they are opposed to it in politics. They consider Unitarianism as a religious democracy; because it relies less on the authority of the Scriptures, than on the manner in which the authority of the clergy expounds them, and retains too little mysticism in its form of worship to strike the multitude with awe.[117]

And James Freeman Clarke found in Kentucky that the "nature of the people" demanded a more emotional discourse than the typical Unitarian sermon provided.[118]

A fairly intensive missionary effort succeeded in establishing Unitarian societies in Augusta, Savannah, Mobile, Nashville, and a few other cities, but most of these dwindled after a brief period of flourishing.[119] As it became plain that the religious radicalism of New England was tending toward anarchy, and more especially as radical clergymen became prominently identified with Abolitionism, Southern religious orthodoxy hardened, and the Unitarian societies became powerless to propagate themselves. General evidence that the South afforded poor soil for religious radicalism may be seen in the following distribution of churches: in 1860 this section had one of the 51 Swedenborgian churches in the United States, 20 of the 664 Universalist, and none of the 17 Spiritualist.[120]

There was a prevalent feeling among Southern people of cultivation that religion should be a settled affair.[121] Restless

[117] Grund, op. cit., p. 158. The Episcopalians were never in a majority in the South, but their influence in certain areas, such as Virginia, could have given that impression.

[118] James Freeman Clarke, Autobiography, Diary and Correspondence (Boston, 1891), p. 226.

[119] For a full discussion of the attempt to establish Unitarianism in the South see Clarence Gohdes, "Some Notes on the Unitarian Church in the Ante-bellum South," American Studies in Honor of William K. Boyd (Durham, 1940), pp. 327-366.

[120] Eaton, op. cit., p. 296.

[121] The apathy with which a cultivated Southern congregation regarded both its faith and the labors of its ministry is illustrated in a story re-

and skeptical minds who disputed its grounds were looked upon as persons inimical to a comfortable and orderly design for living. Refuting a point of doctrine brought one a reputation not so much for intellectual distinction as for perverseness and ill will. New England was contemptuously referred to as the land of "notions." [122] A writer in the *Southern Literary Messenger*, drawing a contrast between Southern and Northern people, found the latter lacking in a sense of measure: "—having liberty which they do not appreciate, they run into anarchy,—being devotional, they push piety to the extremes of fanaticism,—being contentious withal, they are led to attack the interests of others merely because those interests do not comport with their ideas of right." [123]

What the aristocratic Southerner desired above all in religion was a fine set of images to contemplate, as Allen Tate has pointed out.[124] The contemplation of such images was in itself a discipline in virtue, which had the effect of building up an inner restraint. And thus a sense of restraint and a willingness to abide by the tradition were universally viewed as marks of the gentleman; on the other hand the spirit of discontent, of aggressiveness, and of inquisitiveness were associated with those who had something to gain by overturning the established order.

In consequence it is not difficult to see why the Southern gentleman looked upon religion as a great conservative agent

---

ported by Harriet Martineau (*Society in America*, New York, 1837, II, p. 321): "A southern clergyman mentioned to me, obviously with difficulty and pain, that though he was as happily placed as a minister could be, treated with friendliness and generosity by his people, and so cherished as to show that they were satisfied, he had one trouble. During all the years of his ministry no token had reached him that he had religiously impressed their minds, more or less. They met regularly and decorously on Sundays, and departed quietly, and there was an end. He did not know that any one discourse had affected them more than another; and no opportunity was offered him of witnessing any religious emotion among them whatever."

122 *Southern Quarterly Review*, II (July, 1842), p. 137.

123 *Southern Literary Messenger, New Series*, IX (June, 1860), p. 405.

124 *Reactionary Essays on Poetry and Ideas* (New York, 1936), pp. 183-184.

and a bulwark of those institutions which served him. Spokesmen of the South were constantly criticizing Northerners for making religion a handmaid of social and political reform. A critic of Dr. W. H. Channing, writing in the *Southern Quarterly Review*, declared: "It is not very usual for the clergy of our country to enter with zeal upon the arena of politics. The department of a religious teacher is supposed to lie in a different sphere, and to embrace different duties; and the people generally listen to him with aversion and reluctance when he meddles with secular subjects." [125] A dozen years later a writer in the *Southern Literary Messenger* thus described the mixing of secular and religious causes by the North: "Her priesthood prostitutes itself to the level with a blackguard, and enters the secular field of politics, in the spirit of a beerhouse bully: and the politician as carelessly invades the sanctuary of the priest." [126] Although Southern clergymen not infrequently invoked the word of God to defend Southern institutions, especially when these were being assailed, they were on principle opposed to the use of the church as a tool for worldly reform. The evangelical sects aimed at the conversion of the inner man; the conservative ones at the exposition of a revealed ethic; but both regarded themselves as custodians of the mysteries, little concerned with political agitation and out of reach of the winds of political doctrine.[127]

Reverence for the "word of God" is a highly important aspect of Southern religious orthodoxy. Modern discussions of fundamentalism usually overlook the fact that belief in a revealed knowledge is the essence of religion in its older sense. The necessity of having some form of knowledge that will

[125] *Southern Quarterly Review*, II (July, 1842), p. 169.

[126] *Southern Literary Messenger*, New Series, X (November, 1860), p. 343.

[127] A chief cause of the great split between the Southern and Northern Methodists in 1844 was the narrower view which the Southern Methodists took of the church's province. See W. W. Sweet, *The Methodist Episcopal Church and the Civil War* (Cincinnati, 1912), pp. 15-46.

stand above the welter of earthly change and bear witness
that God is superior to accident led Thomas Aquinas to establish his famous dichotomy, which teaches that whereas
some things may be learned through investigation and the
exercise of the reasoning powers, others must be given or
"revealed" by God. Man cannot live under a settled dispensation if the postulates of his existence must be continually
revised in accordance with knowledge furnished by a nature
filled with contingencies. Nature is a vast unknown; in the
science of nature there are constantly appearing emergents
which, if allowed to affect spiritual and moral verities, would
destroy them by rendering them dubious, tentative and conflicting. It is therefore imperative in the eyes of the older
religionists that man have for guidance in this life a body of
knowledge to which the facts of natural discovery are either
subordinate or irrelevant. This body is the "rock of ages,"
firm in the vast sea of human passion and fallibility. Moral
truth is not something which can be altered every time science widens its field of induction. If moral philosophy must
wait upon natural philosophy, all moral judgments become
temporary, relative, and lacking in those sanctions which
alone make them effective, as the more perspicacious Southern theologians pointed out. And though possibly no people
were more ignorant of the *Summa Theologica* than the little-
read and inarticulate Southern rural population, the dualism
of Aquinas supports their instinctive opposition to scientific
monism, one of the last of the South's medieval heritages.
Both are responses to the same need. Ill-equipped intellectually, the South established a habit of being right in the
wrong way, or correct with a poor set of reasons. Then, as
now, this heritage explains its dogged adherence to what is
taught "in the Book," and its indifference to empirical dis-
proofs.

Emerson and his colleagues founded their revolt against

New England orthodoxy upon the principle of the continuity of knowledge and the prerogative of the individual mind to judge and determine. They were successful, and the country concluded that the victory was won everywhere; but in the South the battle has not yet been fought. In the present century, when publicity attending the theory of evolution forced the issue, there was widespread amazement that legislatures representing sovereign states were prepared to vote revealed knowledge precedence over natural, for such in a broad view of the matter is the significance of the so-called anti-evolution laws. This could not have surprised anyone who knew the tradition, for here there had never been any impeachment of the "Word," and science had not usurped the seats of the prophets. It may therefore be proper to describe the South as "backward" if one employs the word not in some vaguely prejudicial sense, but with reference to the continuum of history. The South was striving to preserve a centuries-old distinction which the North was condemning as error.

Indeed, it has been a settled practice with Southern spokesmen to describe the differences between North and South in religious language. When the period of sectional separation came, more than one Southern churchman could be found placing the blame for the sin of New England, the chief of which was abolitionism, upon "the great Socinian heresy." [128] This was bidding open defiance to the whole movement of deism and rationalism, which by the middle of the eighteenth century had captured the cultivated orders of Europe, and by the middle of the next much of New England and the North. At the height of the Gilded Age the Reverend R. L. Dabney, a celebrated Southern Presbyterian divine, was pronouncing pragmatism the equivalent of atheism, and fundamentalist leaders today regard the purely scientific view of man as only the modern pose of godlessness.

[128] R. L. Dabney, *A Defence of Virginia and Through Her of the South* (New York, 1867), pp. 131 ff.

It cannot be denied that during the period of the French Revolution there was much religious skepticism in certain Southern educational centers and among elements of the Southern upper class. It was, however, a transient phase, confined while it lasted to small cultivated groups, and it disappeared so completely in the antebellum years that it can be properly ignored in any account of the molding of the Confederate South. Skepticism is always the achievement of an intellectual aristocracy, who by education and through access to libraries have become accustomed to the critical handling of ideas. At the close of the eighteenth century, and for perhaps two decades afterward some Southern aristocrats considered it fashionable to embrace deism and to flaunt a disrespect for the Bible.[129] Jefferson, who in this period translated twenty chapters of Volney's *Ruins,* is of course the best-known Southern exponent of free-thinking. The irreligion of the day turned Williamsburg, home of venerable William and Mary College, into a veritable seat of infidelity; it flourished surprisingly at the University of North Carolina; it crept across the mountains and infected illustrious Transylvania in the Blue Grass region of Kentucky; and it penetrated the University of Georgia, then in its early years.[130] Despite such progress, however, it remained distinctly an upper-class attitude, sharply localized, and without power to affect the essential religiousness of the Southern populace. After 1830, when the South as if by prescience turned to a defense of all conservative ideals, it declined almost to the point of extinction.

One might suppose that the powerful example of Jefferson would have started a school of rationalism below the Poto-

129 Robert Carter of Nomini Hall was a Virginia patrician who broke with the Established Church and became a deist. He and Jefferson conducted some correspondence about the "human origin" of religion. See Louis Morton, *Robert Carter of Nomini Hall* (Williamsburg, 1941), p. 233.

130 For a full account of religious skepticism in the Old South, see Eaton, *op. cit.,* pp. 10-18.

mac, but in this matter, as in others, Jefferson failed to take root in his section. His doctrine of state rights and his agrarianism were cherished, but his religious liberalism, like most else that he learned from the French radicals, was ignored. His influence waned rapidly, so that within a few years after his death the Presbyterians were able to force the resignation of an atheist professor from the University of Virginia, which Jefferson had hoped to make the very citadel of unfettered thought.[131] In the same period South Carolina fundamentalists compelled the removal of President Cooper of the state university because he had questioned the authority of the Pentateuch.[132]

The influence of nineteenth-century science upon the religious temper of the Old South was never great. It has been the prevailing view that Southerners devoted their minds to politics, the classics, and the novels of Sir Walter Scott, remaining blandly innocent of the discoveries in which this century was so fruitful. Like other generalized descriptions, this one is effectually true, but omits some details which would qualify the picture. Thomas Cary Johnson, in a survey of scientific activity in the antebellum South, has corrected a number of overstatements of Southern indifference to the spirit of the age.[133] He found natural science taught not only in colleges, where sometimes it led the list of elective subjects, but even in female seminaries; and he names a number of Southerners who proved themselves fertile in theory and invention. His study, however, affords little if any evidence that this scientific interest, more widespread than is popularly supposed, issued in a skeptical habit of mind. The truth seems clear that the Southern scientist did not carry his scientific speculation to the point at which it becomes an

131 W. B. Hesseltine, *A History of the South* (New York, 1941), pp. 340-341.
132 Eaton, *op. cit.*, p. 287.
133 Thomas Cary Johnson, *Scientific Interests in the Old South* (New York, 1936).

interpretation of the whole of life. This author ascribes the failure of the South to become eminent in scientific thought to the individualism of its people and their unwillingness to cooperate in enterprises. It seems more accurate to say, on the contrary, that although the traditional mind of the South recognized in science a fascinating set of means, it refused to become absorbed to the extent of making it a religion. Unlike the technician of the present day, the typical Southerner did not feel that he must do a thing because he found that he could do it. It is significant that neither the Jacobinism of the French Revolution nor the scientific materialism of the century which followed was able to draw him from the view that man holds a central position in the universe under divine guidance.

In this way the Southern people reached the eve of the Civil War almost untouched by the great currents of rationalism and skepticism, and their allegiance to the older religiousness was reflected in their fighting men. Into the strange personnel of the Confederate Army, out of "regions that sat in darkness," poured fighting bishops and prayer-holding generals, and through it swept waves of intense religious enthusiasm long lost to history.[134] And when that army went down to defeat, the last barrier to the secular spirit of science, materialism, and democracy was vanquished.

It seems an inescapable inference that in the sphere of religion the Southerner has never been friendly to the spirit of inquiry. He felt, with what may now appear prophetic instinct, that a religion which is intellectual only is no religion. In contrast to his cousin in the North, he has been willing to accept the mystery. Traditionally his has been a

---

134 *The Confederate Veteran* (V, August, 1897, p. 411) estimated that in the Army of Northern Virginia alone there occurred more than 15,000 conversions. For comment on the part which religious conviction played in Confederate morale see Basil Gildersleeve, "The Creed of the Old South," *Atlantic Monthly*, LXIX (January, 1892), p. 76.

natural piety, expressing itself in uncritical belief and in the experience of conversion, not in an ambition to perfect a system or to tidy up a world doomed to remain forever deceptive, changeful, and evil. For him a moral science made up of postulates and deductions taking no cognizance of the inscrutable designs of Providence and the ineluctable tragedies of private lives was no substitute. Whether he was a Virginia Episcopalian, dozing in comfortable dogmatic slumber, or a Celt, transplanted to the Appalachian wilderness and responding to the wild emotionalism of the religious rally, he wanted the older religiousness of dreams and drunkenness— something akin to the rituals of the Medieval Church, and to the Eleusinian mysteries of the ancients.

❧❧❧❧

CHAPTER TWO

Writing The Apologia

=================================

"THINGS REVEAL THEMSELVES PASSING AWAY," SOMEONE remarked to William Butler Yeats, and it is an historical fact that every established order writes its great apologia only after it has been fatally stricken. When the forces of the old and the new come into crucial and dramatic conflict, then spokesmen appear to formulate the traditional assumptions and to defend what it had always been supposed could never be indicted. At best these win only a forensic victory, for the revolution is in full course, and the body politic dies while they are yet arguing its right to survive. In Europe the opponents of the Reformation did not awake to the dissolution of medieval Christendom until the process had gone too far to be checked; then they fought it stubbornly. More than a century later the principle of government by divine right, which had been effectually killed by the English Civil War, received brilliant expositions in Thomas Hobbes' *Leviathan* and in the Earl of Clarendon's *History of the Rebellion*. In 1790 Edmund Burke, a child of the aristocratic eighteenth century, viewed the "red fool fury of the Seine" through the eyes of a traditionalist and correctly foretold the political character of Jacobinism. In each case some accomplished facts were required to reveal all that was involved in the new order, but by that time the appeal of a conservative was the voice of a lost cause.

The situation was similar in the American South. There a few had vaguely predicted what social revolution would mean, but it took the events of war and Reconstruction to demonstrate that this new order would alter not only men's lives but also their perspectives. "Union" and "Abolition" were political cries, innocent-seeming, but the policies they entailed meant political centralization, a parallel to the destruction of feudalism; the ending of fixed social relationships, a parallel to the equalitarian measures of the French Revolution; and the substitution of pecuniary standards of conduct for the old code of chivalry and *noblesse oblige,* a parallel to the rise of industrialism and the money-economy in Europe. Only after the war did the interconnection of these changes become fully apparent to the leaders of the South.

The defeated people of the Confederacy may be said to have made two great dying struggles before becoming adjusted to the reality of their fall. The first of these, which was in the politico-military sphere, went by the name of the Ku Klux Klan, and was in effect an invisible government formed to combat the immediate aims of the conquerors then investing the land. Although this organization has since covered itself with odium by becoming the tool of bigotry, it may properly be thought of as the last expression of Southern political genius, and a not unworthy one in view of the conditions of the period. The second, which was waged on the literary front over a period of about fifteen years, was designed to refute the claim that the North had upheld the cause of law and humanity.[1] The reader who studies the

[1] Writing of an experience in the summer of 1881 Edwin Alderman could say (*Library of Southern Literature,* Atlanta, 1909, I, p. xxii): "Southern literature had, to that period, largely meant to me orations, polemics, threnodies, defenses."

works which this effort produced—and it is not without some patience that they may be perused—has no difficulty in recognizing their antebellum ancestry. They are the writings of the political soldier, carrying on in order that what was lost on the field by unlucky wager of battle may in some form be preserved.

The realization which especially angered the Southern apologists was that they were held up as traitors or subverters of the established order, whereas it appeared plain to them that the North, led on by fanatical reformers, had promoted a revolution on principles rejected by the Founding Fathers. It seemed to them that in the light of history the South was the loyal section, for it had poured out its blood and treasure in defense of the common inheritance of laws and customs. Without exception, therefore, the Southern apologists begin with a careful review of history, in which they point out how constitutional stipulation and legislative precedent justified both slavery and the recourse to secession. Their central aim was to prove that the South formed the Constitutional Party.

The period following Appomattox, moreover, was rife in what a later generation has come to know as "war guilt lies," through which each side accused the other of having inaugurated violence by destructive attack upon the *status quo.* According to the Northern view the South, having become disaffected, set about the criminal business of wrecking the Union, and this, had it been successful, would have reduced the states to political nonentities in the great world. The South, on the other hand, saw the North as an aggressive usurper, disregarding the Constitution whenever it stood in the way of sectional ambition, and seeking to reduce hitherto sovereign states to mere administrative provinces. It regarded as final proof of this design the transfer of the basis of government from compact to conquest, which destroyed the concept of a free union resting upon the consent of the members.

To the Southern political soldier this type of contest was particularly congenial, for he was, as we have seen, a religionist and a metaphysician, and a defender of more or less dogmatic ideals. Things which are eternally right in the mind of God may be wickedly perverted in the world, but the perversion must not go unopposed. The Earl of Clarendon wrote his monumental *History* "that posterity may not be deceived by the prosperous wickedness of these times"; and two centuries later Jefferson Davis could find nothing more apt for the flyleaf of his *Rise and Fall of the Confederate Government* than Seneca's *Felix et prosperum scelus virtus vocatur.* It is, of course, part of the duty of chivalry to serve the eternal verities. The code of honor, the duello, the universal contempt for cowardice were all parts of a system of belief whose central point was that a gentleman may risk destruction but not dishonor. These ideas rest upon a basic assumption that the most important thing in life is the cultivation of truth and the preservation of good form, which entail living up to one's obligations and refusing to act from a sense of what will pay. When the Southern political soldier undertook to prepare his defense after the failure, therefore, his object was to show that his people had acted not from a motive of profit but from a sense of right and obligation. Few words were wasted upon the expediency of a course of independence, but chief spokesmen such as Alexander Stephens, Albert Taylor Bledsoe, and Robert Lewis Dabney were at great pains to demonstrate that the South fought to maintain principles which were better defended in the Union than out, but better out than not at all.

1. The Case at Law

By supposition, he who appeals to the verdict of the sword should abide by it, should "be silent and take defeat," but when the contest has been stubbornly maintained, on what seemed fair grounds, the temptation to try another court of adjudication is sometimes too much for human nature to resist. It is not surprising then to find that shortly after the cannon had ceased Southern publicists were appearing before the tribunal of world opinion in arguments formidably charged with law and history. The prediction by Jefferson Davis that if the South lost the war its history would be written by the North was destined to be realized in the sense that the Northern history of the South came to be the accepted one, but a Southern history was nonetheless written.

Southern spokesmen could take heart from the fact that however deep the cup of woe, they had the almost unanimous moral support of their people. It is, indeed, an important index to the Southern character that in this total overthrow they showed no disposition to turn against their leaders. The advocates of secession had led them into a complete disaster, and had the South been a nation divided over the justice of the war, as some have tried to prove, these leaders might have been singled out for repudiation and even acts of vengeance. But the Southern people have always been characterized by a stubborn "loyalty to loyalty," and the manner in which the war was conducted by the North only confirmed the belief that there lay a deep-seated difference between the two people, a difference great enough to warrant separate political destinies.

Perhaps the most brilliant of all the Southern apologists was the curious eccentric, Albert Taylor Bledsoe. Born in

Frankfort, Kentucky, in 1809, Bledsoe attended Transylvania University and then West Point, where his associates included Jefferson Davis and R. E. Lee. After a varied career as soldier, preacher, and college professor, he joined the bar of Springfield, Illinois, among whose members was Abraham Lincoln. Of the lawyers pleading before this court Bledsoe appears to have been the most successful, for it is reported that he more than once carried off the basket of champagne awarded the winner of the greatest number of cases in a year.[2] Only one curious fact is known of his association with Lincoln: when the future president was challenged to a duel by General James Shields, Bledsoe, drawing upon his West Point training, undertook to teach his colleague the art of using the broadsword.[3]

A born intellectual, Bledsoe had the omnivorousness of mind which seeks strange bypaths of knowledge and finds a challenge in lost causes. He first gave evidence of his great gift as a controversialist in a slender volume entitled *An Examination of President Edwards' Inquiry into the Freedom of the Will,* which he described as "a complete triumph over the scheme of moral necessity." [4] A few years later he produced a *Philosophy of Mathematics,* and in 1856, when the slavery controversy was at the boiling point, he published a book-length tract, *Essay on Liberty and Slavery,* in which he justified the institution in terms of the Miltonic doctrine that liberty must always be proportioned to moral and intellectual worth.

When the Civil War began, Bledsoe left his post as professor of mathematics in the University of Virginia to become Confederate Under Secretary of War. J. B. Jones in *A Rebel War Clerk's Diary* has given an unflattering picture of him

2 Sophia Bledsoe Herrick in *The Library of Southern Literature,* I, p. 395.

3 Albert J. Beveridge, *Abraham Lincoln* (Boston, 1928), I, p. 349.

4 Albert Taylor Bledsoe, *An Examination of President Edwards' Inquiry into the Freedom of the Will* (Philadelphia, 1845), p. 11.

engaged in the work of this office; puffy, indolent, and un-
methodical, he groaned under official routine until in 1864
President Davis sent him to Europe on an important propaganda mission.[5] Davis, feeling that the North was getting in
too many telling blows with its publications on slavery and
treason, and cherishing until the last the delusive hope of
European intervention, entrusted him with the task of preparing a statement which should set forth the Confederacy's
right to existence. For this purpose he was to use European
libraries and to seek European publication, but before he
could complete the task the war was over, and he returned
home with his materials. Finding that the Southern leaders
were being threatened with punishment for treason, he sat
down, and "in white heat," it is said, wrote the classic Southern apologia, *Is Davis a Traitor, or Was Secession a Constitutional Right Previous to 1861?*

In a preface written, one may suppose, to preclude the
charge of seditious literature, the author stated fairly the object of his polemic:

> It is not the design of this book to open the question of seces-
> sion. The subjugation of the Southern States and their accept-
> ance of the terms dictated by the North, may, if the reader
> please, be considered as having shifted the Federal Govern-
> ment from the basis of compact to that of conquest; and
> thereby extinguished every claim to the right of secession for
> the future. Not one word in the following pages will at least
> be found to clash with that supposition or opinion. The sole
> object of this work is to discuss the right of secession with
> reference to the past; in order to vindicate the character of the
> South for loyalty, and to wipe off the charge of treason and
> rebellion from the names and memories of Jefferson Davis,
> Stonewall Jackson, Albert Sidney Johnston, Robert E. Lee,
> and all who fought and suffered in the great war of coercion.
> Admitting then, that the right of secession no longer exists,

5 Herrick, *op. cit.,* p. 396.

the present work aims to show, that, however those illustrious heroes have been aspersed by the ignorance, the prejudices, and the passions of the hour, they were nevertheless, perfectly loyal to truth, justice, and the Constitution of 1787 as it came from the hands of the fathers.[6]

In the pages which follow he presented in narrow compass the familiar argument for state sovereignty, which may be briefly summarized thus: the thirteen original states, after "seceding" from the Articles of Confederation (which were, by the way, supposed themselves to constitute a perpetual tie) formed a new compact, or union, which was given a delegated authority, and to which the various states "acceded" after making important reservations, including the prerogative of sovereignty. Fear that such a consolidation might be manipulated to the hurt of individual members led Virginia, under the urging of Patrick Henry, expressly to provide in her ordinance of ratification for the resumption of powers.[7] Several members of the Constitutional Convention, in describing the entry of a state into the federation made use of the term "accede," which Bledsoe thought might fairly be taken as the antonym of "secede." Moreover, the word "compact" was freely employed, and the argument that the Constitution was not a compact was never heard until 1833, when it was brought forward by Daniel Webster, who was basing an interpretation on the commentaries of Justice Story.[8] The Constitutional Convention repudiated the term "national government," [9] and a motion to have the Constitution approved by a national convention failed to win a second.[10]

To the terms of this original compact the South has been faithful, and if there was to be a proscription of traitors, he

6 *Is Davis a Traitor?* (Baltimore, 1866), p. v.
7 *Ibid.*, p. 159.
8 *Ibid.*, p. 7.
9 *Ibid.*, p. 18.
10 *Ibid.*, p. 62.

argued that it should begin with such Abolitionists as had
denounced the Constitution as "a covenant with hell." Fourteen Northern states, despite their professed respect for the
Union, had passed laws obstructing the recovery of fugitive
slaves and thus had not only contravened congressional law
but also had nullified part of the constitutional compact.[11]
This was the beginning of real treason to the American
Union as it was originally established.

Bledsoe was exempt from the deadly lack of humor which
makes so much Southern political writing a test of patience.
He possessed a fine talent for satire and mockery, and he
loved to use these weapons in dealing with what he considered New England sanctimoniousness. It may be doubted
whether the chapter "Mr. Webster vs. Mr. Webster" is surpassed by any American philippic. Webster's celebrated exposition of the Constitution was "merely a thing of words,"
and the Webster of 1833 was to the Webster of 1850 as
"Philip drunk to Philip sober." The first was a shameless
popularity-seeker; the second a man appalled by the mischievous consequences of the doctrine he had set loose.

> Especially after his race was nearly run, and, instead of the
> dazzling prize of the presidency, he saw before him the dark-
> ness of the grave, and the still greater darkness that threatened
> his native land with ruin; he raised the last solemn utterances
> of his mighty voice in behalf of "the compact of the Constitu-
> tion"; declaring that as it had been "deliberately entered into
> by the States," so the States should religiously observe "all its
> stipulations." [12]

Bledsoe was a master controversialist, writing always with
tremendous directness and compression and appearing to aim
not at a mere limited success, but at crushing victory. To

11 *Ibid.*, p. 101.
12 *Ibid.*, pp. 102-103.

Northerners who express a belated curiosity about loyalties which moved the South to make its immense sacrifices, *Is Davis a Traitor?* will make it plain why Southerners believed they were fighting within their rights. The work of an experienced legalist, citing constitutional provision, law, and precedent, it is the brief of the Confederacy.

At some date after Appomattox General Lee said to Bledsoe, "Doctor, you must take care of yourself; you have a great work to do; we all look to you for our vindication." [13] *Is Davis a Traitor?* was destined to be of immediate use in the defense of Southern leaders, for Charles O'Conor and Robert Oulds, attorneys for former President Davis, lacking time of their own for research into constitutional history, employed it in the preparation of their case.[14] By 1867, however, passions had begun to cool, and charges against the Confederate chieftain were *nolle prossed* before the issue could be unfolded in a courtroom drama.

Having thus made the first Southern counterattack, Bledsoe went to Baltimore to establish an organ for the continuous presentations of his views.

The next writer to enter the list was Edward Albert Pollard, the most prolific of all who argued the Southern cause. Pollard had experienced a colorful life before his fiery career in Southern journalism. Following periods at Hampden-Sydney College and the College of William and Mary, he spent several years vagabonding about the world. Returned home, he became shortly before the outbreak of war co-editor with the brilliant John M. Daniel of the Richmond *Daily Examiner*, in which capacity he was the first to discern and make public the serious limitations of Jefferson Davis. In the course of the war he produced no fewer than eight volumes

13 Edwin Mims, in *The South in the Building of the Nation*, VII, p. 464.
14 Herrick, *op. cit.*, p. 396.

dealing with its issues and events and became notorious for his outspoken criticism of the government's policies, although he protested that his utterances were motivated by "pure devotion to a great cause." [15] In 1864 he, like Bledsoe, was dispatched to England, his mission being to serve as a journalistic representative of the South. He was captured on the high seas, however, and brought to prison, where Secretary Stanton had him kept in solitary confinement for a time. Upon being exchanged early in 1865 he returned to Richmond to continue writing.

Of Pollard's voluminous output, the greatest contribution to the Southern apologia was a work which appeared in 1866 under the somewhat fulsome title *The Lost Cause: A New Southern History of the War of the Confederates, Comprising a Full and Authentic Account of the Rise and Progress of the Late Southern Confederacy—the Campaigns, Incidents and Adventures of the Most Gigantic Struggle of the World's History*. In the introduction the author described his work as "a severely just account of the war." [16] The description scarcely applies; for a just account it plainly is not, although on some topics the writer displays a candor not often met in protagonists of the Southern side. He was more interested in the real causes of the war than in the abstract rights which the opposed parties claimed to be upholding, but he found it necessary to consider the position of the South with reference to the Constitution.

Pollard viewed the Constitution as a highly defective instrument, the ambiguity of which had allowed two political parties to develop over a fundamental point of interpretation. The final document was a vote-getting compromise, salvaged from a convention which had met with vague purposes and had deadlocked over sectional differences. "The lan-

15 *The Lost Cause* (New York, 1866), p. 1.
16 *Ibid.*, p. iii.

guage of the call of the Constitution," he wrote, "was singularly confused. The men who composed it were common flesh and blood, very ignorant, very much embarrassed, many of them unlettered, and many educated just to the point where men are silly, visionary, dogmatic, and impracticable." [17] Yet the agreement which they contrived, though "actually one of the loosest political instruments in the world," had been celebrated as of almost divine origin by three generations of "American demagoguism." All that with certainty could be deduced from it was that the central government could reach individuals within the states through some restricted channels of authority. And yet when the South presented its interpretation of the restricted authority of the Constitution, the North through the use of cunning political nomenclature fastened on its spokesmen the names of "nullifier" and "disunionist." It will require a long time, Pollard declared in a summary passage, for the world to learn "that the system of negro servitude in the South was not Slavery; that John C. Calhoun was not a 'Disunionist'; and that the war of 1861 brought on by Northern insurgents was not a 'Southern rebellion.' " [18] Calhoun, known in the North as the man who would have destroyed the Union, had introduced a proposal which "certainly would have realized a beautiful idea of political association." [19] But from 1787 to 1861, as it happened, the South and the North had lived together as two political aliens, with slavery furnishing "a convenient line of battle between the disputants." [20] From this analysis Pollard passed on to a history of Northern aggression, and to the diverse characters of Southerners and Northerners, which seemed to him the decisive factor in the case.

[17] *Ibid.*, p. 37.
[18] *Ibid.*, pp. 43-44.
[19] *Ibid.*, p. 46.
[20] *Ibid.*, p. 47.

The next man to discuss the legal case of the South was one of its fallen leaders. Alexander H. Stephens, diminutive Vice President of the Confederacy, had always been known as a moderate, and for a number of reasons his voice came more pleasing to Northern ears than that of any other man identified with the Southern cause. Stephens had been one of the die-hard Unionists who fought the movement of secession until, as they thought, the official action of their states deprived them of further choice of course. He had, in fact, a consistent record as a pacificator. As late as November 14, 1860, he had addressed his state legislature in a powerful plea to preserve the Federal Union; during the war he made earnest if unsuccessful attempts to alleviate the sufferings of Northern soldiers in Southern prison camps; and in January, 1865, he was a delegate to the Hampton Roads Conference, where Lincoln met representatives of the South in a good-humored if fruitless exchange of views.

Disagreeing with Davis on many policies, and recognizing the inevitability of defeat, Stephens left his post in February, 1865, and journeyed to his home, "Liberty Hall," in Georgia, there to await like a philosopher whatever fate might befall the leader of a lost cause. In May he was arrested and taken to Fort Warren in Boston Harbor, and although he suffered considerably there through aggravation of an already poor state of health, he received touching signs of kindness from some eminent citizens of Boston and was afterwards able to speak of his period of incarceration without bitterness.

Following his release he returned South, displaying a disposition to adapt himself unreservedly to the changed state of affairs. Of all the Southern apologists, Stephens showed the least interest in recrimination, but he was too representative of the political soldier class to remain silent while issues, even those dead beyond hope of resurrection, were being gone over. Consequently when in 1867 a Philadelphia publisher suggested to him that he write a history of the war, he undertook the task and in three years' time produced one of the unique works in American political literature. This was *A Constitutional View of the Late War Between the States; Its Causes, Character, Conduct, and Results Presented in a Series of Colloquies at Liberty Hall.* It is a treatise consisting of more than twelve hundred pages of dialogue, perhaps the most extended work of this character in existence. Taking Cicero's *Tusculan Disputations* as his model, the author introduces a symposium of four speakers, whose views embody the conflicting theories of the American Union. Three are visitors at Liberty Hall from the North: Judge Bynum, a Radical Republican from Massachusetts; Professor Norton, a Conservative Republican from Connecticut, and Major Heister, a War Democrat from Pennsylvania.

Stephens was the only writer among the apologists to preface his work with a dialectic of history, which is worth noticing for the light it sheds on the type of mind that presided over Southern councils. All communities, he explained, have organic laws which may be called their constitutions. These laws are principles which react upon society, but society reacts in turn upon them, and from this interaction come the changes and revolutions in the human order. Just as the afflictions of the human body proceed from neglect of the "vital laws of its organization," so political convulsions in the body politic proceed from neglect of its principle of organization.[21] Accordingly, he who writes history "with Philosophic hand" will never lose sight of the reciprocal bearing of laws and society.[22] "Principles," he wrote, "constitute the subject matter of this work." [23]

[21] *A Constitutional View of the Late War Between the States* (Philadelphia, 1868-1870), I, p. 9.
[22] *Ibid.*
[23] *Ibid.*

The discussion proper begins on the veranda of Liberty Hall when Judge Bynum, in a tone of friendly curiosity, asks his host why after making his famous pro-Union speech at Milledgeville he followed Georgia when she seceded. Stephens' answer begins an exposition which makes up the twelve colloquies of the first book. He argues that his course was the only one open to a conscientious believer in state rights. Since by the doctrine in which he had been schooled his primary allegiance was to the state, it was his duty to follow her political destiny wherever it might lead.[24] There were, in fact, no citizens of the United States;[25] there were only citizens of the separate sovereignties which made up the Union; and sovereign states cannot be deprived of their sovereignty by implication.

The states of Virginia, New York, and Rhode Island expressly provided in their acts of ratification for a resumption of delegated powers in case these should ever be perverted to their own hurt,[26] and it was not without significance that all of the states retained complete control of their militias. The right of secession was so well understood a part of American political doctrine that Lincoln himself had given an admirable exposition of it in the House on January 12, 1848.[27]

Stephens' central thesis was summed up in the maxim *Contemporanea expositia est optima et fortissima in lege.*[28] But one may inquire why, since the doctrine of state rights had been exhaustively argued for thirty years, he felt it necessary to make this tedious restatement. He told his interlocutors that he knew they had been schooled in a different theory,

24 *Ibid.,* pp. 20-23.

25 *Ibid.,* p. 34.

26 *Ibid.,* pp. 254-255, 270-271, 290-291.

27 This speech, in which Lincoln committed himself to the principle of self-determination of peoples, is found in the *Congressional Globe,* New Series, 1847-48 (First Session, Thirtieth Congress), pp. 93-95.

28 Stephens, *op. cit.,* I, p. 501.

and that because "Men's opinions or convictions on such subjects do not so readily or so easily change," he aspired to leave something by which the future might form an impartial judgment.

It is better, therefore, to leave these questions for the verdict of posterity—for the enlightened and unimpassioned judgment of mankind. By this, we or our memories must abide. All that any of us can hope to do in the premises is, to see that all the facts, as well as a true account of our actions, shall be transmitted to that august tribunal. This is the work of history. The only anxiety I have in the matter is, that this work shall be faithfully performed—that the record shall be rightly put.[29]

With this in mind Stephens tried strenuously to identify the War for Southern Independence with the struggle for constitutional liberty everywhere. And a constitutional lawyer to the last, he maintained that what the South had surrendered was not the federative principle, but only the right to defend it by force—certainly a sufficiently vain distinction. "So you see," he concluded in a characteristically prolix passage,

my opinion is, that the Cause which was lost at Appomattox Court House, was not the Federative Principle upon which American Free Institutions was [sic] based, as some have very erroneously supposed. This was far from being one of the Results of the War. The Cause which was lost by the surrender of the Confederates, was only the Maintenance of this Principle by arms. It was not the Principle itself that they abandoned. They only abandoned their attempt to maintain it by physical force.[30]

This would, of course, leave the Confederacy in the van-

29 *Ibid.,* p. 522.
30 *Ibid.,* II, pp. 651-652.

guard of those nations which perished for freedom's sake, and
such a thought might well become the cherished possession of
her sons. Stephens had a dark view of the tendency of the
American government:

> If centralism is ultimately to prevail; if our entire system of
> free Institutions as established by our common ancestors is to
> be subverted, and an Empire is to be established in their
> stead; if that is to be the last scene of the great tragic drama
> now being enacted: then, be assured, that we of the South will
> be acquitted, not only in our own consciences, but in the
> judgment of mankind, of all responsibility for so terrible a
> catastrophe, and from all guilt of so great a crime against
> humanity.[31]

A Constitutional View is a remarkable *tour de force*;
verbose and repetitious, it is an extreme example of the
Southern habit of couching principles in voluminous rhetoric; yet at the same time it is admirable for its unyielding
insistence upon the point and its determination to refer all
circumstances to basic issues. With the society in which he
had been nurtured undergoing one of the most drastic transformations in recorded history Stephens was able, with something recalling the philosophic manner of the ancients, to
discuss with erstwhile enemies the constitutional life of the
state. But the reader who, wearying of law and precedent,
hopes his author will somewhere descend from the Olympian
height of abstraction and take a human view of the struggle,
is disappointed. It is true that a reading of *A Constitutional
View* has its associations with Job, as Douglas Southall Freeman has remarked; [32] yet there is no work which will better
display the unpragmatic and unempiric quality of the Southern mind. If one divides all humanity into Don Quixotes and
Sancho Panzas, according to a suggestion of George Santa-

31 *Ibid.*, p. 669.
32 *The South to Posterity* (New York, 1939), p. 33.

yana, he must allow Stephens a prominent place with the first who, because they serve ideals only, appear mad to men who take counsel of circumstances.

The political chieftain of the Confederacy was in his seventy-first year when he began the preparation of his apologia. His life since the collapse of the struggle had not been uneventful. He had spent two years in a cell in Fortress Monroe, part of the time in irons; he had gone abroad, where the British especially lionized him as the leader of a lost cause; and he had made an unsuccessful venture into the insurance business. It was plain, however, that he was a parting guest, for whom the world had no further use; and as ill health had then become constant, he settled at "Brierfield" on the Mississippi coast to spend his last days as a recluse. There Jefferson Davis, with the blue waters of the Gulf before him and an expanse of Southern pine and cypress behind, wrote his story of the growth of sectionalism, and of the nation which was born, lived, and died amidst war.

Davis had a stiff-necked quality, which had made him impervious to pressure while he was in office and which left him irreconcilable when conquered. He never sued for pardon, and it is related that Winnie Davis, "Daughter of the Confederacy," refused a highly eligible New Yorker because she knew that the alliance would pain her stern father. *The Rise and Fall of the Confederate Government,* although published as late as 1881, was written wholly as a vindication of the past, and bespeaks a man whose real interest in life ended with the old regime.

Davis had a special reason to render his account to posterity, for he had been the chief target of Southern criticism; and although impressive evidences of loyalty were shown him following his release from prison, these had to be interpreted as signs of sympathy for his harsh treatment at Federal hands, not as an endorsement of his administration. He had been reproached for the failure to attack Washington after Bull Run, probably the finest military opportunity offered the Confederacy during its existence; he had been charged with preserving an obstinate faith in poor advisers such as Braxton Bragg long after events had demonstrated their limited competence, and it was obvious that he had abandoned too late the fatuous hope of European intervention.

Davis had, therefore, not only the duty of arguing the Confederacy's case at law but also the task of justifying his own policies. *The Rise and Fall* begins as a conventional rebuttal of Northern contentions, with the author declaring in his preface:

> The object of this book has been from the historical data to show that the Southern States had rightfully the power to withdraw from the Union into which they had, as sovereign communities, voluntarily entered; that the denial of that right was a violation of the letter and spirit of the compact between the States; and that the war waged by the Federal Government against the seceding states was in disregard of the limitations of the Constitution, and destructive of the principles of the Declaration of Independence.[33]

The first volume leads through a maze of legal argument: the terminology of the Constitution, the various compromises, Northern precedents for secession, and the last attempts at amicable settlement, all are analyzed in the light of the doctrine of strict construction. The Federal Government, he claimed, went so far along the road of usurpation that it finally came to regard itself as the sole judge of its own powers, and when the Lincoln administration was inaugurated "timid vacillation was then succeeded by unscrupulous cunning."[34] South Carolina was maneuvered into a position

[33] *The Rise and Fall of the Confederate Government* (New York, 1881), I, p. v.
[34] *Ibid.*, p. 220.

where she had either to fight or to abandon the principle on which she struck for independence.

> The invasions of the Southern States, for the purpose of coercion, were in violation of the written Constitution, and the attempt to subjugate sovereign states, under the pretext of "preserving the Union," was alike offensive to law, to good morals, and the proper use of language. The Union was the voluntary junction of free and independent States, to subjugate any of them was to destroy the constituent parts, and necessarily therefore, must be the destruction of the Union itself.[35]

Upon the men guilty of this breach of law lay the charge of "whatever of bloodshed, of devastation, or of shock to republican government has resulted from the war." [36]

Many of the steps taken by the central government to meet the novel crisis of a civil war have been recognized as of doubtful legality, and Davis frequently interrupts his military narrative to point out infringements of the Constitution and of local rights. Federal rule in New Orleans had shown little respect for precedent; the subversions of the state governments of Maryland, Kentucky, and Missouri had been high-handed in the extreme; and all through the North there had been arbitrary arrests for suspected disaffection, which look strange in the history of a constitutional republic. Davis had by this time convinced himself that the whole of Northern policy was directed toward establishing a centralized despotism, and that the liberty-loving men in the North as well as the South needed to be warned against its encroachments. "The contest is not over, the strife is not ended," he wrote. "It has only entered upon a new and enlarged arena"; and there the champions of constitutional liberty might fight "until the Government of the United States is brought back to its constitutional limits." [37]

35 *Ibid.,* p. 439.
36 *Ibid.*
37 *Ibid.,* II, p. 294.

The Rise and Fall of the Confederate Government contains elements of the tract, the military history, and the personal diary; but it is perhaps best described as an extended political essay, presenting the whole conflict, from the earliest beginnings through the first years of Reconstruction, from the point of view of the constitutional lawyer. Its primary object was to show that the North, as the party of revolution, had in the fanaticism of its program committed great wrongs against the conservative section of the nation. The premise was that faith among contracting parties depends upon observance of the contracts as written, not as whittled away by tenuous reasoning, or eroded by what one party pleases to call progress.

> Much of the past is irremediable; the best hope for a restoration in the future to the pristine purity and fraternity of the Union, rests on the opinions and character of the men who are to succeed this generation: that they may be suited to that blessed work, one, whose public course is ended, invokes them to draw their creed from the fountains of our political history, rather than from the lower stream, polluted as it has been by self-seeking place-hunters and by sectional strife.[38]

Davis's history, though consisting largely of self-exculpation, is in style grave and noble throughout. The tired old man who composed its exhaustive pages realized that the sun had long set on an order whose living head he once was, but for all that he would not bow the knee to expediency or cease to gainsay his opponents. When he died in 1889 at the age of 81, the last of the political soldiers left the scene, and their sons, having little disposition to revive old issues, were looking about for places in the new order.

Men of varied talents were called by a desire to defend the South in her course of secession, but of them all Bernard J.

[38] *Ibid.*, I, p. viii.

Sage best represents the combination of erudition and vehement spirit which distinguishes the entire Southern apologia. Sage was born and educated in Connecticut, but at an early age he removed to New Orleans to practice law, became a sugar planter, and so generally identified himself with the life and aspirations of the section as to earn the right to be considered a Southern spokesman. He was among those sent abroad in 1864 to help check the adverse tide of European opinion, but it was 1865 before the fruit of his labor appeared, and then it was published in England as *The Republic of Republics; or, American Federal Liberty*, by P. C. Centz, Barrister. This transparent pseudonym, which he meant to stand for "Public Common Sense," went unquestioned, and the book was long looked upon as the work of an English advocate devoting his trained mind to the issues of the American quarrel. After passing through three English editions, it was brought out in Boston in 1881, the year in which Davis completed his *Rise and Fall,* and a year which may be regarded as setting a term to the major apologias.

Sage shows some close parallels to Bledsoe, but there is much in this volume not contained in the compact *Is Davis a Traitor?* and its central thesis is quite original. He argued that although the states had a right to secede under the constitutional compact, in the absence of grounds for restraining them, still the North had a right to make war on the South under the *jus gentium,* by which any people is entitled to take extra-legal steps to preserve its threatened integrity. But this right carried a limitation. After the North had gained the victory, it could not then invoke the Constitution, which had in the meantime been set aside, and treat the vanquished as rebels against a national authority; it could proceed against them only as the conquered people of a foreign nation.

This ingenious analysis is supported by the most painstaking reading of law and history to show the difference between what the founding fathers had laid down and what the Lincoln administration had assumed. Sage was as positive as the others in his view that the states had never sacrificed their sovereignty, and that Federal coercion of them was usurpation. This was "A Roman Chapter of American History," and he quoted Burke's solemn warning, "This change from an immediate state of procuration and delegation to the course of acting as from original power, is the way in which all the popular magistracies of the world have been perverted from their purposes." [39]

"An invidious and fraudulent revolution is now going on." he wrote, "which by subjugating the people to a self-determining government placed the United States on the road travelled by all moribund republics." [40] Long before the gloomy German prophets of the twentieth century, Sage thought he saw signs of what could be called "Caesarism" at the end of Western democracy.[41]

The author found, moreover, an interesting source for the consolidationist philosophy of Story, Webster, and their school. It lay, he argued, in the views of the original enemies of the Constitution, who had sought to defeat its adoption by exaggerating its prerogatives. These opponents had attempted to frighten the hesitant states by describing the contract as a kind of "American Divine Right," an instrument "heaven-inspired, perfect, and to last forever" until they were refuted and voted down by its champions. Lincoln became the heir of their views, not knowingly, but through ignorance, and so was in a position to be misled by cunning advisers.

The *Republic of Republics* is a careful, patient, learned report based on a systematic study of the origins of the Amer-

39 *The Republic of Republics* (Boston, 1881), p. 431.
40 *Ibid.*, p. 17.
41 *Ibid.*, p. 13.

ican nation. It appeared at a time, however, when objections such as it raised were but as chaff before the wind; of course it regained nothing for the states, but it did make plain why Davis and Lee could not be tried as traitors. Northern leaders, having consulted their own sources, arrived at a similar conclusion, and thus in a sense the two "traitors" were saved by the perdurance of the principles for which they had fought.

Bledsoe, Pollard, Stephens, Davis, and Sage all wrote with the object of confuting what they believed to be monstrous aspersion, a "war guilt lie," which if allowed to stand, would leave the character of the Southern people permanently vilified. All wished to clear the record, but all, with the single exception of Bledsoe, realized the hopelessness of trying to reverse the trend of history. A doctrinaire and perhaps the most perfect intransigent of his age, Bledsoe appeared to thrive on frustration. Opposition and failure only inflamed his curious temper. He alone felt it profitable to throw up a new line of defenses from which continuous war might be waged, not only against the Republican Party, but also against the vastly more harmful secular theory of government to which he believed the North committed.

In January, 1867, at the beginning of the year in which the Northern policy of Reconstruction took a turn toward severity, Bledsoe brought out in company with William Hand Browne, later to become a distinguished teacher at Johns Hopkins University, the first issue of a new quarterly entitled the *Southern Review*. Both men signed an announcement which appeared on the back cover. The *Southern Review*, it was declared, was being established to fill the need of an organ for Southern men of letters. "We desire the REVIEW to represent the South, not as a party, but as a people." Politics, however, was not to be excluded as topic matter for discussion. "The causes and consequences of the late war, and the various consequences to which it has given rise, will, from time to time, be temperately discussed; not with the view of awakening acrimonious and vindictive feeling, but of drawing profit from the experience of the past." It was a futile disclaimer. Bledsoe was too combative in nature to remain on the academic level of discussion, and however sincerely he may have meant this profession, he was soon back in the bitter accusatory tone of *Is Davis a Traitor?* One can, indeed, mark a steady rise in the acerbity of the *Review* as its objectives become more remote of accomplishment. The first issue contained several articles of polemic intent, among which were "The Legal Status of the Southern States" and the "Imprisonment of Davis." The former stated the case for the restoration of the South, based on the principle that "in civil war there is no treason" and that "in adhering to a *de facto* government there is no treason" [42] The second was a strong appeal to Americans in general not to start the tradition of political persecution, filled with abuse of those guilty of having caused Davis needless suffering. The denial to a people of the right of self-determination was bad enough, Bledsoe argued, but the martyrdom of leaders captured after an abortive struggle for independence would mark the end of that spirit in which the American government had been conceived.

> The children are yet clinging about our knees, who were born before "State prisoners" were imagined as a possibility upon our soil, and the generations who preceded them—scarce half-grown even now—were taught the stories of the Doge's Palace, the Tower and the Bastille, of Olmutz and St. Helena and Ham, as a warning against the wickedness of kings and lords, and a lesson of thankfulness to the good God, who had made a republic their birth-place.[43]

42 *Southern Review,* I (January, 1867), p. 95.
43 *Ibid.,* p. 233.

Although the primary purpose of the *Review* was to continue the old argument over state rights and secession, part of the herculean task the editors assigned themselves was the inspection of Northern histories of the war as they came from the press. These were appearing in increasing number, and the *Review* undertook to judge them in terms of their interpretation of the struggle. Upon most of them it fell with a determined savagery. One can almost detect the note of glee as Bledsoe warms up for such exercise. He thus approaches John William Draper's *History of the American Civil War:* "The author of course gives himself credit for perfect fairness and impartiality. . . . The promise is fair, but what of the performance? We shall judge the tree not by its blossoms but by its fruits. If these happen to be misrepresentations, calumnies, and lies, what do we care for the author's good intentions? Or for any other hollow, hypocritical thing that bears such deadly fruit." [44] George Bancroft was saluted in similar fashion. "There have been bad men and bad teachers always," Bledsoe wrote, "but society was safe as long as it shut them up in its moral lazarhouses. When it makes them its high priests and spreads its garments and palm branches for them to tread on, those who love it may begin to despair." [45] School histories of the United States of Northern authorship excited him to the highest pitch of indignation, for they were spreading the very kind of doctrine the *Review* had been established to counteract. Characterizing them as "crude compilations of malice and mendacity," he said he could not afford to follow "their innumerable lies, great and small," but he warned Southern parents to keep their children out of schools in which such books were used.

The *Southern Review* had a difficult time, for the people whom it championed would neither read it nor support it, and had it not been for the unflagging energy and determina-

[44] *Ibid., V* (January, 1869), p. 3.
[45] *Ibid., IV* (July, 1868), p. 149.

tion of Bledsoe himself, who sometimes supplied half the content of an issue,[46] it might have perished in the first year. The Southern people as a whole believed in the principles which it advocated, but they did not constitute a reading public; and on those infrequent occasions when they did read, they preferred anecdotes of the camp or criticisms of campaigns, neither of which the *Review* included. The discouragements were great, and in 1870 the founder, "deeply impressed with the vanity of all earthly things," [47] decided to dedicate the magazine thenceforward to the glory of God. Accordingly in January, 1871, it became an official organ of the Methodist Church. Strong political articles continued to appear, but it was made to serve primarily as a vehicle for the theology of Bledsoe, who seized the opportunity to revive a dispute of extraordinary bitterness with the Reverend R. L. Dabney, another doughty Southern spokesman. After Bledsoe died in 1877, his daughter carried on the publication until 1879, when the Methodist Church withdrew its support.

The *Southern Review* was in reality the old antebellum sectional journal fighting for life and recognition in the new era. In the political field its victories were victories in debate only, and its religious theory of the social order went unheard amid the crude materialisms of the Gilded Age, but it remains unquestionably the best repository of the views of the unreconciled Southerner.

2. The Attack Upon Secular Democracy

Another part of the Southern defense, which has received less publicity than the legal case, but which in implications was more profound, was the opposition to all secular theories of the state. The French Revolution had established the prin-

46 Edwin Mims in *The South in the Building of the Nation*, VII, pp. 464-465.
47 *Southern Review, VIII* (July, 1870), p. 443.

ciple that man is the measure of all things; his freedom, his welfare, his opportunity for "the pursuit of happiness" were acclaimed the objectives of all just governments—a sort of political humanism which had the effect of deifying an abstract concept of man. But for hundreds of years before this there had prevailed a contrary notion, which formed part of the medieval world-picture. This taught that the state is the mortal god under the immortal god, that man owes allegiance to the state because it is divinely instituted, and that the carrying out of its commands is a divine appointment for which one must not expect rewards in the utilitarian sense. The fruit of its work, like the fruit of all human effort, was something tending toward "the greater glory of God." After this concept had been eliminated by eighteenth-century rationalism, the state came to be looked upon as a mere instrumentality in the hands of the majority, without relationship to revealed religion, and charged only with the ordering of temporal affairs.

Southern authoritarians felt that rationalism had accomplished as much harm in politics as in religion. In its first issue after the war, *De Bow's Review,* of New Orleans, was cautioning its readers against exclusive reliance upon reason, which, unless "limited, balanced, and counterpoised, always leads to false, and often dangerous conclusions." The application of this truth was to be seen in the present state of the South:

> Every bloody revolution in Christendom, as well in Church as in State, for the last three hundred years, has been brought about by following the too often deceptive guide of reason. And reason now, except in the South, is everywhere at work busily undermining and upsetting all laws, governments, faiths and institutions, with no visible result except the shedding of blood, and the rapid and vast increase of pauperism.[48]

A few Southern churchmen well grounded in history and

[48] *De Bow's Review,* After the War Series, II (November, 1866), p. 494.

philosophy and a few laymen who shrank before the picture
of a godless world undertook the forlorn task of pleading for
a restoration of religious sanctions. Among the divines was
Robert Lewis Dabney, a Virginia Presbyterian, who had
served in the war as chaplain on the staff of Stonewall Jackson. Dabney conceived an intense admiration for the eccentric character of this commander, and as early as 1863 memorialized him in *The Life and Campaigns of Lieutenant-
General Thomas J. Jackson.* At the beginning of events Dabney had opposed secession, but as time passed he came to
view the war as a conflict between the Christian South and
the anti-Christian North. Occurrences following the peace
confirmed him in this view, and he decided that it was his
duty as a teacher of religion and morals to make a statement
of the righteousness of Southern civilization. Therefore he
appeared in 1867 with *A Defence of Virginia and Through
Her of the South in Recent and Pending Contests Against
the Sectional Party.* It is at once the bitterest and the most
eloquent of the major apologias.

The thesis is an argument for an hierarchic society, made
in terms of a combined religious fundamentalism and a
searching political dialectic. No one can fail to be impressed
by the wide and solid scholarship of the better Southern
churchmen of this period, and Dabney was perhaps foremost
of them all. Constitutional lawyers might argue the defects of
the original contract made between the states, but he realized
that the ideas inspiring the recent social revolution did not
have a contemporary origin. They had started with Hobbes
of Malmesbury and "pious John Locke, a sort of baptized
image of that atheistic philosopher," [49] and their propagation
was owing to the "infidel democrats" of the French Revolution. He attacked Locke's theory of the origin of society as
false in fact and impossible in theory. All freedom rests upon

[49] Dabney, *op. cit.,* p. 242.

a true perception of moral distinctions. A man's liberty, accordingly, is not the liberty to do whatever he wants to do, but only a right to do what he has a "moral right to do." [50] Hence membership in civil society is not a matter of one's electing; it is native with every human being, for God, knowing that man is a fallen creature, whose will is disordered, ordained that he live under authority. From these principles Dabney deduced the authority of magistrates and the responsibility of citizens.

Dabney's view in substance was that unless our first postulate be that God designed a moral universe, everything must dissolve in meaningless contention. To set up man's secular advantage as the only ultimate good and then to invest every majority with irresponsible power is to instigate endless strife. "What fruit has radical democracy ever borne, except factious oppression, anarchy, and the stern necessity for despotism?" [51] The thoughtful reader will not miss the resemblance between this and the doctrine of the divine right of kings. In its clearest form the doctrine of the divine right of kings invested the king with a *de jure* right which made it impossible that there should ever be a *de facto* king. The logic of this conception is that society must be authorized to be respected, and that the accidents of history, such as wars and revolutions, must not be allowed to become the criteria of right. In such a society the whole administrative organization is the instrumentality of God's will. "If asked whence the obligation to obey the civil magistrate, who, personally, is but our fellow, we answer from God's will, which is the source and measure of duty." [52] Society is not a product of the flux of history, but of design, and hence one's position in it must be determined by his virtue, that term being understood, of course, through the teachings of religion.

50 *Ibid.*, p. 252.
51 *Ibid.*, p. 259.
52 *Ibid.*, p. 251.

From this point of view there is but a short step to the vindication of slavery. Since persons in a society differ greatly in "power, knowledge and natural relations to each other," no mere assumed equality will serve, and therefore "the civic liberties of all classes of society ought not to be the same." [53] The privileges accorded to anyone, like the duties he must bear, should reflect his powers and moral qualifications. Those who fall below the established level of virtue and reason have to be restrained, and any degree of restraint is righteous that conducts to a righteous end. Inasmuch as all moral obligation proceeds from God, abolitionism, which is a repudiation of moral responsibility, is heresy. "Modern abolitionism in America had, in fact, a Socinian birth, in the great apostasy of the Puritans of New England to that benumbing heresy, and in the Pharisaism, shallow scholarship, affectation, conceit, and infidelity of the Unitarian clique in the self-styled American Athens, Boston." [54]

Dabney was convinced that the whole Southern theory of society was grounded upon a sober study of divine teachings and human history, whereas that of the North was only a reflection of ignorance and obsession. Thus the doctrines of the abolitionists were made up of a "set of miserable and shallow sophisms, which Southern divines and statesmen have threshed into dust and driven away as the chaff before the whirlwind, so long ago, and so often, that any intelligent man among us is almost ashamed to allude to them as requiring an answer." [55] It was anomalous to find the literature of the victorious side "poor, beggarly, and false," while that of the losing was "manly, philosophic, and powerful." [56]

Dabney felt so assured of the correctness of his principles that he promised his readers the North would one day be

53 *Ibid.*, p. 257.
54 *Ibid. p.* 131.
55 *Ibid.*, p. 14.
56 *Ibid.*

overtaken by the consequences of her own misdeeds, and that the wild notions brought down to disrupt Southern society would return to plague their inventors. For its revenge the South would have to look forward to that "anarchy and woe" which the "disorganizing heresies" would eventually produce among its conquerors.[57]

Albert Taylor Bledsoe joined Dabney in preaching the necessity for a religious authoritarian government, and few issues of the *Southern Review* appeared without some attack upon the godless doctrines of the French Revolution. Bledsoe was chiefly opposed to the chimerical notion that man is by nature good. He argued that on the contrary no government can hope to survive which does not proceed on the assumption that man is a fallen being. The first article to appear in the *Review,* ambitiously entitled "The Education of the World," established a point of view which was steadfastly maintained during its twelve-year existence. It contended that in giving up the religious sanctions of his laws and institutions, man hands himself over to the chaos which must always proceed from passion unchecked by higher discipline. To substitute a sentimental optimism and humantarianism for the old and proved doctrine of man's natural depravity is to prepare the way for a new fall. The more there is left open to the whims and passions of men, the wider will be the field of folly. "With the absolute supremacy of the French School, whose doctrines are so flattering to the pride and ignorance of man, there arose the self-idolatry of the men of 1789, and also 'the dominant idea of the last century,' that governments and institutions make the people." [58]

He mocked the favorite notion that people can be regenerated by "an idea." [59] Because the government of the United States had not been "adjusted to the great facts and laws of

---

[57] *Ibid.,* p. 356.
[58] *Southern Review,* I (January, 1867), p. 15.
[59] *Ibid.,* VI (October, 1868), pp. 292-295.

the moral world," it became "a gigantic and degrading tyranny." [60] Because the founders of the American Union had not taken into account the natural depravity of man, the system which they devised, however unexceptionable from the secular point of view, was unable to stand the test of history. "The causes of the late war," he wrote, "had their roots in the passions of the human heart. Under the influence of those causes almost everything in the new system worked differently from what was anticipated." [61] At the founding of the Union the North and the South struggled together like Jacob and Esau in the womb "with almost fatal desperation." [62] After the government had been established, this struggle was continued through seven great crises, and following each the majority section grew bolder and more tyrannical as it grew stronger. The fundamental error of the designers of the Constitution proved to have been the clothing of man instead of law with supreme power. " 'Man is free by nature,' says Locke, but according to the infinitely more profound aphorism of Aristotle, 'man is a tyrant by nature.' " [63] Hence when the majority found that it could rule, it trampled the law into the dust, and so it will always be when man either singly or collectively is made the arbiter. "The legislators of 1787 did not know that man is a fallen being; or, if they did, they failed to comprehend the deep significance of this awful fact." [64]

With this example of human failure before him, Bledsoe could return to the errors of the French radicals. The great mistake of those theorists, he continued, was the constructing of an imaginary man who was not to be found when the actual task of making institutions was commenced. "The

60 *Ibid.*, I (April, 1867), p. 319.
61 *Ibid.*, I (January, 1867), p. 263.
62 *Ibid.*, p. 268.
63 *Ibid.*, p. 270.
64 *Ibid.*, p. 272.

more shallow the theory on which our politics are based, the sooner will they be ground to powder and scattered before the angry winds." [65] The theme of man's natural depravity challenged his resources as a theologian, and he would at times rise to the earnestness and intensity of an Old Testament prophet. "The new Republic of '87, being founded on a presumptuous confidence in man, was doomed to fall, or to undergo sad changes and transformations." [66] He moralized further in the same passage: "As often as the experiment may be made, it will be demonstrated in the grand theatre of history, that the purity, the equality, and the freedom of all men, is one of the most fatal delusions that ever issued from the brain of theorist, or convulsed the world with horrible disorder." [67] This entire philosophy was summed up in the apocalyptic cry: "Woe betide all the proud polities of self-idolizing man." [68]

Even before Bledsoe founded his militant *Southern Review,* General D. H. Hill had established in Charlotte, North Carolina, a journal devoted to "the vindication of Southern history." General Hill had experienced his share of the vicissitudes of war, and feeling now, like Lee, that the sole hope of the Southern people lay in a reorientation through education, he commenced a publication with which he hoped to diffuse a knowledge of the applied sciences among his chauvinistic countrymen as well as argue the justice of the South's cause. On most topics of sectional controversy *The Land We*

---

[65] *Ibid.*

[66] *Ibid.*

[67] *Ibid.*, VIII (July, 1870), p. 19. It was natural that Bledsoe should oppose with equal determination the extension of the franchise to women. He noted with satisfaction that in this program Northern women were "the chief mischief makers," Southern women having shown little appetite for "the forbidden fruit." He foresaw a collapse like that of the Roman Empire if "the spirit of infidel reform, which, in proud contempt of the world and the providence of God, has inaugurated the woman's rights movement, should triumph" (*ibid.*, X, October, 1871, p. 941).

[68] *Ibid.*, I (January, 1867), p. 273.

Love was conspicuously moderate; it made a full confession of Southern sins and expressed the hope that the "everlasting twaddle about politics" would soon be supplanted by discussions of how best to turn the furrow and prune the vine. The growing secular spirit of the North, however, was a feature of the new order which General Hill could not accept. Articles and editorials viewed with alarm the general decay of religious and moral sanctions. In a striking historical parallel the South was compared to La Vendee, which had suffered destruction by opposing the godless fury of the French Revolution. "The South was the La Vendee of the United States," it was declared.

> Her conservatism, her love of the Constitution; her attachment to the old usages of society, her devotion to principles, her faith in Bible truth—all these involved her in a long and bloody war with that Radicalism which seeks to overthrow all that is venerable, respectable, and of good repute.[69]

He saw the assault upon Southern religious faith taking two forms: one was the carnival of corruption in the entire postbellum country, which shook the faith of many persons in a moral order of the universe; and the other was the new spirit of secular education in the North,[70] which gave evidence of moving South. "Everything has been done to debauch the moral perceptions of our unfortunate section," he exclaimed in an editorial.[71]

The spirit of pragmatism, too, was creeping over the nation, and R. L. Dabney was wise enough to realize that it was the most insidious of all the foes of religion. *The Land We Love* published his lecture on "The Duty of the Hour," in

---

[69] *The Land We Love*, V (September, 1868), p. 447.

[70] The author of "Religion in the Public Schools of the North" asked (*ibid.*, VI, January, 1869, p. 247): "Are we a Christian nation? A short ten years ago men daily thanked God that this was not a question."

[71] *Ibid.*, V (September, 1868), p. 444.

which he sought to convince the students of Davidson College that under God's inscrutable providence the right does not always meet with temporal success. "It is only the atheist who adopts success as a *criterion* of right. It is not a new thing in the history of men that God appoints to the brave and the true the stern task of contending, and falling, in a righteous quarrel." [72]

Writing in the *Southern Magazine,* a second periodical established in Baltimore to support the Southern cause, Henry Eubank pleaded for a society based on distinctions in morality and culture. Northern "utilitarianism," he urged, must not be allowed to prescribe for the Southern ailment, for the North was "a civilization progressive only in its increasing knowledge of evil." [73] General Lee had been great because he had recognized his commission as "derived primarily from Heaven." [74] The writer had the aristocrat's fear that the jealous masses were seeking to destroy all exclusiveness.

There is a latent radicalism in the lower strata of society in a chronic condition of receptivity for any and every doctrine that asserts the perfect equality of men regardless of moral and intellectual culture, and aims directly or indirectly at the overthrow of all "rights" claimed as distinctive on grounds of such culture.[75]

The explanation was that such rights are difficult of attainment and are "incomprehensible to those who have acquired no title to them." [76]

Thus the religious part of the Southern polemic advanced three points: that society is of divine ordination; that man is by nature wicked and requires protection against his own

[72] *Ibid.,* VI (December, 1868), pp. 117-118.
[73] *Southern Magazine,* XII (May, 1873), p. 606.
[74] *Ibid.*
[75] *Ibid.,* p. 609.
[76] *Ibid.*

impulses; and that temporal success alone is never a test of right. The victory of the North was seen as threatening to extinguish each of them. Lincoln's "government of the people, by the people, and for the people" is, of course, the classic statement of secular democracy, discarding the older notion of the civil magistrate as God's vice-regent. Majority rule, which in the antebellum union had been somewhat restricted by the nature of the compact, was now beyond challenge. And the practice of judging men's actions by a divine deliverance, or by any code superior to what he himself could frame, was fast vanishing. Southern writers tried as best they could to point out the dangers in this rising tide of empiricism.

3. The Particularism of Peoples

The issue of Southern separatism inevitably raised the question of differences between Southern and Northern people, and it was natural that champions of the lost cause would make the most of comparisons advantageous to them. If two peoples are so unlike that they can be happy only in separate political courses, the yoking of them together is an act of violence which can be justified only by casuistry, or in terms of some mystical belief in a joint mission. Southern spokesmen realized that in the right of self-determination of peoples they had a powerful argument—somewhat vitiated, it is true, by the awkward presence of the Negro—and they were not slow to quote the Declaration of Independence on the necessity of dissevering political bonds.

While many Southern people were conscious that they did not like Yankees, there was little general agreement over what constituted their chief imperfection. Some objected to them as Puritans; some regarded them as a people in whom the commercial instinct, with its degrading effects, had become dominant; and a number of the clerics saw them as anti-Christians, who had been seduced by the heresies of Arminianism and rationalism. Such charges are to be found in various forms in many published sources. A fair example of the kind of indictment which an embittered Southerner could compose comes from the pen of R. B. Rhett, Jr., of the Charleston *Mercury*, who upon suspension of this journal addressed a letter to his subscribers. In reviewing the calamities which had brought the South low, he said:

> The truth is, there is an incongruity between the two peoples from their very natures. . . . The one is cautious and reticent; the other frank and open in communication. The one is penurious; the other free in the use of money. The one cannot comprehend the meaning of the word honor; the other values it beyond life. . . . The one loves gregariousness and does everything by association; the other cultivates privacy and individuality, and acts with difficulty with others. The one is skeptical, prying, officious, harsh, dogmatic, aggressive, and fond of novelties, misnamed progress; the other is more genial and more tolerant, distrusts change and reverences the past. The one looks upon government as an instrument of aggrandizement, to make money or to rule others; the other regards it simply as an instrument of protection, for securing justice and leaving to all under its authority the privilege of seeking their own happiness in their own way. Is it possible that two people of such different characteristics and antagonistic views can live voluntarily under the same Free Government? [77]

Some writers, of whom the brilliant E. A. Pollard is an instance, attached great weight to the Cavalier tradition. "There could be no congeniality," he wrote in *The Lost Cause*, "between the Puritan exiles who established themselves upon the cold and rugged and cheerless soil of New England, and the Cavaliers who sought the brighter climate

[77] "A Farewell to the Subscribers of the Charleston *Mercury*," n.d., n.p.

of the South, and drank in their baronial halls in Virginia confusion to roundheads and regicides." [78] As a result both of his heritage and of the conditions of his life, Pollard continued, the Southerner had developed a superiority of manner which inspired resentment in the Yankee commoner; and when the Yankee saw an opportunity to destroy this affront to his pride, he took it enthusiastically.

> The South had an element in its society, a landed gentry which the North envied, and for which its substitute was a coarse ostentatious aristocracy that smelt of the trade, and that, however it cleansed itself, and packed its houses with fine furniture, could never entirely subdue a sneaking sense of inferiority. There is a singularly bitter hate which is inseparable from a sense of inferiority; and every close observer of Northern society has discovered how there lurked in every form of hostility to the South the conviction that the Northern man, however disguised with ostentation, was coarse and inferior in comparison with the aristocracy and chivalry of the South.[79]

The Northern public, which had deliberately set out to destroy "the distinctive civilization of the South," with its "higher sentimentalism" and "superior refinements of scholarship and manners," he viewed as a mob, rude, fickle, gregarious, with a mind "volatile, superficial, and theatrically inclined." [80] To the charge of lack of refinement he added the graver one of over-addiction to self-interest, which violated the Southern custom of *noblesse oblige*.[81]

In one sense Pollard was but echoing the journalistic abuse

---

78 Pollard, *op. cit.*, p. 49.

79 *Ibid.*, p. 51.

80 *Ibid.*, *p.* 186.

81 In support of this point Pollard quoted a letter written by Washington in 1775 relative to the appointment of officers in the Continental Army. The letter spoke of the unsoldierly conduct of some of his New England subalterns, claiming that "these people seem to be too inattentive to everything but their interest." The letter appears in *The Writings of George Washington from the Official Manuscript Sources* (Washington, 1931-1940), III, p. 451.

of the preceding half century; but in another, if allowance is made for his extreme terminology, he was outlining a difference in background and outlook which has persisted in the face of all changes until today. The North was fast becoming urban and industrialized, and at this very moment there was appearing that disturbing factor, the mass mind. Signs of modernism were everywhere. "Sensations, excitements on slight cause, fits of fickle admiration, manias in society and fashion, a regard for magnitude, display and exaggeration, all these indications of a superficial and restless civilization abound in the North and are peculiar to its people." [82] In comparison the people of the South were slow in their reactions; they had a settled way of life; they maintained "a sober estimate of the value of men and things"; and their favor was neither given nor withdrawn lightly. But hostile critics could, and often did, interpret these features as proceeding from ignorance, insensibility, and indolence. How far these specific descriptions apply may, of course, be debated, but the very currency of such conceptions indicates why many Southerners viewed the Civil War as a war of peoples.

One may be disposed to take Pollard's indictment of Northern character more seriously after learning that he was preparing to look at the adverse side of Southern character. One of the recurrent themes of *The Lost Cause* is that the South failed to gain its independence because of gross mismanagement, which proceeded largely from habitual Southern inefficiency. He went so far as to make the keenly resented charge of shiftlessness. "It has been remarked that the shiftlessness of the people of the South, their want of commercial tact or *business knowledge,* so to speak, however it may have been doubted before, was fully proved in the war, and that this cause, as much as anything else, contributed to the ruin and prostration of the Confederacy." [83] He repeat-

[82] Pollard, *op. cit.,* p. 52.
[83] *Ibid.,* p. 488.

edly referred to the absurd vanity of the Southern people, to their over-confidence, and to their incapacity for analysis. He turned a disapproving eye upon Southern chivalry,[84] and in a later work, *The Life of Jefferson Davis,* he attacked it pointedly, calling it mere excessive admiration for "low physical courage" or "animal combativeness." In the same pages he argued that the widely advertised generosity of Southern character should not be allowed to obscure the insularity of outlook from which most Southerners suffered.

> There are great defects in that character—peculiar defects of accident; but there is also the sum of many virtues. The people of the South are brave to a fault; they are generous to credulity, polite, hospitable, cherishing many noble virtues which the commercial spirit of the age has elsewhere outgrown; but they have all the peculiar faults of an *untraveled people*—a people who pass their lives in local neighborhoods, and who, having but little knowledge of how large and various the world is, easily take conceit of their own powers and virtues.[85]

Yet at the close of *The Lost Cause,* when Pollard looked back over his story of the war, he decided that it was the distinctive Southern character which must be salvaged from the ruins, regardless of its palpable liabilities; for it had permitted the people to emerge from the conflict feeling, even in defeat, that they were "THE BETTER MEN." [86] Abandonment of that distinctive character would prove "immeasurably the worst consequence of defeat." [87] That the people of the South should maintain their superiority "in all the standards of individual character over the people of the North" was but "the plain syllogism of common sense." [88] Civilized habits

84 *Ibid.,* p. 404.
85 *The Life of Jefferson Davis* (Philadelphia, 1869), p. 192.
86 *The Lost Cause,* p. 729.
87 *Ibid.,* pp. 751-752.
88 *Ibid.*

and political scholarship were the two things in which the South had excelled the North, and he feared, not unreasonably as events have showed, that Southerners might be persuaded to give up what was good along with what had no right to survive.

The chief merit of Pollard's approach is that it avoids entirely the cloying attitude of reverence which impedes so much Southern historical writing, even when it does not lead to unconscious falsehood. His allusions to the complexion of the Confederate Congress, to the rows in its secret sessions, and to the general decay of patriotism indicated by the conscription laws and by desertions allow it to appear that the Confederate war effort was not altogether whole-souled and gallant. It is well to notice, consequently, that one who took note of so many of the discreditable occurrences behind the lines could still argue that Southern character had proved its mettle in the ordeal.

Bledsoe's stormy *Southern Review* pressed the matter of difference in more violent language, as was to be expected. The editor remarked with approval that a collection of Southern war poetry reflected "an intense, unquenchable, personal hate of Northerners as a race and as individuals." [89] Always eager to explore historic and philosophic backgrounds, he saw the Southerners as a representative agrarian people, pure, peaceful, and loyal, pitted against the depraved population of Northern cities. He began an extended contrast with the remark of a Spanish author to the effect that *Don Quixote* was one of the most mischievous books ever written because it took the noblest characteristics of human nature and rendered them contemptible. The North had committed the same crime in its caricature of Southern civilization. Bledsoe assumed the agrarian position, previously given expression by Jefferson and John Taylor of Caroline,

[89] *Southern Review,* I (January, 1867), p. 278.

that the cultivation of the earth is the most innocent vocation, and therefore the best training in virtue. "For such reasons as these," he wrote, "by universal consent, an agricultural population has always been deemed the most virtuous, and their characteristics, whatever they may be, the most unchangeable." [90] Consequently, during its seventy-year hegemony the South had ruled the North not by weight of numbers, for it was always a minority, but by integrity.[91] "Every element of purity, stability and greatness is with the South." [92] While Southerners had clung to the old values and had remained a religious people, he argued, the North had become progressively irreligious.

> The great defect of Northern civilization is in its materiality. It is of the earth earthy, and ignores the spirituality of our nature. Its grand motive and object is the accumulation of money, and its prime boast is of the things money can buy— "the lust of the eye, the lust of the flesh, and the pride of life." Mammon is its god, and nowhere has he more devout or abject worshippers, or has he set up a more polluted civilization than in the North.
>
> The whole spirit of Christianity is opposed to this sort of civilization.[93]

The Southern character, he said in development of the thesis, is peculiar for its fidelity as the Northern is peculiar for its faithlessness. Because the North could not assimilate a people so different from it in nature, it set out to change that nature by means of emancipating the Negro and by encouraging the immigration of foreigners. But Bledsoe's conclusion was that the North not only would fail in its attempt to change the characteristics of the South, but also that in the

90 *Ibid.*, VI (July, 1869), p. 102.
91 *Ibid.*, p. 103.
92 *Ibid.*
93 *Ibid.*, p. 109.

course of time it might decide to adopt them for itself. The belief that the civilization of the South represented a permanent, settled order, whereas that of the North represented a temporary, transitional one is frequently encountered in postbellum Southern writing.[94]

This reflected the widely held opinion that Northerners were temperamentally unstable, incapable of distinguishing between the superficial and the fundamental, and consequently always victimized by fads and notions. The author of "A Soldier's History of the War" in *Our Living and Our Dead* felt that the difference in mental and moral qualities made it certain that "the vagaries of the Northern mind could never attain a foothold or flourish among the people of the South." [95] Such expressions point to the Southern distrust of the intellectual.

> Then, and at all times since, they and their descendants have evinced an irrepressibility of mind that tends to erratic extremes. . . . Hence all the wild vagaries and foolish 'isms of the age have had their origin in the Northern States, among the people calling themselves the descendants of the Puritans, a name applied to the Pilgrim Fathers of New England.[96]

It has been remarked with truth that the border states joined the Confederacy after the Civil War, and there may be no doubt that in Maryland, Kentucky, and Missouri sympathy for the stricken areas of the lower South increased in the Reconstruction period, partly from a feeling that the objects of the war had not been honestly avowed and partly from a feeling that the North was acting brutally toward a people with whom it had ties of blood and sentiment. The shift from

[94] *Scott's Monthly,* of Atlanta, could remark (II, October, 1866, p. 866): "From the inception of the government, the political ideas and principles of Southern statesmen were dominant in its control. That they will be so again is as certain as the triumph of truth over error."

[95] *Our Living and Our Dead,* I (November, 1874), p. 296.

[96] *Ibid.,* p. 295.

a neutral state of feeling to one of bitter partisanship may be traced in *The Land We Love,* and in the Richmond *Eclectic* and its successors. The latter was founded in 1868 by William Hand Browne and the Reverend Moses Hoge as "A Monthly Magazine of Foreign Literature, Religious and Secular." A year later Hoge took over complete ownership and transferred the magazine to Baltimore, where it re-commenced publication as the *New Eclectic.* A change of tone was soon apparent. Previously it had taken an innocuous line, praying for sectional reconciliation and avoiding allusion to political controversies, but now it became highly sensitive to all criticisms of the South, from whatever quarter they emanated. An example will illustrate this type of reaction. Hepworth Dixon had published an article in the London *Athenaeum* treating Marylanders with flippancy and ridicule. The *New Eclectic* replied with an editorial which is one of the most defiant pieces in the entire Southern polemic. It was a frank stand in favor of the South's famous, or, if one takes the point of view of its critics, infamous anti-intellectualism. Readers were reminded that Dixon had acquired his knowledge of the South in the North.

He was in search of *isms,* of which happily we have none. He was tracing the development of what in New England are called "ideas"—things which the healthy nature of our people loathes, and which we exorcise with bell, book, and candle, as we would the Devil from whom they come. Our faults, shortcomings, vices if you will, have at least this redeeming feature, that they are natural. Our moral distempers are those of a constitution naturally sound and vigorous.[97]

In 1871 this journal underwent another metamorphosis; now becoming the *Southern Magazine* and dropping eclecticism altogether, it took the offensive, boldly assailing Northern character, "radical delusions," and the policies expressive

97 *New Eclectic,* II (July, 1868), p. 354.

of these. It is obvious that attacks upon character are a more serious sign of alienation than mere disagreement and division over propositions. The latter are capable of compromise and settlement, but differences in character are permanent sources of friction, and the editor of the *Southern Magazine* was determined to keep in high relief the distinction between Southerners and Northerners. In the pushing and jostling new urban proletariat with its "aggressive ruffianism" he saw the ruling class of the North. Alcibiades Jones, writing in the issue of March, 1872, thus described it:

> Within a circle of fifty miles around New York, that is, a circle one hundred miles in diameter, there dwells a population that is distinct and dissimilar from all other populations in Christendom. So far as this population has a social creed on which it would build a social status, its cardinal virtue is the old delusion that God has created all men equal.[98]

Its disagreeable character flowed from a Northern heresy which the South had never accepted. "And in the last analysis it will be found that the active principle of aggressive ruffianism is this pestiferous doctrine of equality carried to its legitimate conclusion." [99]

Concurrent with such criticisms were articles and editorials maintaining the superior gentility and elegance of Southern manners. The magazine ran a series of "letters from the South" by a "Northern hypochondriac." This sojourner had gone South filled with the usual fixed ideas and delusions, only to be disabused of them and to be won over to an admiration of Southern ways. The following neat contrast is found in a "letter" written from Mobile:

> The hurry and skurry and eager haste, the effects of which are so plainly depicted upon the countenances of the human tide

[98] *Southern Magazine*, X (March, 1872), p. 257.
[99] *Ibid.*, p. 259.

in the engorged streets of the Northern cities, are never seen here. Merchants and others bred in this climate go about their transactions with deliberateness, the gentlemanly propriety and grace of men who "understand the situation"—men who are masters and not slaves of their vocation, whatever that vocation may be.[100]

In a later installment the Yankee confessed that before coming South he had possessed no education at all in the real sense. "It was really worse than no education at all. It possessed neither historical coherency nor logical sequence." [101]

The *Southern Magazine* was bold enough to make lynching, or "irregular execution," as it was termed, a criterion of the difference between the two peoples under consideration. It declared that the desire to inflict prompt vengeance upon a criminal, especially if he is guilty of a monstrous crime, is "perfectly healthy and natural," and that any society content to leave such matters to the police and the courts is "an emasculated and deliquescent society." [102]

Thus Baltimore in the 1870's, with Bledsoe booming away in the *Southern Review* on the constitutional and religious issues, and with Browne in the *Southern Magazine* pursuing the general theme of Southern superiority, must have appeared more rebellious than in 1861, when her citizens mobbed the Massachusetts soldiery. Neither magazine, however, survived the decade.

Our Living and Our Dead, a strongly partisan magazine devoting itself principally to the interests of North Carolina, was proud that Northern scorn had done nothing to diminish the spirit of chivalry. "Yankee ridicule has tried its hand upon Southern chivalry, for three generations past," it declared, "but fortunately for the reputation and happiness of our people, it has signally failed to 'laugh' it 'away,' or to

100 *Ibid.*, VIII (January, 1871), p. 432.
101 *Ibid.*, IX (July, 1871), p. 69.
102 *Ibid.*, XVII (July, 1875), p. 663.

expel it from the hearts of our most ideal types of man-hood." [103] It then went over the military record of Sherman, "a sort of mixture of Vandal and Goth," [104] and of Sheridan, and contrasted their practices with the "knightly courtesy, the generous forbearance, the merciful considerateness" of the heirs of chivalry, which was traced to the spirit of Christianity. These things, it added, "serve to 'point a moral' and to throw great light upon the two peoples who dwell in the two great sections of the Union." The South was "indeed poor," but it still had the inheritance of its character.[105]

Most Southern poetry of the postbellum era is dreary and undistinguished, but there is one little-known poem which deserves recognition by reason of its departure from the heroic, sentimental, lachrymose tradition. This is *The Loves of Jonathan and Virginia*, by William B. Johnson, of Virginia, an allegorical work of 416 stanzas in seeming imitation of Byron's *Don Juan*. Described as "a tribute to the Muse of American history," it is divided into six books, the titles of which roughly convey the story: "Early Romance," "The Smitheid," "Virginia, Queen of the Old Dominion," "The Marriage," "The Divorce," and "Reconciliation or Reconstruction." Since it is an account of an incompatible union, the poet goes at length to distinguish the characters of husband and wife, and therefore adds something to sectional portraiture.

Virginia had been founded as a land of freedom, where there would be "no Puritan to preach and no old Pope to pay," [106] and under these conditions she enjoyed a long prosperity. But as she approached maturity, a marriage was suggested between her and "Cousin Jonathan, a tall, thin lad, religiously inclined." Virginia was reluctant, but she yielded

---

[103] *Our Living and Our Dead*, III (November, 1875), p. 663.
[104] *Ibid.*, p. 664.
[105] *Ibid.*, p. 674.
[106] *The Loves of Jonathan and Virginia* (Philadelphia, 1873), p. 11.

when the venerable George Washington said that the union would mean safety for her people. The marriage contract contained certain reservations which she thought would be respected, but which Cousin Jonathan was even then plotting to evade:

> But Cousin Jonathan, a cunning fox,
> Said not a word; indeed, full well he knew,
> Could he get in his tail, no paper locks
> Could keep his body all from going through.[107]

But for many years, while her destruction was being prepared, Virginia lived a life of innocent happiness:

> Meantime her sons in luxury and ease
> Were bred to medicine, divinity, and law;
> While Northern boys were making bread and cheese
> They frolic, fiddle, fox-hunt, paint and draw,
> And in the parlor pretty women please,
> About the future caring not a straw:
> Wild, graceful, chivalrous in their happy youth
> They yet, when men, become the statesmen of the South.

> To make, to mend, to black their boots they could not
> To cut a coat they did not understand;
> To make a wooden nutmeg they would not;
> Nor did they relish ploughing their own land;
> They spent their father's money as they should not,
> But often gave it with a liberal hand;
> And if one e'er was taxed with what he spent
> Replied, he meant someday to be the President.[108]

Finally Virginia decided to sue for divorce, and the case was taken to "old Judge Battle's Court," where it became so long drawn out that the petitioner at length withdrew her plea. The poem ends with some satirical stanzas on Recon-

107 *Ibid.*, p. 70.
108 *Ibid.*, p. 72.

struction, in which Cousin Jonathan is found trying to convert the Negro to political uses. Virginia warns him that his success will be short-lived because Cuffie "knows the difference 'tween gentlemen and Yankees," [109] and will fall back on the Southern whites as his true friends.[110]

Part of the attack on Northern character took the form of holding up individual men as examples of what was to be reprobated. The Radical leaders in Congress drew nothing except invective, of course; but even President Lincoln, whose utterances had been largely though not altogether free of expressions hostile to the South, was pictured sometimes as the fit leader of a coarse mob, and sometimes as a man incompetent for the job he held. A son of that class universally despised as "poor white trash," Lincoln would have been suspected by Southerners even under the best circumstances; rumors of his uncanonical birth, and reports that in his youth he had written a book defending infidelity were used to make the case against him complete. Newspapers went all lengths to caricature him as "the Illinois ape," and some men with pretensions to intellect and scholarship who had known him personally left estimates which clash sharply with the later legend.

Albert Taylor Bledsoe, tending to grow more shrill as the years passed, took Ward Lamon's *Life of Lincoln* as occasion to give his opinion of the martyred President, with whom, he said, he had held almost daily intercourse at the bar of Springfield.[111] After conceding that Lincoln had possessed a character in some ways remarkable, he attacked the notion, then becoming established apparently beyond all hope of removal, that sympathy with the underdog had been the ruling passion

[109] *Ibid.*, p. 116.
[110] Another long but rather ordinary poem on the general theme of *The Loves of Jonathan and Virginia* was W. G. Kennedy's *Ichabod; or the Glory of the South Has Departed*, published in Sumter, South Carolina, in 1882.
[111] *Southern Review*, XII (April, 1873), p. 326.

of his life. "It is believed by the world at large that hatred of
oppression, coupled with a love of freedom, was Mr. Lincoln's ruling passion. Nothing is farther from the truth." [112]
Rather, thirst for distinction was the "one, intense, all-
absorbing passion of his life." [113] He proceeded to repeat
stories of Lincoln's infidelism, of his extra-legal parentage,
and concluded that in view of these things he was the ideal
man to lead the "Northern Demos" in its war to subjugate
the South. "For if, as we believe, that was the cause of brute
force, blind passion, fanatical hate, lust of power and greed of
gain, against the cause of constitutional and human rights,
then who was better fitted to represent it than the talented
but the low, ignorant and vulgar, railsplitter of Illinois?" [114]
Lincoln was the "low-bred infidel of Pigeon Creek," in whose
eyes "the Holy Mother" was "as base as his own." [115]

Bernard J. Sage, the shrewd Connecticut Yankee who became a Louisiana sugar planter, dismissed Lincoln's abilities
with a statement which carries an odd note of finality. He
wrote of him in *The Republic of Republics*:

> He was a person of fair intellect, slight education, limited
> knowledge, no research, kind heart, jocular disposition; a
> man, in short, of excellent nature—just the man with his in-
> experience in statesmanship, and with his vague and and hazy
> notions of political ethics and constitutional history and law,
> to be misled by the sophists of his party, and to be the instru-
> ment of crafty and unscrupulous politicians.[116]

This estimate corresponds rather closely with that left in *A
Constitutional View* by Alexander Stephens, who in the pre-
war years had been a fairly intimate friend of Lincoln. In
January, 1865, two deputations, each with rather undefined

112 *Ibid.*, p. 340.
113 *Ibid.*, p. 349.
114 *Ibid.*, p. 364.
115 *Ibid.*
116 Sage, *op. cit.*, p. 215.

powers, met at Fortress Monroe to discuss the possibility of concluding the war. Stephens, naturally an earnest soul, was appalled by what he considered Lincoln's flippancy, evasiveness, and cheerful ignorance. In reply to an analogy from English history offered by R. M. T. Hunter, the President blandly stated, "I do not profess to be posted in history. On all such matters I will turn you over to Seward." [117] But on the same occasion Stephens was greatly impressed by Grant, whom he termed one of the most remarkable men he had ever met. He felt that Grant, if he ever became fully aware of his own powers, would exercise a controlling influence on the country, "either for good or for evil." [118]

It remained, however, for the *Southern Magazine* to reach heights of rhetoric in presenting the adverse view of Lincoln. To William Hand Browne he summed up all the unfavorable features of Yankee character. Writing also in connection with Ward Lamon's biography, Browne said:

> The whole story of that career, from beginning to end, is so dreary, so wretched, so shabby, such a pitiful tissue of dodging and chicanery, so unrelieved by anything pure, noble, or dignified, that even to follow it as far as we have, has well nigh surpassed our power of endurance; and when, putting all partisan feeling aside, we look back at the men who were once chosen by their countrymen to fill the place that this man has occupied—a Washington, a Jefferson, a Madison, an Adams, or later a Webster, a Clay, or a Calhoun—men of culture and refinement, of honor, of exalted patriotism, of broad views and wise statesmanship—and measure the distance from them to Abraham Lincoln, we sicken with shame and disgust.[119]

A representative attack upon the Radicals of Reconstruction is to be found in *The Land We Love* of July, 1868. We have seen how General Hill first intended his magazine to be

---

117 *A Constitutional View*, II, p. 613.
118 *Ibid.*, p. 598.
119 *Southern Magazine*, XI (September, 1872), p. 372.

an organ of sectional understanding and conciliation, but the Reconstruction measures of 1867 convinced him that the war was still on, and he accordingly took up the gage for the South. An editorial compared the Radical Reconstructionists to the "monkey-tiger" of the French Revolution, "alternately engaged in murder and monkey-tricks" and "as playful as a young ape until the time comes for decreeing the ruin of ten states, and the lingering death of four million negroes." [120] Of course *The Land We Love* did not overlook the beautiful detail that New York, Pennsylvania, and Ohio had repudiated Negro suffrage by overwhelming majorities.[121] "O, ye hypocrites," cried another editorial,

> protesting about equality even when there is none in your own den of thieves. Oh, ye Pharisees! imposing a burden on the South, which ye will not touch with one of your own loyal fingers. . . . How long will the land be polluted with your hypocrisy, your malignity, your knavery, and your stealing.[122]

From every platform and pulpit came calls to the Southern people to cling fast to their character and to ignore the new philosophy of success, which by axiom as well as by example was commencing to dominate the national life. The *Southern Magazine* sneered at the Yankee concept that "honesty is a policy" [123] and contrasted the "foul-mouthed conspirators of Congress and the unabashed crooks of Wall Street" with the type of men the South had always chosen as leaders. Dabney reminded his readers that self-respect is the beginning of all good things and told the Southern people that they could suffer no worse defeat than a loss of belief in the righteousness of their own civilization.

There was one force in particular, however, which kept the

120 *The Land We Love*, V (July, 1868), p. 279.
121 *Ibid.*, IV (February, 1868), p. 263.
122 *Ibid.*, p. 359.
123 *Southern Magazine*, X (January, 1872), p. 259.

defenders of antebellum ideals in a constant state of alarm. This was the new sensational journalism, which had received a great impetus from the war, and for which the Southern people were displaying such an appetite that the voice of their own propagandists was virtually drowned out. Because it was looked upon by the apologists as an expression of the flippancy, vulgarity, and sensationalism for which Yankees were being castigated, it is of moment in this connection. Defenders of the lost cause were driven almost to despair to see the journals with which they were trying to bolster the courage of the South, and which they kept going only at tremendous sacrifice, ignored in favor of illustrated weeklies from the North, whose stock-in-trade was "rebel atrocities" and pictures of emaciated Confederates.[124] *The Land We Love* of May, 1868, carried an article on "Demoralized Weeklies." It examined the whole list, including the *Police Gazette*, and declared them to be "receptacles for every species of moral filth that cannot find sewerage through other channels." [125] The Southern people, instead of devising means to keep out this poison, were showing an eagerness for it, and a farmer who could not afford the local newspaper would somehow scrape together enough cash to subscribe to *Harpers*. In exasperation the author declared that "actual cautery is the only remedy." [126] But the protests were unavailing; the flood grew, and the editorial columns of succeeding issues were filled with expostulation. In November, 1868, it was being asserted that "the Southern people seem determined to patronize only the pictorials of the North." [127] A following issue attacked them as belonging "invariably to three classes,

---

124 Eliza Andrews (*The War-time Journal of a Georgia Girl*, New York, 1908, p. 371) wrote that she got into a rage every time she looked at *Harpers Weekly* and *Frank Leslie's*. "Nothing is sacred from their disgusting love of the sensational."

125 *The Land We Love*, V (May, 1868), p. 80.

126 *Ibid.*, p. 84.

127 *Ibid.*, VI (November, 1868), p. 88.

the trashy, the sensational, and the libelous." [128] If the children of Confederates continued to be supplied with such reading matter, not only would their characters be debauched, but they would come to feel that "their martyr-sires did fill 'dishonored graves.'" [129] Dabney, with his usual unerring eye for historical factors, saw their source in the new commercialism rampant over the North, with its scorn for the honor, decency, and self-respect of the past generation. "The whole sway of their commercial and political ascendancy," he declared in a speech on the New South, "is exerted to fill the South with false literature. Its sheets come up, like the frogs of Egypt, into our houses, our bedchambers, our very kneading troughs." [130] And George W. Bagby could say in a postscript to his satire *A Week in Hepsidam*, "My fate is no better and no worse than that of other men of a literary turn who live in the South—that South which spends millions every year on books and papers that sneer at it and vilify it." [131]

The particularists were probably correct in recognizing in the new journalism their most dangerous foe. The South which, as the *Southern Magazine* boasted, was poor soil for *isms*, and which refused to reward the efforts of even the indefatigable Bledsoe, nevertheless succumbed to its fascination. Within a few years after the war, it was alleged, the Southern people were treating home productions "as if they had no merit whatsoever." [132] First in the press and later in other fields a glaring and irreverent realism was to take the place of the old literature of elegance, gentility, and reserve.

128 *Ibid.*, VI (December, 1868), p. 176. T. C. De Leon (*Four Years in Rebel Capitals*, Mobile, 1892, p. 288) considered the New York journals to be as "catholic in their scope as unreliable in their principles."

129 *The Land We Love*, VI (December, 1868), p. 176.

130 *The New South* (Raleigh, N.C., 1882), p. 15.

131 *A Week in Hepsidam* (Richmond, 1879), p. 66.

132 *Our Living and Our Dead*, I (October, 1874), p. 141.

4. The Theory of Race

Nothing appalled the white people of the South more than the prospect of four million emancipated blacks endowed with the privileges and powers of freemen in a republic. Happy experience with plantation slaves in wartime had convinced most of them that the fear of a general insurrection was groundless, but this was at best a negative comfort. The true problem lay in what the Negro, who had been through none of the white man's long discipline in self-restraint, would do with political authority. It mattered little to say that the Negro was kind and docile by nature, that he seldom cherished hatred against his "old marster." The urgent question was whether or not the Negroes as a group had a moral aspiration which could be united with, or substituted for, that with which the white people had maintained a civilization. For civilization is nothing more than a set of moral ambitions carried out by organization and self-discipline. The Northern theory was that the Negro was another "naturally good" man, whose aspiring impulses had been thwarted by the chains of slavery. But the Southern people had before them the lessons of Haiti and Jamaica, where the Negro— under somewhat differing conditions, obviously—had shown that his tendency, when he was released from all constraining forces, was downward rather than upward.

Now, with the old breed of statesmen gone, with the gentry fallen in battle, and with little sympathetic assistance to be expected from the victorious section, the South felt itself confronted with an impossible situation. Innumerable were the speeches, pamphlets, and articles prepared to impress upon the North the necessity of proceeding cautiously in the matter of extending full rights and privileges to the Negro. A feature of this writing was the continued clash over

whether the degraded condition of the blacks was owing to
enslavement or to racial inheritance. Virtually without an
exception, Southerners maintained that the Negro was a
primitive whom slavery had assisted forward by enforcing
habits of discipline and industry. This naturally outraged
Northern opinion, which began with the assumption that the
Negro was an equal, and which wished to pin on the Southern slaveholder the guilt for his unlettered, shiftless, and
backward condition. The Northern public has generally displayed a strange credulity with respect to stories of abuses
emanating from the South, and when these are multiplied
tenfold, as they were in Reconstruction days, it is little wonder that many Northerners of good will, whom a visit to the
South would have undeceived, went on believing that slaveholders had subjected their Negroes to deliberate and systematic brutalizing. Somewhere between two opinions distorted by passion lay a truth: on the one hand, Southerners
had done less than they might have toward civilizing the
blacks; and on the other hand, Northerners, accepting the
dogma that the Negro had the white man's nature and capac-
ities, had conceived an imperfect notion of the problem.
"The hopes and expectations of the emancipationists," *The
Land We Love* asserted mildly, "are not in unison with the
judgment and predictions of those who have a right to know,
and better understand the negro character." [133]

Meanwhile the problem was there, and more than any
other journal of the time *De Bow's Review* took cognizance
of the fact that the South's future depended closely upon how
the Negro conducted himself under the new incentives. A
study of its pages is a good lesson in Southern opinion on the
whole race question, which was discussed more or less on its
merits. It might be said that among Southerners there were
no progressives and no conservatives; there were only those

[133] *The Land We Love*, VI (November, 1867), p. 22.

who hoped for much and those who hoped for little; but it would be inaccurate to imagine that a feeling of vindictiveness conditioned the general attitude toward the Negro. That the presence of the African had been the chief source of Southern misfortunes was a common admission; yet his very childlikeness, his extraordinary exhibitions of loyalty, and his pathetic attempts to find his place in the complicated white man's civilization rather had the effect of endearing him to his former owners. The prevailing feeling was one of benevolence; but the white man could not forget that the Negro had always been dependent on him for instruction and care, and that he could not become a new man in a day, even if the most sanguine prophecies of the Yankees should be realized.

There were varied surmises regarding his behavior in freedom. A writer in *De Bow's Review* in the first issue after the war gave a frankly pessimistic forecast.

> We avow openly that we feel the deepest commiseration for the enfranchised slaves of the South; and we earnestly hope that everything practicable will be done to alleviate their condition and advance their interests. But we confess we are not sanguine as to their capability of advancement. The black race is proverbially indolent and improvident, and we cannot shut our eyes to the facts of history.[134]

He proceeded further to add, "Accounts from all parts of the South represent the freedmen as idle and indisposed to labor persistently." He could not, therefore, overcome his "melancholy foreboding as to the capabilities of this class in a state of freedom." [135]

Two years later a writer on "Negro Agrarianism" was developing the same thought. "We shall soon have in the South," he said,

[134] *De Bow's Review*, After the War Series, I (January, 1866), p. 22.
[135] *Ibid.*, p. 23.

not negro rule (for they cannot rule anything—not even their own household), but negro anarchy and agrarianism.

We do not see how this state of things can be prevented by peaceable means, and we have had far too much war. We must submit to negro misrule, cruelty and proscription until the Democratic party of the North gets into power.[136]

The *Southern Bivouac* found in the Negro "an absence of self-respect, an unconscious servility," which left him incapable of a white man's moral perceptions. But it added, "The charge is not to be laid at his door, for the negro is still a slave by inheritance, and the tendencies of many generations cannot be counteracted in one." [137]

"The Abolitionists have been telling us for half a century," said *The Land We Love,*

of the degradation and bestiality of the negro through the baneful influence of the oppression of slavery. But no sooner had slavery been abolished than these same philanthropists contend that the degraded bestialized subject of it is fit to serve upon juries, to exercise the elective franchise, to take his seat in the State or National Legislature, and to discharge all the high and responsible duties of manhood. Now there is an inconsistency somewhere.[138]

Discussions of the Negro frequently took the form of excursions into anthropology and sociology, a fair example of which is the pamphlet *The Public School in its Relation to the Negro.* This work, which is a complete examination of the Negro's role in society, was issued in Richmond after being serialized in the *Southern Farmer and Planter.* Writing to prove that the Negro was doomed by his nature to a subordinate position, the author gave as the first reason his "extreme docility, a most desirable quality in a menial: a most

---

136 *Ibid.,* V (February, 1868), p. 138.
137 *Southern Bivouac,* I (October, 1885), p. 318.
138 *The Land We Love,* IV (January, 1868), p. 262.

dangerous, a fatal one in a sovereign." The second was his "improvidence," and the third the fact that the Negro is "eminently a sweating animal." This qualifies him for outdoor work in low latitudes, but renders him objectionable "in the cars, in the jury box, in the halls of legislation, in the crowds that assemble on the court green." [139] By his actions the Negro, "true to nature and true to truth, stoutly denies the heresy of equality." [140] These assertions and many like them were offered in opposition to equal education for Negroes.

This represents, of course, the adverse extreme; a more balanced study of the Negro's character, coming at the end of the Reconstruction era, was Philip A. Bruce's *The Plantation Negro as a Freedman*. Yet Bruce, though more rational in his approach to the topic and more charitable in allowing the Negro a special set of virtues, leaves him exactly where the others do, in the position of servant and menial. "To bring him to the greatest usefulness," the author declared, "it is necessary that he should be required to conform to certain fixed standards of conduct to which he will not rise of his own voluntary motion, or if he should do so, he will not adhere to them long." [141] He observed in the Negro an "inability to be watchful, prudent, and self-controlled for any length of time without alteration," a trait which he "seems to be incapable of either eradicating or repressing." [142] And although under constant supervision the Negro might attain a fairly high standard of neatness and efficiency, "he does not always show in the character of his own cabin that he has taken to heart the spirit of those admonitions to which he may listen attentively at the moment." [143]

[139] "Civis" (B. Puryear), *The Public School in Its Relation to the Negro* (Richmond, 1877), p. 5.
[140] *Ibid.* p. 16.
[141] *The Plantation Negro as a Freedman* (New York, 1889), p. 35.
[142] *Ibid.*, p. 36.
[143] *Ibid.*, p. 41.

It was generally granted that the Negro was "a lineal descendant of Adam," [144] and not a few saw in him potentiality for development, but none conceded him a future in politics. It was often pointed out that political activity was the one arena in which his lack of a civilized tradition would tell most heavily against him. Thus in 1868 Senator James B. Campbell, of South Carolina, issued a pamphlet which warned that carpetbagger rule could not last and expressed the view that " . . . he is the best friend of the colored man . . . who entices him least into the field of politics, than which there is nothing more corrupting to persons like him, just emerging from a condition of pupilage." [145] Over thirty years later the same thesis was being maintained by Frank G. Ruffin in "The Cost and Outcome of Negro Education in Virginia." A survey led him to the assertion that "an experience of nineteen years has shown all observant Virginians that so far from having been fitted by education for the discharge of civil or social duties, that [sic] they have absolutely deteriorated, and have given no promise of amendment in any direction." [146] Their condition marked a lapse from "a high degree of efficiency as agricultural laborers, in slavery, to a state of utter worthlessness in freedom." [147] The Negroes were "political idiots," and the North by trying to put them into political authority had "sinned against all knowledge." [148]

On the topic of the Negro's natural endowment one finds the beginning of a division of opinion; for though some held that he could never compete with the white man in the arts and sciences, others believed that he had the potential ability to succeed in all of them save that of political management. It is a further commentary on the traditional Southern view of

144 *The Land We Love,* III (August, 1867), p. 352.
145 *Public Affairs and Our Duties to the Colored Race* (Charleston, 1868), p. 4.
146 *The Cost and Outcome of Negro Education in Virginia* (Richmond, 1889), p. 7.
147 *Ibid.,* p. 18.
148 *Ibid.,* p. 14.

the arts that no embarrassment was felt over conceding the Negro even superiority in music, poetry, and oratory so long as politics remained the white man's preserve. The *Southern Bivouac* declared that it would not be surprised to see the Negroes "in another generation" producing artists, poets, and orators surpassing those of the white race. But it regarded talent for self-government as the peculiar gift of the Aryan. The Negro betrayed his unfitness for rule through his "absolute, unqualified veneration for power in its every form and symbol." He could understand only external control. "Nature formed him for obedience, and even when he is riotous and apparently insubordinate it is most generally his expression of contempt for what he deems weakness, and an indirect tribute to that which he esteems the real representative of superior controlling force." [149]

More than one writer took the view that it was impossible for the two races to dwell together unless the blacks remained in a condition approximating slavery, and sometimes traditional religion was invoked to sanction such an arrangement. Thus *The Land We Love* could say of the Negro that "from his history we infer that God has given him a tendency to thrive and multiply in a condition of servitude," and that therefore "the servile condition of the negroes in the South was not contrary to the will of God." [150] If they lived free of white supervision and control, they would assert their natural bent, revert to a primitive status, and so create a country in which no white man would care to remain. *De Bow's Review* suggested that within the foreseeable future the Negro would drive the white man from his domain and so achieve an all-Negro South. This was accompanied by the realistic observation that no inferior race is ever practically and actually free when in contact with a superior, for the latter is certain to find means of exploiting the labor of the former. China,

149 The *Southern Bivouac*, New Series, II (March, 1887), pp. 711-712.
150 *The Land We Love*, V (August, 1868), p. 300.

Japan, and Liberia had met this problem simply by excluding white competition. If the Negro had shown any capacity for management, it was said, there would long since have been in the South a Negro feudal tenantry, which would have displaced the white overseer. "But not a single negro in the whole South, was ever found capable of managing a farm." [151]

A reading of these speeches, editorials, and pamphlets indicates that the Southern people of the postbellum era, frightened and confused, were seeking a rational ground for their feeling. They failed to discover a consistent argument for racial discrimination, but the salient fact emerging from every discussion was that they had no more intention of crediting the Negro with equality than had the generation of the 1830's. Even a courageous reformer like George W. Cable, who battled for the Negro's civic rights, drew the line at social equality. By the standard of humanity which the South visualized—and this must be understood in terms of its heritage—the Negro was an inferior. God had willed it; experience proved it; and except in trifling particulars the great majority felt no impulse to redress the balance.

One of the best summaries of the prevailing opinion is to be found in a speech delivered in Congress in 1874 by Senator Thomas M. Norwood, of Georgia, and later circulated as a pamphlet. Twitting the sponsors of the Fourteenth Amendment, he said that he looked forward to the time

> when the white man and the black, the mulatto and the quadroon, the coolie and the Digger Indian, shall be gathered together, a united family, in one unbroken circle, around one common soup bowl and using the same spoon, while shielded by the Stars and Stripes and regaled by the martial measure and inspiring strain of—
>
> John Brown's soul is marching on.[152]

[151] *De Bow's Review*, After the War Series, III (June, 1867), p. 52.
[152] *Civil Rights* (Washington, 1874), p. 3.

All differences and distinctions are now recognized as mistakes, he continued, and thus we must vote them out of existence, although not without a show of "decent respect for the opinion of the author of these errors." [153] Despite the fact that "the flowers of the field might vary in splendor; the lion might be made monarch of the beasts; one star might differ from another in glory, but absolute equality, moral, mental, physical, political, social, in churches, theatres, graveyards, everywhere in the world and out of it, must be ordained among men, women, and children." [154]

It has been argued that although Americans are by temperament empiricists, in their political thinking they have been rationalists, preferring to deduce truths from axioms and first principles. There is perhaps no better illustration of this conflict of procedures than the handling of the vexed race problem. Northerners, remote from the scene of strife and bearing little if any of the responsibility involved, found the rational approach easy; from the Declaration of Independence and other canons of American liberty they could draw conclusions which Southerners found irrefutable. But the South, finding that the concrete situation made a mockery of the abstract statement, as is often the case, regarded itself as forced to the empirical approach and continued to treat the Negro as a special case. Then the unwillingness of the Americans to compromise an issue, frequently remarked by Europeans, led each side to reduce its views to a more or less rigid credo, in which form they stand today. The inability of Southerners to arrive at first principles which would support this position explains much awkward silence in the years that followed.

The Southern apologia was a minority protest delivered over a period of thirty years. If one judges by practical results, it was almost wholly vain. The legal case was at best a

153 *Ibid.*, p. 4.
154 *Ibid.*

hollow victory. The attack upon secular democracy was so much wasted breath, later to be answered by the more terrible radicalisms emerging from Europe. The particularism of peoples, though it may have heightened the self-consciousness of Southerners and made them suspect when abroad, was soon in futile competition with an enthusiastic internationalism. Only the poorly clarified theory of white supremacy was destined to have immediate efficacy. Near the end of the century it came to overt expression in a widespread campaign to deprive the black man of the franchise, which was done by means sometimes more effective than honest.

CHAPTER THREE

꘤꘤꘤

The Testimony Of The Soldier

FOR MORE THAN THIRTY YEARS AFTER THE COLLAPSE OF THE Confederacy the military leaders of the South continued to be its spiritual captains, from whom advice was taken not only on political, but also on social, educational, and even religious matters. It was a natural consequence of the Southern past that this should be so, for the South was an agrarian, patriarchal civilization, all of whose traditions were of the forum and the camp. Its contributions to *belles-lettres* had been modest; those to science comparatively insignificant; and commercial acumen it not only did not have but professed to despise. On the other hand, the Southern contribution to the political life of the nation had been preponderant, and the hero of each of the Republic's three wars had been a Southern man. Washington, Jackson, and Taylor had led the South to believe that it possessed the fighting talent of the nation. Therefore, when in 1861 this section organized a provisional government and struck for independence, it was putting its faith in its statesmanship and its soldiership—all that it had—into the wager. In a sense the South was in the position of a professional expecting easy defeat of an amateur, and one should not wonder at the shock and humiliation experienced when the amateur won.

Various conditions, most of which have been previously outlined, combined to limit Southern interest largely to these institutions. A population coming in early and settling the wilderness learned to respect the power of the rifle; a vigorous outdoor life was the rule; and no cities appeared to exert the inevitably mollifying influence. The Southern people were a people of deeds, and such reflective thinking as went on ran in the narrow round of politics.

Moreover, the South had a natural belief in leaders, which derived in part from its indigenous social hierarchy, and in part, no doubt, from its strong infusion of Celtic blood. The Scotch-Irish immigrants who filled its uplands brought along their natural clannishness and their habit of passionate devotion to a chieftain. This was to express itself in the hero worship accorded men such as Lee, Stuart, Jackson, and Forrest, an intense personal loyalty, which took little account of reverses and crowned its subjects with something of the divinity that doth hedge a king.

Thus the Southern people entered the war feeling that they had every prerequisite of a great military people—a tradition of victory on battlefields, political soldiers who had proved themselves capable of being first in war and first in peace, and a population accustomed to the horse and the gun and disposed to follow tenaciously its chosen captains. At the beginning it had seemed impossible to all but the most thoughtful that they could lose, and after the war the people as a whole were left groping for an explanation of why their best had failed. In that loss the set of virtues which had made the South what it had been was denied and overthrown, and nothing appeared ahead but a wholly new course of life, to which most of them were neither disposed nor fit to adapt themselves. One must examine this state of mind in order to understand the extraordinary volume of Confederate military memoirs which, beginning before the war was over, poured a torrent for more than forty years and even at the opening of the first decade of the next century had not entirely ceased.[1]

Unquestionably the first motive was to compensate for so sharp a humiliation, to show that Southern qualities had not been found deficient when put to the test. It was naturally feared that silence on their part would be taken as an admission of guilt, or of inferiority. General Sherman once declared that the war of secession was begun in error and continued in pride. Most of the soldiers were willing to let the politicians answer the question of error, but as for the other, if it was continued in pride, it was continued also with good results and with fair hope of ultimate success. It was hard for the ex-Confederate to understand why he, who had fought in almost every battle against odds and who had routed superior numbers on more than one field, should be demoted to the position of failure by the mere technicality of surrender. The facts were there, well enough, but the conclusion did not seem right. He had earned honors in the fight; why were not honors forthcoming? Perhaps one must go back to the Southern unwillingness to take a pragmatic view of anything for the answer. There was still in the back of his head the notion from chivalry that the contest should have been decided by knights in equal combat. And hence his frantic attempts to get recognition for his heroism and steadfastness from a world inclining more and more to judge only by results, attempts which varied from the pitiful to the ludicrous. In proportion as the world seemed conspired to scorn and ignore him, his self-assertiveness increased.

But before one accuses the ex-Confederate of too much

[1] In the issue for January, 1910, the *Confederate Veteran* (XVIII, p. 8) was compelled to state that "the accumulation of manuscripts continues far in excess of the space practicable to use."

remembrance of things past, he should consider what it means to lose the initiative as completely as the South did after 1865. Following this date, he had little choice but to dwell with his memories. Before the Civil War the Southerner had figured large in the councils of the nation and exerted perhaps the decisive influence in the shaping of national politics. Defeat changed this to such an extent that the North was left with all the initiative, and the South was rendered impotent. It is one thing for a nation to lose a war with a neighbor and to suffer only temporary occupation and some loss of territory. But to lose a war and then to have even the means of recuperation withheld is total defeat, and this is what the South experienced in the conflict of the sixties. With her economy ruined, her states kept out of the Union by political machination, her citizens disfranchised, and her representatives to Congress—when they got there—more or less under surveillance, it was obvious that nothing affecting the life of the nation as a whole was going to be decided in the South.[2] The section was for the time being emasculated. It is not unusual for an individual or for a nation to allow its imagination to dwell fondly on a period of prosperity. Colonel Alfred Roman had this situation in mind when he wrote in his life of Beauregard: "The Southern people, shackled by years of poverty and political helplessness, and circumscribed as they are in their sphere of action, cannot forget the teachings which, to them and their posterity, embody the true meaning of our institutions." [3] And Napier Bartlett remarked in his *A Soldier's History of the War* that "Secessia, amid her desolation, looks to the old battlefields, as the Sphinx does to the ruined cities of Egypt." [4] The North,

[2] Reaching Savannah in 1866, Frances Butler Leigh (*op. cit.*, p. 13) found that the people "know and care less about what is going on in Washington than in London."

[3] Alfred Roman, *The Military Operations of General Beauregard* (New York, 1884), I, p. 1.

[4] Napier Bartlett, *A Soldier's History of the War* (New Orleans, 1874), p. 5.

flushed with victory, growing in population, and made even wealthier by the war, could afford to forget it except as an issue, live in the present, and build for the future. The South found in the present only hardship and humiliation, and in the future only vague promises of improvement—indeed, as late as 1879 Sidney Lanier was writing to his brother, "In my soberest moments I can perceive no outlook for that land." [5] So the imagination of her sons who were disposed to reflect went back to her flourishing antebellum days, and to her heroic days during the war, when martial valor bade fair to get her a position among the nations of the earth. Such was the natural tendency to recreate the past in a land where "pretty much the whole of life has been merely not dying." [6]

The peculiar quality of devotion in the Southern people showed itself in a determination to perpetuate the memory of its champions. The public of the South, like others, has sins to answer for, but it is not a fickle public. It regards faith in a leader as a kind of pledge of allegiance, which it would be dishonorable to withdraw in a season of adversity. As a policy, this may be productive of ill as well as good, but it does have associations with the fealty of chivalry and so exalts the imagination. Something of this veneration appears in the saying attributed to a Confederate soldier: "The rest of us may have descended or ascended from monkeys, but it took a God to make Marse Robert." [7] Many Southern soldiers took it upon themselves to celebrate the career of their chief, particularly if he had sealed his efforts with his life, as was not infrequently the case. R. L. Dabney, John Esten Cooke, and Henry Kyd Douglas all early prepared matter on the life of the enigmatic Stonewall Jackson. Of Lee's personal staff, A. L. Long, Charles Marshall, and W. N. Taylor each produced a volume of memoirs, and A. S. Venable wrote his recollec-

5 Edwin Mims, *Sidney Lanier* (Boston, 1905), p. 265.
6 *Ibid.*, p. 67.
7 Stiles, *op. cit.*, p. 20.

tions for *Battles and Leaders.* H. B. McClellan, a nephew of
the Federal General George B. McClellan, who had fought
on the Southern side, employed his leisure while serving as
president of a girls' school in Lexington, Kentucky, to write
The Campaigns of Major-General J. E. B. Stuart. The daring
raiders Turner Ashby and John S. Mosby both were made
the subjects of admiring memoirs by their men. Alfred
Roman produced *The Military Operations of General Beauregard,* and John W. Morton, the beardless youth who com-
manded the artillery of Forrest, paid tribute to that extraordinary leader in *The Artillery of Nathan Bedford Forrest.*
Add to these the countless portraits and eulogies appearing in
The Land We Love, the *Southern Bivouac,* and the *Confederate Veteran,* and one has a view of the influence of personal
loyalty in the production of Southern war literature.

Another motive behind the outpouring of military memoirs, somewhat melancholy to record, was that of self-
vindication. Though they had lost a war, no commanders
were ever more vain of their achievements than the Confederates; and any sense of cooling public favor, or any invidious
comment by an associate was sure to bring them into print;
and the further removed they were in time from their deeds,
the more acrimonious the exchange was likely to prove.
Crusty old Jubal Early was the first to appear, in 1867, with a
defense of his disastrous Valley Campaign. In 1874 J. E.
Johnston published his *Narrative of Military Operations,*
with its severe reflections on General Hood, who up to that
time had exhibited a generous behavior and made no attempt
to excuse his defeats at Atlanta and Nashville. Feeling that he
could not endure in silence a printed condemnation, Hood
devoted nearly one half of his *Advance and Retreat* to a close
rebuttal of General Johnston. In 1891 General Beauregard
renewed his quarrel with General Johnston over the situation at First Manassas in *The Battle of Manassas.* As late as

1896 General Longstreet, who had in the meantime embarked on a spotty political career, replied to those who had
blamed him for the loss of Gettysburg and indulged in some
criticism of Lee sharp to the point of bad taste. These works,
to the extent that they are devoted to the narrow purposes of
controversy, are the least valuable as literature, but they shed
light on temperament and on events. Temptation to enter
the argument was doubtless great, and signs are not wanting
that even the reserved Lee, had he lived longer, might have
set down his opinion on some of the points at issue.

1. Why He Fought

A virtual library of such works makes it possible to look
into the mind of the Confederate captain and see what manner of man it was to whom the Southern people were willing
to entrust their destinies implicitly, in peace as in war. It was,
first of all, a candid mind, not at all disposed to sophisticated
questions, and as free as possible from that guile which the
enemy professed to see in defections from the old government. It was also an unselfish mind, and those who imagine
that the Confederate soldier fought to preserve a property
investment in slavery have not begun to understand Southern psychology. The assumption that only a tangible reward
could inspire the enormous exertions which the South made
to win its independence has lent itself easily to the thesis of
the economic determinists. The emancipation crusade was
occasionally alluded to as "practical robbery," but if one
analyzes the attitudes of the actual combatants, he finds them
primarily concerned with the insult which such "meddling"
carried. It is true that the average Southerner did not propose
to have his domestic establishment disturbed, but the point
was a point of honor, and he would throw the whole thing

into the scales, with good prospect of losing it, rather than
submit to dictation or encroachment. A shrewder and less
idealistic people would have driven a bargain and come off
prosperous. But this is not the way in which knighthood settles an issue.

Not all of them thought deeply about their choice; some,
when they saw their people moving into war, joined them as
if by instinct. Others were convinced nationalists and
weighed long the issue between state and nation; but when
the decision was made, it never occurred to them that anything other than principle was involved. A writer in the
Reconstruction period likened the Civil War to the European wars of disputed succession, in which each side had a
legitimate claim. The question of whether loyalty to state or
nation took precedence has been so vexed that it becomes
interesting to observe the reaction of soldiers, who are sometimes accused of taking a narrowly professional view of alternatives. Since these are the opinions of men without whose
assistance disunion would have been only a political figment,
they throw important light on the trend of separatism. General Lee's letter of April 20, 1861, to his sister must always be
remembered as the best witness of an earnest desire to decide
where the primary duty lay:

> My dear sister: I am grieved at my inability to see you. I have
> been waiting for a more "convenient season," which had
> brought to many before me deep and lasting regret. We are
> now in a state of war which will yield to nothing. The whole
> South is in a state of revolution, into which Virginia, after a
> long struggle, has been drawn; and though I recognize no
> necessity for this state of things, and would have forborne and
> pleaded to the end for the redress of grievances, real or sup-
> posed, yet in my own person I had to meet the question
> whether I should take part against my native state. With all
> my devotion to the Union, and the feeling of loyalty and duty
> of an American citizen, I have not been able to make up my
> mind to raise my hand against my relatives, my children, and

my home. I have, therefore, resigned my commission in the Army, and save in defense of my native State—with sincere hope that my poor services will never be needed—I hope I may never be called upon to draw my sword. I know that you will blame me, but you must think of me as kindly as you can, and believe that I have endeavored to do what I thought right. To show you the feeling and struggle it has cost me, I send you a copy of my letter of resignation. I have no time for more.

May God guard and protect you and yours, and shower upon you everlasting blessings, is the prayer of

Your devoted brother,

R. E. Lee [8]

An interesting companion piece to this exists in a letter of Matthew Fontaine Maury, "the founder of Oceanography," to the Grand Admiral of Russia, who had invited him to continue his studies at St. Petersburg during the period of internecine strife. Maury, in addition to being a world traveler, was a man whose achievements in science had made him an international figure, so that he can hardly be accused of parochialism. He told the Admiral that he was a citizen of Virginia, in whose "green bosom are the graves of my fathers," and that "the political whirlpool from which your kind forethought sought to rescue me has already plunged her into a fierce and bloody civil war." Then, after outlining the doctrine of state rights, he explained his choice: "Thus my sword has been tendered to her cause, and the tender has been accepted. Her soil has been invaded, the enemy is actually at her gates; and here I am contending, as the fathers of the Republic did, for the right of self-government, and those very principles for the maintenance of which Washington fought, when this, his native state, was a colony of Great Britain. The path of duty and honor is therefore plain." [9]

8 J. William Jones, *Life and Letters of Robert Edward Lee* (New York, 1906), pp. 133-134.

9 *Library of Southern Literature*, VIII, pp. 3453-3454.

Most of such testimonials, however, which vary greatly in tone and length, were written after the war. Some were satisfied to describe their choice in a brief paragraph, but the unreconciled went into lengthy and impassioned argument. Foremost in the latter group were Jubal Early and Raphael Semmes. The case of Early is worth close study, for he had been one of the staunchest of all Virginia Unionists. In the state convention he had labored against secession, but viewing himself as bound by the decision of that body, he became a doughty fighter in the Confederate cause and an implacable hater of the North. Rather than submit to the terms imposed upon his conquered country, he fled to Canada, and from there in 1867 he issued his *A Memoir of the Last Year of the War for Independence,* which he dedicated to "the Memory of the Heroic Dead, who fell fighting for Liberty, Right, and Justice."

The preface to this volume is a bitter document. He reminded his readers that he had opposed secession with all his power in the hope that "a returning sense of duty and justice on the part of the masses of the Northern States, would induce them to respect the rights of the South." [10] He recalled that "while some Northern politicians and editors, who subsequently took rank among the most unscrupulous and vindictive of our enemies, and now hold me to be a traitor and a rebel, were openly and sedulously justifying and encouraging secession, I was laboring honestly and earnestly to preserve the Union." [11] He went on to say, however, that any doubts about the right of secession he originally held "were soon dispelled by the mad, wicked, and unconstitutional measures of the authorities at Washington," which compelled him to regard "Abraham Lincoln, his counsellors and supporters, as the real traitors who had overthrown the Constitution, and

10 *A Memoir of the Last Year of the War for Independence* (New Orleans, 1867), p. v.
11 *Ibid.*

established in lieu thereof an odious despotism." [12] He saw
no reason to regret his decision, and he had never known the
moment "when I would have been willing to consent to any
compromise or settlement short of absolute independence of
my country." [13] After a review of Northern policies, particularly those concerning the Negro, he closed by declaring that
posterity "will be lost in wonder at the follies and crimes
committed in this generation." [14] Although Early lived until
1894, he never altered his position, but remained until the
end the essential type of unreconstructed soldier of the Confederacy, as Davis, Bledsoe, and Dabney remained its political
oracles.

Two years after the appearance of Early's work, Raphael
Semmes, commander of the illustrious *Alabama*, published
his *A Memoir of Service Afloat During the War Between the
States*, one of the really fascinating narratives in the literature of adventure. But before embarking on his story, which
furnishes more than seven hundred pages of colorful incident
and description, he wrote a long justification of his entrance
into the Confederate States Navy. Semmes had studied law,
and the remarkable skill with which this case is presented
gives evidence of the ability which enabled him to argue
successfully with harbor officials reluctant to admit his craft
and to accomplish almost as much by legal astuteness as by a
rare knowledge of the ocean and the art of seamanship. The
case is not original, but it is here offered with a polemic
talent which puts it in a class with Bledsoe's *Is Davis a
Traitor?* Semmes reviewed in succession the nature of the
American compact, the early formative stages of the nation,
and finally, for he was a realist, the question of slavery as it
affected secession.

He regarded the action of the national government as

12 *Ibid.*
13 *Ibid.,* p. vi.
14 *Ibid.,* p. x.

usurpation. According to his reading of history, the prophecy of Patrick Henry had been fulfilled: the central government, now sensing unbridled power, was beginning to oppress the states:

> In the course of time the government is perverted from its original design. Instead of remaining the faithful and impartial agent of all the States, a faction obtains control of it, in the interest of some of them, and turns it, as an engine of oppression against the others. These latter, after long and patient suffering, after having exhausted all their means of defence within the Union, withdraw from the agent the powers they had conferred upon him, form a new Confederacy, and desire "to be let alone." And what is the consequence? They are denounced as rebels and traitors, armies are equipped, and fleets provided, and a war of subjugation is waged against them.[15]

He held that the charge of treason was fabricated for a purpose. When the time came for the officers of the Navy to resign their commissions if they intended to cast their lot with the South, there was no talk of disloyalty; that was something produced by the Washington government to add vigor to the war. "There were no such questions then," he wrote, "as rebellion and treason in the public mind. This was a Federal afterthought, when that Government began to get the better of us in the war. The Puritan, if he had been whipped, would have made a capital secessionist, and as meek and humble as we could have desired." [16]

Semmes summed up the issue of slavery with the cynical observation:

> The people of the North were, indeed, opposed to slavery, but merely because they thought it stood in the way of their strug-

[15] *A Memoir of Service Afloat During the War Between the States* (Baltimore, 1869), pp. 48-49.
[16] *Ibid.*, p. 71.

gle for empire. I think it safe to affirm, that if the question of slavery had stood upon moral, and religious grounds alone, the institution would never have been interfered with.[17]

No other surviving Confederate, not even Jubal Early or Robert Toombs, matched Semmes in bitterness of feeling against the Yankees. He believed strongly in the Puritan-Cavalier distinction; to him Yankees and Southerners were different genera who should never have entered a political partnership in the first place. Were it not for its intense partisan spirit, *A Memoir of Service Afloat* would in all probability be one of the most widely read American books of adventure. How his unceasing allusions to the theme of Yankee cupidity and hypocrisy get into the very texture of the work will be noticed in a later connection.

Joseph E. Johnston, a brigadier general in the Army of the United States, was the highest ranking Federal officer to leave the old service and to enter that of a seceded state. An analysis of the mind of this personality would in itself make an interesting study. Cold, precise, and businesslike, Johnston was acknowledged by all competent to judge to be a master of logistics, and W. T. Sherman, usually uncharitable in his opinion of opponents, professed respect for his generalship in the field. Yet personal difficulties, which developed early in the war, appear to have clouded his mind so that he was never able to win a notable success by those plans which looked unexceptionable on paper; and he has gone down in Confederate military history as the hero of successful withdrawals. Where Lee and Jackson saw opportunities, he saw only obstacles, and thus the man who was the ablest theorist on the Southern side seems to have been lacking in that other half of the equipment of a military genius—a case analogous to that of McClellan on the Federal side.

The brief apologia with which Johnston began his *Narra-*

17 *Ibid.,* p. 62.

tive of Military Operations, characterized as it is by logical simplicity, bespeaks such a man. "I believed, like most others, that the division of the country would be permanent," he wrote,

> and that, apart from any right of secession, the revolution begun was justified by the maxims so often repeated by Americans, that free government is founded on the consent of the governed, and that every community strong enough to establish and maintain its independence has a right to assert it. Having been educated in such opinions, I naturally determined to return to the State of which I was a native, join the people among whom I was born, and, if necessary, fight in their defense.[18]

General Johnston had an equally simple solution to the question of treason involved in leaving the old army, though it may be thought a trifle narrow in its conception of duty. "The acceptance of an officer's resignation absolves him from the obligations of his military oath as completely as it relieves the government from that of giving him the pay of the grade he held." [19] This was all he felt needful to say by way of justification, and in strong contrast to the work of Semmes, the *Narrative* is entirely free from political animadversions.

A unique work among the military autobiographies came from the pen of Richard Taylor, a son of Zachary Taylor, and a man who embodied all that was best in the Southern aristocracy. Fortunate in commencing life with a distinguished name, a European education, and a measure of wealth, Taylor built up on his plantation in St. Charles Parish, Louisiana, a fine library, from which he drew an extensive learning in literature and military history. It was inevitable that one with this background should take part in politics, and during the rapid passage of events he acted as an instrument of his

[18] *Narrative of Military Operations* (New York, 1874), p. 10.
[19] *Ibid.,* p. 11.

state, loyal, conscientious, and discerning, but not without something of the scholar's dubiousness regarding the result of the political storm. Thus he wrote:

> At that time and since, I marveled at the joyous and careless temper in which men, much my superiors in sagacity and experience, consummated these acts. There appeared the same general *gaîté de coeur* that M. Ollivier claimed for the Imperial Ministry when war was declared against Prussia. The attachment of northern and western people to the Union; their superiority in numbers, in wealth, and especially in mechanical resources; the command of the sea; the lust of rule and territory always felt by democracies, and nowhere to a greater degree than in the South—all these facts were laughed to scorn, or their mention was ascribed to timidity and treachery.[20]

The men who were sealing the fate of the South seemed "as unconscious as scene-shifters in some awful tragedy." [21]

Taylor left nothing to imply that it cost him an internal struggle to go with the Confederacy, and he rejected entirely one Northern theory of the cause of the war. "Anti-slavery was agitated from an early period," he noted at the beginning of his work,

> but failed to attract public attention for many years. At length, by unwearied industry, by ingeniously attaching itself to exciting questions of the day with which it had no natural connection, it succeeded in making a lodgment in the public mind, which, like a subject exhausted by long effort, is exposed to the attack of some malignant fever, that in a normal condition of vigor would have been resisted. The common belief that slavery was the cause of civil war is incorrect, and Abolitionists are not justified in claiming the glory and spoils of the conflict and in pluming themselves as "choosers of the slain." [22]

20 *Destruction and Reconstruction* (New York, 1879), p. 13.
21 *Ibid.*, p. 14.
22 *Ibid.*, p. 10.

Taylor was a Whig, highly distrustful of popular democracy, and although he went with his people and performed well what seemed the duty at hand, he preserved a skeptical mind, resisting the passions of the hour, and forming sharp judgments of even the most exalted of his associates. The Old South could wish for nothing better than to be judged by this scholar-gentleman type, a fine representative of its men of force, character and distinction.

General P. T. Beauregard, whose unusual gift of rhetoric has perhaps been allowed to obscure his solid merit as a commander, was disinclined to enter the intricacies of the question of secession. In an ably written account of the First Battle of Manassas he noted merely that "The political hostilities of a generation were now face to face with weapons instead of words." [23] As regards the morale of the Confederate Army, he had a single terse comment: "The fact that one army was fighting for union and the other for disunion is a political expression; the actual fact on the battlefield, in the face of cannon and musket, was that the Federal troops came as invaders, and the Southern troops stood as defenders of their homes, and further than this we need not go." [24] The abolition crusade he viewed as "practical robbery," to be resisted as such.[25]

The dull and unimaginative Longstreet showed equal indisposition to explore the issues of the long-impending conflict. In the spring of 1861 he was stationed at Albuquerque, New Mexico, where he waited anxiously for news, though still hoping "that the statesman would yet show himself equal to the occasion, and restore confidence among the people." [26] The fall of Fort Sumter, however, made up his mind, and he started for Virginia despite the efforts of fellow officers to

23 *Battles and Leaders of the Civil War* (New York, 1887), I, p. 203.
24 *Ibid.,* p. 218.
25 *Ibid.*
26 *From Manassas to Appomattox* (Philadelphia, 1896), p. 29.

persuade him to remain with the old army. These he silenced, he said, by asking them what they would do if their own states were to secede. Late in June he reported to the War Department in Richmond and asked to be assigned duty in the paymaster's office, because, as he wrote, "I had given up all aspirations of military honor, and thought to settle down into more peaceful pursuits" [27] During the war he proved himself a splendid tactician, an inferior strategist, and an intractable subordinate. His readiness to ally himself with the Republicans in Reconstruction places him among the less devoted of the Confederate heroes.

A different kind of light is thrown upon the whole question of divided loyalties by General Basil Duke of Kentucky in his *History of Morgan's Cavalry*. General Duke was proud of his state and her people, and he desired to explain the curiously mixed role of Kentucky in the war, which appeared to some simple vacillation and gained her a name for treachery North and South. The politics of Kentucky have always been fantastic, but never more so than in this crisis. First the state declared neutrality; then she threw her weight to the North; and later, after the war was over, in the most quixotic of all gestures, she allied herself in sentiment with the beaten Southern states. But Kentucky had been exposed to many crosscurrents. There had been the strength of the pro-slavery element; the great influence of Henry Clay, the Whig and nationalist; the unwillingness of the advocates of union to accept the idea of coercion; and the conviction on the part of Southern sympathizers that neutrality, in the situation then prevailing, was Kentucky's best contribution to Confederate success. In response to all these impulses there was an honest division of opinion, but there was also an element attached to neither side and interested only in the profit it could make by picking the winner. It was not the excited partisan, but these

27 *Ibid.*, p. 32.

mean calculators of advantage who would earn the contempt of history. Those who had fought each other over principles, General Duke felt, were afterwards able to respect each other; for the rest he had a soldier's scorn:

> But for the men who showed so plainly that they were attached to no cause and no principle, but who were ready to sell and barter each and all, who manifested all through the struggle, that they were moved by the most groveling ambition, influenced by the meanest thirst for self-aggrandizement —for them there is no forgiveness.
>
> All Kentucky has suffered from their duplicity, cowardice, and heartless avarice of gold and power—now they have neither, and none regret it.[28]

When he wrote this, Duke was anticipating the verdict of history, for Kentucky is today filled with monuments to the Confederate dead whom in life she disappointed. He hoped that his state had learned from her trying experience "that safety is never consulted by giving heed to the suggestions of timidity, and that the manliest and most consistent course, is also the most truly expedient, and that the interest and honor of a people go hand-in-hand, and are inseparable." [29]

Thus unlike Early and Semmes, who also wrote in the passion-ridden years immediately following the war, Duke recognized the possibility of honest difference. But one gathers from his *Reminiscences,* which came out many years later, that he was one in love with the *ancien régime* in Kentucky, and that it was to defend this agrarian paradise, and not to vindicate the Resolutions of '98 or any theory of government, that he fought for four years under the Stars and Bars.

For the best statement by a soldier of the grounds of strife, however, one must look to the popular and engaging John B. Gordon, who lived well beyond the turn of the century to

28 *History of Morgan's Cavalry* (Cincinnati, 1867), pp. 55-56.
29 *Ibid.*

personify the "reconstructed" Confederate soldier as Jubal
Early had the "unreconstructed." It was not until 1903 that
Gordon appeared with his *Reminiscences of the Civil War,* a
work which stands alone in its frank and generous approach
to all topics. Striving, as he said, toward "the broad, high,
sunlit middle ground where fact meets fact, and truth is balanced against truth," he presented in his initial chapter the
factors of the conflict as they appeared to one reconciled to
the issue. He conceded slavery to have been only "the immediate fomenting cause." [30] It was "the tallest pine in the political forest around whose top the fiercest lightnings were to
blaze"; but underlying all contention were the opposed
theories of government. The South maintained that "the
Union formed under the Constitution was a union of consent
and not of force; that the original States were not the creatures but the creators of the Union." The North, on the
other hand, maintained, "with the utmost confidence in the
correctness of her position," that the Union "was intended to
be perpetual; that sovereignty was a unit and could not be
divided, and that the right of self-preservation was inherent
in all governments." [31] The North tried to combat the political movement in the South by denouncing it as treason, but
this only added fuel to the fire.

> To the charge of the North that secession was rebellion and
> treason, the South replied that the epithets of rebel and traitor
> did not deter her from the assertion of her independence,
> since these same epithets had been familiar to the ears of
> Washington and Hancock and Adams and Light Horse Harry
> Lee.[32]

He denied the oft-repeated charge that the well-meaning
masses of the South were dragooned into war by ambitious

30 *Reminiscences of the Civil War* (New York, 1903), p. 19.
31 *Ibid.,* p. 21.
32 *Ibid.*

and guileful leaders. "The literal truth is that the people were leading the leaders." [33] The only explanation of the "unparalleled spontaneity that pervaded all classes of the Southern people" was "the impulse of self-defense."[34]

Unwilling to labor this portion of the work, General Gordon stated the issues with admirable succinctness. He paused long enough, however, to deprecate the habit of teaching that either section was "wholly and eternally right." Both had fought and suffered for liberty, but each had seen liberty in a different light, and with this charitable suggestion he abandoned political theory to take up an absorbing narrative.

Robert Stiles thought that "the great conflict will never be properly comprehended by the man who looks upon it as a war for the preservation of slavery." [35] Though never doubting that Southerners had the better of the constitutional argument, he believed that they had actually gone into battle to defend their hearthstones. The Confederate volunteer hastened to the front with the thought in his mind: "With me is Right, before me is Duty, behind me is Home." [36]

From these declarations it should be apparent that the Confederate captains believed they were fighting to protect a distinct people who had lost the political safeguards of their welfare. Every minority problem raises delicate questions of the relationship between parts and the whole. The Confederates were the upholders of a particularism which had been present in 1787, and which had greatly increased by 1860. Lincoln, with his principle that the nation could not exist half slave and half free, was a universalist, denying all tendency toward separation and particularity. The question of whether one shall stand up for what is near and dear to him,

33 *Ibid.*, p. 16.
34 *Ibid.*, p. 17.
35 *Op. cit.*, p. 50.
36 *Ibid.*, p. 51.

which is the meaning of all patriotism, or, putting all sentiment aside, align himself with what is supposed to be the
general drift of humanity, has produced divisions before and
will produce them again. Thus the Civil War becomes only a
version of the argument between universalists and particularists, with the Southern soldiers choosing to defend the part,
made dear by nativity and associations.

There are those who maintain that the true principle of
history is a dynamic universalism, so that all true development is a sloughing off of particularities and individualities
in an approach to the typical. There are others who believe
that life consists in the richness of diversity and that conformity to a universal pattern is a kind of death. The opinion
that the world cannot be one half one thing and half another
is an extremely bold statement of the first view. On the level
of everyday politics it takes the form of democratic resentment against exclusiveness, just as the second expresses itself
in distaste for incorporation into something felt to be alien or
inferior. The backwoods politicians of mid-nineteenth-
century America were unknowingly entangled in the great
debate of the Schoolmen, with the Southern separatists play-
ing the part of Nominalists, and the Northern democrats and
equalitarians that of Realists. This view of the conflict,
though unfamiliar, is not farfetched, and if all questions resolve themselves ultimately into metaphysical problems, as is
not impossible, it becomes the philosophical description of
the event.

2. The Saga of Confederate Valor

It is necessary to turn now from these apologias, brief or
long, embittered or philosophic, to the chronicle of Confederate valor as it proved itself on the field. The Southern

people were a provincial people, inclined to regard their
country as the world and, because of lack of comparisons, to
form exaggerated notions of their own merits.[37] The peculiar type of blindness which results from being thus cut off is
an affliction which will visit any people so circumstanced.
Moreover they lived, for the most part, an easy, almost Arcadian existence, which was free from major excitements. It was
inevitable, therefore, that the war should bring to many of
them the one intense experience of their lives, beside which
all that happened before and after seemed commonplace.
Walter Hines Page, growing up in North Carolina in the
days of Reconstruction, noted how surviving soldiers were
accustomed to consider "the War" as an experience by which
all other experiences could be evaluated. It is clear that in
this event an unschooled and innocent people were introduced to one of humanity's great dramas, the memory of
which never faded. Nor should one wonder that some exaggeration occurred in the reporting of its details. But after he
has made allowance for a natural measure of this, and for
overcompensation in an effort to write "Southern heroism"
large on the scroll of history, one must acknowledge, in view
of the plain facts, that the American Civil War was one of the
bloodiest and most stubbornly fought wars in the long history of military conflict. If comparisons mean anything, it

[37] It was seldom that Southerners spoke the homely truth on this subject,
but John Hampden Chamberlayne, addressing the Society of the Alumni of
the University of Virginia in 1880, used candid language. He said to his
fellow Virginians (*Why Despair?*, Richmond, 1880, p. 4): "Virginia has
always been provincial—provincial in her isolation, provincial in her self-will,
provincial in her strength and unhappily provincial in the weakness which
war discovers. Provincial she was, too, in arrogant appreciation of herself, and
provincial sometimes in an abject depreciation and a false estimate of what
was around her. For long periods of her life she found no excellencies outside of her own borders, sought for no lessons from any history but her own,
grew ignorant of that history purposely as well as all else, and reckoned
herself as needing no teacher." To the extent that this was true of the entire
South, the Civil War constituted a rude collision with external realities,
which brought it out of the habit of self-complacency.

may sober one to learn that whereas at Waterloo the army of
Napoleon, after fighting for eight hours and losing ten per
cent of its strength left the field in a rout, at Gettysburg the
armies fought three days, each suffering a loss of about twenty-
five per cent of its strength with neither yielding ground or
suffering visibly in morale. At Stone's River and at Chicka-
mauga the proportion of slaughter was even greater. Single
Confederate units are on record as having lost eighty-five per
cent of their number without ceasing to exist as military
organizations. It must be granted, therefore, that the saga of
valor was worth telling, and General D. H. Hill, who said
that the Southern soldier "united the élan of the Frenchman
with the dogged obstinacy of the Englishman, the careless
gaiety of the Italian with the uncomplaining fortitude of the
Russian," [38] had grounds for his assertion.

Consequently it is understandable that the recital of
heroic achievements should bulk large in the military memoirs, especially in those of men who went to the war young
and filled with romantic preconceptions. We may begin with
the extreme romantic approach by taking John Esten Cooke's
Wearing of the Gray, one of the first volumes of reminiscence
to be published, and a work unthinkable as coming from
anyone except a member of the Southern chivalry. Cooke had
grown up one of those many unhappy young men in the
South in love with literature but compelled by custom and
limited opportunity to apply themselves to law. The arrival
of war brought a resolution of his difficulty, for in it he could
play the part of a man, as it was understood in the South, and
at the same time enjoy a feast of the romantic imagination.
From the first he was intoxicated by the pageantry of it. For
him war was made up of the deeds of heroes, and he frankly
stated that his book was for "lovers of noble natures." [39] The

[38] *Southern Historical Society Papers,* I (January-June, 1876), p. 396.
[39] *Wearing of the Gray* (New York, 1867), p. xiii.

personal details going into his narrative he excused on the ground that such items "elucidate biography and history— which are the same." [40]

The first part of the *Wearing of the Gray* is accordingly composed of individual sketches of Stuart, Jackson, Ashby, Mosby, Beauregard, and others. The modern reader will be struck by the continuous vein of uncritical admiration in which these portraits are offered. The hero epic of the Anglo-Saxons is everywhere suggested. Stuart, who fired his admiration above all others, is "The Flower of Cavaliers." [41] In moments of battle his voice is "hoarse and strident"; his face is "stormy"; and his eyes are "like a 'devouring fire.' " [42] The enemy, one reads, has learned to dread his "flower-encircled weapon." [43] When he met his death at Yellow Tavern, he "fell like some 'monarch of the woods,' which makes the whole forest resound as it crashes down." [44] Little that would give Stuart and Jackson the stature of demigods is left unsaid. Of the latter one reads that "His poetry was the cannon's flash, the rattle of musketry, and the lurid cloud of battle." [45] In a closing description of this figure, Cooke wrote: "In the man who holds aloft his hand in prayer while his veteran battalions move by steadily to the charge, it will not be difficult to fancy a reproduction of the stubborn Cromwell, sternest of Ironsides, going forth to conquer in the name of the Lord." [46] Equally unrestrained is the description of "gallant Pelham" at Fredericksburg, when it is declared, "All know how stubbornly he stood on that day—what laurels encircled his young brow when night at last came." [47]

No one can read far in these descriptions without becom-

40 *Ibid.*
41 *Ibid.*, p. 30.
42 *Ibid.*, p. 28.
43 *Ibid.*, p. 19.
44 *Ibid.*, p. 43.
45 *Ibid.*, p. 50.
46 *Ibid.*, p. 56.
47 *Ibid.*, p. 133.

ing impressed with the conventionalized pattern of Cooke's heroes. They are members of a chivalry, and they exhibited the traditional qualities of modesty, gentleness, good deportment, and above all, bravery—qualities which recall Chaucer's "parfit, gentil knight." In his eagerness to leave Stuart *sans peur et sans reproche* Cooke stresses his devotion to his family and his abstemious habits to offset this gay blade's well-known reputation for frivolity. "Gallant Pelham," the boy major, is praised as "Modest to a fault almost—blushing like a girl at times and wholly unassuming in his entire deportment." [48] Wade Hampton, of South Carolina, who like a baron of old, equipped at his own expense a regiment of six hundred men, is also the *beau chevalier*, with "the noble pride, the true courtesy, and the high-bred honour of one who amid all the jarring strife of an excited epoch, would not suffer his serene equanimity of gentleman to be disturbed." [49] So runs the constant ascription of courtesy, honor, and unselfishness to the leaders in gray. The entire work confronts one with Cooke's belief that these men gained dignity by participating in the mighty struggle, just as one enobles himself by self-dedication to a cause. The reader continues in this aura of romance and idealism to Appomattox, where "A dreamy, memorial sadness seemed to descend through the April air and change the scene." [50]

Henry Kyd Douglas was another young Virginian who rode off to the war with a notion that it would prove something between a picnic and a tournament. Nor was he ever entirely disillusioned, for he came under the powerful spell of Stonewall Jackson, who had a way of infusing men with his own fierce delight in the soldier's calling. *I Rode With Stonewall* is a diary written in the period 1862-66 and revised thirty years later, when the author resolved to soften its sec-

48 *Ibid.*, p. 132.
49 *Ibid.*, p. 63.
50 *Ibid.*, p. 600.

tional feeling. It remained unpublished, however, until 1940, when the University of North Carolina Press brought it out as a notable contribution to our knowledge of the Cromwell of the Confederacy.

It is difficult for an age which has received so many sermons on the horror and futility of war to credit the light-heartedness with which men of this type went into our great civil broil. The modern spirit of calculation, which counts the cost in advance and speculates timidly about the consequences, was foreign to their mentality. For them it combined a great *devoir* with a rare opportunity for adventure, and those who declined the sacrifice entailed were regarded as simply not made of the proper stuff. With reference to his baptism of fire at First Manassas, Douglas could write: "Ever after I never felt so sorry for the man who was wounded as for the man who was too ill to go in." [51] In this spirit of bravura the story proceeds to the very end.

John B. Gordon also belongs to the group which never outlived a disposition to see the war as a contest of chivalry. Engaged in the development of coal mines in the mountains of northern Georgia when secession came, he organized a company of "Raccoon Roughs," which he led to Montgomery for induction into the service. The scenes which met them in their passage along the route to the Confederate capital are offered in witness of the intense ardor of the Southern populace, as well as of the high-flown notions then current of what constituted war.

The line of our travel was one unbroken scene of enthusiasm. Bon fires blazed from the hills at night, and torch-light processions, with drums and fifes, paraded the streets of the towns. In the absence of real cannon, blacksmith's anvils were made to thunder our welcome. Vast throngs gathered at the depots, filling the air with shoutings, and bearing banners with all

[51] *I Rode with Stonewall* (Chapel Hill, 1940), p. 9.

conceivable devices, proclaiming Southern independence, and pledging the last dollar and man for the success of the cause.[52]

At one station a flag bearing "NO RETREAT" was presented to his company by a group of ladies, and in a speech of acceptance Gordon told them the story of the drummer boy of Switzerland.[53] Such feeling preceded the four years of schooling which led to "the brief little diploma handed to us at Appomattox." [54]

In Gordon as in Cooke, one finds himself back in the heroic age. Every leader is a knight, brave, true, magnanimous; every woman is a high-souled heroine, devoting herself to her lord and comforting him in his hardships. Expressions such as "the knightly man in grey" recur. In relating the death of his brother in the Battle of the Wilderness, Gordon wrote with characteristic effusiveness: "The fatal grapeshot plunged through his manly breast, and the noble youth slept his last sleep in the woful wilderness." [55] Taking his soldiers into York, Pennsylvania, in the Gettysburg campaign, he fairly preened himself upon his chivalric code, as Edward Pollard remarked that Southern soldiers were wont to do, by promising a group of alarmed ladies "the head of any soldier under my command who destroyed private property, disturbed the repose of a single home, or insulted a woman." [56] His account of the cavalry fight at Gettysburg is complete down to booted and spurred horsemen, the sound of bugles, "five thousand plumes" and "fluttering pennants on streaming guidons." [57]

James B. Avirett devoted the introduction of his *Memoirs of General Turner Ashby and his Compeers* to proofs that

52 Gordon, *op. cit.*, p. 10.
53 *Ibid.*, p. 11.
54 *Ibid.*, p. 12.
55 *Ibid.*, p. 65.
56 *Ibid.*, p. 143.
57 *Ibid.*, p. 171.

the Southern people had kept the spirit of chivalry from perishing. "In this materialistic age the idea is rapidly gaining ground that chivalry is effete," he wrote, but the Army of Northern Virginia had "failed to confound war with rapine and arson" and so afforded "irrefragable proof that the principle of chivalry is still alive." The forces hostile to chivalry he termed either "demoniacal or puritanical." [58] He went on to describe Ashby as "a living reality in all that constitutes the peerless cavalier, and the impersonation of those knightly qualities of mind and heart, which will go down to posterity as so aptly delineated in the pages of 'Waverley.' " [59]

In the same way Colonel Alfred Roman praised Beauregard for his "high-toned chivalric courtesy." [60]

Although such surviving concepts of chivalry set the tone of the Confederate officers' corps, it must be pointed out in the interest of the whole truth that there were on the Southern side a few commanders who took a practical and cold-blooded view of war. Johnston's *Narrative of Military Operations* is, as the businesslike title indicates, the account of a professional military man, not exceeded in bluntness and directness even by Grant, whose unadorned style shocked Matthew Arnold. John B. Hood's *Advance and Retreat*, although rendered charming in spots by its simplicity and frankness, contains little besides a straightforward chronicle of events. John S. Mosby, the famous partisan raider, went so far as to say that he was temperamentally disinclined to see anything of romance in war. He wrote in *Mosby's War Reminiscences and Stuart's Cavalry Campaigns:*

> I fought for success and not display. There was no man in the Confederate army who had less of the spirit of knight errantry in him, or took a more practical view of war than I did. The

[58] *Memoirs of General Turner Ashby and his Compeers* (Baltimore, 1867), pp. v-vii.
[59] *Ibid.* p. 16.
[60] Roman, *op. cit.*, I, p. 11.

combat between Richard and Saladin by the Diamond of the Desert is a beautiful picture for the imagination to dwell on, but it isn't war, and was no model for me.[61]

This may sound like something from Sherman; yet it is the declaration of one who, more than any other save possibly Morgan and Forrest, came to be associated with intrepidity and the individual daring exploit which single out the hero. And Forrest himself, though he wrote nothing, left behind certain oracular sayings which betray the most pragmatic view of war possible.

For some the romance of war was bound up with the person of a vivid leader, and when he disappeared from the scene, fighting turned into the dreary business of killing. During the life of a gallant and fearless commander, who filled his men with a belief that they could accomplish anything, and who thus became a source of legend, war remained an art. It became a trade after the cold science logistics began to make headway against individual daring and imagination. Followers of both Stuart and Morgan testified that upon the death of these men, something irreplaceable seemed to depart.

To those who were experiencing it for the first time, war was an education. The simple agrarian people who made up the rank and file of the Southern armies had never before known anything so exciting; but at the same time, they found that its horrors exceeded their anticipation. It is a matter of general observation that humanity has never been able to make peace as interesting as war. Conflict, the essence of all

[61] *Mosby's War Reminiscences and Stuart's Cavalry Campaigns* (New York, 1887), p. 80. It was natural for one of Mosby's forthright temperament to become impatient with the shortcomings of the Richmond government, which were manifold, and the following censure (*ibid.*, p. 100) reveals his dissatisfaction with its view of war as a game: "The martinets who controlled it were a good deal like the hero in Molière's comedy, who complained that his antagonist had wounded him by thrusting in *carte*, when according to rule it should have been done by *tierce*. I cared nothing for the form of a thrust if it brought blood. I did not play with foils."

drama, holds first claim on the human attention; yet the suffering inseparable from this variety of it compels the taking of a moral point of view toward what would otherwise be purely a game. Lee, whose intellectual stature has been over-looked by those wishing to portray him only as patriarch and soldier, took cognizance of this in his famous remark at Fred-ericksburg: "It is well that this is so terrible! We should grow too fond of it." [62] This expresses admirably the paradoxical nature of the institution. Its peculiar fascination exacts a ter-rible price, and although many soldiers of the South tried to confine it within the circumspect rules of chivalry and to see romance in its violence, most of them were forced to admit that it brought out the brutish nature of man.

It is highly important to note, however, that Southern sol-diers came out of the war unrepentant, and as convinced as before that there are things worse than war. The awful cost which the South paid for its defeat does not need detailing here—its manpower decimated; its productive facilities largely destroyed; Atlanta and Columbia reduced to shambles; many of its colleges pillaged and burned; and worst of all, its politi-cal power so broken that the very means of recuperation were withheld. But the Southern soldiers trudged home feeling that all had been lost save honor and spent the next thirty years trying to imagine not how war might be banished from the earth, but how the South might have won this war.

In connection with this topic it might be asked whether the Confederate ever achieved a sufficient detachment from the struggle to view it humorously. The question is impor-tant, because the kind of war waged will depend on the state of mind of the combatant. And the answer is a clear yes, although the earnestness and intensity which pervade most of the written record might arouse a different expectation. How much of this was the incorrigible folk humor of the Southern

[62] John Esten Cooke, *A Life of General Robert E. Lee* (New York, 1871), p. 184.

yeoman and how much of it was a feature of the tradition of chivalry, which requires good cheer in adversity as well as good behavior in triumph, would be difficult to settle. But the number of jokes told at the expense of their own men and institutions reveals a humorous side to the grey knights and tends to discount the general belief that Southern pride is supersensitive. The amount of lashing which Southern character received from Northern journalism did, no doubt, make the average man touchy about criticism emanating from that quarter, but practically any latitude was allowed wit and satire originating within the family. John B. Gordon suspends the impetuous movement of his narrative fairly often for an anecdote, and the following will be found an illustration of the points made above.

A Virginia farmer living near Appomattox announced shortly after the surrender that he would give employment to any of Lee's soldiers who wished to work a few days for their food and a small wage. He then divided those who applied into groups according to their rank in the disbanded army.

A neighbor inquired of him as to the different squads. "Who are those men working over there?"

"Them is privates, sir, of Lee's army."

"Well, how do they work?"

"Very fine sir, first-rate workers."

"Who are those in the second group?"

"Them is lieutenants and captains, and they work fairly well, but not as good workers as the privates."

"I see you have a third squad: who are they?"

"Them is colonels."

"Well, what about the colonels? How do they work?"

"Now neighbor, you'll never hear me say one word ag'in' any man who fit in the Southern army; but I ain't a-gwine to hire no generals." [63]

The *Reminiscences* of General Basil Duke are crowded

[63] Gordon, *op. cit.*, p. 453.

with ludicrous episodes. There is Colonel Roger Hanson who, exasperated by requests for sick leave, gave and enforced an order "that there should be only two sick men at one time in each company." [64] One reads about Champe Ferguson, the mountain bushwhacker, who upon being asked how many men he had killed, replied with true hill-billy understatement: "I ain't killed nigh as many as men say I have; folks has lied about me powerful. I ain't killed but thirty-two men since this war commenced." The chapter "Civil War in Shelbyville" is a group of incidents in the style of Toonerville comics. Even John S. Mosby, who prided himself on a stern philosophy of war, could not resist an occasional indulgence in dry humor.

Scattered through *The Land We Love, Southern Bivouac,* and *Confederate Veteran* are countless anecdotes of the camp, many of which show that a sense of the jocose prevailed even when the Confederacy was *in articulo mortis.* Good humor, tolerance, and a certain easygoing acceptance of the irrationalities of life appear so characteristic of the Southern common soldier that one may be at loss to reconcile these with the heritage of bitterness which followed Appomattox.

3. The Christian Warrior

The Confederate captains not only were conscious of being the standard bearers of chivalry; they also regarded themselves as distinctly a Christian soldiery. It is clear that they partook to a large extent of what has been termed "the older religiousness" of the South.[65] The significance of this fact

64 *The Reminiscences of General Basil W. Duke* (Garden City, 1911), p. 142.
65 According to the Reverend W. T. Hall of Mississippi (*The Land We Love,* IV, December, 1867, p. 128) the Christian soldiers of the South, who believed in revealed religion, had a religious reason for fighting. Since the Yankees, "when all their objections had been answered, were disposed to place their intuitions above revelation rather than yield the controversy," Southerners felt that "the very authority of God's word was at issue."

must not be overlooked, for whether or not a man believes that the universe reflects a moral design means a great deal. Unfortunately, since many of the soldiers considered it unprofessional to digress in their memoirs with discussions of non-military subjects, our testimony on this point is less complete than it might be. No one, for example, could gather from the matter-of-fact pages of Johnston's *Narrative* that he was a genuinely religious man. Others, like Stonewall Jackson, were cut off before they could leave any kind of systematic interpretation of events. We have, nevertheless, enough to proceed on to insist that the Confederates were a religious soldiery, and that their religion provided them with an interpretation of the tragedy of defeat. But they were not theological casuists; their religious view of life centered quite simply about a belief in Providence. God had foreseen all, and our suffering and our defeats in this world were part of a discipline whose final fruit it was not given to mortal minds to perceive. Character and virtue were things that had to be earned in the hurly-burly of life, and great calamities had to be regarded as part of the design of inscrutable Providence.

This spirit characterized Lee perhaps more than any other man in the Confederate armies. He appeared to move through life with a kind of objective allegiance to duty, believing that God had a hand in both his defeats and his victories. This awareness of an overruling power, controlling the destinies of men for a final end which is good, gave him a serenity which was a subject of much comment by his associates. A passage from his writings, first made public by Colonel Charles Marshall in 1887, is the testimonial of a deeply religious nature:

My experience of men has neither disposed me to think worse of them, nor indisposed me to serve them; nor, in spite of failures, which I lament, of errors, which I now see and acknowledge, or, of the present state of affairs, do I despair of the future. The march of Providence is so slow, and our desires so impatient, the work of progress is so immense, and our means of aiding it so feeble, the life of humanity is so long, and that of the individual so brief, that we often see only the ebb of the advancing wave, and are thus discouraged. It is history that teaches us to hope.[66]

This conviction that the final outcome is the work of Providence takes much of the burden off human shoulders and prevents the kind of anxiety one must experience when a temporary defeat is felt to be a total repudiation. Such, apparently, was the secret of the sustaining power of religion with these men.

Some few soldiers, of whom John B. Gordon furnishes a good example, came out of the war with more religion than they took in. He entered the struggle a thoughtless young man of twenty-nine; he left it after four years of looking death in the face with a mystical philosophy which appears on many pages of his *Reminiscences*. This expressed itself in a feeling that God fulfills Himself in many ways, and that all the expense and suffering of a mighty war were but the means by which Providence resolved a conflict which had been present since the founding of the Union. Providence accounts for all that human reason cannot explain. Thus it was by "God's mysterious Providence" that Lincoln and Davis were born in the same state, to take up residence in different sections, and to become the leaders of opposing civilizations. Providence does not always dispose according to human estimates of probability, and so Confederate troops in the Battle of the Wilderness, well aware of Grant's overwhelming numbers, "rejected as utterly unworthy of a Christian soldiery the doctrine that Providence was on the side of the heaviest guns and the most numerous battalions." [67] In a further discussion of the same battle Gordon reiterated his "firm faith in God's Providence, and his control of the des-

66 *Southern Historical Society Papers*, XVII (1889), p. 245.
67 Gordon, *op. cit.*, p. 236.

tinies of this Republic." [68] He attributed Lee's power to "an unfaltering faith in the saving truths of the Bible." [69]

Human conflict thus appears as a working out of God's policies, and the very violence of the strife may be a measure of the fruitfulness which will flow from it. General Gordon presented a vivid figure of this process in an experience drawn from his boyhood. He recalled a time when he witnessed a furious storm:

> Standing on a mountain top, I saw two storm clouds lowering in the opposite horizon. They were heavily charged with electric fires. As they rose and approached each other they extended their length and gathered additional blackness and fury. Higher and higher they rose, their puffing windcaps rolling like hostile banners above them; and when nearing each other the flashing lightning blazed along their front and their red bolts were hurled into each other's bosoms. Finally in mid-heavens they met, and the blinding flashes and fearful shocks filled my boyish spirit with awe and terror. But God's hand was in that storm, and from the furious conflict copious showers were poured upon the parched and thirsty earth, which refreshed and enriched it.[70]

It would be a mistake to see this as mere rhetoric. This was General Gordon's dialectic, an interpretation of inexorable events at least as profound as those offered by some of the more sophisticated theories that followed his day. And it is, of course, a religious interpretation, which insists that the road to salvation is lined with suffering, but tells us that because "God's hand" is in the storm of life, our trials are not mere sound and fury. Strife is the father of all things, according to a Greek maxim, and after one has grasped this significant fact, he begins to view the whole process as a pageant, becomes reconciled to the enemy, and so is purged of all

68 *Ibid.*, p. 260.
69 *Ibid.*, p. 232.
70 *Ibid.*, pp. 188-189.

bitterness.[71] It is not improbable that Lincoln, whose mystical soul has defied all attempts to equate him with merely political sentiments, entertained the same philosophy.

Even the phlegmatic Longstreet was moved to say that "there is today, because of the war, a broader and deeper patriotism in all Americans," and that all the nation needed for a perfect healing was "faith in Jehovah." [72]

Some unusual insights into the religious life of the Confederate soldier are provided by the *Personal Narrative* of Charles Todd Quintard, who went through the war as chaplain of the First Tennessee Regiment. A native of Stamford, Connecticut, Quintard had come South to practice medicine, but he conceived an interest in religion and in course of time was admitted to the Episcopal priesthood. Serving in the double capacity of surgeon and spiritual advisor, he witnessed the spectacle of hardened soldiers yielding themselves to a higher power, of which his short volume contains several vivid instances. Perhaps the most remarkable incident is his interview with General Bragg some time after the bloody and indecisive battle of Murfreesboro. This commander was known to be of sharp tongue and unsociable disposition, and it was only with difficulty that Dr. Quintard got admittance to his tent. After requesting the impatient general to dismiss his secretaries, he talked to him about "our blessed Lord, and about the responsibilities of a man in the General's position," and at length asked him to be confirmed. At this point, according to the narrator, tears sprang into Bragg's eyes, and he declared: "I have been waiting for twenty years to have someone say this to me." [73] Shortly thereafter he was baptized

71 In the same vein John McKintosh Kell of the *Alabama* (*op. cit.*, p. 5) could discern in the fall of the South "God's frowning Providence of disaster for his own wise plans and purposes"; and W. H. Tunnard (*The History of the Third Louisiana Regiment*, Baton Rouge, 1866, p. ix) could declare that "The Southern people accept the issue of the struggle as the unalterable decree of a mysterious Providence."

72 Longstreet, *op. cit.*, p. vi.

73 *Personal Narrative* (Sewanee, Tenn., 1905), p. 79.

and confirmed. Dr. Quintard reports that one night during the same period he and Leonidas Polk remained up until two o'clock in the morning while the bishop-general, destined soon to be killed in the Atlanta campaign, gave a detailed account of how his mind had turned to religious topics while he was at West Point.[74] On another occasion, he reports "a long and delightful conversation with General Hardee about confirmation." [75] On June 1, 1863, "General Hardee had his brigade formed in a hollow square, and the Bishop addressed it briefly upon the religious aspects of the struggle." [76]

Robert Stiles gives an extended account of the religious enthusiasm which swept through the Army of Northern Virginia shortly after the battle of Fredericksburg. The church services were invariably packed, the singing was fervent, there were "cries unto God," and many soldiers delivered testimonials, which were moving if simple homiletics. A feature of the sermons preached to the men was that they contained "the gospel and the gospel only." [77]

The Southern soldier had the same religious impulse as the Southern churchgoer of antebellum times. He was a seeker after faith and hope, and by maintaining a distinction between the rewards of God and the rewards of the world, he survived his downfall without loss of conviction. His God was the old-fashioned God who wielded the thunder and who would punish erring people and test the faith of those who prided themselves on being in his favor. As was true with other departments of his life, the spirit of utilitarianism had not made entrance, and the later doctrine that a proper spiritual life is reflected in worldly prosperity had not yet taken hold of the South, though it was to make its appearance in the postbellum epoch.

[74] *Ibid.*, p. 71.
[75] *Ibid.*, p. 76.
[76] *Ibid.*, p. 77.
[77] Stiles, *op. cit.*, pp. 139-143.

4. The Character of the Enemy

Thus the majority of Confederate officers looked upon themselves as Christian gentlemen, and in the recognized calling of war they sought to maintain that character, often to the point of nicety. The style and spirit of their warfare was a source of great pride to them, but that of the enemy provoked criticism and condemnation, on what grounds we must see. It is well to proceed cautiously here, for as an early English poem says, "In broyles the bag of lyes is ever open," and the enemy is likely to be represented as barbarous in proportion as he proves stubborn and difficult to conquer. But after all precautions have been taken and all corrections have been made, there remains considerable foundation for the assertion that the United States is the first government in modern times to commit itself to the policy of unlimited aggression. This was one of the many innovations which came out of the American Civil War. It is true, of course, that no war is wholly free from atrocities, but a distinction must be drawn between those excesses committed by soldiers who have broken discipline and those which are a part of the determined policy of commanders. Generals Hunter, Sheridan, and Sherman put themselves on record, both by utterance and practice, as believing in the war of unlimited aggression, in the prosecution of which they received at least the tacit endorsement of the Lincoln administration.

This is a matter of prime importance in the history of the American past, because the real significance of the war of unlimited aggression is that it strikes at one of the bases of civilization. As long as each side plays according to the rules of the "game," with no more infraction than is to be expected in any heated contest, the door is left open for reconciliation and the eventual restoration of amity. But when one side drops the restraints built up over a long period and commits itself to the total destruction of the other by any means, no longer distinguishing between combatants and noncombatants, then the demoralization is complete, and the difficulty of putting relationships back on a moral basis is perhaps too great to be overcome. In war, as in peace, people remain civilized by acknowledging bounds beyond which they must not go. Even in military combat there must be a supreme sanction, uniting those who in all else are in opposition, and if this is disregarded, then the long and painful business of laying the foundations of understanding must be recommenced from the very beginning. The expression "Christian civilization," when examined, denotes just this body of fundamental concepts and allegiances, which one may not drop without becoming "un-Christian" and so, in the meaningful sense of the word, excommunicated. When this is understood the term "Christian soldier" ceases to be paradoxical. The Christian soldier must seek the verdict of battle always remembering that there is a higher law by which both he and his opponent will be judged, and which enjoins against fighting as the barbarian.

It is not unusual to read in Southern accounts of the rejection of some procedure as "unworthy of a Christian soldiery." Indeed, by the standard of modern practice, which represents a revolt against all civilized restraints, the matter of regard for rule was carried far.[78] Exceptions were found, naturally, among the disorderly elements which made up parts of the Western armies, but few outrages can be ascribed to the armies of Johnston, Lee, and Bragg, and none of them was condoned.

Great indignation followed the discovery that these ob-

[78] Carlisle Terry, M.D., related (*Century Magazine*, XXXIX, February, 1890, p. 638) that near the end of the war a Southern inventor carried before Jefferson Davis a hollow container fashioned to represent exactly a large piece of coal. His plan was to fill these with an explosive and get them placed in the fuel yards of Federal naval stations. But the Confederate President rejected the proposal with a show of indignation as "an unjustifiable mode of warfare."

servances were not going to be reciprocated by the North. Though few Confederate commanders attempted to reason the matter out in terms of philosophy and history, there was conviction that those violating the code were guilty of an enormity whose consequences would not be limited to immediate acts. Most of them considered it unprofessional to display anger, and we have from Lee only a few passing remarks about the cruelty of war. But the more impetuous members of the fraternity were not unwilling to declare themselves. Jubal Early was bitter against Sherman, and the pages of Semmes are crowded with citations of Yankee knavery. One reads of "the mad fanatics of the North," [79] and of "the coarse and rude Vandal." [80] Semmes explained to the captain of a foreign ship that "we are only defending ourselves against robbers, with knives at our throats." [81] In almost every chapter the reader encounters "the Northern Demos" and "the barbarians of the North." Semmes shared the view of Edward Pollard that the Northern government was the instrument of a coarse and unruly mob, and that the Northern armies were recruited from riffraff, whose outstanding penchant was thievery. "Unfortunately for the Great Republic," he wrote, "political power has descended so low, that the public officer, however high his station, must of necessity be little better than the b'hoy from whom he receives his power of attorney. When mobs rule, gentlemen must retire to private life." [82] This government was "with a barbarity unknown in civilized war, laying waste our plantations and corn-fields." [83]

President Lincoln had originally proposed to execute all captured Confederate sea raiders as pirates, but the promise

79 Semmes, *op. cit.*, p. 90.
80 *Ibid.*, p. 98.
81 *Ibid.*, p. 186.
82 *Ibid.*, p. 233.
83 *Ibid.*, p. 648

of retaliation by President Davis compelled him to abandon the intention. Semmes used this incident to sharpen his moral. "This recantation of an attempted barbarism," he said,

> had not been honestly made. It was not the generous taking back of a wrong principle, by a high-minded people. The tiger, which had come out of the jungle, in quest of blood, had only been driven back by fear; his feline, and bloodthirsty disposition would, of course, crop out again as soon as he ceased to dread the huntsman's rifle.[84]

Semmes had destroyed Northern property on a scale far beyond anything other Confederate commanders had an opportunity to do, and it was natural that in the Northern press he should be singled out for special abuse. He therefore took delight in announcing that he had observed the laws of war more faithfully than the enemy. In connection with his capture of the *Golden Rocket* from the "Black Republican State of Maine" he wrote:

> We were making war upon the enemy's commerce, but not upon unarmed seamen. It gave me as much pleasure to treat these with humanity, as it did to destroy his ships, and one of the most cherished recollections which I have brought out of the war, which, in some sense may be said to have been a civil war, is, that the "pirate," whom the enemy denounced, with a pen dipped in gall, and with a vocabulary of which decent people should be ashamed, set that same enemy the example, which he failed to follow, *of treating prisoners of war,* according *to the laws of war.*[85]

Semmes never abandoned his *saeva indignatio* against the North, and at the end of his long work he recorded his belief that the killing of Abraham Lincoln was

84 *Ibid.,* p. 182.
85 *Ibid.,* p. 131.

just retribution for destruction and ruin brought on twelve
millions of people. Without any warrant for his conduct he
made a war of rapine and lust against eleven sovereign states,
whose only provocation had been that they had made an effort
to preserve the liberties which had been handed down to them
by their fathers. These states had not sought war, but peace,
and they had found, at the hands of Abraham Lincoln, destruction. As a Christian, it was my duty to say, "Lord have
mercy upon his soul! but the d——l will surely take care of his
memory." [86]

The most execrated name in Southern annals is, of course,
that of W. T. Sherman. Joe Johnston, who opposed him in
the campaign from Dalton to Atlanta, wrote nothing in censure of his methods, and in 1891 served as pallbearer at his
funeral. But Johnston was of cold temperament; John B.
Hood, on the other hand, who took over command with the
Confederate army backed up against Atlanta, considered the
policies of his adversary barbarous and addressed to him several communications in rebuke. Hearing of the forcible
evacuation of civilians from Atlanta—a measure mild enough
in comparison with the brutalities of both sides in World
War II—Hood found it impossible to suppress feeling. He
accordingly sent Sherman a heated message: "And now, sir,
permit me to say that the unprecedented measure you propose transcends, in studied and ingenious cruelty, all acts
ever before brought to my attention in the dark history of
war." [87] He followed this with quotations from Vattel,
Grotius, and Halleck to show that Sherman's conduct violated the universally recognized rules, and cited instances
from the Peninsular War, in which both Wellington and
Soult had taken vigorous steps to restrain their troops from
acts of revenge. At first Sherman gave as good as he received,
but growing impatient with what he called "hypocritical ap-

[86] *Ibid.*, p. 821.
[87] *Advance and Retreat* (New Orleans, 1880), p. 230.

peals to God and humanity," [88] he advised Hood that it would be better for them to fight it out like men. Both seem to have concluded that such discussion was "out of place and profitless" for soldiers, and the exchange was soon terminated.

Even E. Porter Alexander, Chief of Artillery of Longstreet's Corps, who became thoroughly reconciled to the issue of the war, and who produced one of the most impartial and judicious of the military histories, could not refrain from an observation on the methods of Sherman. In the closing pages of his valuable *Military Memoirs of a Confederate* he wrote with reference to the devastation of Georgia: "This was excused on the ground that 'War is Hell.' It depends somewhat upon the warrior." [89] This may be taken as expressing the general opinion of the Confederate military fraternity.

Charles C. Jones, Jr., in his *Historical Sketch of the Chatham Artillery* recorded the bitter opinion that "A liberal and dignified consideration for the feelings, necessities and welfare of the vanquished and impoverished apparently belongs to a contemned period of Roman virtue, the dead chivalry of a heroic age, now numbered with the neglected past, and the despised teaching of the New Testament dispensation." [90]

Criticism of Northern military methods naturally led to a criticism of the whole of Northern civilization, which unfortunately was presented to the South in the form of the Abolitionist, representing hypocrisy; the plundering soldier, representing among other things Yankee cupidity; and the carpetbagger, representing political unscrupulousness. The more partisan Southerners looked upon these as natural outgrowths of the Yankee heritage and the Yankee way of life. Raphael Semmes was particularly severe in his estimate of the Northerners as people. A Catholic gentleman from Maryland, he had a deep-seated antipathy toward the Puritan, and

[88] *Ibid.*, p. 232.
[89] *The Military Memoirs of a Confederate* (New York, 1907), p. 581.
[90] *Historical Sketch of the Chatham Artillery* (Albany, 1867), p. 228.

few chapters of *A Memoir of Service Afloat* are free from acid comments on this type. Virginia and Massachusetts he viewed as two incompatible yoke-fellows:

> Virginia and Massachusetts were the two original germs, from which the great majority of the American population has sprung; and no two peoples, speaking the same language and coming from the same country, could have been more dissimilar, in education, taste, and habits, and even in natural instincts, than the adventurers who settled these two colonies. Those who sought a new field of adventure for themselves, and affluence for their posterity, in the more congenial clime of the Chesapeake, were the gay, and dashing cavaliers, who, as a class, afterward adhered to the fortunes of the Charleses, whilst the first settlers of Massachusetts were composed of the same materials, that formed the "Praise-God-Barebones" Parliament of Cromwell. These two peoples seemed to have an instinctive repugnance, the one to another.[91]

Although Semmes could excuse them partially on the ground that their "niggard" environment made them what they were, he kept before the reader his belief that their character was "gloomy, saturnine, and fanatical," with a tendency to "repel all the more kindly, and generous impulses of our nature." [92]

He was stirred to indignation whenever he entered a port and found the Yankee consul practising a trade to eke out the pittance allowed him as a diplomatic official. In Puerto Cabello, Venezuela, for example, he discovered that "the American Consul, who is also a merchant, represents not only 'those grand moral ideas' that characterize our Northern people, but Sand's sarsaparilla, and Smith's wooden clocks." [93] At Maranham, Brazil, he thought the situation more shocking, for there he found the consul "with com-

91 Semmes, *op. cit.*, p. 55.
92 *Ibid.*
93 *Ibid.*, p. 164.

mendable Yankee thrift" practising the trade of dentistry, "the 'old flag' flying over his files, false teeth, and spittoons. It was not remarkable, he thought, that one "charged with the affairs of state of the Great Republic, and with the decayed teeth of the young ladies of Maranham, at one and the same time, should be a little confused, as to points of international law." [94] Similar observations of an insulting nature make *A Memoir of Service Afloat* one of the most partisan books ever written.

The experience of the war confirmed Semmes in his belief that men are naturally depraved, and these sharp judgments of Yankees pass over into yet sharper judgments of all men. He became completely disabused of the notions of the French optimists. War and politics, and contact with low types of seafaring men left him convinced that man is only "an intellectual wild beast, whose rapacity never yet has been restrained by a sense of justice." [95] The aura of idealism which surrounded the establishment of the Union seduced many Americans into believing that they had been somehow mysteriously regenerated, so that the tragic fates of other people could never befall them. But, he explained, "the events which I have recorded, and am about to record, have taught them, that they are not better—and perhaps they are no worse —than other people." [96] He recommended an abandonment of the unrealistic basis of government and a return to self-interest, "the great regulator." This would mean that Americans would never attempt "to bind up in one sheaf, with a withe of straw, materials so discordant as were the people of the North and the people of the South." [97]

In broad outline the victory of the Yankee was viewed by the South as a triumph of the forces of materialism, equali-

[94] *Ibid.*, pp. 212-213.
[95] *Ibid.*
[96] *Ibid.*, p. 69.
[97] *Ibid.*, p. 70.

tarianism, and irreligion. Richard Taylor, who spent much of
his time after the war in the North interceding for Confederates in distress, was appalled by the saturnalia he witnessed
there. It appeared to him that the masses had "lost all power
of discrimination." The new men of influence were those
who had just acquired fortunes, and who showed themselves
"destitute of manners, taste, or principles." The great moral
crusade had ended in a mockery:

> The vulgar insolence of wealth held complete possession of
> public places and carried by storm the citadels of society. Indeed, society disappeared. As in the middle ages, to escape
> pollution, honorable men and refined women (and there are
> many such in the North) fled to sanctuary and desert, or, like
> the early Christians in the Catacombs, met secretly and in
> fear.[98]

Among the voices deploring the new Yankee civilization
was that of the *Southern Bivouac,* which now and then indulged in mild political skirmishing. In a plaintive editorial
it declared that Southern youths were now better acquainted
with the exploits of Jay Gould and Jesse James than with
those of their sires in the late war. It found the current feeling
running strongly towards a "continental nationality," with
an element in the North willing to bury the memory of the
war entirely for the sake of getting trade with the South. This
was interpreted as a further sign that money had become the
ultimate aim in life.[99] If these are the days of money, those
were the days of glory, it was constantly affirmed, and suspicion was strong that the new motivation was not going to
produce all that its champions imagined. The issue of September, 1883, noted that the South was winning much praise
for its business activity. This was pleasant, but reservations
had to be made:

[98] Taylor, *op. cit.*, pp. 256-257.
[99] *Southern Bivouac,* II (February, 1884), p. 284.

It is well to be up and doing, but there are some things more essential to national health than full barns and stupendous factories.

Let us not forget the breed of noble blood. Many say, "We have turned our backs on the past. Opinions and sentiments are false friends. Nothing is real but property and money."

The war, indeed, was a curse, if it brought us to this. Time was when gold could not purchase rank in society, politics, and religion. It is so no longer.[100]

With reference to the airs which freedmen were giving themselves, it stated that if these constituted progress, "we would like to see a little retrograde movement now and then, for the sake of variety."[101]

Such remarks tell plainly enough that the French Revolution had not come to the South by 1860. Southerners of the postbellum epoch were men of the eighteenth century suddenly transported into a nineteenth-century world. The source of their bafflement is a familiar story to the cultural historian. The old formulations were gone, and a previously well defined structure of society was giving way before the parvenu, whose title to place rested upon some special—and not always praiseworthy—achievement. The old idea of rewards was vanishing, and instead of receiving a station dictated by a theory of the whole society, men were winning their stations through a competition in which human considerations were ruled out. Carlyle had bitterly indicted it in England as the age of the "cash-nexus." Everything betokened the breaking-up of the old synthesis in a general movement toward abstraction in human relationships. The individual was becoming a unit in the formless democratic mass; economics was usurping the right to determine both political and moral policies; and standards supposed to be unalterable were being affected by the new standards of rela-

---

100 *Ibid.*, II (September, 1883), p. 191.
101 *Ibid.*, II (January, 1884), p. 239.

tivism. Topping it all was the growing spirit of skepticism, which was destroying the religious sanctions of conduct and leaving only the criterion of utility.

War is a destroyer of patterns, and those who have grown up in one order, familiar with its assumptions and customs, and feeling that the rules of its collective life somehow emanate from themselves, are likely to be seized with nostalgia when struggling with a new pattern. The alteration which came over the whole country after the triumph of the nationalist party was part of a worldwide tendency. It was modernism, with its urgency, impatience, truculence, and its determination to strip aside all concealing veils and see what is behind them. When the men of the new order did strip aside these veils and found that there was nothing behind them, but that the reality had existed somehow in the willed belief, or the myth, they marked the beginning of modern frustration.

To those who believe in the cyclical theory of cultures, growth and decay are real, and hence there is an absolute point of view from which one generation can assert that the next is a step nearer perdition, if by that we understand a failing sense of moral values, a loss of belief in self, and the spiritual debility which flows from these. It is a problem to determine whether the Confederate captains were aware of the deeper implications of the conflict, which seldom got into the catchwords used to rally either side. It seems that they heard the warning voice, but lacked the insight, or perhaps the vocabulary, to make a full demonstration of the danger. It was generally recognized that two opposed systems were struggling for the mastery. The passing of the code of chivalry, the refusal any longer to see war as a game, the rampant spirit of commercialism, brought it home even to the least perceptive that there was something new in the world, that the "unbought grace of life" was being destroyed by forces

The Testimony Of The Soldier 225

beyond a soldier's power to combat. There was a stubborn notion that there existed some necessary relationship between the old way of life, with its emphasis upon sentimental values and personal integrity, so that the modernism ushered in by Northern victory looked to some like the knowledge of evil, which ends man's state of innocence.

The Eden was the agrarian South, whose existence was challenged in 1861. The serpent had brought with him the twin temptations of science and relativism. Among the outcasts of the Garden who did not cease to sigh for their once happy condition was General Basil Duke. After the coming of peace General Duke settled in Louisville, where he served as an editor of the *Southern Bivouac,* a great compendium of Confederate lore. Late in life he published the *Reminiscences of General Basil W. Duke,* a work which parallels his earlier *History of Morgan's Cavalry* in its main features, but which contains far more in the way of anecdote and personalia and shows that the author had matured philosophic views. The mellowing influence of time is evident, but there has crept in also a wistfulness; for Duke was aware that the world was undergoing a transition, the marks of which could be seen not only in human institutions, but also in the visible face of his enchanted Blue Grass. Though wise enough to see that both loss and gain were involved, he could not resist writing an apologia for the old Kentucky. He had a tempting subject, for all contemporaries have testified that the people of central Kentucky, from the period of its settlement around 1800 to the tragedy of internecine war sixty years later, lived an idyllic existence. Man and nature, it would seem, had arrived at terms. The settlers had come into possession of one of the finest regions of earth, and they had achieved a decorous and stable society which permitted singularly satisfying lives. Warming over these recollections, General Duke wrote: "In the immediate antebellum period, this region was in the acme of its loveliness. Then, so to speak, the charm of nature was blended in just degree with the grace of cultivation, making the picture perfect." [102] A landscape which pleased in every prospect was not at this time marred by the viler work of man. He went on to picture one of the fairest of antebellum communities:

> The rural life of Central Kentucky, in the twenty or thirty years preceding the Civil War, was extremely pleasant, and while simple and unostentatious, had some social features peculiarly attractive. Blue Grass farmers were a robust and well-to-do generation; very much inclined to enjoy creature comforts, and well supplied with them; fond, also of good company and hail fellowship. Their farms yielded them abundant provisions for home consumption, and generally a handsome revenue in addition. As people so situated usually are, they were hospitable, and liberal in all matters, save perhaps a few cherished opinions.[103]

The bucolic life of these Kentuckians was to be interrupted by a revolution, the meaning of which could not be fully anticipated, but which would in the course of time practically obliterate their pattern of life. General Duke had a sense of the mystery involved in great social transformations. "The last decade of their antebellum history," he continued,

> must always be regarded by the people of the South and of Kentucky with peculiar interest. A revolution was impending which was to destroy the old order, and to inaugurate another that to them would appear like a new world. Dimly discerning, but not entirely conscious of what was coming, they were thrilled with a feeling of mingled expectancy and apprehension.[104]

When the sons of Kentucky who had gone forth to fight under the Stars and Bars returned to their native state, "they

102 *Reminiscences of General Basil W. Duke* (New York, 1911), p. 20.
103 *Ibid.*, p. 24.
104 *Ibid.*, p. 30.

could no more recognize the old landmarks than could the sons of Noah have identified the old home after the subsidence of the deluge." [105] Duke held that transitions are real, that the time spirit does change, and that the attempt to speak across the gulf of the generations is, except for limited purposes, fruitless. It was not an illusion that the Old Kentucky had gone:

> Whether the "Old" Kentucky was, or was not, better than the Kentucky of today—and it is just as well not to discuss that question—something of her former glory and prestige, as well as an interest and beauty, seems lacking. The land has undergone a metamorphosis, and "the tender grace of a day that is dead" can never return,[106]

he wrote. Taught by experience that no amount of writing and talking can convince the growing generation of the reality of a vanished time, he concluded: "Let age gracefully recognize its limitations and try to be happy. Content with the past and its recollections, and with no pretense that we can enlighten our juniors, we will admit as candidly, if as sadly, as did the Knight of La Mancha when cured of his illusions, that 'the birds of this year are not found in last year's nests.' " [107]

Richard Taylor, whose exceptional learning permitted an historical perspective not enjoyed by those who are soldiers merely, often pondered the contrast between such peaceful agrarian scenes and the desolation and corruption left by war. Campaigning with Jackson in the Shenandoah, he remarked upon the beauty of the region. The great Valley of Virginia, over which there lay a "languid grace," was soon to be ravaged "with a cruelty surpassing that inflicted upon the Palatinate two hundred years ago." [108] Transferred back to

[105] *Ibid.,* p. 401.
[106] *Ibid.,* p. 31.
[107] *Ibid.,* p. 512.
[108] Taylor, *op. cit.,* p. 46.

his native Louisiana, Taylor found similar scenes of rural innocence threatened by some malignant force from without. Here among the dwellers of the bayou country he recognized the French peasant of the era before the Great Revolution. "Tender and true were his traditions of la belle France, but of the France before Voltaire and the encyclopaedists, the Convention and the Jacobins—ere she had lost faith in all things divine and human, save the *bourgeoisie* and *avocats*." [109] And then he observed that "It was to this earthly paradise, upon this simple race, that the war came, like the tree of the knowledge of evil to our early parents." [110] One gets the fulness of Taylor's reaction to what the new era had brought in the chapter devoted to the City of Washington under the Johnson administration, in which he exclaims that "although of a tolerant disposition and with wide experience of earthly wickedness" he could not see why the cities of the plain were overthrown and this place suffered to exist.[111]

James B. Avirett gives a comparable picture of Virginia on the eve of the John Brown raid. It lay, he said, "a very Eden in its loveliness," filled with people "primitive and simple in their tastes." Against its innocence and repose there was plotting the Satan of a "vindictive and jealous fanaticism." Not the least of Virginia's blessings had been her "happy freedom from the multitudinous phases of infidelity and German Neology." [112]

The Southern people as a group were unspoiled in the sense that they were content with simple habits and primitive tastes. Like any other people of this kind, they were distrustful of commercial and intellectual pursuits, regarding both as ultimately demoralizing. The North, on the other hand, had been caught up in the full tide of nineteenth-century

109 *Ibid.*, p. 106.
110 *Ibid.*, p. 107.
111 *Ibid.*, p. 242.
112 *Op. cit.*, p. 26.

progress; science and a money-economy were completely transforming its life, and it was impatient of the social conservatism of a country cousin like the South. Between the two there was a widening gap. Yet if in either case the path is predestined and the end is the same, it seems as idle to reproach the North for making haste as to reproach the South for delaying. But if we abandon the concept of the fixed cycle and say rather that man lives by his myth, by a projection of ideals, sentiments, and loyalties, which constitute the world of truth—not the world of nature—then the conservation of the pattern becomes obligatory, and the underminers of the faith and the mockers of the vision deserve the obloquy which has traditionally been theirs.

Whether the Confederate captains were fighting in response to conscious ideals, or out of the instinctive distrust with which the primitive views the seductive ways of a decadent civilization, is a profound question. Probably they labored better than they knew. The common man could sense that a change was passing over the nation, that something in the soul of the people was dying, that a pristine state of simplicity, likened to that of our first parents, was being destroyed by the forces of an active evil.

The indictment of the Northern revolution drawn up by Southern politicians, clerics, and soldiers parallels in many interesting particulars Edmund Burke's indictment of the French Revolution, of which, in truth, it was the continuation.[113] Behind each was the fear of what happens to a society which decides to cut itself off suddenly from all tradition. "The web of history is woven without a void," and the desire to start anew as if the past were no foundation is itself a sign of sickness and derangement. No society in which a majority of the people say, "Opinions and sentiments are false

---

[113] Raphael Semmes made the comparison (*op. cit.*, p. 548): "Radicalism seemed to be now just what it had been in the Great French Revolution, a sort of mad-dog virus; everyone who was inoculated with it became rabid."

friends," is healthy, and disaster is multiplied if faith in principles is part of the heritage to be abandoned. An ambition to reject traditional beliefs in favor of new "realities" conceals an impulse to escape from beliefs altogether.

Thus a part of the tragedy which brought about the moral collapse of the twentieth century was acted on the stage of America. It required the dislocations of the First World War to show how extensive the internal ravages had grown, and how thin the security of civilization had worn. When the Second World War brought the barbarian into open conflict with civilization, it could no longer be doubted that the systematic destruction of ancient ideals and sentiments leads to **the revolution of nihilism.**

⊷⧸⧸⧸⧸⧸⧸

CHAPTER FOUR

Diaries and Reminiscences Of The Second American Revolution

THE LITERATURE OF MILITARY AUTOBIOGRAPHY, EXTENSIVE AS it became, was matched in volume by the memoirs of civilians who felt impelled to set down their story of the great social upheaval. Their phase of the general report is valuable because it affords many things outside the province of the soldier and because it continues the account through Reconstruction, during which the old ideals were put to the test and some new ideals were forged. By their very richness of detail, moreover, such works helped to crystallize legends of the South and so provided primary material for later imaginative treatments which tended to picture the South as a special region.

Although the soldiers occasionally paused long enough to moralize or to indulge in criticism of Yankee character, their stories are chiefly of the organization of armies and the execution of battles. What went on behind the lines—on the plantations whose white males were at the front; in the cities where inflationary prices reduced the poor to want; in the

hospitals where women volunteered to minister to that curious patient, the common Confederate soldier; in the con-
claves of government, where the heritage of pride and individualism proved so hurtful to cooperation—these and
myriad other matters are to be sought in the memoirs of
civilians, some of which are not the less important for being
brief and little advertised. Indeed, in those writers who neither expected nor wanted a large audience, there are often
a simplicity and a directness which tell more than artful
expression.

Diaries were prepared by people of every station and with
every kind of relation to the war, but in glancing over the
bookshelf one is impressed by the extent to which the preserving of such records fell to the women. A few men only
left works which may be considered of first-rate importance.
Among them was John Beauchamp Jones, who has been
given the not wholly apt sobriquet of "the Confederate
Pepys." Jones was a native of Maryland, who spent part of his
early life in Kentucky and Missouri. Long before the war
period he made a name for himself as a writer of fiction, and
in 1859 he wrote a novel, *Wild Southern Scenes,* which then
and afterward was hailed as an accurate presage of sectional
conflict. In the spring of 1861 he was editing the *Southern
Monitor* in Philadelphia when word came that a fleet had
sailed for the relief of Fort Sumter. He fled South just ahead
of a mob bent on lynching him,[1] and found employment in
the Confederate War Office. He wrote under the date April
29, 1861: "At fifty-one I can hardly follow the pursuit of
arms; but I will write and preserve a DIARY of the revolution." [2] He adhered to this resolution during the four years,
and although his *Rebel War Clerk's Diary* lacks the intimacy
and spiciness of Pepys, it is by far the best extant record of
official Richmond.

1 *A Rebel War Clerk's Diary* (New York, 1886), I, p. 19.
2 *Ibid.,* I, p. 29.

Another was Thomas Cooper De Leon, whose role in the Confederacy is difficult to fix, but whose *Four Years in Rebel Capitals* is not surpassed in its picture of life behind the lines. When war came, De Leon was a clerk in the Bureau of Topographical Engineers and a gay young man-about-town in Washington: but he forsook his Bohemian comrades, who warned him that he would starve in the South, and proceeded to Montgomery. De Leon was a literary artist, and all that came within his view he saw with understanding and imagination, which qualified him to write one of the most enlightening of the inside stories. Many years later, after he had acquired distinction as playwright and novelist, he added to this *Belles, Beaux, and Brains of the Sixties,* a garrulous volume filled with biographical and genealogical lore, but wholly lacking in the graphic power of the earlier work.

If to these we add the short though excellent *Rebel's Recollections* of George Cary Eggleston, brother of the author of *A Hoosier Schoolmaster,* and *The End of an Era,* by John S. Wise,[3] written many years after the war, we shall have noticed the principal contributions by men.

With the women the case is otherwise. Opinion is virtually unanimous that they formed the backbone of the Confederacy; from the thoughtless belle in her teens who asked her lover to "kill me a Yankee," to the mature matron, who knew all the arts of heartening the discouraged male, the women of the Confederacy showed a united front of sentiment such as has been rarely manifested in any population. It is a fact noteworthy in the history of the Southern people, moreover, that their loyalty did not wane in the years of defeat.[4] With exceptions too few to be noted, the Southern women did not

---

[3] Although both Eggleston and Wise saw service as soldiers, their works are best considered descriptions of Southern society.

[4] One of the chief complaints of Northern soldiers returned from the South was of their failure to be received socially. See *passim, The Report of the Joint Committee on Reconstruction;* also W. F. Fleming, *Civil War and Reconstruction in Alabama* (New York, 1905), pp. 318-321.

smile upon the winner; the pomp and circumstance of victory did not endear the Yankee to them; [5] and they busied themselves not only with rebuilding a broken homeland but also with encouraging Southern nationalism. Federal soldiers often declared that Southern women made the fiercest secessionists, and President Davis, after observing their devotion in Reconstruction as in war, felt it proper to dedicate to them his *Rise and Fall of the Confederate Government*.

In sober truth the history of the women in Reconstruction makes better reading than that of the men. Dismayed by failure and left idle by want of opportunity, the men in some cases became poseurs or fribbles, a recognizable type of which is caricatured by O. Henry as Major Caswell in "A Municipal Report." [6] But the women for the most part turned lionesses, took over the direction of their households, in many instances supported their men, and taught their children what they wanted believed about the Southern Confederacy. Their unremitting labor in seeing to it that dead heroes were memorialized is evidenced by monuments from the Potomac to the Rio Grande, and the organization of the United Daughters of the Confederacy is a witness to the vitality of their spirit. It is no small part of the truth to say that after the Civil War the South became a matriarchy, and the decisive hand of its women was seen not only in social life, but also in letters. They produced some of the best of the older type of writing, and they were the first with the new. Consequently, whoever wishes to know the tenor of the Southern mind from 1865 to 1900 and beyond must pay considerable attention to their testimonials.

The women, moreover, had been influenced by the section's intense preoccupation with politics. Many a Southern girl grew up in a home where political discussion was the

[5] Myrta L. Avary, *Dixie After the War* (New York, 1906), pp. 115-117.

[6] Frances Butler Leigh (*op. cit.*, p. 13) found the men "trying, in a listless sort of way, to repair their ruined fortunes."

staple of table conversation. Later she would be taken to Washington or Richmond, to become acquainted with personalities and to hover in the background of history-making councils. It was natural for such women to keep a keen ear for all that came by gossip, rumor, or report. Representative of this group was Mary Boykin Chesnut, daughter of a governor of South Carolina and wife of a United States Senator from that state. After becoming mistress of Mulberry Plantation while hardly more than a girl, she was for twenty years a prominent member of the Charleston aristocracy. It was her husband who carried to Major Robert Anderson the demand for the surrender of Fort Sumter, and when the family later moved to Richmond, she was able to observe from a point of vantage the internal conflicts of the Confederacy. Such topics are faithfully and intelligently presented in *A Diary from Dixie*. Mrs. Virginia Clay, wife of a senator from Alabama and a typical society matron of the old regime, offered in *A Belle of the Fifties* an excellent picture of social Washington in the sultry decade preceding the outbreak of war. The story is continued through the period of strife and into Reconstruction, and the latter parts are an interesting chronicle of the hardships experienced by the planter class. Another diarist who possessed unusual political understanding was Eliza Frances Andrews, the strong-minded daughter of Judge Garnett Andrews of Georgia. Judge Andrews had opposed secession with might and main and kept aloof from the Confederacy, but this did not prevent his family from joining enthusiastically in the struggle for Southern independence. Her *War-time Journal of a Georgia Girl* is a little masterpiece of realistic reporting. In the closing days of 1864 she performed a journey across Sherman's track of desolation with a motley band of refugees, and her descriptions of ruined Georgia are unexcelled.

On turning to the more specialized accounts, one finds an

impressive variety. The earliest of these to reach print was the sensational *Belle Boyd in Camp and Prison,* brought out in London in 1865 with an introduction by "A Friend of the South," who has since been identified as George Augustus Sala. Though none too reliable and without great merit as a narrative, it relates one of the dramatic careers of the war. An entirely different kind of record is found in Phoebe Yates Pember's *A Southern Woman's Story.* Mrs. Pember, believing that the women of the South had been the principal factor in inciting the men to armed strife, made the honorable decision to shoulder her part of the fight. Though reared to a life of ease and refinement, she took over a division of the great Chimborazo Hospital in Richmond, then suffering under the inefficiency which blighted so much Southern enterprise behind the lines. The story of her administration of this unit makes a small epic of ingenuity, courage, and tenacity. A modest but highly revealing account of how the Southern people continued to exist in their starved economy is given by Parthenia Antoinette Hague in *A Blockaded Family.* For the entire four years she lived on a plantation in southern Alabama, where she assisted in the thousand and one expedients which were devised to meet the exigencies growing out of the blockade. It is an amazing story of resourcefulness, in which the little plantation community manages to produce everything from shoes and clothing to such medicinal supplies as castor oil and opium. No survey would be indicative of the range of this writing without mention of Cornelia Phillips Spencer's brilliant *The Last Ninety Days of the War in North Carolina.* Mrs. Spencer was the New York-born daughter of a Presbyterian minister who taught mathematics in the University of North Carolina. A woman of uncommon mental powers, she wrote *The Last Ninety Days* with the object of furnishing a careful, patient, and reasoned indictment of those excesses which made the

American Civil War one of the nost barbarous of modern wars. First printed in the New York *Watchman* as a series of papers, the work was so well received that it was later brought out in book form. Northern birth and a superior education gave Mrs. Spencer a quality of detachment which lent weight to her case.

These are examples of people who, early or late, left their impressions of the great social and political transformation. Naturally, methods of composition differed, and a few of the works here considered did not reach print until the second decade of the following century; but all stem from the period, and all reflect the mentality of war and Reconstruction. Some writers kept records from day to day and sought immediate publication; some laid their manuscripts away in trunks and forgot them until dispute over an event of the war or the interest of their friends demanded a resurrection; and not a few dictated from memory in their old age and left the final preparation to editors.

1. The Northern Aggressor

Although they left a rich mine for the historian of social attitudes, the writers of diaries and memoirs were not very voluble on the topic of the origin of the war. About the vast thirty-year debate which led up to the invoking of the principle of secession they had less to say than the soldiers and immeasurably less than the politicians. It becomes apparent, however, whenever their subject matter led them around to the question, that most viewed the North as the aggressor. Mrs. Clay and T. C. De Leon subscribed to the traditional Southern belief that the war was initiated by a North inspired with envy. The former, who knew Washington well at the period in which the storm was brewing, formed this estimate of the situation: "There was, on the part of the North, a palpable envy of the hold the South had maintained so long upon the Federal city, whether in politics or society, and the resolution to quell us, by physical force, was everywhere obvious." [7] It was no accident that this hostility was strongest in the West, where democracy was most complete, and it is an interesting commentary that this section furnished the best soldiery and the most successful leaders to the Union. "Our physical prosperity, no less than the social security we enjoyed," she continued frankly, "had caused us to become objects of envy to the rough elements of the new settlements, especially of the North-west." [8] On this point Mrs. Clay had the concurrence of Mrs. Roger Pryor, another society matron of the old regime, who recalled that during the administration of President Buchanan Southern women, with their "natural and acquired graces," made their sisters from the North and West feel awkward and embarrassed.[9]

De Leon saw two distinct peoples, each jealous of the mastery. Writing in *Belles, Beaux, and Brains of the Sixties*, a work of his old age, he declared that the North and South had been "two peoples as dissimilar in thought and feeling, in habit and in need, as were the Saxons and the knights of the descent of Rollo the Norman." [10] He thought that when the reasons for the war had been sifted, this would be found the decisive one. The North and the South, living under a single government, had ceased to understand each other, and the only way to understanding was "by arbitrament of blood." [11]

George Cary Eggleston, the Virginia-born Hoosier, tried to explain to his abolitionist friends how what appeared to them

7 Virginia Clay-Clopton, *A Belle of the Fifties* (New York, 1905), p. 143.
8 *Ibid*. pp. 149-150.
9 *Reminiscences of Peace and War* (New York, 1905), pp. 81-82.
10 *Belles, Beaux, and Brains of the Sixties* (New York, 1909), p. 17.
11 *Ibid.*, p. 18.

as a "wicked and causeless rebellion" appeared to Southerners a legitimate resistance to invasion of rights. Patriotism means loyalty to one's own, but what constitutes one's own was precisely the question which had been left open by the founding fathers. This may appear a problem in casuistry, but no more so than the one posed by the American Revolution, when the colonial patriots, in the language of Webster, "went to war against a preamble," and "fought seven years against a declaration." [12] And so the Virginians, without whose valor and military talent the struggle would have been short-lived,

> made war upon a catchword, and fought until they were hopelessly ruined for the sake of an abstraction. And certainly history will not find it to the discredit of those people that they freely offered themselves upon the altar of an abstract principle of right in a war which they knew must work hopeless ruin to themselves, whatever its other results might be.[13]

From the time of the famous Resolutions of '98, in which unconditional submission to the central government was repudiated, Virginia had been a foremost champion of local sovereignty. Now events placed her in a dilemma, in which she had either to oppose the armed strength of the central government or surrender what she believed to be the fundamental principle of the Union. On the one hand was policy, on the other principle, and Virginians, being "brave men and honorable ones," did not have to deliberate between the two.[14]

In their analysis of the causes of conflict, the diarists on the whole were singularly free of rancor, although some of their comparisons may appear invidious.

12 *A Rebel's Recollections* (New York, 1905), p. 5.
13 *Ibid.,* p. 6.
14 *Ibid.,* p. 17.

2. *Southern Leadership*

The Civil War epoch marks the beginning of a decline in that pride which the South had always taken in its political leaders. The soldiers believed implicitly in themselves and seldom questioned the competence of their military superiors. But the diaries of civilians are conspicuously lacking in enthusiasm for government servants, high and low. It was not that corruption of the old ideal had set in: honor was there in full measure, and so were courage and fortitude, but these were offset by an absurd insularity of outlook, a preoccupation with political unrealities, and a great deal of personal friction, which was and still is a part of the price the South pays for producing strong personalities. The cause may have been great, but not all of the protagonists were worthy of it. It is an oft-repeated statement that the thin gray line which held the Confederate fronts for four arduous years was not matched in quality by the men behind who were charged with the conduct of main policies of state. The natural strength of the Confederacy, which was at the beginning but a fraction of that of its adversary, was continually sapped by ineptitude and inefficiency.[15] Most Southerners were willing to admit that they did not equal the Yankees in efficiency, but this shortcoming had not been especially deplored. One must constantly keep in mind that the Southern world had its own set of values, and that efficiency, like thrift, caution, and diligence, was not in the list of upper-class virtues. Only when it became plain, as it did in the course of the war, that inefficiency was a luxury that had to be paid for in pains and in

---

15 Many Confederate soldiers came to realize that their great personal exertions were frustrated largely by the mistaken policies of their government. Thus Thomas Jordan and J. P. Pryor wrote their *The Campaigns of Lieut.-Gen. N. B. Forrest* (New Orleans, 1868, p. viii) to show both "the splendid martial qualities" of the Southern people and "the constant mismanagement of their defensive resources."

failure, was there serious impatience with it. Later, the more far-sighted Southerners were to hope that Reconstruction, with its discipline of poverty and hardship, would root out this expensive habit. But at the beginning of the war it was not fully appreciated that courage and determination by themselves could fail. The result was that from the councils of state in Montgomery and Richmond to the field hospitals and commissariats of the armies there prevailed a toleration of nonessentials and a lack of expedience that amaze the modern reader.

The Confederate Congress especially filled critical observers with dismay. Years in Washington had given T. C. De Leon a poor opinion of popular democracy, but when he reached Montgomery he found that new skies did not make new men, and the House of Representatives there looked to him like "the Washington Congress, viewed through a reversed opera-glass." [16] Instead of devoting itself immediately and unremittingly to the creation of an army which should guarantee Southern independence, it listened to "windy dissertations on the color of the flag," to debates over the establishment of a patent office, and to speeches with no particular point at all.[17] In the Confederate Cabinet it was the same story of narrow views and conceit. De Leon observed in Robert Toombs, one of its more brilliant members, a "hyper-Southern underjudging of the men opposed to him in the North." [18]

On the progress down he had noted the complete lack of preparation and the bewilderment of a people waiting to be told what to do. He remarked with some uneasiness that the intelligence of the average Southern rustic was not high, and that it seemed to drop lower as one moved straight south, whether because of the depressing effect of pine barrens, or

[16] *Four Years in Rebel Capitals*, p. 31.
[17] *Ibid.*, p. 32.
[18] *Belles, Beaux, and Brains of the Sixties*, p. 83.

because of "recurring agues." [19] It was his clear impression that the fate of these people in a contest which was to determine their welfare for generations was in the hands of old party hacks, who had no idea of the perils of the situation, much less of specific things needing to be done.

J. B. Jones, who spent four years close to the center of things in Richmond, arrived at the same estimate of Southern political leaders. "The greatest statesmen of the South," he wrote, "have no conception of the real purpose of the men now in power in the United States." [20] When on April 22, 1861, he called on Governor Wise of Virginia and told him that the 75,000 men Lincoln had summoned would be but the outpost of a host of 750,000, he was pooh-poohed. In the *Rebel War Clerk's Diary* of November 14, 1862, he set down his impression in this striking figure: "Never before did such little men rule such a great people. Our rulers are like children or drunken men riding docile horses, that absolutely keep the riders from falling off by swaying to the right and left, and preserving an equilibrium." [21] Mary Boykin Chesnut added her testimony to the overwhelming evidence that the people were far ahead of their leaders both in demanding secession and in readiness to organize for war. "The fire in the rear is hottest," she quotes someone as saying. "And yet people talk of the politicians leading! Everywhere that I have been the people have been complaining bitterly of slow and lukewarm public leaders." [22]

The feebleness of political leadership and the extraordinary incompetence at business management which so hampered the cause at home are open to several explanations, the most charitable of which is that all the brains and energy went into the army. Eggleston believed that Southerners of

19 *Four Years in Rebel Capitals*, p. 22.
20 J. B. Jones, *op. cit.*, I, p. 26.
21 *Ibid.*, I, p. 189.
22 Mary Boykin Chesnut, *A Diary from Dixie* (New York, 1905), p. 2.

the better class esteemed service behind the lines dishonorable and so left it to those who would have it, with the result that not the smallest part of the Confederate army's claim to distinction was its feat in keeping the field four years with such a government and such a commissary. The Davis government did, he said,

> as nearly as possible, *all* the things which it ought not to have done, at the same time developing a really marvellous genius for leaving undone all those things which it ought to have done. The story of its incompetence and presumption, if it could be adequately told, would read like a romance.[23]

The small men who were willing to remain behind to do the routine work made the administrative organization "at once a wonder of complication and a marvel of inefficiency." [24] The general effect was that in Richmond "everything was done by rule except those things to which system of some sort would have been of advantage, and they were left at loose ends." [25]

There is witness that the same kind of gross mismanagement prevailed in the medical service. Dr. A. Monteiro, who served as surgeon of Mosby's command, could scarcely find words to express his indignation over "the thoroughly organized hell of the medical department of the Confederate States army." [26] In this branch of the service "no surgeon was ever promoted, or even respected, if he was not both stupid and despotic." [27] He said in summary: "To the reader unacquainted with medico-military matters, it would be extremely difficult to convey in language the aggregate stupidity attending the cruel meanderings of the medical depart-

23 Eggleston, *op. cit.*, p. 196.
24 *Ibid.*, p. 199.
25 *Ibid.*, p. 209.
26 *War Reminiscences by a Surgeon of Mosby's Command* (Richmond, 1890), p. 184.
27 *Ibid.*, p. 23.

ment of the army. From the cerebrum to the caudal appendix of this department, individual egotism and general imbecility prevailed." [28]

Persons acquainted with the transactions of the War Department frequently gave way to expressions of helpless exasperation. There was a great deal of dissatisfaction over the conferring of commissions, and the Department seems to have been blind to the value of promoting men on the field for exhibitions of extraordinary valor. "Joe Davis, Jr., said, 'Would Heaven would send us a Napoleon!' " Mrs. Chesnut reported. "Not one bit of use. If Heaven did, Walker would not give him a commission." [29]

The men engaged in administration were not only lacking in competence; they were also inclined to be very sensitive about the prerogatives attaching to their positions. Time and energy which might have gone into the war effort were spent in observing forms, or worse still, in settling quarrels which arose out of offenses to foolish pride. Nothing could better illustrate the kind of friction that proceeds from intense individualism than the following incident related in *A Rebel War Clerk's Diary*. Albert Taylor Bledsoe, who later became the most brilliant Confederate apologist, worked at a desk near the door of the Secretary of War. When one day General Walker of Georgia came in to see the Secretary, the following dialogue ensued:

> Gen. W.: Is the Secretary in?
> Col. B.: [with a stare] I don't know.
> Gen. W.: [returning the stare] Could you ascertain for me? I have important business with him and am here by appointment.
> Col. B.: You can ascertain for yourself. I am not his doorkeeper. There is his door.

[28] *Ibid.*, p. 26.
[29] Chesnut, *op. cit.*, p. 86.

Gen. W.: [after a moment's reflection] I asked you a civil question in a courteous manner, and have not deserved this harshness and will not submit to it.

Col. B.: It is not courteous to presume I am acting in the capacity of messenger or doorkeeper.[30]

Only diplomatic intervention by the Secretary himself prevented this absurd exchange from growing into a duel.

The aristocratic Mary Boykin Chesnut saw enough of such self-pluming and petty dignity to become disgusted. She noted in her *Diary from Dixie:* "I have come to detest a man who says, 'My own personal dignity and self-respect require.' I long to say, 'No need to respect yourself until you can make others do it.' " [31]

The same author was too sharp an observer to overlook the beginning of a process which was to become of great consequence in Southern history, and which even then was making its harmful influence felt. This was the gradual loss of initiative and energy on the part of the old ruling class. "This race has brains enough," she wrote under the date of June 5, 1862,

but they are not active-minded like those old Revolutionary characters, the Middletons, Lowndeses, Rutledges, Marions, Sumters. They have come direct from active-minded forefathers, or they would not have been here, but, with two or three generations of gentleman planters, how changed has the blood become. Of late, all the active-minded men who have sprung to the front in our government were immediate descendants of Scotch, or Scotch-Irish—Calhoun, McDuffie, Cheves, and Pettigru, who Huguenotted his name, but could not tie up his Irish. Our planters are nice fellows, but slow to move; impulsive, but hard to keep moving. They are wonderful for a spurt, but with all their strength, they like to rest.[32]

[30] J. B. Jones, *op. cit.,* p. 61.
[31] Chesnut, *op. cit.,* p. 85.
[32] *Ibid.,* p. 175.

The Yankees, she admitted, had double their energy and enterprise, but "Wait a while. Let them alone until climate and mosquitoes and sand-flies and dealing with the negroes takes it all out of them." [33]

Further light on this situation is thrown by Constance Cary, who as a pupil at M. Lefevre's Boarding School in Richmond had enjoyed an opportunity of knowing daughters from the great plantations of the Deep South, where slavery was the basic institution of economic and social life. From what she saw she concluded that

> the surrounding slave service was inspiring neither to the energy of the body or the independence of ideas which I had been taught to consider indispensable. . . . Many of these pretty languid creatures from the far Southern States had never put on a shoe or stocking for themselves, and the point of view about owning and chastening fellow beings who might chance to offend them was abhorrent to me.[34]

3. The Class System

Notwithstanding these failures at the top, the Southern class system held up with surprising stubbornness. Politicians might be blind to opportunity, and "general imbecility" might frustrate the action of departments, but the Southern aristocracy as a whole did not prove itself inferior in the ordeal of war, and herein lies a secret of Southern social organization after Appomattox. One of the objects of Northern propaganda had been to drive a wedge between the upper class and the plain people of the South by stigmatizing the war as a slaveholders' rebellion. But the actual pressure of conflict had a curious effect upon the social order; it produced a closer alliance of classes, but at the same time it

[33] *Ibid.*, p. 181.
[34] *Recollections Grave and Gay* (New York, 1911), p. 42.

vindicated that element which had always regarded itself as the top stratum—a result precisely opposite that intended by the enemy. The upper-class Southerner, that is to say, the man who owned some property and perhaps a few slaves and who had at least a fair education, proved himself a leader in the field. He proved it by fighting better, by complaining less, and by staying alive longer than the others. Naturally this had the effect of guaranteeing his position at the head of society for a long time to come. Our best source of information on this point is T. C. De Leon; a social butterfly himself, he was eager to see how the gay young blades who were his erstwhile companions would conduct themselves in the trials of war. He summed up his finding as follows:

> When I say that in every Confederate camp, *the best* soldiers of that winter were "crack companies" of the gay youths of cities, I only echo the verdict of old and tried officers. . . . A strange fact of these companies was often stated by surgeons of perfect reliability: their sick reports were smaller than those of the hardiest mountain organizations. This they attributed to two causes: greater attention to personal cleanliness and to all hygienic precautions; and the exercise of better trained minds and wills in keeping them free from the deadly "blue devils." [35]

Gentleman companies, he reported, fought as only gentlemen can, and he came to the conclusion that "the man who tells us that blood has little effect must have read history to very little purpose; or have looked very carelessly into the glass that Nature hourly holds up to his view." [36] Such soldiers as these, "scattered among the grosser material of the army," gave it a true mettle.

During her service in the Chimborazo Hospital in Richmond, Phoebe Pember noted some facts about the Confederate common soldier which she interpreted in terms of class

[35] *Four Years in Rebel Capitals*, p. 142.
[36] *Ibid.*, p. 109.

origin. A hospital ward was a point of vantage from which to study the basic material of the Confederate armies; the gray-jacket was an inspiring figure when charging an open battery, but on closer inspection he was likely to prove long-haired, dirty, tobacco-stained, and ignorant. She found in many of the rank and file an invincible provincialism, which kept them from making even the simplest adaptations. Frequently a soldier would reject a bowl of tastefully prepared soup because "My mammy's soup was not like that," and could never be brought to see why hospital fare was not exactly what he had been accustomed to at home. The average private soldier was, according to Mrs. Pember, a strange ingrate, who accepted the service rendered him without a word of appreciation. She considered this a reflection on breeding.

> The mass of patients were uneducated men, who had lived by the sweat of their brow, and gratitude is an exotic plant, reared in a refined atmosphere, kept free from coarse contact and nourished by unselfishness. Common natures look only with surprise on great sacrifices and cunningly avail themselves of the benefits they bestow—but give nothing in return —not even allowing the giver to feel that the care bestowed has been beneficial. That might entail compensation of some kind and in their ignorance they fear the nature of the equivalent which might be demanded.[37]

A lady told Mary Boykin Chesnut that "the better born, that is, those born in the purple, the gentry" made the best hospital patients. " 'They are hardier, stronger, tougher, less liable to break down than the sons of the soil.' Why is that? I asked, and she answered, 'Something in man that is more than the body.' " [38]

That the man who came out of the Southern backwoods to fight Yankees was not laden with the virtues which make a

---

[37] *A Southern Woman's Story* (New York, 1879), p. 36.
[38] Chesnut, *op. cit.*, p. 182.

polished society must be admitted without argument. He had lived close to the soil in a region by no means wholly rescued from the wilderness, and his tutelage had been confined to the rudimentary type which prepares one to struggle against the elements rather than to contend for place in a highly organized community. Hawthorne, viewing some Confederate prisoners during his visit to Washington in 1862, was struck by what he considered their brutishness,[39] and certainly there was no dearth of primitive humanity in the South. But it is an interesting historical fact that the lowest types were willing to make a united front with the comparatively highly cultivated seaboard aristocrat in defense of what reduces itself to a sentiment. Stories illustrating how the diverse classes came to know and appreciate each other are to be encountered everywhere. Cornelia Phillips Spencer, who wrote of all these matters with a rare degree of objectivity, counted this one of the few benefits which North Carolina got out of the fiery trial. "It has brought all classes nearer to each other," she wrote. "The rich and the poor met together. A common cause became a common bond of sympathy and kind feeling. Charity was more freely dispensed, and pride of station was forgotten." [40] As a matter of fact, there had never been a real breach between the white classes of the South, and the war actually served to strengthen a mutual esteem. John S. Wise observed the easy fusion of rich and poor in Virginia: "the two stood up together side by side, and fought and slept and died together,—never thinking which was rich and which was poor, until a time when such as survived were all poor together." [41] This circumstance was the precursor of the Solid South.

There is room for surmise regarding the superior power of

[39] Op. cit., XII, pp. 331-332.
[40] The Last Ninety Days of the War in North Carolina (New York, 1866), p. 264.
[41] Op. cit., p. 241.

an articulated society, such as George Fitzhugh had defended in *Sociology for the South*, to withstand shock. A classless society is invertebrate. A class society, on the other hand, if it is not so rigid that it prevents the ever-essential recruiting from the lower orders, has in its very structure an element of strength. Though perhaps slackening, this process of recruiting had been continuous over the South, and it had not entered into the head of the Southern yeoman that he was a man of no consideration. General Hooker in his testimony before the Committee on Conduct of the War asserted that although he believed his army to be superior to Lee's in intelligence, in physique, and in equipment, it was never able to equal the enemy in discipline "for reasons not necessary to mention." [42]

Most students have agreed that behind the Confederate soldier's respect for his leaders lay the Southern social system. Unless this type of society is eaten internally by corruption, or weakened by a long history of class oppression, a superior loyalty may infuse and bind the whole. People feel kindly toward a community where each has a station in which he is respected,[43] and where the leaders are men of character and principle rather than popularity seekers and panderers. Deterioration sets in when distrust, selfishness, and the cult of envy destroy confidence in the value of a collective effort. A people who have come to believe that there are no rational grounds for superiority, that ideals are illusions and self-sacrifice only foolishness are morally sick. These conditions prepared France for her destruction in 1940.

It can scarcely be doubted, furthermore, that a fierce attachment to the ideal of a class society lay behind the enthu-

42 *Report of the Joint Committee on the Conduct of the War* (Washington, 1865), I, p. 113.
43 Frances Butler Leigh (*op. cit.*, pp. 61-62) told a Northerner who had expressed surprise over the loyalty of her family's slaves: "Yes, this is a relationship you Northern people can't understand and will soon destroy."

siasm which Southern women showed for the cause. Every Southern woman constituted a citadel of the Confederacy; she was the first to want independence of the North and the last to admit failure, and the chronicle of her war effort comes out in many a small act of heroism and many an appalling sacrifice. These women were born into the last society, with the possible exception of Imperial Germany, in which soldiers and politicians were the true leaders, and probably they sensed by intuition the coming of the age of tired and unromantic businessmen. The Southern gentleman of the old school possessed every quality which women are supposed to admire in men: bravery, generosity, personal aplomb, and a gift for large talk. If we contrast these men with the Babbitts of a later era, whom Vachel Lindsay has caustically described, "with their neat little safety vault boxes, with their faces like geese and like foxes," we need not wait to discover to which the feminine preference will fall, more especially if the women have been reared in a country where romance is breathed in with the air. Add to this the innate feminine belief in social distinctions, and one has the explanation of why the Southern women felt that the society then being threatened by Northern industrialism and political equalitarianism was just the kind of society to satisfy their primary longings. It should be recognized as a truth that romance and efficiency are hostile to such a degree that they can never dwell together; one survives at the expense of the other, so that a choice between them has to be made. The French Revolution, with its elevation of the bourgeois, was coming to fruition in the North, and the virtues traditionally associated with the Yankee are those of the unromantic middle class. They are thrift, sobriety, patience, and the kind of plodding industry which creates bourgeois security. The revolt of the Southern women, therefore, may be seen as an instinctive rebellion against the impending business civiliza-

tion, which by starving romantic impulses sent two generations of American women raking over the ruins of Europe to
make up the deficiency, and which, when the whole story is
told, may be identified as one of the roots of the fascist
movement.

From the very eve of conflict they were filled with the most
ardent spirit. Sallie Putnam tells in her *Richmond During
the War* that long before the secession convention of Virginia
nearly every woman in the city had in her possession a Confederate flag.[44] Mrs. Roger Pryor relates how Virginia girls
refused to become engaged until their lovers had fought the
Yankees.[45] George Cary Eggleston, who was critical of many
things in the Confederacy, devotes a chapter to unsparing
praise of the way in which Southern women sustained their
country. He describes how "with their woman-natures they
gave themselves wholly to the cause, and having loved it
heartily when it gave promise of sturdy life, they almost
worship it now that they have strewn its bier with funeral
flowers." [46] There are numerous anecdotes in *A Rebel's
Recollections* to indicate the bitterness of their hostility. One
young lady, finding herself the involuntary hostess of a Federal officer, severed the strings of her piano with a hatchet
when he sat down to entertain himself with music. "That's
my piano, and it shall not give you a minute's pleasure," was
the angry explanation.[47] Another destroyed her library because that was the only way she could prevent a general officer billeted near her home from enjoying the books each
morning.[48]

If women had been in charge of the direction of the war,
perhaps Lee would have gone into the mountains in 1865,

[44] *Richmond During the War* (Richmond, 1867), p. 22.
[45] *Op. cit.,* p. 129.
[46] *Op. cit.,* p. 57.
[47] *Ibid.,* p. 64.
[48] *Ibid.*

there to prolong resistance indefinitely; for they were more violent in sentiment than the men, and the more grievous their loss, the more stubbornly they identified themselves with the cause. The spirit of the women at the fall of New Orleans, for example, is described in the *Journal of Julia LeGrand*. Wild rumors, first of danger, then of depredation, flew about, but apparently only the female citizens remained undaunted. In the words of the *Journal:*

> Of course, the greatest confusion prevailed, and every hour, indeed almost every moment, brought its dreadful rumor. After it was known that the gunboats had actually passed, the whole city, both camp and street, was a scene of wild confusion. *The women only* did not seem afraid. They were all in favor of resistance, *no matter how hopeless* that resistance might be.[49]

Kate Cumming was horrified by rumors that the ladies of Mobile had extended a warm welcome to the Yankees who entered upon the capitulation of that stronghold. But when she arrived there she was relieved to find it looking like a city of the dead, with no sign that the invader was being greeted.[50] John S. Wise reports that some gay ladies in Richmond who were thoughtless enough to entertain Federal officers within a few days after the surrender were years in regaining their social standing.[51]

On the whole the Southern social system proved itself a tough fabric. The success of its leaders in the field, the loyalty of the lower orders to their traditional superiors, and the determination of the women that a society which took cognizance of rank and degree should not go down before the new impulse of popular control gave it strength during the war and left it vitality for the postbellum struggles.

49 *The Journal of Julia LeGrand* (Richmond, 1911), p. 40.
50 *Op. cit.,* p. 198.
51 *Op. cit.,* p. 461.

4. The Scourge of the Invader

Before the first year of the war was over, the Southern people were beginning to discover what it means to suffer invasion. Plundering and ravaging had commenced in Virginia and in the lower Mississippi Valley by the spring of 1862. It was often the hard lot of the women to remain behind and witness the systematic destruction of their homes while denied the soldier's consolation of inflicting some compensatory damage upon the enemy.[52] A few meek Christian ladies like Mrs. Judith McGuire counselled an attitude of forbearance,[53] but the majority of Southern women displayed a much more human reaction—first, astonishment that such procedures could occur in an enlightened age, and subsequently, moral indignation against the Yankee perpetrator.

A typical experience was that of Sara Morgan Dawson, a young girl who spent most of the war period in Baton Rouge. Miss Dawson began her diary with a high estimate of Yankee kindness and restraint, only to have it shattered after action got under way in earnest. In August, 1862, General Breckinridge attacked the city, driving the Federal troops out of their camp to the protection of their gunboats, and at this juncture the era of good feeling ended. Miss Dawson had taken refuge across the river at "Westover," near enough to see the shells arch over the city and to hear the delayed report of cannon. Here she received what she felt to be a fantastic account of the sacking of her home, but a visit she was able to make a

52 Phoebe Pember (*op. cit.*, p. 105) felt compelled to remark upon the lack of vindictiveness shown by Confederate soldiers in discussing their opponents. Far from exploring the rights and wrongs of the conflict, the rank and file summed it up by saying, "They fit us, and we fit them." After the explosion of the Petersburg mine, however, she noticed a change of attitude, for this was condemned as "a mean trick"—a reappearance of the stubborn chivalric concept.

53 *Diary of a Southern Refugee* (New York, 1867), p. 225.

few days later revealed that nothing had been exaggerated. It was the familiar story of vandalism—smashed mirrors, split furniture, a ransacked library. The following incident tells more about the plundering of the South than a page of generalities:

> A young lady, passing by one of the pillaged houses, expressed her surprise at seeing an armoir full of women's and children's clothes being emptied, and the contents tied up in sheets. "What can you do with such things?" she asked a soldier who seemed more zealous than the rest. "Ain't I got a wife and four children in the North?" was the answer.[54]

After the sacking of Baton Rouge, her descent into hardship was rapid. Having "never before lived in a house without a balcony," [55] she found herself an exile from home, barefoot, sleeping on the floor, and eating, perforce, with her fingers.

The finest document of all those written among the ruins is Eliza Frances Andrews' *War-time Journal of a Georgia Girl*. Late in 1864 Miss Andrews, in company with her sister, performed a sixty-five-mile journey from Camack Station to Macon, an odyssey which, in its trials and interruptions, parallels the flight of Scarlett O'Hara from Atlanta to Tara Plantation in *Gone With the Wind*. Her fellow travellers were an unhappy band of refugees, Confederate officers on leave, wounded soldiers, and nondescripts. Miss Andrews was an exceptionally unsentimental young woman, and she kept her eyes and ears open for the significant occurrences. A bit of dialogue as the procession moves past gaunt chimneys brings humor out of the grim scene. A soldier had joined the party

> with awful tales about the things Sherman's robbers had done; it made my blood boil to hear them, and when the captain

[54] *A Confederate Girl's Diary* (Boston, 1913), p. 209.
[55] *Ibid.*, p. 206.

asked him if some of the rascals didn't get caught themselves
sometimes—stragglers and the like—he answered with a wink
that said more than words.

"Yes, our folks took lots of prisoners; more'n'll ever be
heard of agin."

"What became of them?" I asked the lieutenant.

"Sent 'em to Macon, double quick," was the laconic reply.
"Got 'em thar in less'n half an hour."

"How did they manage it?" continued the lieutenant * in a
tone which showed he understood Sam's metaphor.

"Just took 'em out in the woods and *lost* 'em," he replied in
his laconic way. "Ever heerd o' losin' men, lady?" he added,
turning to me, with an air of grim waggery that made my flesh
creep—for after all, even Yankees are human beings, though
they don't always behave like it.

"Yes," I said, "I had heard of it but thought it a horrible
thing."

"I don't believe in losin' 'em either, as a gener'l thing," he
went on. "I don't think it's right principul, and I wouldn't
lose one myself, but when I see what they have done to these
people around here, I can't blame 'em for losin' every devil of
'em they can git their hands on." [56]

Arrived in Macon, she witnessed the wild scenes of the
evacuation: "All of the intoxicating liquors which could be
found in the stores, warehouses, and barrooms had been
seized by the authorities and emptied on the ground. In some
places the streets smelt like a distillery, and I saw men, boys,
and negroes down on their knees lapping it up from the
gutter like dogs. Little children were staggering around in a
state of beastly intoxication." [57]

By late April she was at her father's home in Washington,
Georgia, and here begins the affecting part of the story.
Washington, in the northeastern part of the state, was on the
arterial route which disbanded Confederate soldiers took

* This apparently should be the captain.—*Ed.*
56 Eliza Frances Andrews, *op. cit.*, pp. 30-31.
57 *Ibid.*, p. 154.

moving south and west, and through it passed one of the saddest processions in history. Moods were varied: some were reckless and devil-may-care; some sullen; some hopeless and even in tears; some buoyed up with false expectations of a renewed fight in the Trans-Mississippi Department; but all knew that their country was ruined and that they faced difficult and uncertain futures. Nor was it yet clear that there would not be some savage proscription with blood shed on the scaffold to make enmity permanent. For a whole month the Andrews family watched this throng file past, first Lee's men and then Johnston's, and fed them what they could from their meager larder of ham and cornfield peas.

Mary Boykin Chesnut, who had been bred to a delightful life "à la Caroline du Sud," was in the path of Sherman's destructive march, and her spirit almost broke under the daily report of atrocities. In the summer of 1865 she could write only: "No words of mine can tell how unhappy I am." [58]

A different approach to the problem of total war as it was posed by General Sherman for the South and the world is found in Cornelia Phillips Spencer's *The Last Ninety Days of the War in North Carolina,* a work which, in its firm and intelligent handling of the subject, is unequalled by anything else of the period. Mrs. Spencer adopted the ingenious device of contrasting the procedures of General Sherman with those of Lord Cornwallis, who seventy years previously had been in the same region on the identical mission of suppressing a "rebellion." What follows makes sad reading for those who might imagine that eight decades of freedom and native American idealism would elevate the character of Americans and separate them from the bloody past of Europe. It is the English lord who bows politely to ladies, preserves discipline and protects property; it is the American general who acts in

[58] Chesnut, *op. cit.,* p. 404.

the manner of the mailed fist of a European tyrant crushing a peasants' uprising. The orderbook of Lord Cornwallis, which Mrs. Spencer had before her as she wrote, is filled with instructions to his officers for "preventing the oppressed people from suffering violence by the hands from whom they ought to look for protection." [59] From his headquarters at Dobbin's House, February 17, 1781, the British commander had written: "Any officer who looks on with indifference, and does not do his utmost to prevent shameful marauding, will be considered in a more criminal light than the persons who commit these scandalous crimes, which will bring disgrace and ruin on his Majesty's service." [60] To the drama of this contrast the author adds extracts from Kent's *Commentaries on International Law,* and from *International Law and Laws of War,* by Halleck, Sherman's erstwhile chief of staff, to show that ravaging is not approved by either law or policy. It is an old story that blows are never dealt by measure, and there is something futile in the spectacle of the beaten party pleading for the respect of abstract rights; yet, as she declared, there was a valid moral lesson to be drawn by the North from the result of its own excesses. Conduct of this kind does not improve an army, but rather demoralizes it and lowers its efficiency. Mrs. Spencer pointed out that "When plunder is to be had, lawless and unrestrained men care little whether it belongs to friend or foe; and that lust, once aroused and let loose, cannot distinguish and is amenable to no laws." [61] In proof of this many contemporary witnesses have testified that once the policy of plunder had been instituted, the blacks suffered as much maltreatment as the whites, the soldiery being as ready to snatch the silver watch of the slave [62] as the gold one of his master, and particularly

[59] Cornelia Phillips Spencer, *op. cit.,* p. 35.
[60] *Ibid.,* pp. 36-37.
[61] *Ibid.,* pp. 211-212.
[62] Susan Dabney Smedes reports (*Memorials of a Southern Planter,* New York, 1900, p. 234) that during the siege of Vicksburg, a party of Grant's

if they were from the Western states, more likely to visit the former with physical violence.

This is an unhappy chapter to record in the history of any nation and the deep psychological wounds it left postponed reconciliation indefinitely.

5. *The Negroes in Transition*

While these great events were in progress, the alien race, which then numbered about four millions in the South, kept its accustomed place, excepting those who through contact with Federal armies were won away from adherence to "massa" and "ol' mistis." They tilled the fields, did the household chores, and performed the special tasks demanded by the exigencies of the situation. The substantial fact is that the Negroes went through the war and well into Reconstruction in a dense ignorance of what beyond the scope of their actual observation was going on. They could see that things were in a turmoil, that their masters were coping with stringencies and hardships hitherto unknown, and that some people called Yankees were coming down as invaders and depredators. A few of them sensed in the air that one of the questions being decided was whether they should be bond or free, but even after this came to be pretty fully appreciated, the response to it was mixed. Romance and sentiment need not conceal the fact that once the land was filled with bluecoats, many a slave, and among them some bearing reputations for special loyalty, bolted the old homestead to taste the intoxicant of freedom; on the other hand one need not delve far to find many a one who considered his lot happy,[63] and

---

soldiers, who looked "like the dregs of some city", stopped at Burleigh, the plantation of Thomas Dabney. They took all the money from every Negro on the plantation. "Uncle Isaac had buried eighty dollars in gold,—the savings of years. This he was made to unearth. He had lately bought a new silver watch, for which he had paid forty dollars. This was taken from him."

63 See Frances Butler Leigh, *op. cit.* pp. 21-22.

who stuck by his white folks in a time when disloyalty would have meant to them the difference between starvation and survival.[64] Mary A. Gay tells an amusing story of fidelity on the part of "King," an old family servant. King had made the novel request that his mistress sell him to a Mr. Johnson, and when asked why he wanted to change owners, he said:

> "When this war is over, none of us are going to belong to you, and I would a great deal rather Mr. Johnson would lose me than you. He is always bragging about what he will do; hear him talk, you would think he is a bigger man than Mr. Lincoln is, and had more to back him, but I think he's a mighty little man myself, and I want him to lose me. He says he'll give you his little old store on Peachtree street for me. It don't seem much, I know, but much or little, it's going to be more than me after the war."

This exchange reached a peak of quixotism when Mrs. Gay declined by saying:

> When our people became convinced that the troubles be-tween the South and the North had to be settled by the sword, that she, in common with all good citizens, staked her all upon the issues of the war, and that she would not now, like a coward, flee from them, or seek to avert them by selling a man, or men and women who had endeared themselves to her by service and fidelity.[65]

Frances Butler Leigh records the faithfulness of "Uncle

[64] After the burning of Columbia by Sherman, the family of Joseph Le Conte (*'Ware Sherman*, Berkeley, 1937, p. xv), who later became a world-renowned geologist, was kept from starvation by the foraging of his Negroes; and in northern Georgia in the spring of 1865 the family of Eliza Andrews (*op. cit.*, p. 286) subsisted partly off the earnings of "Uncle Osborne." A carpenter by trade, he took his wage in provisions and turned them into the family larder. Mrs. Irby Morgan (*How it Was*, Nashville, 1892, p. 90) could not recall a single act of Negro lawlessness during the war; but on the other hand remembered many exhibitions of sincere devotion. "When news would come that an old or young master had been killed, they would weep with the family pure tears of affection."

[65] *Life in Dixie During the War* (Atlanta, 1894), pp. 90-92.

John and Mum Peggy," who, having sold some chickens from the plantation to a Yankee captain near the beginning of the war, carefully hoarded the money for four years until they could give it to the rightful owner.[66]

The Negro was an exceedingly pliable being, and his conduct, both in its virtuous aspects and in its vagaries, can nearly always be correlated with immediate influences. If the influence was good, he was likely to remain the ideal of a devoted subordinate; if temptations fell in his way, he usually had little with which to withstand them. When Joseph Le Conte reflected on the aid rendered him by his slaves in his hazardous flight before Sherman's raiders, he paused to express gratitude: "I must not miss the opportunity of paying tribute to the blacks. Closest association doesn't destroy their sincere homage to the white gentleman, an homage only equalled by the old-time homage to the nobility." [67]

A reading of the diaries and memoirs of the period leaves one assured that the idea of enfranchising the Negroes was exclusively a Northern notion. Not one white person in a thousand, not even those most generously disposed, who wanted to see the blacks begin their new life with advantages, was willing to grant that the freedmen were ready for participation in government. The Northern conception that the Negro was merely a sunburned white man, "whose only crime was the color of his skin," found no converts at all among the people who had lived and worked with him. They viewed him as an African and a primitive, carrying with him a heavy weight of those impulses which it is the duty of civilization to remove or subdue.

It was an almost universal belief, therefore, that if the Negro were turned out on his own, he would soon relapse into savagery. Chief among the grounds for this was his ad-

[66] Frances Butler Leigh, *op. cit.*, p. 23.
[67] Le Conte, *op. cit.*, p. 59.

diction to heathen religious practices. Southerners had been in the habit of justifying slavery on the score that it gave the Negroes opportunity to become Christians. There can be no question of the sincerity of this argument, though an age which regards all religion with mild disdain may imagine it to be hypocritical. But the Christian planters who undertook to bring the Gospel to their Negroes found what many a missionary to the Dark Continent has found, that there was a stronger tendency for Christianity to become Africanized than for the African to become Christianized. Mrs. Virginia Clay, writing of Senator Hammond's Redcliffe Plantation in 1864 told something of the story:

> Senator Hammond's view for the civilizing of the negroes led him to forbid the presence of exciting negro preachers, for the religion of the black man, left to himself, is generally a mixture of hysteria and superstition. The conversion of the negroes under their own spiritual guides was a blood-curdling process in those days, for they screamed to heaven as if the Indians with their tomahawks were after them, or danced, twisting their bodies in a most remarkable manner.[68]

Disturbing reports of Negro voodooism now and then crept in. Myrta Avary states that "trance meetings" and "devil dances" became numerous in the first years of emancipation. "It was as if a force long repressed broke forth. 'Moans,' 'shouts,' and 'trance meetings' could be heard for miles. It was weird. I have sat many a night in the window of our house on the big plantation and listened to the shouting, jumping, stamping, dancing, in a cabin over a mile distant; in the gray dawn, negroes would come creeping back, exhausted and unfit for duty." [69] Frances Butler Leigh records that during the war Negroes on a Georgia plantation tore down a church that had been built for them and set up as a

68 Virginia Clay, op. cit., p. 219.
69 Myrta Avary, op. cit., p. 204.

goddess a Negro woman whom they called "Jane Christ." [70] Fairly early in the war Julia Le Grand was hearing reports of voodooism in New Orleans. Tidings came that there was a secret society among the blacks called "vaudo." She wrote, "These people would be savages again if free." [71]

By far the best account of what Reconstruction meant in terms of the planter's struggle to get on his feet again, to restore the plantation world once more to a harmonious community of agricultural laborers in spite of physical destruction, outside interference, and demoralization of the Negroes is given in Frances Butler Leigh's *Ten Years on a Georgia Plantation*. In 1866 Miss Butler, who had spent the war period in the North, went with her father south to Butler's Island, off the coast of Georgia, to take charge of a rice plantation abandoned since the outbreak of hostilities. The state of affairs proved even worse than had been anticipated; the country had undergone a "complete revolution"; and "chaos" and "barbarism" were the terms she employed to describe what she found.

The physical condition of the plantation was discouraging, but the one great obstacle to transforming it again into a productive enterprise, an obstacle which was never really overcome in her ten years of diligent administration, was the unwillingness of the Negroes to work regularly. The slaves on the Butler Island Plantation had always been treated well, and they showed great loyalty and affection, but such feeling did not translate itself into steady industry. One of her men asked Major D., a Northerner, what was the use of being free if he had to work harder than when he had been a slave,[72] and Miss Butler at length concluded that all the blacks really yearned for was plenty to eat and unlimited idleness. Yankees who came into the region declaring that, on the contrary, the

70 Frances Butler Leigh, *op. cit.*, p. 149.
71 Julia Le Grand, *op. cit.*, p. 57.
72 Frances Butler Leigh, *op. cit.*, p. 55.

Negroes wanted only steady work and decent wages, usually lasted from two to six years and then gave up in despair.[73] Miss Butler and her father introduced the sharecropping system, which was actually a response to the necessities of the situation. The practice of paying the ex-slaves wages at the end of stated periods was considered ruinous, for "the first five dollars they made would have seemed so large a sum to them, that they would have imagined their fortunes made and refused to work any more." [74] Yet the sharecropping system left something to be desired, for with the understanding that they were to get half of the crop, they felt that "if six days' work would raise a whole crop, three days' work would raise a half one, with which as partners they were satisfied, and so it seemed as if we should have to be too." [75] The real comedy occurred when she attempted to get them to sign contracts after some of their Northern friends had told them that this would put them back in slavery. Each would come in with "long explanations, objections, and demonstrations," and even those who had made up their minds to sign would not do so until they had spoken their "discourse." [76] Many tried to insert some ridiculous stipulation, and a few declared that although they would work for her "until they died," they had scruples against signing any paper. The problem of getting the Negroes to show zeal for either work or self-improvement was never solved, and Miss Butler wrote: "I felt sure then, and still think, that the pure Negro is incapable of advancement to any degree that would enable him to cope with the white race intellectually, morally, or even physically." [77]

Nor were the Southern Whites able to take courage from the Negro's general behavior upon induction into the com-

73 *Ibid.*, p. 54.
74 *Ibid.*, p. 26.
75 *Ibid.*, p. 27.
76 *Ibid.*, p. 87.
77 *Ibid.*, p. 93.

munity of free citizens. This change of condition made no immediate difference in the lives of many of these unfortunates, but there were others who assumed that it would mean relief from all work and responsibility, and a few pathetic creatures, for so the story goes, thought it a precursor of physical transformation which would render them indistinguishable from their masters. Myrta Avary has given an unforgettable account of their demonstrations when Lincoln entered Richmond shortly after military occupation of that city by the Federals. The President found the path of his carriage blocked by "a rabble of crazy negroes, hailing him as 'Saviour' and 'My Jesus.' " Some knelt on the ground and kissed his hands. Others went into a "regular voodoo ecstasy" and danced and jerked.[78] The sad-eyed Lincoln, who knew people, realized that the Negroes' troubles were only commencing and tried to get them to accept their new status in a sober frame of mind. Evidence that this sort of exhibition was owing to emotional irresponsibility was provided two years later when Jefferson Davis, after being discharged from Judge Underwood's court, was met by a similar demonstration and cries of "God Bless Mars Davis." [79]

The Negro's first disillusionment came when he tried to grasp in tangible form the benefits which the new dispensation was expected to confer. Stories are told of his coming to town with a sack to carry back the franchise which was to be given him, and of his confusion of the "Freedmen's Bureau" with the well-known article of furniture. " 'Whar's dat bureau?' was sure to be the first question," Virginia Clay wrote. " 'Whar's all dem drawers what got de money and de sugar and de coffee? God knows I neber see no bureau 't all, and dat man at de book-cupboard talked mighty short to me, at dat.' "[80]

[78] Myrta Avary, *op. cit.*, p. 30.
[79] *Ibid.*, p. 241.
[80] Virginia Clay, *op. cit.*, p. 284.

Myrta Avary tells of a Negro child who thought that free-dom would bring with it a change of color. " 'Ole Miss,' asked my mother's little handmaiden, 'now I'se free, is I gwi tu'n white lak white folks?'

" 'You must not be ashamed of the skin God gave you, Patsy,' said her mistress kindly, 'Your skin is all right.'

" 'But I druther be white, Ole Miss' " [81]

The second disillusionment came when he tried to frater-nize or do business with his presumptive benefactor, the Northern invader. He discovered not only that the whites from the North had no intention of recognizing him socially —with the exception of a few who came in a missionary spirit, and a fair number who came with an axe to grind—but also that their efficient methods left no room for the indulgence and humoring to which he had been accustomed. This is an aspect of Negro character not at once grasped by the inex-perienced newcomer. The Negro is one of the most sensitive creatures on earth, but he resents not so much his implied inferiority as the sharp word and the unsympathetic look which tell him that he is not wanted. In the antebellum South the whites and the Negroes had established a *modus vivendi* in which the Negroes—usually referred to as "ser-vants"—were seldom reminded of their status, which was as-sumed as a thing understood on both sides. Behind the fence of a few dearly prized prerogatives he could cultivate a sur-prising amount of self-respect, and if he was decorous and well-behaved, he was in little danger of having his feelings hurt. As a matter of fact a rather elaborate code of courtesy existed between whites and blacks in the days of slavery, and a master was more likely to greet a bondman with "cordial and respectful saluations" than was the Northern employer to notice his wage hands. Myrta Avary wrote that "in old sections where new ways have not corrupted ancient courtesy"

[81] Myrta Avary, *op. cit.*, p. 193.

such signs of consideration and affection were still to be seen in the Reconstruction era.[82]

Many a Negro discovered on first contact that the Yankee had no knowledge of the etiquette of race relations and no idea of treating him with deference. An amusing but pathetic incident is related by Myrta Avary, whose cook, Aunt Susan, had heard that it was now possible to dine with white folks. The new white folks evidently made fun of her, for she returned from her adventure with the remark, "White folks dat 'll eat wid me aint fitten fuh me to eat wid." [83] An ex-slave of the Andrews family returned from his first taste of freedom with the complaint that the Yankees "didn't show no respec' for his feelin's." [84] Experiences of this kind continued to occur far into Reconstruction, and many Negroes were forced to see, despite political shibboleths, that their best friends were to be found among the people who had owned them. It is largely upon such experience that the Southerner bases his claim to understand the Negro better than outsiders ever can. Constance Cary, who went to live in New York after the war, was impressed by the plight of Southern Negroes who had come there seeking a black man's Utopia. "For years after the war," she wrote,

I kept coming upon wretched homesick specimens of their class in New York, praying aid and counsel of us Southerners of the old regime, in whom they instinctively trusted more than in their representative abolition friends. One of the best women I ever knew, a lecturer and a missionary to her race, said to me once, "Some of them call me Miss and ask me to sit in their grand parlors in satin chairs while they tell me how well off my people are. Your kind says, You, Susan Jones! you're just wet through tramping the streets; go straight downstairs to my kitchen and get dry and have your dinner." [85]

82 *Ibid.*, p. 31.
83 *Ibid.*, p. 192.
84 Eliza Frances Andrews, *op. cit.*, p. 183.
85 Constance Cary, *op. cit.*, p. 142.

Twenty years after emancipation plantation Negroes were complaining of the growing impersonality of human relationships. Frances Butler Leigh heard the following reproach from an old Negro, the death of whose wife had gone unnoticed: "Ah, tings different now from de ole times; den if any of de people die, de oberseer hab to write Massa John or Massa Pierce, and tell 'em so-and-so's dead, but now de people die and dey buried, and nobody know noting about it.' " [86]

Perhaps some of these attitudes may be discounted as the inevitable fruit of a system of patronage in a feudal society, but the significant fact remains that the sentiment of loyalty and the sentiment of *noblesse oblige* did not vanish at once when the underpinning of the old order was withdrawn, and therein lies a lesson for students of the "science of society."

The welter of Reconstruction lowered rather than raised the white man's estimate of Negro responsibility, though it must not be lost sight of that many of the black man's follies were recognized as traceable to white instigation. The system of slavery, like that of military discipline, enforces habits of health and regularity, and when it was suddenly removed, the hitherto unknown ills of syphilis, consumption, and insanity made immediate appearance.[87] But the chief obstacle to Negro-white *rapprochement* was the outbreak of crimes against women, a thing practically unheard of in antebellum times. Myrta Avary, who had more than any other writer to say about the Reconstruction Negro, thought that these outrages resulted directly from dressing him up in a blue uniform and talking to him about "social equality." Such acts drove the whites into a blind fury of determination, and the response was the lynching mob which, regardless of its hastiness and brutality, seemed to her an immediate answer to the problem. "Within the circumscribed radius of its influence,"

[86] Frances Butler Leigh, *op. cit.*, p. 236.
[87] Myrta Avary, *op. cit.*, p. 196.

she wrote, without apology, "lynching seems to eradicate the evil for which it is administered." [88]

Julia Le Grand reacted so strongly against Negro misconduct that she turned from an abolitionist into a believer in slavery. After observing the freed blacks in Federal-held New Orleans, she entered the following in her diary:

> I was once as great an abolitionist as any in the North—that was when my unthinking fancy placed black and white upon the same plane. My sympathies blinded me, and race and character were undisturbed mysteries to me. But my experience with negroes has altered my way of thinking and reasoning. As an earnest of sincerity given even to my own mind, it was when we owned them in number that I thought they ought to be free, and now that we have none, I think they are not fit for freedom.[89]

She considered Negroes the only race that labor does not degrade. The white man, freed from cares, strives toward a higher plane, but the Negro lacks the "pride of character" which furnishes the incentive to do this. She wondered about the proper place in the scale of humanity for a creature who was "servile if mastered, and brutal if licensed." [90]

On the other hand Eliza Andrews, whom we must keep in mind as the realist of this group, marvelled that under the twin burdens of ignorance and temptation the Negro did not behave far worse. And she correctly foretold that the resentment of this race, when they finally became undeceived, would be not against the Southerner for having enslaved them, nor against the Yankee for having made them false promises, but against the whites in general. At the same time she regarded Negro suffrage as the greatest calamity that could befall the South. If the Negro were forced into a posi-

88 *Ibid.*, p. 381.
89 Julia Le Grand, *op. cit.*, p. 100.
90 *Ibid.*, p. 101.

tion above his capacity, he would fall, she thought, and in falling drag down everything around him. No stability was conceivable until the country should return to "some system of apprenticeship embodying the best features of slavery." She concluded that "Nothing but experience, that 'dear teacher' of fools, will ever bring the North to its senses on this point, and the fanatics will be slow to admit the falsity of their cherished theories and admit themselves beaten." [91]

Nothing could be more idle than speculation about which race is superior, Mrs. Avary wrote in a chapter entitled "Race Prejudice." The whole question of relative rank can be waived; for the decisive fact is that like eagles and sparrows they will not flock together. "They are different rather than unequal" and "to ignore a difference inherent in nature is a crime against nature and is punished according to nature." [92] The only hope for the future lay in the willingness of each race to mark out its place, and of each to help the other maintain that place.

6. The Tragedy of Defeat

Such citations indicate how the Southern people bore themselves under the hardships of war and the problems of Reconstruction, but in describing the complex Southern psychology which emerged from the fierce trial, one must notice especially the reaction to the total meaning of defeat. This is a difficult theme, which few of the diarists themselves attempted to handle at length, but incidental remarks enable one to piece out the underlying philosophy of the majority. The religious explanation was, as might be expected, popular. It rested on the assumption that there is a god of justice, and that sometimes people are punishd for sins of which

91 Eliza Frances Andrews, *op. cit.,* p. 316.
92 Myrta Avary, *op. cit.,* pp. 392-393.

they are not conscious. Since only a minority of Southerners believed that slaveholding is a sin, and since many of them felt that they surpassed the Yankee in nobility of character—an impression deepened, unfortunately, by the conduct of Federal soldiers in the South—it was necessary to fall back on the theory of an inscrutable providence. Remarks typical of the religious mind lie scattered through the *Journal of Hospital Life* of Kate Cumming, a woman who saw as much as anyone else of the human waste of war. "Our sins must have been great to have deserved such punishment," she wrote after viewing a harrowing hospital scene.[93] In a reflective passage she declared, "Why the enemy are permitted to work their fiendish purposes is still in oblivion," but she took comfort in the thought that "God is his own interpreter." [94] It was in keeping with her character that the war should teach her not some exalted political truth, but rather the vanity of all earthly things. "O, may we learn the lesson that all this is designed to teach," she wrote near the end of her story, "that all things sublunary are transient and fleeting." [95]

Phoebe Yates Pember, who also served as a hospital nurse, was bitter over the condition of Southern prisoners returned from Northern prison camps on exchange. Among the emaciated wretches whom she made a special but vain effort to nurse back to life was Richard Hammond Key, grandson of the author of "The Star Spangled Banner." [96] Describing them as "pictures of famine and desolation," she declared they made one feel "that the Atonement had failed, and that Christ had died in vain." [97] Yet she wrote in review that her experiences in the Richmond hospitals had exerted a purifying and ennobling effect on her character.[98]

93 Kate Cumming, *op. cit.*, p. 20.
94 *Ibid.*, p. 195.
95 *Ibid.*, p. 198.
96 Phoebe Yates Pember, *op. cit.*, p. 123.
97 *Ibid.*, p. 121.
98 *Ibid.*, p. 192.

Mrs. Judith McGuire was a noble Christian lady, capable of praying for the enemy when the torch was at her door, but she confessed herself unable to understand why God had seen fit to destroy the South, "with the fairest land, the purest social circle, the noblest race of men, and the happiest people on earth." [99] She affirmed, however, that her faith was not shaken, and she prayed for a return of "the healing balm of love" and "the spirit of Christ." [100]

Parthenia Hague in *A Blockaded Family* interpreted the war as proving that "a man's family is the nearest piece of his country and the dearest one." [101] When she returned to her home in Georgia and saw the desolation in Sherman's track, the sight reduced her to tears, but she recorded: "Yet after all our great and sore afflictions, I found only cheerfulness and Christian resignation at the end of these troublesome wartimes, and the hope that we might yet rise above our misfortune." [102]

All of these expressions proceed, it must be admitted, from an unsophisticated level; but they reflect the majority mind, and they explain the event as satisfactorily for the believer in a God-created universe as do the later Marxist interpretations for the materialists.

For another variety of interpretation we must turn to Eliza Frances Andrews, whose *War-time Journal of a Georgia Girl* has been mentioned favorably before. For Miss Andrews was that *rara avis in terris,* a Southern-reared economic determinist. By what route she arrived at her view is not clear, but she saw only economic forces in the creation and destruction of Southern civilization. It was, she said, "a case of belated survival," against which economic tendencies had long been marshalled. The children of the South should ac-

99 Judith McGuire, *op. cit.,* p. 7.
100 *Ibid.*
101 Parthenia Antoinette Hague, *A Blockaded Family* (Boston, 1888), p. 3.
102 *Ibid.,* p. 176.

cordingly be taught that it fell "not because it was evil or vicious in itself, but because, like a good and useful man who has lived out his allotted time and gone the way of all earth, it too has served its turn and must now lie in the grave of the dead just." [103] This change was signalized when "changed conditions transferred to another class the economic advantage which is the basis to all power." [104] Slavery and feudal society, whatever their intrinsic merits, in the latter part of the nineteenth century stood in a hostile world. This was common opinion everywhere, but Miss Andrews is conspicuous by her frank espousal of the economic thesis, opposed as it was to the Southern religious and the Northern moral interpretation.

The men who wrote diaries and reminiscences showed perhaps less inclination to wrestle with the topic of the significance of defeat. William L. Royall, whose practical temperament found it easy to bid farewell to the past, composed a very brief epilogue: "It may be thought," he wrote, "that after these bitter reflections I am still an 'unreconstructed rebel.' But I am not. I have come to believe that the thing turned out as it ought to have turned out. Slavery and the principle of secession had to be got rid of and the only way they ever could have been got rid of was to fight the war to a finish." [105] T. C. De Leon took the view in *Belles, Beaux, and Brains of the Sixties* that the war was a baptism of blood out of which a true nationalism was forged, and that it was therefore worth the cost—a theory which must have closely paralleled that of Lincoln.[106]

[103] Eliza Frances Andrews, *op. cit.*, p. 11.
[104] *Ibid.*
[105] *Some Reminiscences* (New York, 1909), p. 44.
[106] *Op. cit.*, p. 19. De Leon was, however, very cautious about predicting a new South. He knew that the phoenix which arose from the ashes would not be wanting in signs of its heritage. Those who taught that the New South would be only another New England in lower latitudes were, he thought, raising false hopes.

As one looks at these civilians behind the lines, who in either active or passive roles watched their country go down in ruin, the feeling must grow upon him that they were essentially tragic victims. Although the judgment of history went against them, it is difficult to establish a moral scheme by which they may be condemned. In both personal and public morality they were at least the equals of their foes; and as for the political crime of disunion which the North sought relentlessly to fix on them, it is plain that the letter of the law was on their side, even if the spirit in which they faced the issue belonged to 1776 rather than to 1860. Somewhere there was a tragic fault—a fault compounded of pride, exclusiveness, and self-absorption. To say that the tendency against which they fought was world-wide does not demean their role. The victory of centralism in the American Civil War was one of those "unifications" with which the century was replete. But we are brought back to the tragic quality of the event when we realize that in every tragic resolution the good goes down with the bad, and the loss of the good stirs our compassion. Much was lost in the destruction of the Old South that men have not ceased to regret. Most of the poetic virtues—honor, dignity, fealty, valor—were made to look outmoded and futile, and have had since to sneak in by the back door and apologize for themselves. There were different ideals to oppose them, of course, and just because it was a sharp clash of ideals, the Civil War will remain "the war" indefinitely to those who study the making of America. Not until one has passed beyond the pragmatic view of history and studied the tragedies of failure as well as listened to the raucous claims of success does he see into the life of things.

Yet when one tries to discover whether the Civil War taught the Southern people a "lesson" in the conventional sense, he learns that it did not. Despite some seeming diversity of feeling, it appears that the traditional Southerner emerged from the war—a grand attempt to coerce him into the stream of "progress"—not only unreconstructed but relatively unreconstructible. His faith in politicians was, indeed, shaken, and he was to suffer three generations of rabble-rousing public servants in place of the old political metaphysicians and declaimers who had once held his faith. But his soldiers had secured for him a great consolation prize—the conviction that man for man he belonged to a superior breed; the Southerners, being less mercurial than their Northern brethren, tend to have longer memories and to cherish such comforting suppositions until a favorable time for acting on them presents itself. His belief in the class system, especially the class system defined by racial lines, was confirmed. His belief in the primitive way of life, too, endured, and with it the anti-intellectual tradition permeating even his institutions of higher learning. Northerners who exclaimed in exasperation that the Southern people were like the Bourbons, having learned nothing and forgotten nothing, were in a sense correct, but the force they were indicting was much more deep-seated and pervasive than they realized. It was a force which was to assert itself several decades later in Europe in the form of the "revenge of instinct" and the revival of primitive ideologies.

ᴥᦞᴥ ᦞᴥᦞᴥ

Fiction Across The Chasm

A TIME OF WAR IS A GOOD TIME TO WRITE ABOUT BUT A POOR time to write in, as Abraham Cowley remarked. For four years the South had been engaged in one of the fiercest wars in history, a war which left no source of its energy untapped and no department of its life untouched; and for thirty years preceding the actual outbreak of hostilities, it had been in a virtual state of siege, preparing itself for the assault which its prophetic soul knew must come. After the matters at issue had been settled by arbitrament of the sword, deep as were the vexation, the humiliation, and the despair, there prevailed in some quarters a sense of relief. There was a feeling that in slavery the South had been saddled with an incubus, and some wry satisfaction could be derived from the knowledge that it had been "blown hellward from the cannon's mouth." On grounds of prudence a less costly excision might have been preferred, but Southerners were never famous for prudence or for knowing their own interests, and many felt that it was better to see their country go down in red ruin than to submit tamely to outrageous interference. After the war more than one Southerner could be found asserting proudly that he had fought well in a wrong cause.[1] The important circumstance, however, was that the never-ending battle to defend slavery was now over, and that Southerners who had pens to write could now present the story of their country without thought of immediate controversy and in terms which the world would accept.

A heavy duty lay upon them. Wise counsellors were reminding the Southern people that since their sword was broken, their tongue must be doubly eloquent. In the spirit of that King of Prussia who said of his country, "The body is dead; we must awaken the spirit," a host of Southern writers of varying degrees of talent and with various attitudes toward the history and traditions of their native section began to present in fiction the world's last feudal society.

But if a sense of realism and a fresh orientation were what the South after Appomattox needed, the first works to appear gave little promise of amendment. This was not unnatural, however, for when passions were aroused, the response to total condemnation is likely to be unqualified endorsement; and the charge of Northern journalism that the South was sunk in barbarism received a retort equally extreme, which was that the antebellum plantation was an idyll of comfort and harmony, and that the men who fought in gray constituted a blameless chivalry. John Esten Cooke, Thomas Nelson Page, and Thomas Dixon were the chief exponents of this view.

1. Advocates of the Old Régime

The literary apologists of the Old South were less tough-minded than its political and military defenders, and one

[1] Dr. A. Monteiro, surgeon of Mosby's command, certainly expressed a contemporary attitude when he declared of his countrymen (op. cit., p. 180): "Though conquered we were like other men—vain even of our defects and proud even of our follies."

must begin them prepared for a vast amount of conventionalized portraiture, sugary romance, and nostalgia. Cooke, who
was earliest, represents the ultra-romantic approach. It was
said of him that he had been born into most of the good
connections in Virginia and had married into the remainder,
and no one more instinctively identified himself with the life
of the old commonwealth, or better expressed the virtues of
its ruling class. After four years of service with Jackson,
Stuart, and Pendleton, through which he went unscathed,
Cooke buried his silver spurs in the earth at Appomattox in
token of defiance and cast about for a mode of life in the
new order. He had providentially remained single during the
period of the war, and when he married in 1867, at the age
of thirty-seven, he acquired possession of a farm. Previously
he had entertained thoughts of leaving the country, or of
trying his luck in New York, that mecca of twenty thousand
uprooted Southerners, but now he decided to attempt subsistence farming and to seek a cash income by literary work.

Despite his intense Southern sympathies, Cooke knew that
he would have to write for a Northern audience, and his
works may therefore be regarded as an early part of that
bridging of the bloody chasm which commenced when Lee
advised his countrymen to forget local animosities and to
make their children citizens of the nation. His writings which
draw upon contemporary subject matter may be conveniently
divided as follows: works of history with fictional subplots;
"novels," which are only history written with some degree of
color, detail, and animation; and a single novel setting forth
the problems of Reconstruction. Because Cooke wrote with
great rapidity, and because he wrote only that for which he
had an immediate market, one cannot draw conclusions from
the chronological order of his books. The first was *Surry of
Eagle's-Nest* (1866), a story which takes its hero from the
secession convention in Richmond through the death of Jack-

son at Chancellorsville. In the opening chapter the author addresses the reader with an explanation: "How Lee looked, and how Stuart spoke—how Jackson lived that wondrous life of his, and Ashby charged upon his milk-white steed—of this the coming generation will talk, and I think they will take more interest in such things than in the most brilliant arguments about secession." [2] These figures are present throughout in semi-legendary form, but Cooke deemed it necessary for the reader's interest to complicate his story with mysterious strangers, a duel at dawn, an abduction, and various unexplained relationships in patent imitation of the older romance. Fact and fiction contend for the mastery: the reader is first absorbed by a faithful depiction of Jackson's quixotic appearance as he reviewed his troops at Harper's Ferry, and then plummeted into the unreality of disguised conspirators and pale heroines. It is, in short, a combination of romance, as the South had learned it from Sir Walter Scott, and the Civil War as it was recalled by one who worshipped the Army of Northern Virginia. The reality for Cooke at this time was the charging lines of gray beneath the Stars and Bars, beside which inventions based on his reading of fiction appear weak indeed. As he confesses in the last chapter of *Surry:*

> At all times—everywhere—the Past comes into the Present and possesses it. As I awake in the morning, the murmur of the river breeze is the low roll of drums from the forest yonder, where the camps of infantry are aroused by the reveille. In the moonlight nights, when all is still, a sound comes, borne upon the breeze, from some dim land—I seem to hear the bugles. In the thunder of some storm, I hear the roar of artillery.[3]

In *Mohun: The Last Days of Lee and His Paladins* one

2 *Surry of Eagle's-Nest* (New York, 1894), p. 9.
3 *Ibid.,* p. 483.

finds again history with an embroidery of fiction. This work
is a continuation of *Surry of Eagle's-Nest*; the chain of events,
here commencing after Chancellorsville, extends down to
1868, and there are new and even more bizarre characters to
provide an accompaniment of romance. Certain passages,
such as the description of Gettysburg, must be noted as especially fine, and a few pages on Richmond, touching speculation and the defection of individuals, contain matter which
ordinarily got only into the records of the diarists. Yet even
more than *Surry*, *Mohun* reveals Cooke's constitutional
faults: his habit of stereotyping characters and then employ-
ing them in wooden fashion, his florid and exaggerated style,
his wearisome repetition of phrase, and his insistence on setting down what he had seen and heard at crucial points,
sometimes irrespective of its connection with the narrative.

Cooke loved the Confederate cavalier with such whole-
souled devotion and sent him charging through his pages
with such joyous abandon that one is surprised to find him
telling George Cary Eggleston, "I never liked the business of
war. There is nothing intellectual about fighting." He went
on to say, "It is fit work for brutes and brutish men. And in
modern war, where men are organized in masses and con-
verted into insensate machines, there is really nothing
heroic or romantic in any way calculated to appeal to the
imagination." [4]

Perhaps this was a natural reaction against the "business of
war," which settled down on the Federal army after the removal of McClellan and on the Confederate after the death
of Jackson, when the struggle became a slugging contest with
superior weight certain to prevail at last. But such a declaration does not comport with the tone and attitude of his war
books. Everywhere in these glowing pages one feels that here

[4] Quoted in J. O. Beaty, *John Esten Cooke, Virginian* (New York, 1922), p.
109.

is a man who would not love life so much loved he not honor more. The period succeeding Appomattox was for the average Virginian a pretty sad vacancy; the war was still the absorbing topic, and there was no sudden accession of riches to compensate for wounds or to dull the memories of the bivouac. In a prologue to *Mohun* Cooke had tried to define his attitude toward his subject matter:

> But is it wrong to remember the past? I think of it without bitterness. God decreed it—God the all-wise, the all-merciful —for his own purposes. I do not indulge in any repinings, or reflect with rancor upon the issue of the struggle. I prefer recalling the stirring adventure, the brave voices, the gallant faces: even in the tremendous drama of 1864-65, I can find something besides blood and tears: even here and there some sunshine.[5]

By and large, Cooke was content to illustrate what was noble in the tragic contest that proved fatal to his idyllic Virginia, to call back his days spent with great soldiers, and to show the world that the South, no less than proud Scotland, provided subjects for enduring romance.

In *The Heir of Gaymount* (1870) Cooke undertook to tell the struggles of a Southern landowner during Reconstruction, but even here he could not abandon the vein of facile romance, nor could a closely autobiographical framework save it from the excesses of his former stories. Edmund Carteret, who must be taken to represent the author, returns from the war to find himself the possessor of an ancestral house and forty acres of land, the upkeep of which is beyond his means. After pondering the notion of emigrating to Mexico, he decides to remain on his land and try the experiment of truck farming. The roseate story of success which follows is incredible. Cabbages, tomatoes, celery, and melons sprout as

5 *Mohun* (New York, 1869), p. 9.

if by magic; later come wine-producing grapes, and within three years Carteret has $6,000 in the bank and is on the point of taking up a loan. One may read all this in perfect innocence of the existence of unfavorable weather, of marketing difficulties, and of ruinous price levels; Cooke's conception of agriculture, as one critic has expressed it, is that the grower puts a seed in the ground and gets a coin back.[6]

This is only part of the story, however, for a sinister figure lurks in the background. Israel Tudmuddle is an ex-overseer, who by hard work and cunning business practice has risen to wealth. It is his ambition to buy Gaymount and marry his son into the Virginia aristocracy, who despise his kind. Through a dishonest contrivance he has induced Carteret to sign a deed which will give him possession of the estate unless the aspiring young farmer can meet a note for $8,000. A cashier's defalcation prevents Carteret from doing this with the proceeds of his farming, and villainy has almost triumphed when an accident brings about the discovery of an uncle's buried treasure and a recorded will, which provide him respectively with enough money to meet his obligations and title to a neighboring estate of 3,000 acres. Thus the story ends with Tudmuddle foiled, and with Carteret and his friends Hartrigger and Lance forming a Christmas tableau of happy couples.

From this charming if impossible story of rehabilitation Cooke intended that his Southern readers should draw two comforting thoughts. One was that the lands of the South, so long wastefully given over to cotton, corn, and tobacco, could be profitably turned to intensive cultivation, although, as has been indicated, his demonstration of the new system imposes somewhat on credulity. The second was that the Southern people have true friends in the North. Here they are represented by Frank Lance, a cheery, expansive, happy-go-lucky

6 Beaty, *op. cit.,* p. 125.

New Yorker, who fought the Johnny Rebs, but who now appears on the scene to encourage his erstwhile enemy and to bring succour at critical moments. He is the Northern well-wisher who comes South not only to see for himself but also to lend the hard cash which, in a land stripped of its capital, spells the difference between victory and defeat in any struggle to regain position.

The Heir of Gaymount is thus a highly romanticized picture of Cooke's own experience as a Virginia farmer in the late sixties, interwoven with the same kind of melodramatic plots he placed in his war stories, and primarily designed, as one must suppose, to entertain an uncritical audience rather than to come to grips with the problems of the Southerner in the new order. Its hero is still wearing the gray and seeing his torn and broken world through the eyes of a Southern romantic. Cooke was temperamentally incapable of realism, regardless of his theme, but the novel is interesting as showing how pervasive was the tendency to idealize and how eager Cooke was to have the Southerner succeed as Southerner. Despite these brave attempts, he was candid enough to admit that his type of fiction belonged to the literary order which was passing. When the new realism commenced with William Dean Howells, he acknowledged the essential rightness of its approach but realized that he was too old to acquire a new attitude and learn a new technique.[7]

Cooke's successor in the work of idealizing the South was Thomas Nelson Page, another Virginian of similar background, and a writer who found a much wider audience for his romantic stories of Southern life. Page, however, wrote chiefly about Reconstruction. He devoted the greater part of a fairly productive literary career to the portrayal of Virginians in the restored Union, and no other author was more sensible of the differences between the old and the new civili-

[7] M. J. Moses, *The Literature of the South* (New York, 1910), p. 328.

zations and of the far-reaching effects, extending even to trifling matters, which a reorientation must enforce. Son of a soldier of the Army of Northern Virginia, Page was born too late to have a part in the war, but his impressionable years were spent in that period when it seemed natural to South-erners to compare all things, including the beauty of the moon, with what had obtained in the fabulous times "befo' de wah." He was told what his people had done in that war, and he could see how cruelly they were struggling to re-establish their fortunes.

These two themes furnish the staple of a line of fiction which began in 1884 with "Marse Chan." An accident led to the writing of this story. Page was shown a letter which had been taken from the body of a Georgia private killed in one of the battles around Richmond. It was an ordinary love let-ter except for one item: the writer, after begging her soldier lover to return, added the following postscript: "Don't come without a furlough; for if you don't come honorable, I won't marry you." This accorded so well with all that had been said about Southern women's devotion to the cause that Page re-solved to put it in a story, and so began a successful career of letters. "Marse Chan" appeared as one of a collection of tales issued in 1887 under the general title *In Ole Virginia*. In 1894 came another collection containing the highly charac-teristic "Burial of the Guns." This is the story of an artillery regiment which, upon receiving word of Lee's surrender, finds itself holding an impregnable position in the moun-tains. Rather than give up their guns, which they have served through four bloody years, they resolve to roll them over a cliff into a river. First, however, they prepared a statement of the unit's record, which is rammed into a muzzle. It read in part:

> We're all volunteers, every man; we joined the army at the beginning of the war; and we've stuck through to the end;

sometimes we ain't had much to eat and sometimes we ain't
had nothin', but we've fought the best we could 119 battles
and skirmishes as near as we can make out in four years, and
never lost a gun. Now we're agoin' home. We ain't surrendered; just disbanded; and we pledge ourselves to teach our
children to love the South and General Lee; and to come
when we're called anywhere and anytime, so help us God.[8]

Notwithstanding its sentimentality, this statement may be
taken as the epilogue of every Confederate soldier who felt
that he had won the fight but lost the war, and there were
many such.

Confederate loyalty and valor are subjects Page never lost
sight of, but his long novels deal with Reconstruction, and
here the struggle is usually against the more insidious forces
bred in the competitive business life of the Gilded Age. *Red
Rock* is the earliest and the most typical, for it dramatizes the
two most pressing necessities of the hour: the saving of old
estates and the defeat of those outside elements which tried to
take charge of affairs while the old commonwealths were
being "reconstructed." In this story Jacquelin Cary and Stevenson Allen win a long fight against the carpetbagger
Jonadab Leech, who is backed up by corrupt supporters and
the military arm of the United States Government. In *Gordon Keith* it is the son of old General Keith, master of
Elphinstone, who becomes an engineer, helps develop the
mineral resources of his state after outwitting the dishonest
entrepreneurs, and wins the right girl in the meantime. Page
had a fixed idea that the best way to bring about a reunion of
the nation was to promote the marital union of Southern
belles with Northern youths, or, as second best, of Northern
belles with Southern youths. Such matings occur not only in
Red Rock and *Gordon Keith* but also in "Meh Lady: A Story
of the War."

[8] *The Burial of the Guns* (New York, 1894), p. 80.

The rapprochement is always made by the younger people; the older figures learn to respect one another's character but do not find it possible to change themselves. The fiction of Page is filled with dignified generals, colonels, and majors who have nothing left but their pride and the manners of a gentleman; they are anxious to see their young people succeed but are a little suspicious of the new conception of success. The author remarks of General Keith, whose son proved himself capable of surviving in the rough-and-tumble world of an expanding industrialism: "He knew the Past and lived in it; the Present he did not understand, and the Future he did not know." [9] His education had left him totally ignorant of business and of natural science. "I know no more of science, sir, than an Indian," he declared. "The only sciences I ever thought I knew were politics and war, and I have failed in both." [10] In *John Marvel, Assistant* the hero says of his sire, "My father was naturally adapted to the conditions that had created such a character, but as unsuited to the new conditions that succeeded the collapse of the old life as a shorn lamb would be to the untempered wind of winter." [11] Sometimes, as in "The Christmas Peace," it is the energetic and practical daughter, a harbinger of Scarlett O'Hara, who salvages the estate, but always the old man lingers in the background, a picturesque figure of unbending rectitude, often a trifle absurd in view of his narrow circumstances and usually able to pass on as patrimony only a good name and some advice regarding human nature, the shrewdness of which his children one day discover.

A favorite device of Page was to bring a Northerner to the South and to let him see for himself the condition of the country and the character of the people whom his press at

9 *Gordon Keith* (New York, 1912), I, p. 2.
10 *Ibid.,* I, p. 52.
11 *John Marvel, Assistant* (New York, 1910), I, p. 5.

home was representing as rebels and banditti. In *Red Rock,* Major Welch, a Union soldier, comes to Virginia to buy property, finds that the title to his purchase is faulty because of the machinations of carpetbaggers, turns against those whom he has regarded as missionaries of reform, and finally loses his daughter to the leader of the local conservatives. In most of these plots there is an effort, frequently overdone and therefore pathetic, to exhibit the best qualities of the Southerner in an open bid for Northern esteem. The old family, the sense of honor, natural capacity, and a desire to settle matters through law rather than through violence—these the hero unfailingly illustrates, never missing an opportunity to point out inferior Northern standards and examples. Jacquelin Cary and Stevenson Allen show Major Welch what Southern probity means; young Gordon Keith gives Miss Alice Yorke a lecture upon manners and later proves that business acumen is not exclusively a Yankee possession.

These constitute an ill-concealed note of special pleading, the object of which is to rehabilitate the South in Northern eyes. One encounters at intervals in Page's characters a feeling of exasperation aroused by the prejudices they must overcome when thrown in contact with Yankees. The Southern hero cannot understand why the Yankee will not perceive that he is of sterling character, that he intends to work within the restored Union, and that, when exempt from outside interference, he prefers court procedure to gunplay. In an effort to combat such prejudice, Page tended to make his characters paragons. In "The Spectre in the Cast" a Virginia lawyer harangues a mob which is bent on lynching a Negro and threatens individual prosecution of its members. The Ku Klux Klan appears in *Red Rock,* but it is an absurdly genteel Klan, a parody on those organizations which with terrible effectiveness secured white supremacy in the early period of Reconstruction. Obviously in these incidents Page is making the South put its best foot forward. He is trying to believe that its conquerors fought for principle, but he is insisting firmly that Southerners be credited with having done the same. More especially he is always pointing out that the salvation of the section can be worked out only by the well-disposed local elements, whom the coercive measures of Reconstruction rendered powerless.

It scarcely needs adding that the characters in Page's early novels and stories are stereotyped. The Southerners are Cooke's heroes in gray, now fighting the battle of Reconstruction. There is always the representative of the old order living on in the new, a character formal and courtly, and though disillusioned, indomitable. There is the son who inherits his father's ethical code, but who is enabled by youth, adaptability, and practical idealism to achieve a success. On the other side there is the carpetbagger, a trickster who avoided service in the war, but who when the war is over and the South's bones are to pick, comes down with an itching palm and a mouth full of pious platitudes. Offsetting him is the Northerner of good character, who fought a good fight, but who joins the conservative party when he comes south and finds the people suffering real oppression. Not until 1909, when he wrote *John Marvel, Assistant,* which is not a novel of Reconstruction, did Page consider those differences which do not proceed from political division, and create a character with a convincing mixture of human traits.

His Negroes fall entirely within the legend. They remain loyal after slavery; they take pride in their white folks' social position; they offer those shrewd, oblique observations on conduct which are peculiar to the race; and they display amiable weaknesses which stamp them as wards. No less than the whites they idealize antebellum times, and Page's one picture of the educated free Negro is distinctly satirical.[12]

12 "Mam Lyddy's Recognition," *Bred in the Bone* (New York, 1912), pp. 219-252.

It is not surprising after all this that the plots adhere to formula, and that the situations are contrived in the facile style of the period. Page was not, in view of these limitations, a literary craftsman; he was rather an exponent of a time and a place. He wrote out of the kind of knowledge which comes by acquaintance, and he wrote with simple sincerity, which means in the last analysis that he failed to attain a complete awareness. It is to his insistence upon the nobility of the Virginia gentlemen, however, that much of the crystallized Southern legend is due. One envisages him a late member of the patrician race, extending his hand to the new order with true but modest friendliness, but inflexible in personal standards, and convinced that whatever fads in morals and behavior may seize the public, a character founded on honesty and manners, on consideration for others, will not suffer permanent eclipse. Like certain others who loved the South best, he was most in favor of reconciliation and reunion. In an introduction to *In Ole Virginia* he could say with perfect candor that he had "never written a line which he did not hope might tend to bring about better understanding between the North and the South, and finally lead to a more perfect Union." [13] But the road to understanding would have to lie through an appreciation of the value of sentiment and of the manly virtues.

While the men were thus eulogizing the Southern code of honor and valor, the women writers were working in a less direct but no less effective way to restore the Southern ideal of society. By far the most celebrated of them was Augusta Jane Evans, the first of a long line of Southern women novelists who, without so much as approaching the top grade of literary excellence, nevertheless have managed to capture the popular imagination and to create characters of universal appeal. A native of Columbus, Georgia, Miss Evans wrote two novels, both of slight significance, before the war. During the

13 *In Ole Virginia* (New York, 1912), p. xi.

struggle itself she was passionate in the Southern cause, and
in after years she remarked, "The sole enthusiasm of my life
was born, lived, and perished in the eventful four years of the
Confederacy." [14] As an expression of this enthusiasm she
published in 1864 *Macaria: or, Altars of Sacrifice,* a tragic
romance filled with fierce denunciations of Northern political leaders and breathing intense loyalty to the South. It is
said to have proved so damaging to the morale of Federal
soldiers that officers ordered it confiscated and burned.[15]

A year after the war she appeared before her publishers in
New York with the manuscript of *St. Elmo,* a novel which
was to to have a tremendous vogue. It is difficult for a later
generation to imagine the kind of taste that found satisfaction in this story, embroidered as it is with a strange medley
of historical allusions, scientific digressions, and moral discourses. Its heroine is Edna Earle, a pure-minded, idealistic
girl who by sheer nobility of character reforms and thereafter
marries the wealthy but depraved St. Elmo Murray. Although
it is nothing more than a florid and sentimental love story,
the two serious convictions of Miss Evans' life nevertheless
creep in, and these reveal her a champion of the old order.
One was belief in a fixed code of morals, and the other was a
feeling, which became more fervent as she grew older, that
the emancipation of woman entailed her degradation and
would lead to the dissolution of society.

In general, the battle to save the old way of life was a battle
to preserve distinctions—the distinction between man and
woman, between master and slave, between gentlemen and
men without honor, between decorum and impropriety. The
erasure of distinctions which made up the gradations of quality was seen as the chief menace of "Northern barbarism."
Miss Evans pointed to signs of peril in the moral collapse of

14 Louise Manly in the *Library of Southern Literature,* XIII, p. 5842.
15 "Augusta Jane Evans," *DAB,* VI, p. 196.

the Reconstruction period, about which every person of conscience had something to say. "Statesmen were almost extinct in America—," she wrote,

> a mere corporal's guard remained, battling desperately to save the stabbed Constitution from howling demagogues and fanatics, who raved and ranted where Washington, Webster and Calhoun had once swayed a free and happy people. The old venerated barriers and well-guarded outposts, which decorum and true womanly modesty had erected on the frontiers of propriety, were swept away in the crevasse of *sans souci* manners that threatened to inundate the entire land; and latitudinarianism in dress and conversation was rapidly reducing the sexes to an equality, dangerous to morals and subversive of all chivalrous respect for woman.[16]

Accordingly Edna Earle set herself to fight these forces of corruption, taking her stand on the principle that woman can be most influential in society as woman.

> Believing that the intelligent, refined, modest Christian women were the real custodians of national purity, and the sole agents who could arrest the tide of demoralization breaking over the land, she addressed herself to the wives, mothers, and daughters of America; calling upon them to smite their false gods, and purify the shrines at which they worshipped. Jealously she contended for every woman's right which God and nature had decreed the sex. The right to be learned, wise, noble, useful, in woman's divinely limited sphere. The right to influence and exalt the circle in which she moved. The right to mount the sanctified bema of her own quiet hearthstone; the right to modify and direct her husband's opinion, if he considered her worthy and competent to guide him; the right to make her children ornaments to their nation, and a crown of glory to their race; the right to advise, to plead, to pray; the right to make her desk a Delphi, if God so permitted; the right to be all that the phrase "noble Christian

16 *St. Elmo* (Chicago, n.d.), p. 394.

woman" means. But not the right to vote; to harangue from the hustings; to trail her heaven-born purity through the dust and mire of political strife; to ascend the *rosta* [*sic*] of statesmen, whither she may send a worthy husband, son, or brother, but whither she can never go, without disgracing all womanhood.[17]

When Miss Evans published *A Speckled Bird* in 1902 she was still convinced that the decay of morals and the relaxing of standards were of Northern inspiration, and the sectional clash is here made quite sharp. Like *St. Elmo* this is a love story, detailing in a style much the same the complicated romance between Eglah Allison, granddaughter of a Confederate general and daughter of a Reconstruction Federal judge, and the fabulously wealthy Noel Herriott. Mr. Allison's membership in the United States Senate, with the frequent journeys between the South and Washington which it requires, offers opportunities for political asides. The author was now maintaining that the preservation of womanhood was identical with the preservation of the South, and Eglah is a stout opponent of female emancipation. She holds the following spirited dialogue with Miss Higginbotham, a Westerner who advocates the new freedoms for her sex. Miss Higginbotham is chiding Eglah about the narrowness of Southern views:

"Oh, but your mother was Southern, and you represent not heredity but sheredity, a sociological factor of immense potency, which must be reckoned with, let me tell you, in the near future, when women fully emancipated come to the full enjoyment of all rights so long withheld from them. The mothers, and not fathers will wield the destiny of this great country; and already female colleges are spreading the blessed gospel of free and equal rights. Last week someone asserted that you were a graduate of ―― ―― college, but I contradicted it as flatly impossible and absurd."

17 *Ibid.*, p. 395.

"I am sorry I do my dear *alma mater* such lamentable discredit; but unfortunately, we were not taught to wear our diplomas on our hats as advertisements of scholarship."

"You certainly amaze me."

"Perhaps you will excuse me in assuring you that the sensation is at least mutual."

"With your educational advantages, you lock up your mind in a stockade of provincialism. Desectionalize yourself."

"May I ask whether you spell your last verb with an x or a ct? I should prefer to understand first which process is demanded of me."

"Your Southern bigotry is a mill-stone around your neck. The very word emancipation is a red rag to old slaveholders and their progeny. You can never forgive us for breaking the shackles of groaning millions held in bondage."

Following this catty exchange, Eglah sums up her view of woman's proper sphere:

Indeed, I have the most affectionate and jealous regard for every right that inheres in my dower of American womanhood. I claim and enjoy the right to be as cultured, as learned, as useful, and—if you please—as ornamental in society and at home as my individual limitations will permit. I have no wrongs, no grievances, no crying need to usurp lines of work that will break down the barriers God has set between men and women. I am not in rebellion against legal statutes, nor the canons of well-established decency and refinement in feminine usage, and, finally, I am so inordinately proud of being a well-born Southern woman, with a full complement of honorable great-grandfathers and blue-blooded, stainless great-grandmothers that I have neither pretext nor inclination to revolt against mankind.[18]

Miss Evans was at this stage so violent a partisan that *A Speckled Bird* is not free from expressions of bitterness. "Nutwood is a mere shadow of older and happier days," says

[18] *A Speckled Bird* (New York, 1902), pp. 119 ff.

Mrs. Maurice in bidding farewell to Herriott. "Ichabod is printed all over the ruined South, and we live only to guard our graves." [19] As time passed and the tendencies she decried grew in force and number, the old Southern homestead took on a symbolical meaning for Miss Evans. It stood for permanence in a world of change, for fixed human relationships, just laws and proper customs against a welter of aberration and experiment then surging up. Thus Nutwood appeared:

> Outside conditions, social and domestic, had changed utterly; new canons prevailed; new canons of strange laxity rolled over the former dikes of purity, refinement, and decorum; but the turbid tide of up-to-date flippancy broke and ebbed from the tall iron gates of the house on the hill. Here decadence was excluded, and one coming into a long-closed mansion inhaled a vague haunting aroma, as if old furniture, glass, china, books, paintings and silver had been sprinkled with powdered sandalwood, lavender, and rose leaves blended with the subtle pervading atmosphere of hereditary social pride.[20]

Standing over these relics of a higher civilization she saw the Southern woman, a guardian vigilant and incapable of betrayal. Whatever the terms her men made with their conquerors, the Old South, with its personalities, its deference towards women, and its general social distinction was the world in which she cared to live, and she declined, as many of them actually did, even to go through the pretense of reconstruction. "To the truly typical Southern woman who survived the loss of family idols and her country's freedom, for which she had surrendered them, 'reconstruction,' political and social, was no more possible than the physical resurrection and return of slain thousands in Confederate graves all over the trampled and ruined South." [21] The mistress of

19 *Ibid.*, p. 34.
20 *Ibid.*, p. 246.
21 *Ibid.*, p. 14.

Nutwood shuts out agents of "union and reconstruction" as promptly as she would have excluded carriers of smallpox.

In further exposition of these views Miss Evans wrote her last novel, *Devota,* a work composed when she was at the advanced age of seventy-two. This develops in particular the thesis that it is treason for woman to desert her God-given sphere. Along with passionate arguments for a revival of family life, it contains tirades against socialism, humanitarianism, and all efforts to destroy the old standards. But the worldwide impulse to wipe out all distinctions, both those made by nature and those provided by social systems, was answering it with new and more radical theories of equalitarianism.

While Augusta Jane Evans was thus defending the institution of womanhood and the old-fashioned morality, Julia Magruder was producing a line of fiction the chief point of which was the superiority of Southern manners. A niece of the Confederate General "Prince John" Magruder, she grew up in Virginia, where her preference for Southern habits and attitudes was established, and although later she saw much of the great world, she remained conscious of her sectional character.

Her device was the simple one of bringing Southerners and Northerners together and exhibiting the difference in their reactions to situations. Her Southern protagonists are young ladies in a Northern environment, who surprise their supercilious Yankee hosts by solving problems which only a Southern background could prepare one to cope with, or by showing that Southern courtesy rests upon consideration for feelings rather than upon calculation of profit. Her first venture in this direction was significantly entitled *Across the Chasm* (1885). Its heroine is Margaret Trevennon, a young lady from a tiny community in Virginia, who goes to Washington to visit her fashionable married cousin, Mrs. Gaston Margault. Here she is shocked to discover that her cousin, who is in no sense a *parvenu*, thinks it necessary to consider her social engagements in terms of the prestige they will bring in the *haute monde*. This is disturbing to one to whom it is instinctive to associate with the right people, regardless of whether they are in a position to confer benefits.

> "I was only going to say that I thought a lady, born and reared, never had to think of anything like that," she remarked to Mrs. Margault one evening.
> "Like what?"
> "Where she is seen and whether her association will be considered correct. I thought it would all come of itself—that a lady would not be in danger of making mistakes of that sort, because what she did would be the natural outgrowth of what she was."
> "Those may be Southern ideas, but you'd not find them to answer here."
> "I don't know whether they are Southern ideas or not. I never knew they were ideas at all. Certainly I have never heard them formulated before, and I don't quite know how to express myself. They simply seem to me instincts." [22]

Other Southern visitors to Washington are made to appear equally ingenuous and to display an annoying indifference as to whether they are meeting the proper persons.

Miss Magruder, no less than her sentimental countryman Thomas Nelson Page, found inevitable the notion of wedding North and South through the marriage of a Northern man and a Southern woman. And so Margaret, after utilizing several opportunities to show her hosts their deficiency in natural courtesy, succumbs to the charm of her cousin's brilliant brother, and the novel closes with her exclaiming: "Doesn't it seem funny, such a Yankee and such a Rebel as you and I. Let us set an example by letting by-gones be by-gones, and shake hands across the bloody chasm." [23]

22 *Across the Chasm* (New York, 1885), p. 83.
23 *Ibid.*, p. 309.

The author employed a similar method of contrasting North and South in "Miss Ayr of Virginia." In this short story Miss Carter Ayr goes to visit her fashionable cousin in New York, only to find that Southerners are at a discount generally, and that her clothing, which had looked fine enough back home, moves her rich and stylish relatives to derision. She begins to win respect by displaying kinds of knowledge quite beyond the scope of town-bred people. Her relatives find, moreover, that though they have the means, she has the airs, and she irritates them by a presumably typical Southern indifference to money. "Carter Ayr," says one of them, outraged by her decision to reject the affluent Jim Stafford, "I'd like to know what you are thinking of and what you expect. You Southern people act as if you owned the earth." [24] But Carter, after delivering some pronouncements on the irrelevance of money to love, returns to marry her rustic fiancé in Virginia.

Light as they are, however, Miss Magruder's stories are sprinkled with tart criticisms of Southern manhood for what she regarded as its serious failings—indolence, and an absurd self-conceit which arose from nothing but a paucity of contacts with the world. Back in her little hamlet of Bassett, Margaret Trevennon could look about and recall "a system of things of which the inertia and the irresponsibleness that jarred upon her so, in the people around her, seemed the logical outgrowth." [25] She concluded that "servitude itself seems to me a nobler kind of life than idleness," [26] and she told her lazy Southern suitor, Charley Somers, "It isn't the first time I've advised you to take lessons from the Yankees." [27]

She had no patience with Southerners who felt that "a Southern man had better take the wrong way in any issue

24 *Miss Ayr of Virginia* (Chicago, 1896), p. 54.
25 *Ibid.*, p. 24.
26 *Ibid.*, p. 6.
27 *Across the Chasm*, p. 255.

than learn the right way from a Yankee," [28] and she wished above all to see a type who loved his own land best "because he had compared it with others, and not because he was ignorant of everything beyond it." [29] In young Alan Decourcy Miss Trevennon recognized a Southern man who "had had sufficient contact with the world to get rid of that colossal belief in himself and his own methods and manners, as the only commendable ones which she felt to be one of the chief failings of her countrymen." [30]

A few simple tales, in which Southern provincialism is scored, and Southern chivalry and idealism are praised, form Miss Magruder's contribution to the growing legend.

The state of Georgia was as prolific in sectional peacemakers as was Virginia in irreconcilables. Joel Chandler Harris has always been grouped with the exponents of the New South, largely because of his association with Evan P. Howell and especially with Henry W. Grady, whose celebrated oration "The New South" has been received as a general Southern recantation. But a full study of the writings of Harris reveals that his position is somewhat difficult to fix. Two things may be said of him with certainty: the first, that he was a strong opponent of sectionalism; and the second, that he lived long enough into the new era to perceive that a civilization whose every value is predicated upon profit and loss is not an unmixed blessing.

Harris grew up in the Reconstruction period in middle Georgia, a region "which was then, and is now the most democratic in the world," [31] with nothing in his antecedents or experience to give him a predilection for the old order. He could see little sense in the Civil War and less in the partisan

[28] *Ibid.*, p. 144.
[29] *Ibid.*
[30] *Ibid.*, p. 143.
[31] Joel Chandler Harris, *Gabriel Tolliver: A Story of Reconstruction* (New York, 1902), p. 95.

spirit which sought to fan its fires after 1865. As early as 1879 he was attacking sectionalism as a chief obstacle to the welfare of the nation:

> We do not regard this question of sectionalism as at all political in the usual acceptance of the term. We look upon it as a disaster of the most deadly aspect—a disease that slays the social instincts of the people and destroys commercial enterprise and national progress. We have protested against it, not as Georgians, or as Southerners, but as Americans.[32]

At the same time he was criticizing unceasingly the provincialism of Southern literature, which he thought productive of tendencies "preposterous in themselves," and "deadly in their effects upon literary art." [33] He attributed it to "the social and political isolation in which the South sought to preserve its peculiar property investment." [34]

Yet Harris recognized that the partisan spirit was fully as furious in the North as in the South, and he could not refrain from contrasting Southern statesmen of the old régime with the type of men whom the Republican ascendancy had placed in the saddle:

> It seems like a dream to remember the giants who grappled in intellectual contests in the Senate Chamber in Washington during the decade previous to secession, and to think of their shadows now. These men had principles, and they upheld them: after all, the best that could be said of them—the best that could be said of any man—is that they were honest. No Credit Mobilier manipulations clung to their skirts, and the "Art of Addition, Division, and Silence" was to them unknown.[35]

[32] Quoted in Julia Collier Harris (ed.), *Joel Chandler Harris, Editor and Essayist* (Chapel Hill, 1931), p. 41. From the Atlanta *Constitution*, December 6, 1879.

[33] *Ibid.*, p. 47. From the Atlanta *Constitution*, June 29, 1881.

[34] *Ibid.*, p. 44. From the Atlanta *Constitution*, November 3, 1879.

[35] *Ibid.*, p. 12. From a contribution of undetermined date in the Savannah *Morning News.*

With such remarks in mind, we may turn to the one novel in which Harris presented the issues of the postbellum settlement. In 1902, many years after he had won the plaudits of the nation with the unforgettable Uncle Remus, he wrote *Gabriel Tolliver: A Story of Reconstruction*. It is a work of very poor literary quality; its blurred characters, loose plot, and stale incidents leave it far below the comparable productions of Cable, Page, and Dixon. But the historian of the Southern mind will find highly interesting certain passages which express a now fully grown distrust of the new business civilization. It may not be without significance, moreover, that these are not always placed in the mouths of characters, but sometimes proceed from the author *ex cathedra*. The first chapter, for example, begins with a sermon-like paragraph which might well raise the shades of the clerical apologists:

> In all ages of the world and in all places, there are men of restless and superficial minds who mistake repose and serenity for stagnation: no doubt then, as now, the most awful sentence to be passed on a community was to say that it was not progressive. But when you examine into the matter, what is called progress is nothing more or less than the multiplication of the resources of those who, by means of dicker and barter, are trying all the time, to overreach the public and their fellows, in one way, and another. This sort of thing has now a double name; it is civilization, as well as progress, and those who take things as they find them in their morning newspaper, without going to the trouble to reflect for themselves, are no doubt duly impressed by terms large enough to fill both ear and mouth at one and the same time.[36]

Southern writers in the antebellum period had praised the superior sentimental values of Southern civilization, and there was widespread fear that these could not survive the advance of rationalism, science, and commerce. By the turn of

[36] *Gabriel Tolliver*, p. 18.

the century, Harris had become convinced that the fear was justified. As he declared in another part of *Gabriel Tolliver:*

> It has been demonstrated recently on some very wide fields of action that the atmosphere of commercialism is unfavorable to the growth of sentiments of an ideal character. That is why wise men, who believe in the finer issues of life, are inclined to be suspicious of what is loosely called civilization and progress, and doubtful of the theories of those who clothe themselves in the mantle of science.[37]

Apparently it had been brought home to Harris, as John Donald Wade has said, that the irreconcilables were in their blundering way right.[38] But not being given to self-deception, he could see nothing but an increase in this destructive spirit when he looked ahead. Near the close of the novel he makes Mrs. Claiborne dourly remark:

> You will have plenty of company in the money-grabbing business before long. I can see it now, and every time I think of it I feel sorry for our young men, yes, and our young women, and the long generations that are to come after them. In the course of a very few years you will find your business to be more respectable than any of the professions. You remember how, before the war, we used to sneer at the Yankees for their money-making proclivities? Well, it won't be very long before we'll beat them at their own game; and then our politicians will thrive, for each and all of them will have their principles dictated by a Shylock and his partners.[39]

When Gabriel Tolliver, after his escape from Federal detention, addresses the crowd at Halcyondale, he takes for his thesis the narrow and somewhat pragmatic question, "Why should a parcel of politicians turn us against a Government

[37] *Ibid.*, p. 111.
[38] "Profits and Losses in the Life of Joel Chandler Harris," *American Review*, I (April, 1933), p. 33.
[39] *Gabriel Tolliver*, p. 404.

under which we are compelled to live?" This was a statement
in brief of the whole issue. That the idea of union, apart
from its perversions and abuses, was tolerable most Southerners would have agreed. But now it seemed clear to Harris,
as to the disunionists of half a century before, that union was
a device through which the assault upon a civilization of
"higher sentimental values" was being carried to completion.
And it was not clear that acceptable compensations were
being made for the old chivalry, generosity, and romantic
idealism. However much he might abjure the false ideals and
the sectional preferences of Southern orthodoxy, he lived to
regret that the old spaciousness of life had flown, to be supplanted by the meaner, calculating spirit of commercialism.

The last member of the group with strong Southern bias
was Thomas Dixon. Nearly forty years had elapsed since the
close of civil strife, and the Spanish-American War—which
saw the appointment of "Fighting Joe" Wheeler to a major
generalship in the United States Army—had found the two
sections united against a foreign enemy, when Dixon undertook to tell the story of Reconstruction from the extreme
Southern point of view. Thomas Nelson Page had attempted
the task, but his desire to have the North recognize the worth
of the Virginia gentleman, and his gingerly method of handling both personalities and incidents, kept him from coming
to grips with the subject. Both James Lane Allen and Grace
King had in the same period touched on the many difficulties
of adjustment, but it was reserved for Dixon to present the
struggle as a conflict of good against unvarnished evil.

In view of Dixon's early life, one might have expected a
different course. He was a native of North Carolina, that
peculiar Southern state, so valiant to defend the old order
while there seemed a chance of saving it and so enterprising
to get on with the new once its inevitability became apparent. He was not unacquainted with the North moreover, for

as a minister he had held pastorates in both Boston and New York. Neither was his fiction the work of youthful impulse; at a fairly young age, it is reported, he had resolved not to publish until he had "come to forty year," and he was in fact thirty-seven when he began his Reconstruction trilogy with *The Leopard's Spots: A Romance of the White Man's Burden.*

Teeming with characters who embody the conflicting forces of the time, this novel begins with the surrender of Lee's army and ends with that day years later when the white people of North Carolina, "the typical American democracy," wrest the government of their state from the Negroes and their unscrupulous allies. Unquestionably the dominant figure is the Reverend John Durham, an admirably conceived representative of the conservative Southern clergy, for whom Dixon had the models of R. L. Dabney, A. T. Bledsoe, and Moses Hoge. The Reverend Mr. Durham is a traditional Southerner who believes that society is instituted by God; and he has no more notion of retreating before the dogmas of the new radicalism than he has of yielding to the devil.

> As a preacher he spoke with authority. He was narrow and dogmatic in his interpretation of the Bible, but his very narrowness and dogmatism were his flesh and blood, elements of his power. He simply announced the Truth. The wise received it. The fools rejected it and were damned. That was all there was to it.[40]

The feeling of righteousness made him hard, and when a Boston lady reformer with time and money on her hands sought his aid towards establishing a school for the freedmen, she received a statement of his views which did not leave much room for customary Southern politeness:

> "Your mission is to teach crack-brained theories of social and political equality to four millions of ignorant negroes, some of

[40] *The Leopard's Spots* (New York, 1902), p. 40.

whom are but fifty years removed from the savagery of the African jungles. Your work is to separate and alienate the negroes from their former masters who can be their only real friends and guardians. Your work is to sow the dragon's teeth of an impossible social order that will bring forth its harvest of blood for our children."

He paused for a moment, and suddenly facing her, continued, "I should like to help the cause you have at heart; and the most effective service I could render it now would be to box you up in a glass cage, such as are used for rattlesnakes, and ship you back to Boston." [41]

Throughout the vicissitudes of this indescribable era the Reverend John Durham remains the voice of the white South, opposing reason to ignorant fanaticism and counselling his people against despair.

In the novel one encounters the Negro, bewildered and pathetic, expecting that the new freedom will bring "eternal rest, not work." [42] He is the tool of crafty scalawags, who say, "He thinks he's going to heaven, but we'll ride him all the way up to the gate and hitch him on the outside." [43] The Ku Klux Klan is brought in as a "Law and Order League" and credited with having ended chaos in the hapless South in a brief matter of weeks.

But in addition to these incidents, which reflect the political passions of the hour, one finds observations on the place of the South in the nation profounder than those ordinarily incorporated in fiction. For Dixon saw the South as the great flywheel of all American society, temporarily worsted in its contest with Northern radicalism, but destined to survive and to combat the possibly more insidious radicalism of the future. He makes the Reverend Mr. Durham say to a deacon from Boston, come down to entice him to a Northern pastorate:

41 *Ibid.,* pp. 46-47.
42 *Ibid.,* p. 69.
43 *Ibid.,* p. 106.

I've studied your great cities. Believe me the South is worth saving. Against a possible day when a flood of foreign anarchy threatens the foundations of the Republic and men shall laugh at the faiths of your fathers, and undigested wealth beyond the dreams of avarice rots your society until it mocks at honor, love, and God—against that day we will preserve the South.[44]

But deeper and more meaningful than this is the doctrine of particularism, which lies at the bottom of his choice. This teaches that internationalism and cosmopolitanism are but disguises for those who have no true character. Thus Charles Gaston, reviewing the program of his party before an excited political convention, declares:

I am in a sense narrow and provincial. I love mine own people. Their past is mine, their present mine, their future is a divine trust. I hate the dishwater of modern world citizenship. A shallow cosmopolitanism is the mask of death for the individual. It is the froth of civilization, as crime is its dregs. The true citizen of the world loves his country.[45]

He goes on to rejoice that the South "has sneered at paper-made policies, and scorned public opinion," that she is "old-fashioned, medieval, provincial, worshipping the dead, and raising children rather than making money," that she is never found "knowing her own interests, but living her own life in her own way." [46] It is a defiant address, celebrating every feature of Southern individualism and recalcitrance even more boldly than the political apologists had done, and in a sense focussing the meaning of a powerful propaganda novel.

The story of *The Leopard's Spots* is so strong in its implications that the author felt it necessary to provide an historical note in which he affirmed that the incidents narrated

44 *Ibid.*, p. 334.
45 *Ibid.*, p. 441.
46 *Ibid.*

either were drawn from authentic records or had come within his personal knowledge, and that the only liberty he had taken was "to tone down the facts to make them credible in fiction." [47] Even so they brought him hundreds of letters of inquiry.

Each member of the trilogy, however, is weaker than its predecessor both as propaganda and as literature. *The Leopard's Spots* concerns chiefly the Negro in politics; *The Clansman*, which comes next, deals with the operations of the Invisible Empire. Among its characters are Lincoln, Grant, Johnson, Charles Sumner, Ben Butler, and "The Hon. Austin Stoneman," a thin disguise for Thaddeus Stevens, the arch-enemy of Southern civilization. To preserve the basic conflict, Dixon brings Stoneman South for his health, where the old man, though responsive to Southern kindness, remains implacable in his decision to force Negro supremacy. But events make a mockery of his decision. His daughter falls in love with the leader of the Ku Klux Klan; his son narrowly misses execution for killing a Negro, and in a final passage unsurpassable for melodrama the evil genius of Northern radicalism himself repents, blaming his course on a desire for personal vengeance and the blandishments of a mulatto mistress.[48] In some scenes, nevertheless, the melodrama derives from the kind of truth which exceeds fiction; the suicide of Mrs. Lenoir and her daughter, who leap hand-in-hand from a precipice after the latter has been violated by a Negro, was based on an acutal occurrence in the vicinity.[49]

The Clansman devotes less space than its forerunner to a citation of Southern virtues, but is careful to make the point that the Ku Klux Klan, instead of being a symbol of lawlessness, is on the contrary an expression of Southern determination to have law and order. The Southerner is described

---

[47] *The Bookman*, XX (February, 1905), p. 500.
[48] *The Clansman* (New York, 1905), p. 371.
[49] *The Bookman, loc. cit.*

as "an ultraconservative, and the last man on earth to become a revolutionist." [50] That was why he battled for the Constitution against Yankees, who had denounced it as a covenant with hell.

The Traitor presents the dissolution of the original Klan, whose titular head was Nathan Bedford Forrest, and its reorganization by less responsible elements for irregular purposes. The political theme is here too slight to support the novel, which turns into a story of the romance of John Graham, a member of the Klan loyal to its first purposes, and Stella Butler, the daughter of a scalawag judge. By this time Dixon had given ample statement to his thesis, and the reader misses the vigor and passion of *The Leopard's Spots*.

Although they will not stand the test of close inspection as literature, these three novels must be remembered for their influence in molding the mind of the time. Shrewd observers back in the sixties had known that there was in the North a large body of people who responded to the ideals for which the South declared it was fighting. The general reception accorded *The Leopard's Spots* was the first indication that the South might yet win the ideological battle. The fact that a work of such militant spirit could be widely read in the North was a sign that the old division into rebel and loyalist, or Bourbon and democrat was weakening under the tendency to look more closely at the social complex.

2. *The Beginnings of Critical Realism*

While this battle was in progress, however, there was developing in other quarters a spirit of criticism, for the Reconstruction South produced also a group of writers of fiction whose adherence to Southern ideals was not unqualified.

50 *The Clansman*, p. 277.

These were, for the most part, artists who loved the Old South, and the remnants of it still surviving, for its color, romance, charm, and unreasonableness, but who were continuously disturbed by an inner voice of social justice. One finds in their work sympathetic pictures of the vanishing order and a general endorsement of those virtues on which the South prided itself, but he finds also many uneasy questions, either direct or implied. All were consciously Southern, and all seem to have felt that reality subsists in the particularities which their section furnished so abundantly. Yet an impulse to drop the inherited ideology and to examine the claims of the South in terms of more modern conceptions deflected to some extent the work of each. They saw that Southern society was filled with tragedies, but they felt that Reconstruction, though painful and destructive of much good, was an inevitable adjustment to realities. George W. Cable and James Lane Allen were the chief representatives of this school, to which Grace King, Charles Egbert Craddock, and John Fox in a measure belong. Of the five, Cable and Allen ended their lives in self-imposed exile in the North, and the other three, after touching on the seemingly unresolvable conflicts in their section, chose to immerse themselves in local color.

Cable was the first to discover basic inconsistencies in the conventional Southern attitude. Descended on the one side of German, and on the other of New England Puritan ancestry, he grew up in New Orleans a child of the place, absorbing the ideals and beliefs of a multi-racial community. At nineteen he joined the Fourth Mississippi Cavalry, fought skillfully, and suffered a severe wound. During his life in the army he found many hours for serious study and after his return to New Orleans some clever contributions to the *Picayune* won him a position on the staff of that paper. He held this until conscientious objection to Sunday drama led him to refuse an assignment to write theatrical criticism.

This incident marks the first appearance of an intense moral earnestness, which is the focus of much of his fiction, and which drove him to grapple with the tremendous and complicated problem of the Negro. It resulted eventually in his flight from the Deep South to Northampton, Massachusetts, where strictures upon the Southern whites would not incur ostracism. Other Southerners had felt the stifling effect of creeds unanimously supported. Mark Twain, for example, after two weeks of inglorious service with the Confederate army, fled West, and in his career as a writer thereafter, never ceased to satirize anything that could be identified with the romantic Old South. But Cable made the experiment of staying home to cope with the problem *in esse,* not with the idea of achieving a working compromise, but with the object of demonstrating a theory of race relations which should endure because it was based on fixed principles.

It is indicative of Cable's Puritan conscience that he was first made thoughtful by the easy and evasive reasoning with which some Southern newspapers were accepting the result of the war. He had gone into what he considered a struggle for principle; if the principle was right last year, it could not be wrong this year merely because one side had made more cannon and mustered more men than the other. Such reflections led him to a critical study of the issues of the conflict, and from this he passed to a study of that highly surcharged subject, the general position of the Negro in the South.

Cable's first stories, which appeared in book form under the title *Old Creole Days,* revealed him especially sensitive to the curious relationships produced by mixed blood in Louisiana. Certainly no student of human justice could overlook the problems posed by that New Orleans caste known as the quadroons. Here was a group of women possessing one quarter part of Negro blood, yet in whom the African inheritance was so little perceptible that they often more than measured up to the Caucasian standard of attractiveness. Cable noted their faultlessness of feature, their perfection of form, their varied styles of beauty,—for there were even pure Caucasian blondes among them,—their fascinating manners, their sparkling vivacity, their chaste and pretty wit, their grace in the dance, their modest propriety, their taste and elegance in dress. In the gentlest and most poetic sense they were indeed the sirens of this land, where it seemed "always afternoon"—a momentary triumph of an Arcadian over a Christian civilization, so beautiful and so seductive that it became the subject of special chapters by writers of the day more original than correct as social philosophers.[51]

In consequence they were much sought after by the pure-blooded aristocrats of the community, but no alliance with them could receive the sanction of law or the approval of society. Although they were capable of every reciprocation of love and faithfulness, and often exhibited life-long loyalties to their white paramours, a race discrimination of cast-iron rigidity denied them acknowledgement and opportunity. Cable first stirred the resentment of his fellow townsmen by alluding to their sense of hopelessness, and to the quiet, long-enduring tragedies which were their lives. Madame Delphine dramatizes the situation with a flare-up of rebellion when she asks the priest why her daughter cannot make a legal marriage.

"Why did they make that law?" he replies. "Well, they made it to keep the two races separate."

Madame Delphine startled the speaker with a loud, harsh, angry laugh. Fire came into her eyes, and her lips curled with scorn. "Then they made a lie, Père Jerome! Separate! No-o-o! They do not want to keep us separated; no, no! But they do want to keep us despised."

She laid her hand on her heart, and frowned upward with physical pain. "But very well! from which race do they want to keep my daughter separate? She is seven parts white. The law

51 *Old Creole Days* (New York, 1927), p. 15.

did not stop her from being that; and now, when she wants to be a white man's good and honest wife, shall the law stop her? Oh, no."

She rose up, "No; I will tell you what that law is made for. It is made to—punish—my—child—for—not—choosing—her—father! Père Jerome—my God, what a law." [52]

In "Tite Paulette" a mother says to her daughter, who is known throughout the neighborhood for her rare beauty: "You will be lonely, lonely all your poor life long. There's no place in the world for us poor women. I wish we were either black or white." [53]

The strong reaction which met these overt expressions of sympathy drove Cable into a series of highly interesting social studies, which even today must rank among the solid contributions to the literature of the great race problem. The first of them, *The Creoles of Louisiana* (1884), was a fairly full examination of those people who have maintained a Latin civilization in their part of the continental United States. In the following year, however, he boldly attacked the more serious theme of the Negro in *The Silent South*. This is the most searching and the most outspoken analysis of the great race question presented up to this time by a Southerner, if we except the sociologists of the antebellum period, who were equally frank with another point of view. On many of these issues raised by Reconstruction Cable agreed with his countrymen. He felt that the carpetbaggers had deserved their fate; [54] and he even believed that the Negro, in comparison with the cultivated white man, was an inferior being; but he stoutly maintained that the perpetual state of pupilage contemplated for the Negro by the Southern whites would prove an injustice to him and an injury to themselves. It would mean for the South a frozen solidity in politics, and

52 *Ibid.*, p. 62.
53 *Ibid.*, p. 221.
54 *The Silent South* (New York, 1885), p. 97.

for its people evasions, dishonesties, and all the corruptions which proceed from an attempt to conceal a moral enormity.

"Social equality," he said peremptorily, "is a fool's dream." [55] It is made impossible not only by such palpable differences as color and feature, but also by those infinite sources of gradations recognized as operative among men. "Social equality can never exist where a community, numerous enough to assert itself, is actuated, as every civilized community is, by an intellectual and a moral ambition." [56] Civil rights, on the other hand, are different things: they are every man's birthright, and the conferring of them upon the Negro would not destroy the principle of segregation. The South could give the Negro simple justice by according him these and still retain the social divisions it had always preferred. Five years later Cable returned to the subject in a yet more positive frame of mind. *The Negro Question* (1890) is a re-exposition of the status of the race, and an affirmation that despite the revolution wrought by the North, the South still preserved the slaveholder's attitude toward the blacks.

It is not surprising in view of his experience as a Confederate soldier, his encounters with Southern sensibility in the matter of mixed blood, and his frank espousal of Negro rights that Cable should produce one of the few realistic novels about Reconstruction. In *John March, Southerner* (1894), the reader finds the sharp clash of character, the divergence of interests, and the honest confusion of mind naturally to be expected of a people who must make a great transition at the same hour in which they are endeavoring to rebuild a ruined country. The setting is Suez, a small county seat and shipping port on the fringe of the mountains, where the planter, the Negro, the hillbilly, and the Northern émigré mingle in colorful contrast.

55 *Ibid.*, p. 54.
56 *Ibid.*

Never very successful at describing characters in the full, Cable here apparently designed them to represent prevailing points of view; yet it may be said that what they lack in round human qualities is compensated for by the fierceness of the political passions they embody. Major Garnet is the unreconstructed Southerner, who cannot honestly regret the overthrow of slavery, but who feels that its passing confronts the white race with new and scarcely less serious problems in dealing with the black man. "In the depths of a soldier's sorrow for the cause he loved and lost, there had been the one consolation that the unasked for freedom so stupidly thrust upon these poor slaves was in certain respects an emancipation of their masters." [57] He lies awake at night to ponder the destiny of "the whole Southern world, with its two distinct divisions—the shining upper—the dark nether—," and at length he concludes that "a man who, taking all the new risks, still taught these poor, base, dangerous creatures to keep the only place they could keep with safety to themselves or their superiors, was to them the only truly merciful man." [58] Another member of the unreconstructed element is "Professor" Pettigrew, an unhappy Virginian in exile, for whom "the premises and maxims of religion were refuted by the outcome of the war." [59]

As foil to Major Garnet, there is General Launcelot Halliday, a reconstructed Southerner. He comes home bringing a Yankee from the very command to which he surrendered and gives such signs of having "harmonized" and "accepted the situation" that even his oldest friends are outraged. The General meets so much disapproval that he composes a sententious letter to the press about those "who, when their tree has been cut down even with the ground, will try to sit in the shade of the stump," and who "now that slavery is

[57] *John March, Southerner* (New York, 1918), p. 38.
[58] *Ibid.*, p. 40.
[59] *Ibid.*, p. 195.

gone, still cling to a civil order based on the old plantation
system." [60] As if this were not enough, he works with the
freedmen and brings into the local political struggles the
same Southern stubbornness and pride with which he battled
the Yankees.

There are numerous Negro characters, together with a
large amount of Negro dialogue, most of which cannot be
taken as flattering the intelligence or promoting the political ambitions of the race. It is humorous, genial, and sprinkled with those malapropisms into which the Negro is likely
to fall when striving to be impressive. Clearly Cable did not
continue his argument for the Negro by making him a political or social hero, but he did point out the irrationality of the
whites' position in regarding the Negroes as so many indistinguishable work animals.

> On the way back, while Garnet explained to Mr. Gamble, the
> heavier guest, why negroes had to be treated not as individuals
> but as a class, John had been telling Mr. Fair why it was wise
> to treat chickens not as a class, but as individuals, and had
> mentioned the names and personal idiosyncrasies of the favor-
> ites of the flock.[61]

Throughout the novel the general scuffling of Reconstruction is in progress, as "a rain of pitch and ashes" showers
down upon the unhappy South. The freedmen are first confused and then misled; communities live in dread of con-
certed Negro action; bluecoats clatter through the streets on
their errand of keeping the South peaceful and "loyal"; and
white men of social station ride hooded through the night,
whipping and killing. Despite its lack of consecutive narrative *John March* gives a better picture of the years of chaos
than other novels written with neater plots and more obvious
professions of sympathy.

60 *Ibid.*, p. 51.
61 *Ibid.*, p. 83.

Cable continued his theme of North-South polarity by taking some inhabitants of Suez north of the Mason-Dixon line, but his carelessness about settings and the disconnected nature of the story prevent a fruitful result. The Southerners search their hearts to discover why they are "different" and conclude that it is a spiritual rather than a physical South which makes them a distinct people. John March and Barbara Garnet muse together as the train speeds along:

> "It's not," returned March, "a South of climate, like the Yankee's Florida. It's a certain ungeographical South-within-the-South—as portable and as intangible as—as—"
>
> "As our souls within our bodies," interposed Barbara.
>
> "You've said it exactly. It's a sort of something—social, civil, political, economic—"
>
> "Romantic?"
>
> "Yes, romantic! Something that makes—"
>
> "No land like Dixie the wide world over."

Cable was unique in possessing both the New Englander's conscience and the Southerner's complexity of attitude. The South which he depicted, and which afterwards he had to contend against, was a real South, but the broad ethical generalizations on which he based his argumentative writings were typical of the outsider and explain his eventual exile. From another point of view it might be said that Cable was the South's liberal self speaking, but a self too inexperienced, harassed, and uncertain to prevail generally against passion and exigency, more especially at a time when the public mind, both North and South, was not prepared to accept realities.

James Lane Allen is the most interesting example of this group, for he illustrates in the progress of his thought a transition from the genteel, romantic view of the world to which his generation was born to an acceptance of rationalism and nineteenth-century science. A native of the Blue

Grass region of Kentucky, he grew up in one of the garden spots of the globe, the beauty and fertility of which are said to have made the first settlers exclaim that Heaven could only be another Kentucky. Here he attended Transylvania University, whose corridors had already echoed to the footsteps of Jefferson Davis, Stephen Austin, Thomas Holley Chivers, and Albert Taylor Bledsoe. After a short career as a teacher, he applied himself seriously to writing, caught by the romantic possibilities of Lexington, gracious "Athens of the West," and the surrounding Blue Grass countryside. He performed a filial service by describing this section in *The Blue Grass Region of Kentucky,* and he was to use it as an idyllic backdrop for most of his stories. But this preoccupation with the charm and softness of Kentucky's agrarian paradise was only the first step of a course which led him finally to accept the bleak necessities of naturalism.

In 1891, before he had become absorbed in the problems presented by the new science, before indeed he had peered beneath the mask of conventional human relationships, he published *Flute and Violin,* a series of sketches treating of Kentucky in sentimental, romantic vein. Among them "Two Gentlemen of Kentucky" unfolds in the story of contrasted lives central to Kentucky's change from a Garden of Eden supported by slavery into the new state of confused and uncertain trends, a change so great that survivors of the old order were left baffled and lonely, and members of the new were projected beyond any sympathy with the beliefs of their forebears. Colonel Romulus Fields is a character drawn to represent those landed gentlemen of Kentucky, the political and social leaders of their day, whose position was so much altered by the war that they left their native acres and moved to town, there to lead "idle, useless lives." He is attended by Peter Cotton, an ex-slave and the very nonpareil of a devoted darkey.

Colonel Fields had taken no part in the conflict, but its cruel hatreds, nowhere more fierce than in the border states, had come to blight a life hitherto innocent of the harsher human passions. His younger brother had early fallen in battle; his saintly mother had perished from grief over the loss; political differences estranged him from the family of his sister; and all of his servants except the faithful Peter decamped: thus did the war break and scatter to the winds fixed human relationships, dividing the populace "as the false mother would have severed the child."

Because destiny had formed Colonel Fields to be "an ornament in the barbaric temple of human bondage," he was left without a vocation when that temple was destroyed. Feeling that the world was slipping from him, he made pathetic attempts to renew his contact with reality. He hung about Lexington's Cheapside and conversed with farmers; he opened a hardware store in order that he might enjoy the society of his customers; he even tried politics, only to be convinced that "he had no part in the present." Peter Cotton, too, was unable to make the adaptations required by the age. When Colonel Fields informed him that under the new dispensation he was obligated to pay him a salary, the Negro replied truthfully that he had "no use fur no salary." [62] He served as minister of a congregation, which asked him to resign because he wore Colonel Fields' second-hand clothing and "preached in the old-fashioned way." [63] In Allen's elegant image: "The sun of their day had indeed long since set, but like twin clouds lifted high and motionless into some gray quarter of the twilight skies, they were still radiant with the glow of the invisible orb." [64] When Colonel Fields inquired of Peter whether he thought they could pass as repre-

62 *Flute and Violin* (New York, 1925), p. 188.
63 *Ibid.*, p. 117.
64 *Ibid.*, p. 119.

sentatives of the New South, the philosophic Negro summed up the situation by saying, "We got to pass for what we wuz." [65]

The gulf between the generations appears again in "Sister Dolorosa," another story from this collection. The hero is Gordon Helm, a young man of good extraction who comes into his inheritance just at a time when his society is being forced "to the discovery of new ideals." [66] More explicitly, this meant "putting into his relationship with his fellow-creatures an added sense of helpfulness, a broader sense of justice, and a certain energy of leadership in all things that make for purer, higher, human life." [67]

In many passages such as these one sees Allen drifting slowly into sympathy with the new age, speaking a good word for what was noble in the past, but displaying an increasing intolerance with its narrowness and pretentiousness. With *The Reign of Law*, published in 1900, he definitely allied himself against traditionalism, and in doing so aroused considerable hostility in the local community.

The Reign of Law is one of the unique books of Southern fiction; bringing in nineteenth-century biological science to shatter the earlier view of man and his position in the universe, it is a wholly unexpected novel to come from a purveyor of the old romance. It recounts the histories of two creatures of the great transition, but to the background of social ferment present in all Reconstruction novels it adds an intellectual ferment. One of the characters is David, son of a small Kentucky hemp farmer, who upon hearing that an institution of higher learning is to be established in Lexington —an institution which shall stand in the borderland, knowing neither North nor South, a symbol that "the animosities were over, the humanities re-begun—" determines to acquire an

65 *Ibid.*, p. 127.
66 *Ibid.*, p. 204.
67 *Ibid.*, p. 203.

education. With the proceeds of two years' labor in the hemp fields, David goes up to Morrison College, filled with that supreme reverence for learning found only in the uniniti- ated. All goes well until he begins to visit the various churches of the city and finds each opposed to each, and each maintaining its position on grounds adduced from Apostolic Christianity. Tortured by doubt, David seeks out his pastor, only to be met by coldness, incomprehension, and scorn. This is the beginning of a course which can have but one end. Doubt leads to inquiry, and soon he is reading the works of the exponents of the new theory of evolution, which tell him that the world runs according to scientific law and not ac- cording to the whims of a capricious deity. When he furtively opened his copy of *The Origin of Species,* he felt that "It was the first time in his life that he had ever encountered outside of the Bible a mind of the highest order." [68] Summoned be- fore a committee to explain his irregular conduct, the best he could say was, "Lord, I believe, help thou mine unbelief." Allen goes somewhat out of his way to connect this inquisi- torial body with the religious persecutors of all ages, includ- ing those who made use of fagot, rope, and rack.

David returned home, confessed to his outraged and heart- broken parents, for whom his apostasy was a sign of failure, and sank back into the inarticulate and meaningless life of a rural laborer.

Later in the novel he meets Gabriella, who had come from the other half of Kentucky life. She was one of those "penni- less and unrecognized wards of the Federal government," [69] whose portion in life had been swept away by war and eman- cipation. Born in a big white house in Lexington, brought up to expect a life made easy by income from property, she, like numberless other Southern girls, found herself left neces- sitous by a vast social upheaval:

68 *The Reign of Law* (New York, 1900), p. 119.
69 *Ibid.,* p. 259.

All that could be most luxurious and splendid in Kentucky during the last deep, rich years of the old social order, was Gabriella's: the extravagance, the gayety, the pride, the lovely manners, the selfishness and cruelty in its terrible, unconscious, and narrow way, the false ideals, the aristocratic virtues. Then it was that, overspreading land and people, lay the full autumn of that sowing, which had moved silently on its way toward its fateful fruits for over fifty years. Everything was ripe, sweet, mellow, dropping, turning rotten.[70]

Instill into one group of people the idea of the right of self-government and the idea that a man may do what he will with his own until these become passions; and instill into another the idea of nationalism and the idea that all slave-holding societies are morally abominable until these two become passions; bring these two groups into collision so that a resolution of opposites is hammered out by war, and one sees what happened to the two parts of the American Union in 1861-65. Gabriella, "one little girl living in Lexington, Kentucky," had her own task of coping with this awful settlement. Too proud to adopt the recourses familiar to an aristocracy after its economic support is withdrawn, she procured a teacher's certificate and went into the country to take charge of a small school, feeling that the farther she travelled from the Lexington she had known in happier days, the easier would be her spirit. Like Dandridge Mountjoy in Ellen Glasgow's *The Battle-Ground,* only after she had been discarded by the society into which she had been born did she discover how cruel it could be. In the country she found David, and after some meetings which give him a chance to unfold his newly acquired scientific view of the world, they decide on a life together. In a final bitter touch Allen makes David conclude that he must leave Kentucky and go North: "I must be where people think as I do." [71] But there is con-

70 *Ibid.,* p. 255.
71 *Ibid.,* p. 379.

solation in the thought that "The whole world will believe in evolution before I am an old man." [72] And with this, the son of a poor farmer, defeated by traditional theology, and the daughter of a proud aristocracy, who had to shoulder the defeat brought on by its arrogance and presumption, depart to find a new life in a new atmosphere.

Allen himself, having offended his local public even more deeply by exploring the psychology of marital incompatibility, moved to New York City, where he spent the latter part of his life away from the scenes which had first allured his imagination.

Perhaps the best historian of the breakup of the old class system was Grace King, of Louisiana. Born into the antebellum New Orleans aristocracy, she received a fashionable education of the French mode at the Institut St. Louis. But her family was impoverished by the war, and the New Orleans she knew was a city of *nouveaux pauvres,* in which, as she was to remark in *Balcony Stories,* typewriting girls were as numerous as heiresses had formerly been. All about her she saw pitiful attempts to keep up the forms and grandeurs of the old régime, and many of her stories are developed around incidents which tell of the transition from patrician splendor to the plebeian level of life.

There is the tale of Marie Motte, whose father had been killed in the war and whose mother shortly thereafter died. For thirteen years she had been kept at the aristocratic Institut St. Denis supposedly by the charity of an uncle. But upon her graduation it is revealed that her true benefactor had been Marcelite, an ex-slave of the family, who had earned sufficient money as a hairdresser to give her mistress the kind of education a young lady of station should have.

The lords of the old society are everywhere cast low. In "The Old Lady's Restoration" an aged *grande dame* is shown

[72] *Ibid.*

tottering down Royal Street, where she sells to an antique shop the remaining valuables of a disappearing estate. In "La Grande Demoiselle," Idalie Sainte Foy Mortemart des Islets, who had grown up on a sugar plantation in something approaching oriental luxury, becomes after the war a teacher in a public school, hiding her face from the world by a veil, until she is found and married by "old Champigny," who himself "dwelled in the wretched little cabin that replaced his former home." [73] Most poignant of all is the story of "Bonne Maman." Struck to the heart by the defeat of her country, and unable to learn the methods of business, the heroine loses the last acre of her possessions. "They came in a royal grant; they went in a royal cause. There were law quibbles; but was she one to lose a creed to grovel for coppers?" [74] Accordingly she decides, "As the men fought, let the women suffer against overwhelming odds." [75] She seeks out an old slave cabin in the quadroon section of New Orleans and lives a recluse until her death. She forwent all amelioration of her lot, because she was convinced that this was the life to which she was committed "by fate and by principle." [76]

Throughout her stories, as an omen of the South's distraught future, there is the rise of the hitherto unrecognized classes to power and leadership. The aristocrats are outraged by the thought that the Institut St. Denis will be taken over by Madame Joubert, who, it was complained, "had not a single qualification, nothing, except an education." [77] Morris Frank, the son of a despised German overseer, rescues the abandoned St. Marie Plantation, becomes a respected part owner, and leads the state in yield of sugar cane. "That is the

[73] *Balcony Stories* (New York, 1892), p. 32.
[74] *Tales of a Time and Place* (New York, 1892), p. 86.
[75] *Ibid.*, p. 87.
[76] *Ibid.*
[77] *Monsieur Motte* (New York, 1888), p. 168.

way with those revolutionnaires," says the indignant Tante
Pauline in "The Drama of an Evening." "They come from
the depths; not from the bourgeoisie, my dear, but from the
people,—the people." [78]

Miss King had a pervasive sense of irony, and the misfortunes which fell upon her class in the South are made to
appear but specimens of those reversals which capricious destiny deals out to everyone. Life has a way of mocking expectations. Says a speaker in "Monsieur Motte":

> Look at our schoolmates: not one has turned out as she ex-
> pected. Those who had a vocation to lead religious lives, who
> would be nothing but nuns, they were the first ones married
> and having children christened. Those who were ready to fall
> in love with every new tenor at the opera, they became *de-
> votés*. Those who cared only for money fell in love with poor
> men; and those who made their lives a poem with love for the
> hero,—they married money.[79]

Such disposition to see social transformations in a larger pattern gave her a status somewhat above that of the mere local
colorist. Though lacking in intensity and profundity, Miss
King composed thoughtful and sometimes witty stories of the
transition, and she told them with an objectivity which divides her from the apologists.

A mixed attitude toward Southern institutions, compara-
ble with that of Cable and Allen, is found also in Charles
Egbert Craddock, whose criticism tends on the whole to be
more incisive than theirs. Although interested mainly in the
local color afforded by the Tennessee mountains, she took a
Reconstruction theme for her novel *Where the Battle was
Fought*. The hero of this tale is Captain Estwicke, a Southern
Unionist, and the chief Confederate actor, General Vayne,

[78] *Ibid.*, p. 222.
[79] *Ibid.*, p. 158.

narrowly misses being a comic figure. There is satire in her description of the latter, who covers up a lack of business capacity with the Southern habit of lofty speech. He holds everything up to a "moral magnifying glass." Thus "In the rickety court-house in the village of Chattalla, five miles out there to the south, General Vayne beheld a temple of justice. He translated an office-holder as the sworn servant of the people. The state was this great commonwealth, and its seal was a proud escutcheon. A fall in cotton struck him as a blow to the commerce of the world. From an adverse political fortune he augured the swift ruin of the country." [80] Even when he is in private conversation, "His method of enunciation might suggest to the literary mind the profuse use of capital letters." A guest in his home is likely to be addressed with rotund periods such as "Conservatism, sir, is the moral centripetal force that curbs the flighty world." It is a cruel but probably just remark which Maurice Brennett makes of the General as he watches him holding an audience spellbound in the town square: "If that man had even a modicum of common sense, he could do anything—anything." [81]

Nor was she disposed to grow sentimental over the South's adherence to departed glories. She describes the loafers congregated about the square in the morning, rehearsing incidents of the war until even the language of their narrative becomes cliché. Overhearing them, one could realize "that all their interest lay in the past, and that they looked upon the future as only capable of furnishing a series of meagre and supplemental episodes." [82] A feminine impatience with the lack of initiative on the part of Southern men, visible too in Julia Magruder, shows in many passages of this work, and stamps Miss Murfree as at least a partial realist.

80 *Where the Battle was Fought* (Boston, 1892), p. 4. Craddock is, of course, Mary Noailles Murfree.

81 *Ibid.*, p. 284.

82 *Ibid.*, p. 174.

John Fox, Jr., presents an ambiguous case. Little concerned with the issues of the conflict, he apparently arrived at the conclusion, satisfactory to the sentimental on both sides, that the North deserved the victory and the South deserved the glory. *The Little Shepherd of Kingdom Come,* his one novel dealing with the Civil War, describes without a trace of partisan bias the struggle as it was fought out in Kentucky. Chadwick Buford, the central character, like mountaineers from most of the Appalachian area, sides with the Union. But the ground of his decision is not made very specific, and he moves through the story a colorless embodiment of duty while his friends and benefactors, having taken the Confederate side, monopolize the glamor. Indeed, John Hunt Morgan becomes the hero of this novel in the same perverse way that Satan does of *Paradise Lost,* and it is the rebel soldiers who win the encomiums. "They were born fighters," Fox wrote in his chapter on "Morgan's Men":

> a spirit of emulation induced them to learn the drill; pride and patriotism kept them true and patient to the last, but they could not be made by punishment, or the fear of it, into machines. They read their chance of success, not in opposing numbers, but in the character and reputation of their commanders, who in turn, believed, as a rule, that "the unthinking automaton, formed by routine and punishment, could no more stand before the high-strung young soldier of brains and good blood, and some practice and knowledge of warfare, than a tree could resist a stroke of lightning." [83]

With this kind of introduction, the blue-blooded Kentuckians dash from state to state and perform all the spectacular actions.

At a dinner given in Lexington in 1860 Chad had heard a brilliant lawyer say: "The struggle was written in the Consti-

[83] *The Little Shepherd of Kingdom Come* (New York, 1909), p. 276.

tution. The framers evaded it. Logic leads one way as well as another and no man can logically blame another for the way he goes." [84] And when he determines to leave his friends and don the blue, he is not conscious of sharing the prevalent animosities, least of all those generated by slavery. He had the typical mountaineer's attitude toward the Negro. "To him slaves were hewers of wood and drawers of water. The Lord had made them so, and the Bible said it was right." [85]

He went into the war in response to an older loyalty, identified with the spirit of '76, and having fought gallantly and successfully, he emerges not only without animus, but with something of a yearning for the affection of his old friends. The solution "every man, on both sides, was right, who did his duty" [86] suits him perfectly. Although one may think that this is surrendering to the problem rather than solving it, he should recall that Basil Duke, John B. Gordon, and a large number of others could find no different epilogue.

3. Humorous Satire

As the century neared its close, a third motive appeared in Southern fiction, alien alike to the sentimental romance of Cooke and Page and to the moral earnestness of Cable, Allen, and other nascent realists. This was sympathetic satire, which took over the Southern legend, now grown to vast proportions, and poked some sly fun at its creatures. The two sons of the South who led in this delightful type of comedy were Opie Read and F. Hopkinson Smith, the one a vagabond journalist and *bon vivant*; the other a professional engineer and builder of lighthouses when he was not engaged in art and letters.

[84] *Ibid.*, p. 210.
[85] *Ibid.*, p. 239.
[86] *Ibid.*, p. 400.

It would be improper to call these writers critics of the South, for they were rather exploiters of local color, who saw great opportunity for humor in contrasting the legend with the reality. Neither was sufficiently immersed in the Southern tradition to have felt in danger of being damned with it; yet, on the other hand, neither felt the duty of remonstrance. There is nothing prescriptive in their pages and no hint that they would have had the Southern colonel anything other than what he had always been. They were literary satirists who perceived that much could be made of Southern quixotism, although neither appears to have considered the sobering thought that reason appears sometimes as madness, and that the wisdom of the world may be foolishness with God.

Opie Read was one of those Southerners who by reason of temperament and fortune found it easy to adapt themselves to the postbellum settlement. The greater part of his life he spent in the North, but it was the South which held his interest and peopled his imagination. Although the bulk of Read's fiction appeared in cheap, paper-bound volumes, which were frequently peddled on trains, no one can read this gifted storyteller without feeling that in him a great talent was made to serve inferior ends. Few authors of the period could match him in contrivance of situations, in perception of human motives, and in delineation of character. Endowed with the artist's eye for the significant detail and a fine sense of the sardonic, he went through life serving up the picturesque, eccentric, and shiftless aspects of the Southern scene for no other object than that of simple entertainment.

A representative specimen of Read's work is *A Kentucky Colonel*. In this amusing tale Philip Burwood, a newspaper reporter out of work, becomes amanuensis to Colonel Remington Osbury, who has determined to win literary fame by writing a history of Shellcut County. The plot, which leads through various complications to the young man's marriage with the daughter of his employer, is unimportant. The substance of the work is the fine description of life on a Kentucky manor, with its naturalness, its laziness, and its come-day-go-day indifference to the passage of time. The Colonel himself is the traditional compound of generosity, irascibility, vanity, absurdity, and indolence. Like F. Hopkinson Smith's Colonel Carter, he is proudly innocent of the ways of the commercial world, and upon being warned that his *History* may meet adverse criticism from the reviewers, settles the matter by declaring that "The books were sent out as presents, and that no gentleman would criticize a present." [87]

The dominant characteristic of Read's Southern types is shiftlessness. The Colonel; Uncle Buckhorn, who sits all day in his chair and follows the shade around the porch; the son Henry, who turns away a client from his real estate office rather than interrupt a chat about literature; the worthless tenant farmer Jack Gap; and the Negroes are all studious avoiders of exertion. Unquestionably Read thought of this as the South's inheritance from slavery, for in the opening sentences of the book he speaks of Burwood as "a fair type of that class of Southern young men whose prospects of a life of thoughtlessness and ease had been destroyed by a decree which we all now cheerfully admit was issued by the God of justice." [88] The Colonel and Uncle Buckhorn, moreover, are parodies of Confederate fierceness. The former confesses, "I was a hot-headed secessionist, but there is one thing I am proud of—in fact, I don't know but that I was proud of it all along—and that is the fact that old Kentucky did not go out of the Union. Thank God it is all over now and settled as it was." [89] Uncle Buckhorn had made a number of secession speeches, declared that he was ready to die for the cause, and then neglected to join the army.

87 *A Kentucky Colonel* (Chicago, 1891), p. 302.
88 *Ibid.*, p. 5.
89 *Ibid.*, pp. 41-42.

The second noticeable characteristic of the Osbury clan—and they are intended to represent the average Kentucky family of the better class—is an intense provincialism. They display the puzzling Southern capacity to be cordial in all personal relationships while remaining very narrow in range of sympathies. Colonel Osbury and Burwood hold the following illuminating conversation about New Orleans:

> "You say you like New Orleans?"
>
> "It is a quaint and interesting city."
>
> "I don't care much for it," he rejoined. "I am used to hearing negroes talk English, and, suh, when they begin to jabber in French, why, that settles it with me. Don't want to live in a town where negroes can't talk as they should."
>
> "Out in some places where I have been," Fred remarked, "they talk Spanish."
>
> "Well, I don't want any of them to come talking Spanish to me," said the Colonel. "English is good enough for me. It was good enough for old Andrew Jackson and the men who planted this government, and I don't believe in scattering foreign jabber among the people." [90]

In a similar way Uncle Buckhorn is on the alert to scent Yankee innovations. After having had his pronunciation corrected by the Colonel's daughter, Luzelle, he explodes:

> "Oh well, if you want to call it 'Such,' you can do so. When I was a boy and folks was honest, 'sich' was good enough for people who didn't have to borry from the neighbors every time they wanted to get a bite to eat; but now that everything is gittin' to be Yankeefied, we have to twist up our mouth and say 'Such.' " [91]

If the South is provincial within the nation, Kentucky may be said to be provincial within the South. Little hints of its individuality come out on many pages. The Colonel first

[90] *Ibid.*, p. 294.
[91] *Ibid.*, p. 37.

greets Burwood in his customary fashion, "showing that he was a true Kentuckian with a sort of miscellaneous and unanalytical courtesy." [92] He informs his guest irritably, and yet one suspects with underlying pride, "Well, suh, I'll warrant you that Kentucky has more shiftless fellows than any State in the Union. All they care for is to drink licker and talk about women and horses." [93]

In *A Tennessee Judge* Read brings a Chicagoan down and initiates him into the illogical Southern way of life. Mr. Hawley soon discovers that the way to win acceptance by local society is to forget the profit motive and take a sentimental view of all things. As the Judge remarks to him, "You are a man of sentiment and therefore a gentleman. But I had my doubts when I heard you were from Chicago, a city that respects nothing old or venerable." [94]

In *The American Cavalier* (1904) Read turned essayist and wrote extensively in praise of the New South of practical education and of successful business men. Yet here the familiar dichotomy comes out: whenever he needed an anecdote or paused for a flight of imagination, it was the intractable Old South which supplied the material—golden eggs of a goose which his program would kill. An American reared as a Southerner is in a sense like a man born into the Church of Rome; it is questionable whether he ever finds it possible to repudiate the South entirely. He may show himself torn between an inherited sympathy, and an exasperation with its inertia, narrowness, and pretense. Yet its famous prejudices tend to form a matrix for his thinking; even overt rebellion may testify to its hold upon him; and in the end he is likely to return to its easier and more primitive ways as to something that conforms better with his nature. The rebellion will be intellectual; it is strenuous and costly to maintain,

92 *Ibid.*, p. 19.
93 *Ibid.*, p. 24.
94 *A Tennessee Judge* (Chicago, 1893), p. 40.

and there is always the impulse to let the "natural" resume its sway. From an abstract social creed and a self-devised religion one turns instinctively to anything that seems to have the authority of tradition. In this case, though Read saw justice in the great revolution which brought about a general leveling of society, he must have realized that the South of the past, with its distinctions, anachronisms, paradoxes, and conflicts—in short, with its "human" society—was the great storehouse of the raconteur, for in the course of a long life he drew upon it for more than a dozen works.

Smith, on the other hand, was a versatile mind, whose preoccupation with the traditional South was only one of several interests. Born in Baltimore, a descendant of the Francis Hopkinson who signed the Declaration of Independence and wrote "The Battle of the Kegs," he found himself at the close of youth too impecunious to afford the Princeton education for which he had been prepared. After some experience at odd jobs, he went to New York, with a Southern boy's natural foreboding of that great Yankee hive. But an endowment of valuable personal qualities, plus a capacity for hard work, enabled him to become in course of time an outstanding mechanical engineer, among whose constructions the Race Rock Lighthouse and the foundation of the Statue of Liberty are notable.

Though interested in painting and literature from an early age, Smith was past fifty when he secured literary recognition with *Colonel Carter of Cartersville*. This study of a Virginia patrician, obviously emanating from a sympathy with the type, and yet delightfully satirical, has probably done as much as any other book to fix the public's conception of the Southern colonel. Its leading character is an embodiment of all that is fine and much that is dubious in Southern character; he is honest, proud, loyal, and affable on the one hand, but on the other visionary, indolent, a trifle inclined to pamper the physical man, quick-tempered, and prone to invoke violence in the settlement of disputes. He has to a high degree the insular mind of his class, and he gives his address, "Col. George Fairfax Carter, of Carter Hall, Cartersville, Va.," in the innocent assurance that it will be recognized throughout the universe. Smith describes him as

> a Virginian of good birth, fair education, and limited knowledge of the world and men, proud of his ancestry, proud of his State, and proud of himself; believing in States' rights, slavery, and the Confederacy, and away down in the bottom of his heart clinging to the belief that the poor white trash of the earth includes about everybody outside of Fairfax county.[95]

Blind to most of the changes about him, the Colonel keeps faith in the old standard of personal honor, and he relates with obvious relish and approval the action of his neighbor Colonel Talcott, who shot a Yankee postmaster dead for the discourtesy of refusing him credit for a three-cent stamp. The only thing left "for a high-toned Southern gentleman to do," he added.[96]

An underlying theme of the novel is the Colonel's child-like incompetence at business affairs. He proposes to retrieve his fortunes by promoting "The Cartersville and Warrenton Air Line Railroad," the chief recommendation of which as an investment is that it will pass by several old estates of the Virginia landed gentry, including Carter Hall. The Colonel's practical friend Fitzpatrick, who loves him for being a character true to type, and who humors him in his fancies, confesses to someone, "I couldn't raise a dollar in a lunatic asylum full of millionaires on a scheme like the colonel's, and yet I keep on lying to the dear old fellow day after day, hoping something will turn up by which I can help him out." [97] The venture succeeds when it is revealed that the

95 *Colonel Carter of Cartersville* (New York, 1908), p. 10.
96 *Ibid.*, p. 21.
97 *Ibid.*, p. 43.

Colonel's estate contains a rich coal deposit, an item which he, in his enthusiasm for the history and prestige of Carter Hall, had ignored as of no material importance. An amusing complication is the Colonel's challenge to a duel of a New York stockbroker, who had spoken slightingly of the investment project. Colonel Carter had prepared his will and has his seconds on hand when he learns that the challenge was never delivered, because with characteristic casualness he had forgotten to affix the necessary postage to his letter.

The author followed *Colonel Carter of Cartersville* with *Colonel Carter's Christmas* which, like most sequels, fails to reach the level of its predecessor. It describes in detail the reconciliation between the Colonel and his broker rival, Mr. Klutchem. In an exuberant burst of Southern generosity the Colonel invites the Vermonter and his daughter to Christmas dinner, and here one meets the customary solution in which the Yankee, after a close look at Southern life and manners, becomes entranced and departs pronouncing them good.

Smith wrote also short stories of Southern life, most of which treat of conventional types and subjects. "Six Hours in Squantico" is a clever satire on Southern impecuniousness and business ineptitude. "A Gentleman Vagabond" is a parallel to *Colonel Carter of Cartersville*. Its chief character is "Major" Tom Slocombe of Pocomoke, who by current reports attained his title by marrying the widow of Major John Talbot. Major Slocombe, who owns an island in Chesapeake Bay, is land poor. He puts on the airs of a magnifico nevertheless, and when he entertains shooting parties from the North, he pretends that he has a splendid estate so successfully as to make them half satisfied with the illusion.

In these stories even the wrongs of Reconstruction take on a burlesque character, for Smith was never a partisan. He was merely among the first to see that the Old South, by its very contrast with the business civilization then completely triumphant in the North, would inevitably gain attention. It is important to bear in mind that the South of legend has been the nation's escape from the reality of the industrial world; and creations like those of Smith have done much to confirm the popular notion of its romantic character and to make artistic reconstruction of its past one of the fruitful fields of American letters.

On a still more fruitful level, however, such contrasts might call forth inquiry. To the extent that modernism represents the breakdown of cultural forms, the traditional South surviving in the present is a rebuke, teasing in its persistence, disturbing in the reasonableness of its "unreasonable" predilections, a warning to arrogant presentism that deep thoughts lie in old customs. But there are many ways of missing these implications, and the satirists, through their absorption in the details of localism, illustrated one of them.

4. Realism

The question of whether the South could be presented in fiction with a degree of objectivity was thus held in abeyance for more than forty years after the war. Its realities had been obscured, its presumptions exaggerated, and the lesson of its splendid past drawn on a very narrow basis. The advocates of the old régime had composed stories which were charming because impossible, but because impossible, in the end barren. The critics of Southern life never rose to full stature, and the whole phantasmagoria of Reconstruction, which might have produced a school of Zolas, received but a cursory telling. The satirists floated on the surface of the stream, keeping the nation amused with oddities of Southern life and character. But at the end of the century there appeared in the field a young Virginian who was to take the first solid step toward giving the South a literary expression free on the one hand from mawkishness and unwieldy political theses, and on the other from the superficiality of local colorism. If Ellen Glasgow was not the first to perceive that what the South needed above all else was blood and irony, she was at least the first to try the experiment of providing them. Born in Richmond to the sheltered life, she is proof that the artist is not made by the accident of environment, but by an imagination which strives to seek out and understand the issues of the world.

Miss Glasgow was only twenty-three when she published her first novel, *The Descendant,* which is not a Southern story at all except by the reflection it throws on the Southern caste system. The protagonist is Michael Akershem, an extra-legal child, who flees from Virginia to New York and there experiences to the fullest the heartlessness and brutality of the great city. Later, his successful career as an editor is brought to an end by a tragic love affair. The conclusion is decidedly stern, and one does not wonder that the literary taste of the day pronounced the work "disagreeable." But Miss Glasgow had demonstrated that she could handle a story of human relationships without becoming maudlin, a real achievement in the decade of the nineties, especially for a lady author from below the Potomac.

Three years later she wove the society and politics of postbellum Virginia into *The Voice of the People* (1900). This is in brief the story of the rise of a plebeian to the governorship of the Old Dominion, narrated with an expert knowledge of the class system of that state and of the impediments which it places in the way of the unfriended. The setting is Kingsborough, which "dozed through the present to dream of the past, and found the future a nightmare." [98] The hero is Nicholas Burr, who, like Michael Akershem, belongs to the

---

[98] *The Voice of the People* (New York, 1936), p. 12.

disinherited. His father is a peanut planter, oppressed and spiritless; his mother a dour woman, distrustful of book-learning and fretted by the hopelessness of their condition. Through the compassion of a wealthy neighbor Nicholas is invited to share in private tutoring, in the sessions of which he is first made to feel the cruelty of upper-class hauteur. But by virtue of single-mindedness and a capacity for hard work he perfects himself in the study of law.

The crisis of his life turns upon a personal relationship. There had been a ripening understanding between himself and the aristocratic Eugenia Battle, but Eugenia's brother Bernard, seeking to escape the opprobrium of extra-legal fatherhood, falsely accuses Nicholas. The emotional havoc wrought by this piece of perfidy is so great that from this point on Nicholas becomes a less human figure; aloof and self-righteous, he refuses to mellow even after attaining the governor's chair and remains a stiff embodiment of his own conception of justice, scorning to trade favors in the traditional style. Finally he loses his life in a quixotic attempt to save a Negro from lynching, an opponent of social discrimination to the last.

Virginia society appears in ample cross-section. The aristocrats of Kingsborough, "where there isn't enough vitality to make one first-class savage," earnestly fight the battle for their class. A prominent character is the haughty Mrs. Jane Dudley Webb, who points to the Confederate button at her throat and tells a Northern visitor, "Sir, the women of the South have never surrendered." [99] It is she who tries to drive Nicholas from the school by telling Judge Bassett, "It is folly to educate a person above his station," but it is the Judge who saves him by insisting firmly, "Men make their stations, madam." [100]

[99] *Ibid.*, p. 95.
[100] *Ibid.*, p. 98.

The political meetings, which are described with cruel truth, are rife with sentimentality, rhetoric, bombast, and cant. Yet in all such gatherings "one would have recognized instinctively the tiller of the soil." [101] For it is this kind of man, "the sole survivor of the Virginia pioneer," who listens patiently to appeals to the old fidelities while he learns fumblingly the devious methods of a new political day. In this sphere more than in any other the author turns the light of realism upon topics hitherto obscured with artifice and sentiment. "The Mother of States and Statesmen" affords in her deliberative gatherings only a carnival of vulgarity and ridiculous pretense. At twenty-three Nicholas Burr has gone to Richmond "to meet an assembly of statesmen; he had found a body of half educated and wholly unprofitable servants." [102] He was quick to perceive that "The day when a legislator meant a statesman was done with; it meant now merely a representative of the lower average, a man to be juggled with by shrewder politicians, or to be tricked by more dishonest ones." [103] It is Burr, a son of the lower orders, who places himself at the head of these people, whom he sees to be "honest in everything except convictions" and "faithful where their prejudices or interests lead them," [104] and by one of those ironies in which Miss Glasgow finds satisfaction, illustrates the path of incorruptibility and justice.

She had by now written three novels in which the Civil War appears only by reference and indirection, but in *The Battle-Ground* (1902) she took up this most tempting of all subjects to the Southern writer. In a preface composed many years after the first publication of the novel she admitted a realization that no one could touch upon that "desperate if fantastic struggle" without touching romance, because the

101 *Ibid.*, p. 251.
102 *Ibid.*, p. 261.
103 *Ibid.*
104 *Ibid.*, p. 262.

War for Southern Independence must always remain one of the romantic episodes of the world's history. "For Virginia the Civil War was the expiring gesture of chivalry." [105] But at the same time its profound effects upon the society and civilization of the old commonwealth convinced her that no one, however realistic, satirical, or even cynical his purpose in depiction, could ignore it.

The chief actor of this story is Dandridge Montjoy, son of scapegrace Jack Montjoy and of Jane Lightfoot, who permanently estranged herself from her aristocratic family by eloping. Following the death of his mother, young Dandridge comes trudging two hundred miles to Uplands, where old Major Lightfoot, after inspecting his countenance, owns the tie of blood by saying, "Come in, sir, come in: you are at home." [106]

Apart from the interest of its special episodes, *The Battle-Ground* is noteworthy for showing the coalescence of classes under the fierce heat and pressure of war. Young Montjoy grows up in a very arrogant household—indeed, the Lightfoots hold themselves a bit above the Washingtons. In the midst of her misfortunes his mother had said to him:

> The Lightfoots were never proud, my son; they have no false pride, but they know their place, and in England, between you and me, they were more important than the Washingtons. Not that the General wasn't a great man, dear, he was a very great soldier of course, and in his youth, you know, he was an admirer of your Great-great-aunt Emmeline.[107]

In his grandfather's house Dandridge gets a rearing appropriate to his class; gay and spirited, he leads a joyous and thoughtless existence until a scandal at the University puts an end to his cordial relations with the old Major. It was not the

105 *The Battle-Ground* (New York, 1939), p. ix.
106 *Ibid.*, p. 31.
107 *Ibid.*, p. 28.

fact that the young man fought a duel that mortally offended the Major; it was that he had tried to "murder a Virginia gentleman for the sake of a barroom hussy." [108] He had lowered himself and had capped the social error by spending a night in gaol. After an altercation, Dandridge leaves the ancestral place in anger, but the war comes along almost at once to provide him with a four-year occupation.

In camp Dandridge meets Pinetop, a specimen of that sturdy Southern yeomanry who, with hazy ideas about the political issues and with indifference to whether or not the aristocracy preserved its stake, appeared to defend native soil against invasion. Pinetop had come "with easy strides, down from his bare little cabin in the Blue Ridge, bringing with him a flintlock musket, a corncob pipe, and a stockingful of Virginia tobacco."[109] At first the butt of every jest from the high-toned gentlemen about him, he wins by means of imperturbability, doggedness, and courage in the field the respect of those who had contemned him for his origins. Something new in the social history of the South occurs when Dandridge and Pinetop realize that whatever the diversity of their heritage, both are proved men in the test of battle, beside which differences of class fade into insignificance. As the untutored philosopher of the hills expresses it when they part at Appomattox:

I reckon you'll go yo' way an' I'll go mine, for there's one thing sartain an' that is our ways don't run together. It'll never be the same agin'—that's natur—but if you ever want a good stout hand for any uphill plowing or shoot yo' man an' the police get on yo' track, jest remember that I'm up thar in my little cabin. Why, if every officer in the country was at yo' heels, I'd stand guard with my old squirrel gun and maw would with her kettle.[110]

108 *Ibid.*, p. 183.
109 *Ibid.*, p. 252.
110 *Ibid.*, p. 424.

Few men born to high-caste existence realize the cruelty of the caste system until they are forced outside it and made to witness its operations from another point of view. The tragedy of it broke upon Dandridge the night he found Pinetop beside the camp fire absorbedly trying to teach himself to read out of a primer. When he saw this uncomplaining and self-poised stalwart groping after "the primitive knowledge which should be the birthright of every child" [111] he understood the great woe which slavery had brought by degrading the underprivileged white. From Major Lightfoot's arrogant statement that slavery is an institution for gentlemen only to this elementary perception of its social consequences lies the great gulf between the Old and the New South.

And in the experience of Dandridge there is mirrored the whole tragic story of the section—its stubborn pride going before a catastrophic fall, its descent through war to the ultimate privations, and its idealistic decision to build a new order without losing that part of the old order which deserved to survive. When he returns to Uplands and greets Betty by telling her that he is now a worse beggar than upon his first forlorn appearance, to find himself accepted with joy and affection, he symbolizes the resurrection.

Miss Glasgow was the first Southern author to treat without predilection these two different eras. Her Virginia nobility is a true nobility, firm in its virtues but limited in its sympathies, and its shortcomings are held up to full view. But it is especially significant that her new men too are real; in Michael Akershem, in Nicholas Burr, and in Pinetop one meets the offspring of the vital lower orders who will not be denied their entrance upon the stage of the world.

In one sense it can be said that the whole body of Southern fiction published between 1865 and 1910 is auxiliary to the apologia. Whatever diverse aims the authors had in mind,

111 *Ibid.*, p. 384.

they contributed to the vindication of the South by making it a concrete reality, a part of the stubborn fact of the world, against which political delusions must always break. The artist, as D. H. Lawrence has remarked, is by nature a damn liar, but if he is an artist, he will tell you the truth about his time. The writer who can show that Major Lightfoot is just as real as Pinetop, because he is the product of conditioning factors just as solid, is a creator of the truth of art.

In another aspect, this body of writing indicates a progressive emancipation from the peculiar "mind of the South." The complete absorption of Cooke and Page gave way to criticism, however vague in direction and ineffective. This was succeeded by humorous satire, which requires a certain detachment; and then came full realism, with all that it implies of freedom from obsessions and systematic delusions. It was no accident that Southern literature became mature when it first became capable of irony, for the road to maturity lies through the ironic understanding of life. Because irony proceeds from critical awareness, it opens up alternatives and leaves one confronted with the multiplicity of the actual world. The early Reconstruction writers who undertook to defend the antebellum South by picturing it as without fault were making a mistake. Thomas Nelson Page and Harriet Beecher Stowe are ridiculous by the same test. Distortions have a way of being found out, and there is no reason to believe that the political zeal which today manifests itself in sociological caricatures will not also be recognized and judged. Only when the impulse to justify is replaced by the impulse to see the thing in the round does something like an enduring justification become possible.

The development of Southern fiction is not so much a repudiation of the antebellum ideal as a reflection of changing conditions, which inevitably called attention to its narrowness and exclusiveness. The artists are always the first to sense

impending changes, and thus fiction was changing its ground
while the politicians, less perceptive, were still declaiming
the old ideas. But "the South," which in some form or other
is an inescapable inheritance, has remained with the novelists
of every persuasion as a part of their self-consciousness.

CHAPTER SIX

The Tradition And Its Critics

IN 1890 THE SOUTH CROSSED A DIVIDING LINE, FOR THIS YEAR was for it the most significant date since 1877, when President Hayes, in partial fulfillment of a "deal," withdrew the Federal garrisons. The close of the previous decade was marked by the silencing of two symbolic Southern voices. Jefferson Davis, returning by boat from an inspection of his dilapidated estate Brierfield, caught a chill and expired peacefully in New Orleans on December 6, 1889. Just seventeen days later Henry Grady, universally known as a champion of the New South, died in Atlanta after a meteoric career of only three years, which had carried him to the front rank of American orators. In the popular mind these two figures represent opposite poles of Southern thought and feeling, but if one examines the whole body of their utterances, he finds that they stood fairly close together in support of orthodox Southern ideals. On the matter of sectionalism they differed, but the speakers who today declaim, "There was a South of slavery and secession—that South is dead" are usually unaware that in succeeding speeches Grady spent most of his time defending the social creed of antebellum civilization.

Davis had taken his stand on the narrow point of constitutional interpretation; and his massive *Rise and Fall of the Confederate Government* is an exposition of the Constitution as a preservative agent. But Grady looked at the whole drift of modernism, and instead of attempting to bury Southern traditionalism, he deplored, in those speeches which he prepared for home consumption, the very tendencies which were opening a way for the New South.

Grady was among those who discerned a collapse of the structure of society. "Anarchy, socialism—that leveling spirit that defies government and denies God—has no hold upon the South," he asserted.[1] He viewed apprehensively the new division of the people into self-seeking classes, envious, distrustful of one another, and ready to make use of political machinery to further special interests. "The universal brotherhood is dissolving," he declared in an address, "Against Civilization," given at the University of Virginia, "and people are huddling into classes." [2] This was a poor exchange for the old feudal unity which everyone was consigning to the irrecoverable. In a speech on "The Solid South" he asked, "Can a Northern man dealing with casual servants, querulous, sensitive, and lodged for a day in a sphere they resent, understand the close relations of the races in the South?" The increasing rootlessness of people was a sign of dangerous things to come, and he praised the farm as the best nursery of character.[3] It would be difficult to find stronger preachments against the breaking of the ancient bond of sentiment and duty than Grady's addresses to his fellow Southerners.

But the most alarming portent of the times to Grady, conservative to the core where matters of religion and conduct were involved, was the growing "bitterness of unbelief." He

1 *The New South* (New York, 1890), p. 185.
2 *The Complete Orations and Speeches of Henry W. Grady* (New York, 1910), p. 137.
3 *Ibid.*, pp. 168-169.

told an audience that "culture has refined for itself strange religions from the strong old creeds," and he advised the South not to seek immigrants who would bring in heresies and discordant ideals. Speaking at Augusta, Georgia, he urged his listeners to invite only such as would come "to confirm and not to estrange, the simple faith in which we have been reared, and which we should transmit unsullied to our children." He was glad that the homogeneous character of the South "has left us the straight and simple faith of our fathers, untainted by heresy and unweakened by speculation." [4] Like the traditional Southerner again, he retained a belief in divine Providence, and he cherished the characteristic dogma that the position of the races is ordained by God. Apart from the disavowal of sectionalism, which was certainly nothing new in 1886, Grady thus stands much nearer to the apologists than to the liberals and reformers; and his disposition to see the future of the South in some kind of sublimated reunion with the nation should not be allowed to obscure his belief that the section offered "the last hope of saving the old fashion in our religious and political government." [5]

If the career of Grady were the only augury of a "New South" to appear by this date, the advocates of a new set of values and a differently constituted society could have hoped for little, but in 1890 there occurred an event which prepared the way for a real change by making it unlikely that the South would again have to assume the purely defensive role. This was the defeat in Congress of the "Force Bill." Introduced into the House by the suave and scholarly representative from Massachusetts, Henry Cabot Lodge, this measure would have authorized Federal supervision of elections in all districts where there was evidence of fraud or intimidation. Although Representative Lodge politely pointed out

4 *The New South*, p. 185.
5 *Ibid.*, p. 186.

how the bill would be of advantage in certain Northern areas, its intention was plainly to secure the franchise for the Negroes of the South. The debate which it occasioned in Congress, though lengthy, was good-humored and happily free from the acerbities of Reconstruction days. There it passed the House by a narrow margin of six votes, but it failed in the Senate.

This was in effect a victory for the upholders of white supremacy, for it indicated that the national legislature, whether because it was wearying of the fight or because the Southern arguments were beginning to make converts, was growing minded to let the South run its own household. But memories of Reconstruction were less than twenty years behind, and fear that the Southern states might again be turned over to Negroes and bureaucrats produced a flurry of alarm, particularly among the business elements, who were beginning to feel that finally they had the South on even keel. With the object of forestalling a revival of this disastrous policy, fourteen spokesmen, including such well-known names as Zebulon Vance, Robert Stiles, and Bernard J. Sage, undertook to explain the Solid South to what may be termed the New North. In April, 1890, they published a symposium *Why the Solid South? or Reconstruction and its Results.* This book is more truly a document of the New South than the speeches of Grady, for whatever else may be said of the work, it was free from the old Southern rallying cries, and it was designed frankly to appeal to the self-interest of a business class. The authors were men who had been in the thick of the affairs they described, and they believed that they could win their case by making Northern business men, whose pecuniary stake in the South was growing, realize what Reconstruction had cost in money, in public morale, and in cultural retardation.

Dedicated specifically to "the business men of the North," *Why the Solid South?* has a distinctive tone of sobriety. Absent are the posturing and attitudinizing of ex-rebels, and in their place is a straightforward account of what carpetbaggery and Negro rule had meant in terms of responsible government, so needful to business. Hilary Herbert of Alabama, who served as editor, expressed the thought in a preface:

> Its object is to show to the public, and more especially to the business men of the North, who have made investments in the South, or who have trade relations with their Southern fellow-citizens, the consequences which once followed an interference in the domestic affairs of certain states by those, who either did not understand the situation or were reckless of results.[6]

There followed factual histories of Reconstruction in each of the ex-Confederate states, including West Virginia and Missouri, which also had suffered from the fraud, repression, and vicious partisanship of the postwar settlement. All in all, it is one of the most dismal stories ever told, unrelieved by a single ray of light, unless a revelation of how much people can endure and how they will struggle to attain their hopes even *in extremis* be such. Governor Vance of North Carolina in a particularly mild and philosophic chapter pointed out that during what was supposed to be a moral and political rebirth "the criminals sat in the law-making chamber, on the bench and in the jury-box, instead of standing in the dock." [7] It has become the fashion nowadays to regard Reconstruction as a kind of chamber of horrors into which no good American would care to look, but Governor Vance reminded his readers that no portion of our history better deserves study "by every considerate patriot." [8]

From the comparatively uneventful story of North Carolina's experience, the chronicle moves on to the wild saturnalia of South Carolina, where amidst riotous spending of

6 Hilary Herbert (ed.), *Why the Solid South? or Reconstruction and its Results* (Baltimore, 1890), p. xvii.
7 *Ibid.*, p. 70.
8 *Ibid.*, p. 71.

public funds the State House was turned into a combination of saloon and brothel. Yet the ordeal of South Carolina was matched by that of Louisiana, where in four years' time the incredible Warmoth regime squandered an amount equal to half of the wealth of the state.[9] "Corruption is the fashion," Governor Warmoth, an ex-soldier who had been dishonorably discharged from the Federal army, remarked with laudable candor. "I do not pretend to be honest, but only as honest as anyone in politics." [10]

The concluding chapter, which the editor entitled "Sunrise," was well supplied with figures to show how good government means appreciation of capital assets, and it closed with the earnest plea "that the American people may not need to take another lesson in the school of Reconstruction." [11]

Why the Solid South? was decidedly a fresh tack for Southern spokesmen, who seem here to have concluded that policy could accomplish more than principle. It showed recognition of the fact that the postbellum North was in charge not of Puritan zealots trailing clouds of Transcendentalism, but of the money-seeking class which, as *De Bow's Review* had once declared, "cared nothing for the negroes unless to dislike them," and "nothing for the Abolitionists, unless to wish that they would hold their tongues and stay their pens, or transport themselves *en masse* to Exeter Hall, never to return to America." [12] But obviously it was a step in the direction of pragmatic acquiescence.

However important *Why the Solid South?* may seem as a sign of change, it would be unfair to regard it as setting the keynote of the decade, for the period beginning in 1890 was one of mixed trends in the South, with the old and the new battling on fairly even terms. There was the beginning of

9 *Ibid.*, p. 405.
10 *Ibid.*, p. 429.
11 *Ibid.*, p. 442.
12 *De Bow's Review*, After the War Series, III (April and May, 1867), p. 428.

industrial exploitation, to which many Southerners were ready to lend an eager hand, and to which *Why the Solid South?* was in a sense an invitation. There was a great upsurge of Confederate sentiment, expressing itself in reunions, with glowing memorial addresses at the unveiling of monuments, where the veterans, now gray and unsteady, grew tearful over the eulogies of dead leaders. But perhaps most important of all there was the appearance of a group of Southern scholars, trained in the new disciplines, who tried to see the history of their section in the pattern of world history, with indifference to the old partisan slogans.

1. The Last Confederate Offensive

A realization that "the Cause" was slipping into the past produced a strong resurgence of Southern feeling, which took form in a last attempt to express to the world the ideals for which the soldiers of the South had fought. The final Confederate offensive got under way in 1890 with the organization of the United Confederate Veterans. There were already in existence separate survivors' organizations, but because of the Confederate's preoccupation with the rebuilding of his shattered fortunes, and because of a strong distrust of "rebel societies" prevalent in the North, there had been no group comparable to the Grand Army of the Republic. In this year, however, a great host of the wearers of the gray assembled in Chattanooga, with the ever-popular John B. Gordon commanding. A constitution was drawn up which declared the purpose of the organization as follows:

> to gather authentic data for an impartial history of the War between the States; to preserve relics or mementoes of the same; to cherish the ties of friendship that should exist among

all men who have shared common dangers, common sufferings and privations; to care for the disabled, and extend a helping hand to the needy; to protect the widows and orphans, and to make and preserve a record of the services of every member, and as far as possible of those of our comrades who have preceded us in eternity.[13]

Actually the association through its annual meetings served to keep green the memory of sectionalism, and not infrequently to breathe defiance at Yankee civilization.

Three years later there was established the *United Confederate Veteran*, which defied the customary fate of Southern periodicals by maintaining existence for forty years. Notwithstanding its good humor and camaraderie, the prevailing note of the *Veteran* is pathos. The minds of most Southern soldiers had been stopped by the war as a clock is stopped by an earthquake, in the graphic figure employed by Walter Hines Page; but the war was now almost thirty years behind, and a new generation, wearying of old men's stories and marking the contrast between the wealth of the North and the poverty of the languid and still tatterdemalion South, was taking over the scene. It was increasingly hard to interest the younger men in what had been the one great, illuminating, passionate experience of the soldier's life. Plaintive hints that the old order and the values which alone make living significant were being buried together began to appear. "We are drifting away from the old anchorage" [14] became a theme. The upholders of the civilization of "superior sentiment" recognized their true enemy in the spirit of commercialism, which would judge everything by tangible results. "Enterprise and thrift are well enough," wrote Daniel Bond in the issue of February, 1896, the content of which may be regarded as typical, "but there are some signs in this desire for

13 *First Annual Convention, United Confederate Veterans* (Chattanooga, 1890), p. 4.
14 *The Confederate Veteran*, II (June, 1894), p. 166.

an exchange of old ideas for new that seem but taking the false for the true." [15] Even such sacred things as the ancient custom of hospitality were threatened. "Business suggests that we entertain those who entertain us, or worse still, that we do it as a stroke of business advertising." [16] Filled with resentment against the matter-of-factness of the commercial spirit, he went on to remind his readers that "There is something better than wealth, something dearer than success." With the failure to discriminate between the weighty and the trivial which is characteristic of much writing in the *Veteran*, he closed with a plea for general cooperation toward saving "that glorious songster of the Southland, the mockingbird." [17]

A self-imposed ban upon political topics kept speculative writing at a minimum, but whenever the *Veteran* essayed the subject of the future, it expressed a desire for perpetual union—then practically a formula in all Confederate writing —together with the hope that the Old South, "the South of chivalry," might continue through the years. Here lay a difficulty which many ingenious rationalizations were never able to overcome. Manifestly the South could not keep march with "progress" if it condemned a business civilization, resisted the penetration of new ideas, and insisted on class distinctions which grew out of a different order. A few writers attempted the solution in general, if not evasive terms, but for the most part it must be said that the South which the soldiers apotheosized remained a memory world, in which they lived in time's despite, but which they did not earnestly try to square with the world of present realities. [18]

Paul Buck has noted in expressions at Confederate re-

---

[15] *Ibid.,* IV (February, 1896), p. 54.

[16] *Ibid.*

[17] *Ibid.,* p. 55.

[18] This may recall a statement made two decades earlier by Sidney Lanier (Edwin Mims, *Sidney Lanier,* p. 267): "Our people . . . whirl their poor old dead leaves of recollection round and round, in a piteous eddy that has all the wear and tear of motion without any of the rewards of progress."

unions an undercurrent of satisfaction that the cause had been lost.[19] This was accompanied, however, by a conviction that submission to the demands of the North would have been a betrayal of manhood, and that the only honorable decision was to meet force with force. It was the custom of the *Veteran* to publish the more significant speeches delivered before each annual convention, and this justification was frequently heard. John H. Reagan, of Texas, appearing in Nashville before the seventh annual gathering, gave a typical review of the South's feeling with reference to the contest:

> Such a sacrifice as that which was demanded of the Southern people has not in the world's history been submitted to by any people without an appeal to the last dread arbitrament of war; and ours were a chivalric, intelligent, proud, liberty-loving people, who, had they submitted to this sacrifice without a struggle, would have proved themselves unworthy of the proud title of being Americans. And I say now, with deliberation and sincerity, in view of all the calamities of that war, if the same condition of things could again occur, I would rather accept those calamities than belong to a race of cowards and surrender the most sacred rights of self-government to the clamor of a majority overriding the Constitution and demanding terms so revolting to our sense of justice.[20]

The *Veteran* stubbornly refused to see the war on a profit-and-loss basis. Filled with the belief in sentiment as an integrating power, speakers frequently defended its part in the social constitution. The Reverend J. B. Hawthorn, in an address before the same meeting, declared:

> I am sometimes confronted by a cold-hearted, self-seeking, mammon-worshipping man who wants to know what good will come from keeping alive such sentiments. . . . My reply is that the poorest, weakest, and meanest country on God's footstool

19 *The Road to Reunion* (Boston, 1937), p. 241.
20 *The Confederate Veteran*, V (July, 1897), p. 345.

is the country without sentiment. A nation without sentiment is a nation without character, without virtue, without power, without aspiration, and without self-respect.[21]

In addition to all this there was a tendency, stronger as the veterans grew older and animosities faded, to see the struggle as a transfiguration. Discipline and suffering awaken men to the eternal verities, which thoughtlessness and ease obscure. Truth was carried to Cavalry and there crucified that all men might know it. The Reverend James S. Vance expressed in a sermon before the group the thought in which many Confederates found chief solace:

> The South is not ashamed of the lost cause, which can never be lost as long as men preach patriotism, glorify valor, and worship sacrifice. The period of struggle was the period of discipline. It was providence placing the idle ore in flame and forge. God said, "Go up and die," but already the South has learned that the summons to death was a summons to life. It was a call to transformation rather than to a grave, and so, lying down on the rugged summit of her defeat and despair, the South is awakening to an inheritance that eclipses her past.[22]

For the real note of defiance one must look not so much to the editorial columns of the *Veteran* as to the memorial addresses which were being made at dedications in every part of the South. Many of these were conspicuously lacking in conciliatory spirit, and tended, if anything, to aggravate the sense of loss. The Reverend R. C. Cave in a speech at the unveiling of the Soldiers and Sailors Monument in Richmond renewed the claims of Southern civilization. "On one side of the conflict was the South," he said:

> led by the descendants of the cavaliers, who with all their

[21] *Ibid.*, V (August, 1897), p. 411.
[22] *Ibid.*, V (July, 1897), p. 351.

faults, had inherited from a long line of ancestors a manly contempt for moral littleness, a high sense of honor, a lofty regard for plighted faith, a strong tendency to conservatism, a profound respect for law and order, and an unfaltering loyalty to constitutional government. Against the South was arrayed the power of the North, dominated by the spirit of Puritanism, which, with all of its virtues, has ever been characterized by the pharisaism which worships itself, and is unable to perceive any goodness apart from itself, which has ever arrogantly held its ideas, its interests, and its will higher than fundamental law and covenanted obligations, which has always "lived and moved and had its being" in rebellion against constituted authority.[23]

In the same city two years later, Bradley T. Johnson of Maryland carried further the distinction between the "free mobocracy" of the North and the "chivalry" of the South.

There was forming in the South a military democracy, aggressive, ambitious, intellectual, and brave, such as led Athens in her brightest epoch and controlled Rome in her most glamorous days.

If that was not destroyed the industrial society of the North would be dominated by it. So the entire social force, the press, the pulpit, the public schools, was put in operation to make destructive war on Southern institutions and Southern character, and for thirty years attack, vituperation, and abuse were incessant.[24]

And when implacable old Jubal Early died, John W. Daniel assured the audience gathered in commemoration that the cause was sufficiently characterized by the men who upheld it. "Indeed, my countrymen, it is impossible to conceive that a cause espoused and led by such men as Davis, Lee, Jackson, the two Johnstons, Early, and their compatriots was wrong, whilst that led by Lincoln, Seward, Stanton,

23 *Southern Historical Society Papers*, XXII (1894), p. 361.
24 *Ibid.*, XXIII (1895), p. 367.

Sherman, Thad Stevens, and Ben Butler, *et id omne genus*, was right." [25]

It was growing late for justifications in the form of full-length books, but one more title must be noticed before the topic is closed. There was feeling that the history of the United States everywhere taught and accepted placed the South in the role of criminal, and in 1894 J. L. M. Curry, an Alabama soldier, statesman, and teacher, prepared a volume, *The Southern States of the American Union,* which met with such wide approval that a special edition, complete with questions, was compiled for school use. "History as written," he said, "if accepted in future years will consign the South to infamy." [26] Accordingly he wrote to show that the history of the section had been "rich in patriotism, in intellectual force, in civil and military achievements, in heroism, in honorable and sagacious statesmanship." [27]

The work itself is little more than a succinct re-exposition of the Southern theory of the Union, but it added a chapter on "The Horrors of Reconstruction" and claimed that the South was vindicating itself "under the stimulus of new institutions and a Christian civilization." That the work was not wholly ingenuous may be seen from some of the questions appended: "How did New Englanders ease their conscience on the subject of slavery?" "What constituted the Southern states the true defenders of the Constitution and the Union?" "What efforts were made to humiliate the Southern people?" [28]

The last and most ambitious attempt to put forward a Southern history of the war occurred in 1899 with the appearance of the twelve-volume *Confederate Military History,* prepared under the general editorship of Clement Evans.

25 *Ibid.,* XXII (1894), p. 283.
26 *The Southern States of the American Union* (Richmond, 1895), p. 5.
27 *Ibid.*
28 *Ibid.,* pp. 266-270.

The first and last volumes of the series covered the general
subject, and the intermediate ones related the story of the
war as it affected the several states. The *History* was thus a
compendium bringing a great deal together, but it may be
doubted whether it furnished much that was new, and one is
surprised to find at this late date a concealed sense of inferiority lying behind portions of the argument. Gone is the
firm assurance of Bledsoe, Dabney, and Pollard, and one de-
tects what was perhaps the unavoidable result of thirty years
of defense-mindedness and the psychological problems created by involuntary adjustment.

The greater part of the *Confederate Military History* is too
familiar to bear review, but special notice may be taken of a
chapter by J. William Jones, "The Morale of the Confederate Soldier." Much has been said about the religious zeal of
Southern soldiers, but this is a revelation of "religiousness" as
a factor in their remarkable stamina. Jones pointed out how
these men, "all reared under the religious faith prevailing in
the South, which was singularly free from skepticism, carried
their moral convictions with them to keep company with
their ardent patriotism." [29] And the kind of religious service
the soldier wanted was the kind he had been accustomed to
before the war. He did not want a lecture on ethics or a
course in the higher criticism, or even a discussion of religion
in relation to the war. He wanted "the simple truth" and
"the old, old story of salvation," and the welling up of an
inner feeling of acceptance and faith. Jones gives a graphic
description of a meeting held in the Episcopal Church of
Fredericksburg, Virginia, some time after a bloody struggle
had left hecatombs of dead in the streets of that historic city.
Soldiers run to reach the building before all the seats are
taken, and the sermon is "Gospel." The preacher does not
discuss " 'the relation of science to religion,' or the slavery
question, or the causes which led to the war, or the war itself.

[29] *Confederate Military History*, XII (Atlanta, 1899), p. 146.

He does not indulge in abusive epithets of the invaders of our soil, or seek to fire his hearers with hatred or vindictiveness toward the enemy. He is looking in the eyes of heroes of many a battle, and he knows that the long roll may beat in the midst of his sermon, and therefore he 'speaks as a dying man to dying men.' " [30]

Jones believed that not even the army of Cromwell contained so many genuinely religious men as that of the Confederacy, and it is doubtful whether the following scene, enacted while the fighting raged around Atlanta, has had many parallels since the seventeenth century. "Yesterday," he quotes an Episcopal bishop as writing,

> in Strahl's brigade, I preached and confirmed nine persons. Last night we had a very solemn service in General Hood's room, some forty persons, chiefly generals and staff officers, being present. I confirmed General Hood and one of his aides, Captain Gordon of Savannah, and a young lieutenant from Arkansas. The service was animated, the praying good. Shells exploded nearby all the time. General Hood, unable to kneel, supported himself on his crutch and staff, and with bowed head received the benediction.[31]

Like the mass of the people for whom he fought, the Confederate soldier approached religion in an uncritical spirit. It was not for him a clarification of events, but a power to sustain in dealing with the ineluctable. Those Confederates who in the depths of disillusionment kept faith in the cause but lost faith in religion were not typical. The Southern refusal to correlate religion with temporal successes and failures was never better demonstrated than in the war, and ministers reported that men of their congregations came home from the field better Christians than before.[32] Many new church members of the postbellum era were men who had found

---

[30] *Ibid.,* p. 151.
[31] *Ibid.,* p. 186.
[32] *Ibid.,* p. 167.

"Christ in the camp," [33] and the experience of the war induced not a few to enter the ministry.

If the last expression of the Confederate apologia grows
wearisome, this is from the staleness of repetition rather
than from waning ardor on the part of the apologists. They
continued to voice the contentions of thirty years earlier.
That the South had been legally right in its action, that
Southern civilization was superior in that it honored the
claims of sentiment and duty, and that its religion was a
strong creed which scorned speculation—these were enduring
themes of Southern patriotism. In speech, however, it may be
said that they were growing old-fashioned. The last Confederates knew what to fight, but they did not know how to fight
it in a way that would attract recruits from youth, an evidence that under "progress" the generations were becoming
estranged.

2. The South in the Perspective of History

Thus the soldiers, aided by the clergy, who were closer to
them in sympathy than any other group,[34] continued to
write the story of the Southern past in as large letters as they
could at the close of the century. But there was commencing
a different kind of interpretation, which, without being measurably less pro-Southern, had the invaluable aid of historical
perspective. Previously nearly all of the postbellum writers
who had undertaken the theme of the war had become so

33 *Ibid.* Basil Gildersleeve (*Atlantic Monthly*, LXIX, January, 1892, p.
76) recalled the power of religion in the Confederate army: "Here let me say
that the bearing of the Confederates is not to be understood without taking
into account the deep religious feeling of the army and its great leaders. It is
an historical element, like any other, and is not to be passed over in summing
up the forces of the conflict."

34 This close understanding of soldier and churchman is itself an important
survival of feudalism.

engrossed in its details, or so moved by its passions, that they had failed to see it as anything more than a sectional contest, sectional in the ideologies of the opposing sides, and sectional in the glories to be apportioned out. The more obvious comparisons had, of course, been made: the Confederates were high-minded Cavaliers fighting fanatical Roundheads; or, thrust into the position of the colonists of 1775, they were resisting a tyrannous subjugation; or, the South was La Vendée, destroyed and desecrated by infidel armies. Not until the 1890's, when Southern men again began to be vocal not as special pleaders, but in wider fields of expression, and when sectional allegiance ceased to be carried about like a banner, were the first attempts made at objective analyses.

Two of the best of these came from the pen of Basil Gildersleeve, the learned philologist of Johns Hopkins. While a young professor at the University of Virginia, Gildersleeve had "spent his vacations" serving in the army until the campaign of 1864, when he received a disabling wound. Thus he was later able to confront the North not only as an ex-Confederate bearing the marks of battle, but also as that unfortunately rare creature, a Southerner able to compete with Yankees in something other than political scholarship. In 1892 he contributed "The Creed of the Old South" to the *Atlantic Monthly,* and in 1897 he followed it with the provocative "A Southerner in the Peloponnesian War."

The first article was an attempt, which he feared would be futile, to give the rising generation some notion of the form and pressure of the time which had sent blue and gray armies into the field. "That the cause we fought for and our brothers died for was the cause of civil liberty, is a thesis which we feel ourselves bound to maintain whenever our motives are challenged or misunderstood, if only for our children's sake." [35]

35 "The Creed of the Old South," *Atlantic Monthly,* LXIX (January, 1892), p. 87.

Two thoughts give "The Creed of the Old South" the flavor
of "unreconstructed" Southern writing: pride in having belonged to "an heroic generation" and satisfaction in having
served an intensely felt particular loyalty rather than a general and diffuse one. Southern men, he reminded the reader,
were often rebuked for a baseless pride, but the pride itself,
however disputable its grounds, was a factor to be reckoned
with. For

> the very pride played a part in making us what we were proud
> of being, and whether the descendants of the aforesaid "de-
> boshed" younger sons of decayed gentry, of simple English
> yeomen, of plain Scotch-Irish Presbyterians, a doughty stock,
> of Huguenots of various ranks of life, we all held to the same
> standard, and showed, as was thought, undue exclusiveness on
> this subject.[36]

Whether excessive addiction to a local patriotism may
reach the point of treason is debatable, but Gildersleeve saw,
as others have seen after him, that attachment to the place of
one's nativity is an indispensable element in any larger patriotism. Andrew Carnegie, "a canny Scot who has constituted himself the representative of American patriotism, not
without profit," had mentioned how under the new settlement one felt prouder of being an American than of being a
citizen of any particular state. To this Gildersleeve's answer
was: "What it means to be a native of any state in the country, especially an old state with an ancient and honorable
history, is something Mr. Carnegie cannot possibly understand." [37] For those who brought up the matter of the "expense of independence" he had an equally scornful reply:
" 'Counting the cost' is in things temporal the only wise
course, as in the building of a tower, but there are times in
the life of an individual, of a people, when the things that are

36 *Ibid.*, p. 76.
37 *Ibid.*, p. 78.

eternal force themselves into the calculation, and then the abacus is nowhere." [38] And if a state is resolved upon a career of independence, it must resist the slightest encroachment as well as the greatest; to do otherwise means submission and slavery. It may happen, he conceded, that the effacement of state lines will prove "the wisdom of the future," but nothing is more certain than that "the poetry of life" will find its home in the old order, among those who chose to fight for home and fireside.[39]

"A Southerner in the Peloponnesian War," a half-serious comparison of the American civil conflict with the famous war of antiquity, follows the truism that all wars are one war. Gildersleeve proceeded to show how the American struggle could be described down to astonishingly small details in the language of Thucydides. The ancient affair was "a war between two leagues, a Northern Union and a Southern Confederacy. The Northern Union, represented by Athens, was a naval power; the Southern Confederacy under the leadership of Sparta, was a land power. The Athenians represented the progressive element, the Spartans the conservative. The Athenians believed in a strong centralized government. The Lacedaemonians professed a greater regard for autonomy." [40] Slavery happened not to be an issue, for all ancient civilizations were slave societies, but there were the trade jealousies between Athens, Megara, and Corinth. Megara, like the South, was blockaded: the cry in the South for sugar was matched by the cry of the Peloponnesians for honey, and the dearth in the South of materials for lighting purposes finds its counterpart in the scarcity of oil, an Attic product, among those fighting Athens.

It would be misleading to read much serious intent into

38 *Ibid.*, p. 79.
39 *Ibid.*, p. 87.
40 "A Southerner in the Peloponnesian War," *Atlantic Monthly*, LXXX (September, 1897), pp. 334-335.

this comparison, but if one regards it for its significance rather than for what it specifically says, he finds a beginning of that detachment which would enable Southerners to put themselves back in the world picture and drop the embarrassing role of a singular nation and a singular people.[41]

In the same year which saw "The Creed of the Old South," William Peterfield Trent published a life of William Gilmore Simms, the chief purpose of which was to lay the blame for Simms' lack of recognition on the "primitive nature" of the Southern people. Since the work is a critical study of Simms in his relationship to Southern civilization, it may be considered as an important part of the revaluation. Trent displayed here a Tennysonian faith in the certainty of progress, and the picture was easy for him to decipher: the North was prepared and determined to go forward; the South, with equal determination and more temper, was resolved to go her way, which was backward. Yet when Trent brought the struggle into the higher reaches of speculation, he could do only what many a less sophisticated person had done before him, which was to invoke destiny as a prime mover. "All life is a struggle; and the higher planes of existence, individual as well as national, are reached by toil, by slow degrees, by pain." [42] There is little difference between this and an infinitude of postbellum sermons. He continued upon the assumption that "it was the forces of destiny in the main that placed the South in her direful position; and it was the forces of destiny that made the North the instrument by which the whole country, North and South, was finally saved for what we all believe will be a glorious future." [43]

Five years later in an article entitled "Dominant Forces in Southern Life" Trent took a yet closer look at the Southern

41 *Ibid.*, p. 342.
42 *William Gilmore Simms*, p. 287.
43 *Ibid.*

people in an attempt to explain to the nation their "unity in diversity." He wished to determine whether it is profitable in any discussion to refer to Southerners as a distinct group, and his finding was that it is profitable despite the libels, half-truths, exaggerations, and misnomers which had been bandied about in sectional controversy.

He would at the beginning make certain concessions to the traditional view of the South. It was true, for example, that Southerners were descended from those Englishmen who retained longest a part of the "feudal notion." Thus the familiar claim that the South had a Cavalier heritage had a small but real basis in fact. It was also a proved reality that slavery encouraged a patriarchal attitude among the ruling whites. But acknowledging these to be elements in the general complexion, he found disparities which had to be accounted for in any complete stocktaking of the Southern people. Southerners were sufficiently attached to their states to fight for them, and one can discover on examination that the people do differ roughly by states. The Virginian is the eighteenth-century English squire, fond of bonhommie and good living, and although to the country as a whole he typifies the Southern aristocrat, he is measurably more democratic than his cousin, the South Carolinian. The South Carolinian is the seventeenth-century Royalist, masterful, conscious of his position, and because of an infusion of Huguenot blood, somewhat stern. He is the most provincial of the Southerners. He "actually wishes to be rooted in a particular parish or town. The *genus loci* is the god he worships, and he stands for everything that is not cosmopolitan." [44] North Carolina, the most bourgeois of states, is the home of the typical Southern democrat, less fancy than his neighbors, but willing to work for a good thing; and Georgians are properly denomi-

[44] "Dominant Forces in Southern Life," *Atlantic Monthly*, LXXIX (January, 1897), p. 44.

nated the Yankees of the South. Louisianians have learned
how to enjoy life, but have been conspicuously lacking in
ambition, and the Tennesseean may well be considered more
Western than Southern, or as "with" the South rather than
"of" it. All this prepares for the generalization that the
Southern people are "heterogeneous in manners, but homogeneous in ideas." [45]

These are discriminating sketches, and no one versed in the
Southern regions could take exception to them unless on the
basis of local patriotism, but there remains the question of
what can be predicated of these people as they take their
place in the picture of the reconstructed nation. The first
lesson to be mastered is that the South has not escaped from
its yesterdays. The Negro is still there, and with him a drag-
weight on the industry, independence, and personal industry
of the whites. The poor white is still there too, with his unfortunate heritage and his comparative unteachability. The
rural South is a decayed country; the calling of gentleman
farmer has vanished except in a few localities where the lush-
ness of nature makes failure difficult. Cities develop, and with
them the urbanized Southerner, who inevitably gains
shrewdness and loses some of the traditional virtues. Politics
remains abysmal; orthodoxy enfeebles the press and retards
education; and there is no literature "except in the narrow
field of provincial storytelling." [46] The general view is dis-
maying, but Trent thought he spied a source of hope in the
slow disintegration of old creeds, which would leave room for
some free play of the mind. The salvation of the South lay in
the "growing liberalization of ideas, which is visible in politics and literature and religion, and which renders it certain
that no long time will elapse before the advent of both philosophy and statesmanship." [47]

45 *Ibid.*, p. 49.
46 *Ibid.*, p. 51.
47 *Ibid.*, p. 53.

Just as this article is less severe in its strictures than the life of Simms, so the life of Robert E. Lee, which Trent prepared for the Beacon Biographies, represents a further stage of mellowing. This work, which he admittedly commenced in a skeptical spirit, believing that much of the praise of Lee had been partisan fustian, turned into something approaching a panegyric, in which the great Virginian is charmingly set forth as a knight *sans peur et sans reproche,* and "a master of the art—not the trade—of war." [48]

It would be broadly true to say that Trent's writings upon the South constitute a progressive extenuation of the Southern cause, for in the next year he appeared with "Gleanings from an Old Southern Newspaper," a gracious study of an antebellum community, in which he concluded that slaveholders as a class were "kind-hearted men who made the best of a bad system handed down to them from an epoch callous to human rights and suffering." [49]

To the list of trained scholars who undertook to re-evaluate the figures of the Southern past must be added Edwin Mims, whose *Sidney Lanier* is an attempt to do for the chief poet of the South what Trent had done for its chief novelist. Though uncertain in point of view and perhaps complacent in the face of contradictions, it presents Lanier as one of the more determined voices of the New South. The author proceeded at some length to score the advocates of the old régime as men who "failed to understand the meaning of defeat." [50] They saw the war as a triumph of brute force; they regarded the Negro as incapable of improvement; they fought stubbornly for an exclusive system of education; they made puerile overestimates of Southern achievement. He found Lanier distinguished from these by his conviction that "belief

48 *Robert E. Lee* (Boston, 1889), p. 61.
49 "Gleanings from an Old Southern Newspaper," *Atlantic Monthly,* LXXXV (September, 1900), p. 364.
50 *Sidney Lanier,* p. 272.

in the sacredness and greatness of the American Union among the millions of the North and of the great Northwest is really the principle which conquered us"; [51] by his sympathetic feeling toward the erstwhile enemy; by his opposition to "the looseness of thought among our people"; [52] and by his strong interest in science and improved agriculture as a means of recreating the fallen section.

Pragmatic in his approach, Mims found the "New South" as employed by Lanier not a reproach to the "Old South," but a "recognition of changed social life due to one of the greatest catastrophes in history." [53] Lanier is placed with Atticus Haygood, Benjamin Hill, and Henry Grady as one of "a group of far-seeing, liberal-minded, aggressive Georgians," who pioneered the work of "upbuilding."

With the opening of the new century, even the *Atlantic Monthly* was ready for a re-appraisal of the chapter of American history most inflamed by partisan dispute. Beginning in January, 1901, it published a series of ten articles, mostly by Southerners, re-assessing the years since Appomattox. Woodrow Wilson led the list of contributors with the "Reconstruction of the Southern States," a learned but formal and austere study, which betrays in one pregnant and perhaps unguarded statement what the restored union meant to this future President: "It is evident that empire is an affair of strong government, and not of the nice and somewhat artificial poise or of the delicate compromises of structure and authority characteristic of a mere federal partnership." [54] Hilary Herbert, who ten years earlier had edited *Why the Solid South?*, reviewed the general problems of Reconstruction, and Daniel H. Chamberlain recounted South Carolina's melancholy ex-

---

[51] *Ibid.*, p. 266.
[52] *Ibid.*, p. 267.
[53] *Ibid.*, p. 276.
[54] "The Reconstruction of the Southern States," *Atlantic Monthly,* LXXXVII (January, 1901), p. 14.

perience, expressing the unequivocal opinion that "To all who feel a real solicitude for the welfare of the Southern negro, it ought to be said that the conditions of his welfare lie in reversing at all points the spirit and policy of Reconstruction." [55] William Garrott Brown of Alabama described the Ku Klux Klan, and though he asserted, like nearly all other Southerners, that it had been a necessary device of the hour, he could not overlook its crippling effect upon society. "Southern society was righted"; but a paralyzing solidity holds the Southern people prisoner. "They outdid their conquerors, yet they are not free." [56]

Thomas Nelson Page contributed a notable essay, "The Southern People During Reconstruction." Although Page was an exponent of the Old South in all he wrote, one would go far to find a discussion more judicious than this, or more earnest in its purpose to discern the motives and understand the limitations of all involved in the great disturbance. He emphasized the attachment of the Southern people to the soil. Because they "loved the land on which they had been reared with a devotion little short of idolatry," and because they were "habituated to rule," they believed in personal defense of their rights, whether by the ceremonious code duello, or by ruder methods. Such attachment always results in intense provincialism.

> They knew little more of the modern outside foreign world than they knew of Assyria and Babylon; that is, they knew it almost exclusively from books. They knew no more of New England and the rest of the North than New England knew of them, and that is not a large measure.[57]

These insular people, however, came home from the war

[55] "Reconstruction in South Carolina," *ibid.*, LXXXVII (April, 1901), p. 483.
[56] "The Ku Klux Movement," *ibid.*, LXXXVII (May, 1901), p. 644.
[57] "The Southern People During Reconstruction," *ibid.*, LXXXVIII (September, 1901), p. 289.

feeling that man for man they were superior to their opponents, and this conviction, together with the already potent
pride of race, formed a spirit which enabled them to weather
Reconstruction.

One indignant Northerner, at a date immediately after the
war, had compared the Southern people to the Bourbons;
they had learned nothing, he said, and they had forgotten
nothing. Though the conquered side, they came swaggering
up in the old spirit of arrogance to dictate the terms of the
peace. How this impression could be given may be seen from
the following story related by Page: A tattered and worn
Confederate soldier, trudging to his home after the war, was
asked what he would do if the Yankees got after him. "Oh,
they ain't goin' to trouble me," he said. "If they do, I'll just
whip 'em again." [58]

Page did not dwell on the evils of Reconstruction, but he
remarked that when the North approached the Negro problem in a spirit of arrogance and bigotry, it was met by the
same spirit; and where it had expected settlement, it produced only aggravation. He concluded his article with a
statement which the editors of the *Atlantic* looked upon as
begging the question. Its intent, however, was plain: "That
intelligence, virtue, and force of character will eventually
rule is as certain in the states of the South as it is elsewhere;
and everywhere it is as certain as the operation of the law of
gravitation. Whatever people wish to rule in those states
must possess these qualities." [59]

The scholars rendered no mean service to the South by
bringing universal considerations to bear upon her history,
but they did not, except in local contests, labor for reform.
Aristocrats by temperament for the most part, they wrote
with detachment. Their interest was mainly in discovering

[58] *Ibid.*, p. 293.
[59] *Ibid.*, p. 304.

the *causa causans* of Southern society. They helped Southern self-confidence, perhaps, by showing that antebellum civilization could receive sympathetic interpretation by the learned. Under the conditions then existing their audience, however fit, could not be numerous. The work of arousing the populace was reserved for journalists and politicians, and it was they who first gained attention for the attack on Southern tradition.

3. *The First Liberals*

Though the decade of the '90's saw the United Confedeate Veterans at the peak of their strength and witnessed the formation of the political Solid South, it saw also the first stirrings of Southern liberalism. Since this birth was a rebellion against what Walter Hines Page, its bravest and best equipped champion, called an "unyielding stability of opinion," it was perhaps right that it should begin in the field of education. Page himself was born in North Carolina, the son of a father out of sympathy with dominant Southern ideals. Although his education, which included a period under the incomparable Basil Gildersleeve, was such as might have made him another defender of the faith, he developed a hostility to those forces which kept Southern thought conservative, narrow, and uncritical. While a very young man he had described a typical small Southern community for the *Atlantic Monthly* in "Study of an Old Southern Borough." In this he tried to demonstrate that the South could build something fine upon the foundation of its inheritance, but already he gave signs of resenting the constrictions of the tradition. There could be little opportunity for improvement in a society where every man "considers the influence of his opinion either *pro* or *con* on a given subject of the greatest importance, and . . . looks to its finally conquering all opposition." [60] He had seen other young men rebel against the inertia resulting from this condition: "The only successful rebellion, however, is an immediate departure" [61]—a dictum which foreshadowed his own course. At the height of his career as an editor, Page collected and published his indictments of the old order under the title *The Rebuilding of Old Commonwealths*. Judged as a piece of crusading journalism, this little volume is almost beyond praise.

Page believed that whatever the needs of the past—and he was never bitter against the ideal of the Old South—the time for self-satisfaction and self-flattery was now over, and he proposed to tell his people exactly what their perverse dogmas had done for them. In the first section, which had been prepared as a speech on "The Forgotten Man," he observed:

> Thus we have come to put a false value on our social structure, and we have never looked ourselves in the face and seen ourselves as others see us. This false view has done an incalculable hurt. All social progress must begin with a clear understanding of men as they are. We are all common folk, then, who were once dominated by a little aristocracy, which, in its social and economic character, made a failure, and left a stubborn crop of wrong social notions behind it—especially about education.[62]

He illustrated this with a story about his classmate in a famous boys' school, who one day had come into his room and burst into tears of humiliation "because his father was not a Colonel." [63] In the days of aristocratic domination the two molders of public opinion had been the stump and the pul-

[60] "Study of an Old Southern Borough," *Atlantic Monthly*, XLVII (May, 1881), p. 649.
[61] *Ibid.*, p. 654.
[62] *The Rebuilding of Old Commonwealths* (New York, 1905), p. 9.
[63] *Ibid.*, p. 7.

pit; and both of these had generated false philosophies of education. The aristocrat, with his conception of education as a special privilege, had given the masses a notion that for them learning was not attainable, and from this they had drawn a conclusion—still of startling prevalence in the South —that it was not desirable. Religious leaders had a somewhat broader outlook, but the training they provided was for the sake of the church and not for the sake of the people, and they preached to the forgotten man a doctrine which only confirmed him in his inertia. In some of the boldest sentences ever spoken in Southern halls, Page put down the politician and the preacher as the chief impediments to Southern progress and invited them to step out of the way while North Carolina got on with her educational program.

In "The School that Built a Town" he took a concrete instance to show how public education could revolutionize the life of an entire community. This town had been led to abandon the usual view of the teaching profession as a refuge for needy women, or as the monopoly of the old-fashioned schoolmaster "who made the boys learn the Latin grammar by heart, and who flogged them when they failed." It sought instead instructors in applied arts and sciences. Page based his case on the theory that no country can be great unless it possesses sufficient social mobility to allow its citizens to find places consonant with their gifts. The unanswerable argument in favor of democratic education is that it enriches the community by discovering aptitudes. "Society forever needs re-inforcements from the rear." [64] Slavery, by "pickling Southern society" had made impossible that rise through talent and industry which is the selective process of the world. Now that slavery was gone, and with it the old aristocracy, it was a simple necessity for the South to establish an educational system in order to find its leaders. People who failed to see this

[64] *Ibid.*, p. 89.

truth, Page told his readers, were one of the reasons why property in the South was not worth five times what it was: "You are a frayed-out 'knight' of feudal times with a faded plume, and you think in terms of the Middle Ages; and the sooner you know it the better for the community, and I am glad of a chance plainly to tell you so." [65] But he was sure that no man "who can distinguish dominant from incidental forces" doubted that education and industry would in the course of time defeat the reactionary impulses, now "respectable" but "spent."

A few years later Page put these concepts into a novel, which he entitled *The Southerner, or the Autobiography of Nicholas Worth*. It is a work replete with brilliant insights into Southern and Northern character, and remorseless, though not bitter exposures of those elements which the author viewed as blocking progress in his native section. Nicholas Worth is a young Southerner who grows up an eyewitness to the deeds of war and Reconstruction, goes to Harvard for an education, and returns home puzzled over what to do about the discrepancy between his poor South and the wealthy, educated, and progressive East. His efforts to get his people to see the value of education and to rally them behind some political program which will incorporate something more than the old fustian and bombast constitute a complete course in the sociology of the South. Page opposed the Confederate mind, but he understood it, and that means he knew by what process it had come to be. The psychological effect of the war on the surviving Southern males he viewed as more unforunate than the physical devastation.

It gave everyone of them the intensest experience of his life, and ever afterwards he referred every other experience to this. Thus it stopped the thought of most of them as an earthquake stops a clock. The fierce blow of battle paralyzed the mind.

[65] *Ibid.*, p. 76.

Their speech was the vocabulary of war; their loyalties were loyalties, not to living ideas or duties, but to old commanders and to distorted traditions. They were dead men, most of them, moving among the living as ghosts; and yet, as ghosts in a play, they held the stage.[66]

A typical figure is Colonel Stringweather, representative of the politically potent "rebel brigadiers." One learns that "The poor old Colonel gloried in the poverty of our people. He used to say that the South was the only country left in the world where men are content without money, believe in God, read Scott's novels, bake sweet potatoes properly, and vote the Democratic ticket." [67]

But when Nicholas Worth tries with the firmest intention to break away from a sectional attachment and to escape the hampering effect of a sectional label, he finds himself in a dilemma. Neither in his own section nor outside it will he be accepted as a member of a common genre. In the South his compatriots expect him to behave as a "Southerner," and if he goes beyond her borders, his opinions are listened to as those of a "Southerner." Every Southern-born man carries about with him a ghost, which somehow remains master of his actions. And this ghost is "the old defensive man." [68] The crippling self-consciousness which comes of always being judged as a problem or a special product has done more than anything else to keep Southerners from a full and free participation in the national life. Page saw that other sections were in a measure to blame for this situation.

In such a position many Southern young men chose the simple alternative of flight, and rehabilitation in a region without such encumbrances. Nicholas Worth lost his teaching post when it was bruited about that he represented forces "Against the Church, and the ex-Confederates and the Pious

66 *The Southerner* (New York, 1909), p. 46.
67 *Ibid.*, p. 388.
68 *Ibid.*, p. 390.

Lady and our Honored Dead and Anglo-Saxon Civilerza-
tion." [69] Many another so aspersed had deemed the odds
hopeless and fled, diminishing by that much the already
scanty talent of the South. Page was outlining the most melancholy trend in postbellum history when he wrote: "The
backwardness of the Southern people is to a large degree the
result of this forced immigration of many of its young men
who would have been the leaders of the people and the
builders of a broader sentiment." [70] But with the curious
ambivalence which arises in the breasts of even her most
offended sons, Worth stays on and resolves to fight it out with
the rebel brigadiers.

After losing the election to forces of the old order, comprised of men who will deal with him in private in a kindly
and sincere fashion, but who, once the old issues of race, caste
and fealty are raised, will oppose him in public with every
unscrupulous device of demagoguery, Worth perceives a further split in the Southern character: one half of it is genuine,
natural, sensible; the other is a strange medley of poses, fixed
reactions, and lofty professions completely out of line with
reality.

The keynote of the book is struck when his friend, "Professor Billy," declares "we can't at once work a revolution for
education among a people who do not yet care to be educated." [71] Page thus realized what many persons born outside
the culture are never able to grasp, that the Southern resistance to "education" and "progress" is not just a negative
thing—not merely a matter of torpor—but a positive one; it is
part of the old pride in being a military, outdoor, unbookish,
"sound" people, who prefer to be wrong in their own way
rather than right in another's, and who have no desire to

69 *Ibid.*, p. 181.
70 *Ibid.*
71 *Ibid.*, p. 294.

emulate the triumphs of New England, the "section of long-haired men and short-haired women." If it were only a matter of gaining physical access to them, or of bringing them to wakefulness, the revolution would have been accomplished years ago. It is instead the far more difficult task of winning them over to a completely different scale of values.

Although Page was easily the best-known voice of Southern liberalism, he was not without allies, especially in his own state of North Carolina. The history of North Carolina liberalism affords a topic in itself. Settled by a thrifty and self-reliant population of Scotch-Irish and Germans, this state never had to face the heritage of powerful traditions such as conserved the old order in Virginia and South Carolina. Its inhabitants were for the most part small farmers and tradesmen, without pretensions, who felt no embarrassment over severing with the past and accepting the practical tasks necessary to build up a commonwealth. Even with these advantages, however, it got a late start; for political corruption and the threat of Negro rule made systematic development impossible until 1900, when Charles Brantley Aycock was elected governor on a platform of white supremacy and universal education. From this point forward North Carolina led the Southern states in what the remainder of the nation styled progress.

Governor Aycock was a man of exactly the right kind to promote such a movement. Although at the University of North Carolina he had distinguished himself in the humanities and in the then generally admired art of oratory, a short perusal of his speeches will show that his was not a great intellect. He was a man well endowed with the bourgeois gift of common sense; he was a sagacious student of people; and he possessed just enough book learning to realize the value of it and to covet it for others. He was, in brief, another common man, writ large in his own state. So he went up and down North Carolina and later over the South, carrying the message of education, often appealing to his audience with homely anecdotes and parables which presumed very slight acquaintance with book learning. Like Page, he offered the people of his state the cogent argument that whereas in the old days an aristocracy was depended on to send qualified leaders to the front, today that aristocracy was no more, and only the schools could perform this work of selection.

It is very nearly true to say that if one scratches a Southern liberal, he finds, perhaps not a conservative, but at least one with strong convictions about individualism and local prerogative. The liberalism of Aycock, as that of Grady and others who could be named, took the form of a battle for specific improvements, but did not include a surrender to rationalism, or "the dishwater of modern world citizenship," to recall the expressive phrase of Thomas Dixon. The great substratum of Southern conservatism in Aycock's character occasionally betrayed itself in a distrust of the skeptical habit of mind, and in an affirmation, not heard everywhere, that virtue and literacy are not interchangeable terms. Speaking on "The Genius of North Carolina Interpreted," he boasted: "Illiterate we have been, but ignorant never. Books we have not known, but men we have learned, and God we have sought to find out." And he accepted it as a matter for congratulation that North Carolina had "nowhere within her borders a man known out of his township ignorant enough to join with the fool in saying 'There is no God.' " [72]

Governor Aycock was, moreover, a patriot in the sense that Walter Hines Page was not. Speaking in New York City in 1901, he made the defiant pronouncement: "There are two subjects on which I take it there can be no debate—that the States had the right to secede in 1861, and that they no longer

[72] *The Life and Speeches of Charles Brantley Aycock,* ed. R. D. W. Connor and Clarence Poe (New York, 1912), p. 277.

have that right"; [73] and in the following year at the Charleston Exposition, in the presence of President Theodore
Roosevelt, he rebuked the Governor of South Carolina for
making a concession on this point. Governor McSweeney, in
a burst of warm feeling, had expressed regret that the South
did not share the Northern view of the war. Whereupon
Aycock, to the sound of tumultuous applause, said, "There is
a South and a glorious South, and we are not ashamed of
what our fathers wrought in the days from '61 to '65." [74]

It was characteristic of the student of men rather than of
books that Aycock did not call for an abdication of character.
Universal education did not mean for him a general "Yan-
keefication" of North Carolina and the rest of the section,
but a cultivation of local virtues and aptitudes. In an address
before the Southern Educational Association in 1903 he
urged the point that

> No people can ever become a great people by exchanging their
> individuality, but only by developing and encouraging it. We
> must build on our own foundation of character, temperament,
> and inherited traits. We must not repudiate but develop. We
> must seek out and appreciate our own distinctive traits, our
> own traditions, our deep-rooted tendencies, and read our des-
> tiny in their interpretation.[75]

Closely allied with Page and Aycock in their work to forward the educational system of North Carolina was Charles
Duncan McIver. Active principally as a teacher and a super-
intendent of education, McIver wrote little that will be remembered, but the eloquent memorial volume prepared by
the North Carolina State Normal and Industrial College testi-
fies to the universal esteem in which he was held. His liberalism rested on a conviction that "the distinguishing charac-

[73] *Ibid.*, p. 153.
[74] *Ibid.*, p. 269.
[75] *Ibid.*, p. 281.

teristic of Americanism is its theory, and I am glad to say its usual practice of giving every man, woman, and child a fair chance in life." [76]

The record of the liberal group would be incomplete without mention of Edgar Gardner Murphy, a minister of the Episcopal Church, who during a residence in Montgomery, Alabama, made some intelligent studies of the vexed race question. His work, *The Problems of the Present South*, published in 1905, approaches several old topics from fresh angles. Murphy interpreted the extreme sensitiveness of Southerners to criticism from the outside not as a sign that they felt guilty of evading plain duties, but on the contrary as proof that they had worthy goals in view and that they were painfully conscious of tardy progress toward them. He thought that the old aristocracy, instead of being a dead weight on all advance, would prove the real strength of the new democracy. The day of aristocratic ascendancy was over, but he felt that the qualities of that class, the finest of which was a sense of responsibility, lived on to impart valuable features to the new social alliance. [77] And the white race, now back on its feet after surviving several decades of attack, was in a position to include the Negro in the general program of responsibility. But like Governor Aycock, Murphy saw the Negro problem with the eyes of a realist, and he argued that a separate development of the races is the only workable solution. The purpose of segregation was not to degrade the Negro, but to give him his only conceivable chance to progress. "There is no hope for a race that begins by despising itself," and nothing could be worse, he thought, than to teach the Negro that he must go outside himself for any share in the world of enjoyment and knowledge. The Negroes must instead be taught "race sufficiency," which would mean the production of "its own leaders and thinkers, its own scholars,

[76] From McIver's biennial report of 1902, *Charles Duncan McIver* (Greensboro, N. C., 1907), p. 271.

[77] *The Problems of the Present South* (New York, 1909), p. 17.

artists, and prophets." [78] The South was acting with instinctive wisdom when it realized that good fences make good neighbors and that an indiscriminate mingling such as visionaries at the North had urged would only multiply the points of friction, leaving the dreamed-of "equality" as chimerical as ever.

These are the views of one who studied the problems of a bi-racial community on the ground, and not in the textbooks of revolutionaries.

Murphy not only championed a fair discussion of the race question; he was also among the first to expose the shameless exploitation of Southern child labor by Northern industrial interests, and his efforts eventually led to the organization of the National Child Labor Committee.

The program of the liberals may be summed up as a belief in general education, a plea for a more fluid society, a call to recognize the main currents of the world's life. They contended that the forces of the *ancien régime* had lost creativeness and were spending themselves in the celebration of past glories. Had there been a different conservatism, able to present better the values it defended, and ready to make the adjustments inevitably required by passing time, the contest might not have seemed, as it did to Page and others, an opposition between the dead and the living. The liberal attack was against petrifaction. Actually there was not much in the program which the conservative Southerner could not have accepted, unless he was abnormally fearful of thought and recreant to his own "proper sentiments."

4. The South in the Nation

While the scholars were endeavoring to explain the place of the South in the continuum of history and the liberals were striving to make it more responsive to current impulses,

78 *Ibid.*, p. 274.

another group of spokesmen, difficult to label in terms of party or predilection, were acting as ambassadors of goodwill to the nation at large.

No man was more eagerly heard in all sections than Henry Watterson, editor of the Louisville *Courier-Journal.* Watterson had been "in and out" of the Confederate army for four years; at Chattanooga he had edited a propaganda paper of distinguished quality called *The Rebel;* and settled in Louisville after the war, he had opened the fight on carpetbaggery "when the *Courier-Journal* was one day old." After thirty years of speechmaking North and South, in which he strove as resolutely as anyone to bury sectionalism as a political force, he published his discourses as *The Compromises of Life.* A study of their leading ideas reveals an anomaly which is by now familiar: a repudiation of the abstract doctrines for which the Confederacy stood, and a defense of those things which were the substance of the Old South—the art of good living, provincial pride, and a dislike of "modern impiousness." He could cheerfully bid goodbye to a "system which, because it was so contented, refused to realize, or to be impressed by the movements of mankind"; [79] yet he was conscious of a loss of values. Confessing that postbellum Kentucky was no match for the old commonwealth to which the entire nation had looked for eloquence and leadership, he asserted that "the present generation of Kentuckians is relapsing into a state of mediocre indifferentiality and a relaxation of that provincial pride which lay at the bottom of the supremacy once enjoyed by the commonwealth." [80] The decline of Kentucky was simultaneous with that of "the soldierly and gentleman-like school." [81] It resulted from a "heaven-defying modern impiousness, which scorns the old, slow, and homely methods, in a vain and wicked effort to

[79] *The Compromises of Life* (New York, 1903), p. 101.
[80] *Ibid.,* p. 269.
[81] *Ibid.*

formularize society under certain universally recognized conventional limitations." [82] He went further to say, "The provincial spirit, which is dismissed from polite society in a half-sneering, half-condemnatory way, is really one of the forces of human achievement. As a man loves his provincialism he loves, in part, his originality, and, in this way, so much of his power as proceeds from his originality." [83] He added the striking paraphrase, "What is life to me if I gain the whole world and lose my province?" [84] Even while defending provincialism and attacking "miserable, cosmopolitan frivolity," Watterson made himself a national influence and the last great figure of personal journalism.

In this same period Edwin Alderman, distinguished president of the University of Virginia, was diligently setting before the nation the virtues of Southern life and society. He described the gift of the South as a spiritual heritage, which had met some checks, as any spiritual force in a material world is bound to do, but which had never failed to display its intrinsic value. Like Thomas Dixon, Alderman held the view that Southern conservatism and pride of locality, plus a pure attitude toward government, might prove in some future crisis the salvation of the country. He entertained the fear of all traditionalists that the destruction of old customs would bring not the millennium, but chaos and the rule of blind passion. In an address at the University of California he told his audience that they could count on the South in the day of that distress:

> And so when the age of moral warfare shall succeed to the age of passionate gain-getting; when blind social forces have wrought some tangle of inequality and of injustice, of hatred and suspicion, when calculation and combination can only weave the web more fiercely: when the whole people in some

[82] *Ibid.*, p. 270.
[83] *Ibid.*
[84] *Ibid.*, p. 273.

hour of national peril shall seek for the man of heart and
faith, who will not falter or fail, in the sweet justice of God,
hither shall they turn for succor as once they turned to a
simple Virginia planter.[85]

Men of this type served to make the South an articulate
minority while encouraging it to remain a conscious one.

In the opening decade of the century the South was advancing so rapidly in courage and prosperity that a determined bid for recognition seemed due. Henry James had
described the section as "disinherited of literature," and
Southern intellectuals were made sensitive by the habit of dis-
counting whatever came from below the Mason-Dixon line,
or of regarding it superciliously as "pretty good for the
South." Obviously the only answer to this prejudice was a
lesson in the facts of Southern achievement, and a group of
Southerners prepared to give this to the nation. Trent,
Alderman, Mims, W. L. Fleming, and a few others were the
moving spirits behind two impressive collections, the *Library
of Southern Literature* (1907), and *The South in the Building of the Nation* (1909).

The first was a fifteen-volume anthology of the best in
Southern writing under a rather inclusive principle of selection. As Charles W. Kent said in the general preface, it was
not intended to prove anything, but "to set forth much." No
other section of the Union, he declared, had been so little
given to exploiting its own accomplishments, and the small
figure which the South cut in the nation's culture was due
primarily to its reluctance to join the jostling throng and
clamor for recognition. Alderman undertook to explain the
sectional perspective by pointing out that sectionalism, which
"is naive and even sinister when its votaries merely distrust
those who do not live where they do," nevertheless, when
thoughtfully cultivated, is a source of "force, fruitfulness, and

[85] *The Spirit of the South* (Berkeley, 1906), p. 15.

beauty." [86] He recalled how Homer, Shakespeare, and Burns
had drawn from narrow locales the materials needed to mirror the world's experience. This afforded ground for the assertion that the South, which was of all sections the "richest
in romanticism and idealism, in tragedy and suffering, and in
pride of region and love of home" offered the same sources of
strength.

The second was an even more ambitious undertaking, for
it would record the whole achievement of the section, its
history, its notable lives, its literature and press, its arts and
sciences. In his introduction to the volume on "The Literary
and Intellectual Life of the South" Trent also felt it necessary to mention the indifference of Southerners towards advertising their deeds before the great world. Though he
would not pretend that the South had rivalled New England
or the Middle Atlantic states in contribution to intellectual
life, he believed that no other section had produced so admirable a group of political sages. Instead of trying to become Yankees,

> It seems much more desirable that we should endeavor to
> comprehend what our fathers stood for, especially in all mat-
> ters relating to self-government, then study calmly our own
> situation, and resolutely acknowledge and adapt the princi-
> ples and policies that seem most consonant with our welfare.
> So far as my own studies allow me to judge, no other people or
> fraction of a people has a more admirable body of publicists
> from whose writings inspiration and guidance may be derived.[87]

But he cautioned the Southern people to ask themselves
"whether . . . they are sufficiently trained in clear thought
and expression, and sufficiently bold, to make their political
and social ideals prevail." [88] Though most of the writers in

86 *Library of Southern Literature,* I, p. xix.
87 *The South in the Building of the Nation,* VII, p. xxiv.
88 *Ibid.,* VI, pp. xxvi-xxvii.

this symposium emphasized the liberal features of Southern life, the entire work was predicated on an assumption that there lay in the Southern inheritance much which should be brought forth, studied, and preserved in so far as it met the test of critical inspection.

Chancellor James H. Kirkland of Vanderbilt University saw the intellectual history of the South as a story of gradual emancipation. "Southern intolerance was the distinct legacy of slavery," [89] he wrote. This was true because in the South slavery had fought its last battle, the length and bitterness of which "attested the intellectual power, the resourcefulness of the defendants." [90] He felt that the advancement of the South would be measured by the intelligence shown in handling the Negro problem, for "we shall necessarily live by the standard of conduct we apply to him." [91]

Other contributors reviewed less publicized aspects of Southern culture, such as folklore, wit and humor, classical scholarship, and Southern influence upon the character and culture of the North.

One of the clearest signs of increased Southern vitality was a sudden outburst of magazine publication. The first decade following the war had witnessed the establishment of numerous journals of protest, none of which endured long. Little of consequence followed these with the exception of the *Sewanee Review,* whose honorable career, beginning in 1892, extends down to the present. Between 1905 and 1910 there appeared, as substantial evidence of life if not of literary competence, four periodicals of varying degrees of promise. Bob Taylor, the folk hero of Tennessee, began *Bob Taylor's Magazine,* which divided its content between a dreamy, poetic re-creation of the Old South and a sober estimate of business possibilities; John Trotwood Moore, Tennessee his-

89 *Ibid.,* VII, p. xli.
90 *Ibid.,* p. xlii.
91 *Ibid.,* p. xliv.

torian, inaugurated *Trotwood's Monthly,* which featured, for
the one part, Southern history, and for the other, the lore of
the horse breeder; Tom Watson removed his *Tom Watson's
Jeffersonian* from "hateful, calculating New York" to
Thomson, Georgia, where it became the militant champion
of a strange congeries of movements; and Joel Chandler
Harris undertook with the *Uncle Remus Magazine* to publish more of his great fund of Negro stories.

Bob Taylor's Magazine took its stand for the Old South, but
a great gulf lies between it and the belligerent, uncompro-
mising Southern organs of forty years earlier. There was no
longer the arduous work of coming to grips with an argument, of defending every inch of disputed territory. All was
mellow, nostalgic, and just evasive enough to allow one to
know that hope for a real restoration had been abandoned. A
sentimentality breathing of moonlight and magnolia and
urging goodwill to all men replaced the knotty syllogisms of
the great apologists. It was an extreme example of the tendency, by now widespread, to bury issues without caring to
analyze them, and to indulge in comforting recollections
without interest in marking their relevance to the present.

Trotwood's Monthly confined itself principally to descriptive and expository writing, but it was almost rabidly anti-
Negro. "For the South being a pure race is wise," wrote John
Trotwood Moore in endorsement of Ben Tillman's position
on the Negro issue, "and it knows that black and white may
be mixed to the end of time and never produce anything but
yellow. And yellow is now and will be forever the flag of the
mongrel." [92]

Apart from its dealings with racism, however, *Trotwood's
Monthly* preserved a fairly objective reportorial tone and
published historical monographs of real merit.

Tom Watson's Magazine, a strangely conceived attempt to

[92] *Trotwood's Monthly,* III (November, 1906), p. 153.

promote the theory of Jeffersonian democracy, spoke for the South on living political issues. Watson was a powerful but often quixotic personality; and to the traditional Southern stand in favor of state rights and racial exclusiveness, he added an intense hostility to the Roman Catholic hierarchy, to Big Business, and to the theory of socialism. Referring to the Negro, he declared that "The Southern man has his experiences and his necessities to fix his attitude; the Northern man has only his philosophy and his prejudices." [93] Later issues of the magazine attacked "Jew-hired and Jew-blinded journalists."

It is certain that all programs based on universalism will meet their greatest resistance in America in the individualistic, tradition-loving South. The socialist premise that patriotism is but a nickname for prejudice, for example, gave him a wonderful opportunity to attack the movement on grounds that Southerners would understand. Yet Watson was distinguished from other Southern editors of his time by an understanding of the true effects of the Northern financial invasion of the South. Many had prattled about "wealth" and "signs of progress" while deploring only the brusqueness of commercial ways. He understood that this wealth could lie in the South without belonging to it, that it could be exploited without raising the South's pitiful rank in the national economy. He saw, moreover, that there was a group among his own people willing to become the instruments of Northern domination while wearing the garb of sectional loyalty. To betray an ideal at the very moment one praises it is an ancient ruse, and some of those who talked most glibly of the antebellum South were the readiest to drive a bargain with Northern financial imperialism. They did not escape notice by the man who had learned politics in hard struggle against the money-power.

[93] *Tom Watson's Magazine*, I (April, 1907), p. 500.

The South moved into the new century feeling confidence in its future, and striving manfully to put its case before the nation, but actually conceiving that case rather badly. With hopeful exceptions here and there, its people suffered from intellectual stagnation. They were paying a heavy price for the old boast that the South affords poor soil for ideas. More alert minds, who realized that no people can really remain indifferent to the course of humanity, pleaded for a little more self-examination, a little more receptivity to new vision, a little more creative enterprise in place of the old threshing about of the dead leaves of recollection. The ultra-conservative Southerner, who worshipped the South in its crystallized form, was as much at fault as the devotee of "progress," who turns his back upon history and thinks of the past as so much error. But the Southern press retained just the right degree of orthodoxy to keep things settled at home while disarming criticism from abroad; the arduous work of thinking out problems to their ultimate conclusions was eschewed; and there was developing a tendency to rest content with second-rate achievements while pluming oneself on possession of the old-fashioned virtues. An increasing number of persons showed all the signs of final acceptance of defeat: a weariness, a dedication to the less dangerous occupation of money-getting, and a willingness to turn collaborationist and cooperate with the victor on all points.

The South which entered the twentieth century had largely ceased to be a fighting South.

Epilogue

HISTORY IS A LIBERAL ART AND ONE PROFITS BY STUDYING THE whole of it, including the lost causes. All of us are under a mortal temptation to grant the accomplished fact more than we should. That the fall of Rome, the dissolution of medieval Catholicism, the overthrow of Napoleon, the destruction of the Old South were purposeful and just are conclusions that only the tough-minded will question. But such events, hammered out by soldiers and politicians, by adventurers and traders, are hardly a guide to the moral world. They are text for the lesson, not the lesson itself, which should go beyond the waywardness of events. Behind all there must be a conception which can show the facts in something more than their temporal accidence. In this research, therefore, I have attempted to find those things in the struggle of the South which speak for something more than a particular people in a special situation. The result, it may be allowed, is not pure history, but a picture of values and sentiments coping with the forces of a revolutionary age, and though failing, hardly expiring.

The South possesses an inheritance which it has imperfectly understood and little used. It is in the curious position of having been right without realizing the grounds of its rightness. I am conscious that this reverses the common judgment; but it may yet appear that the North, by its ready embrace of science and rationalism, impoverished itself, and that the South by clinging more or less unashamedly to the primitive way of life prepared itself for the longer run.

It is an old Southern custom, however, to take too sanguine a view of the section's record, and before going further with this prophecy, one should make a candid examination of failures. The South committed two great errors in its struggle against the modern world, errors characteristic for it, but of disastrous consequence. The first was a failure to study its position until it arrived at metaphysical foundations. No Southern spokesman was ever able to show why the South was right *finally*. In other words, the South never perfected its world view, which determines in the end what we want and what we are. Legal arguments like those of the apologia are but a superstructure resting upon more fundamental assumptions; journalistic defenses, however brilliant in phrase, are likely to be even less; and fiction may serve only as a means of propagation. The South spoke well on a certain level, but it did not make the indispensable conquest of the imagination. From the Bible and Aristotle it might have produced its *Summa Theologia,* but none measured up to the task, and there is no evidence that the performance would have been rewarded. It needed a Burke or a Hegel; it produced lawyers and journalists. Perhaps the sin for which the South has most fully though unknowingly atoned is its failure to encourage the mind. Some fringes of excess it has thereby avoided, but it has had to compete against the great world with second-rate talent, and to accept the defensive where an offensive was indicated. One may understand the feeling which could boast of the South's freedom from *isms,* but this implies the existence of a satisfactory theology and metaphysics, which were not on hand. The lack continues, and today we behold Southern writers of amazing resource and virtuosity—I should instance here Thomas Wolfe—thrashing about in the world and almost terrifying us with their potentiality, but leaving in the end nothing but the record of an enormous sensibility. The average Southerner, pushed beyond the rather naive assumptions with which he sanctions his world, becomes helpless and explodes in anger.

Another great failure, and one for which people cannot be readily forgiven, is the surrender of initiative. So little has this section shown since 1865 that one is prompted to question whether the South ever really believed in itself. It is not that the South is uncreative; on the contrary it is pregnant and full of dreams; it is always sending abroad some novelty to be adapted and perfected; the list would be long and astonishing. But it seems to have no faith in its own *imprimatur*. It has been unwilling to buy books and magazines unless they came with the prestige of a Northern publisher; indeed this preference has extended over a vast range of things. Does it bespeak some deep-lying sense of incompetence, of inadequacy? The supposition clashes with the widely noticed presumption and conceit of the Southerner, with his faith in the rightness of his way of life, which have irritated numberless people from the outside.

I believe there is at bottom a consciousness of failure. Probably the decision of 1865 has been interpreted too literally. It has been regarded as casting a cloud over all Southern endeavor, so that the Southerner, despite efforts at compensation, has been unable to convince himself.

And more than likely this is to be traced to the first failure, the lack of a fundamental position from which he could judge his achievements with some assurance that the judgment would be vindicated.

In summary, I would say that the South needs now, as much as ever before, a metaphysic of its position, and that it must recover initiative at least to the point of following a right course without waiting for the North or for Washington to express approbation. Only this can diminish its hypersensitivity to criticism, which makes the task even of its friends difficult.

One might hesitate to say that the South, with such weaknesses, has anything to offer our age. But there is something in its heritage, half lost, derided, betrayed by its own sons, which continues to fascinate the world. This is a momentous fact, for the world is seeking as perhaps never before for the thing that will lift up our hearts and restore our faith in human communities. The search is not new; it began before the brashness of nineteenth-century confidence had worn away, and Henry Adams, wearied with the plausibilities of his day, looked for some higher reality in the thirteenth-century synthesis of art and faith. In a parallel way victims of the confusions and frustrations of our own time turn with live interest to that fulfillment represented by the Old South. And it is this that they find: *the last non-materialist civilization in the Western World.* It is this refuge of sentiments and values, of spiritual congeniality, of belief in the word, of reverence for symbolism, whose existence haunts the nation. It is damned for its virtues and praised for its faults, and there are those who wish its annihilation. But most revealing of all is the fear that it gestates the revolutionary impulse of our future.

Looking at the whole of the South's promise and achievement, I would be unwilling to say that it offers a foundation, or, because of some accidents of history, even an example. The most that it offers is a challenge. And the challenge is to save the human spirit by re-creating a non-materialist society. Only this can rescue us from a future of nihilism, urged on by the demoniacal force of technology and by our own moral defeatism.

The first step will be to give the common man a world view completely different from that which he has constructed out of his random knowledge of science. Without this the various schemes of salvation are but palliatives. What man thinks about the world when he is driven back to his deepest reflections and most secret promptings will finally determine all that he does. We might well ask for a second coming to

accomplish this change. Multitudes would wait with eagerness to learn

>   . . . What rough beast, its hour come round at last
>   Slouches toward Bethlehem to be born?

But we must put aside the temptation of literalism and consider from what source we are likely to get the needful revelation. Barring the advent of an illumination by some fateful personality, the task falls upon poets, artists, intellectuals,
upon workers in the timeless. We must again hearken to
these unacknowledged legislators of mankind. They alone
can impress us with some splendid image of man in a morally
designed world, ennobled by a conception of the transcend-
ent. They will have to abandon, and I am sure they will be
ready to abandon, the tortured imaginings of our vexed
decades. The rift between them and the people has not been
a rift of their own making, but the symptom of a deep lesion,
and its cure will have to be a part of the "healing of the
nations." The common man is now ready to discard his bas-
tard notions of science and materialism, intellectual hobbies
of a hundred years ago. Nor do I speak cynically here of a
pendulum movement in fads; non-materialist views of the
world have flourished for most of our history, have inspired
our best art and held together our healthiest communities.
This is, indeed, the "natural" view, whereas the other is
symbolic of spiritual decadence. The South had this view and
fought for it long, behind the barricades of revealed Christianity, of humanism, of sentiment; it battled somewhat
ineptly for lack of adequate weapons, but with inner conviction. Now it can return as to the house of its fathers.

The creation of a religious moral world will bring an end
to the downward conversion which today threatens institutions and culture. Equalitarians have always understood that

men must be equated through a lowest common denominator, which is appetite. All men are equal in that they get hungry and deserve to be fed; this is admissible on every side and should not be made a debating point in discussions of the future start. But as soon as we begin to refine the tests and to look for positive qualifications, we are at the threshold of those divisions which make society. We can then hope to distinguish between good and bad, between the wise and the foolish; we can have centers of power and influence; we can undertake the great task of demassing the masses. There will result a pluralistic world, in which one will not have to choose between being first at Rome and having no authority at all.

For the present tendency of the world's great states is in the direction of dictator or emperor worship. It is not a chosen course; the emperor will be elevated to his throne by science; he will be the source of control of power too dangerous for distributive ownership. Today we are running from our inventions, hiding from them, trying to reason away their awfuller potentialities. We shall soon have to perceive that science is democratic only in a treacherous sense. True, it brings the same thing to everyone, war to the babe in the cradle; it compels virtually all men to listen to radio edicts. But what of the source of the edicts? We are being narrowed down to one nation, to one world, in which nobody can move an elbow without jostling those in the farthest corner; and the danger of friction is so great that liberty of opposition must be decreased, channeled, and there must stand ready a supreme authority ready to strike down any menace to peace, to its peace, to the status quo. The emperor or dictator, of completely pervasive authority, backed by an oligarchy of scientists—that is the situation into which forces are hurrying us. The state becomes a monolith, rigid with fear that it has lost control of its destiny. We all stand today at Appomattox, and we are surrendering to a world which this hypostatized science has made in our despite.

By restoring the moral and aesthetic medium, we shall have a leverage on this. We can will our world, and retrieve our defeat by an upward conversion. This will revive those differences which mean as much to living as rules mean to a game, which are indeed the living that is not sustained by bread alone. Then man can again see his life as a drama and know the transfiguring interest that comes through conflict. The conflict will not be a meaningless strife of forces, into which scientists and utilitarians sought to usher him, but a conflict in the old sense of religious drama, between him, with what he can apprehend of the good, and the powers of evil.

Distinctions of many kinds will have to be restored, and I would mention especially one whose loss has added immeasurably to the malaise of our civilization—the fruitful distinction between the sexes, with the recognition of respective spheres of influence. The re-establishment of woman as the cohesive force of the family, the end of the era of "long-haired men and short-haired women," should bring a renewal of well-being to the whole of society. On this point Southerners of the old school were adamant, and even today, with our power of discrimination at its lowest point in history, there arises a feeling that the roles of the sexes must again be made explicit. George Fitzhugh's brutal remark that if women put on trousers, men would use them for plowing has been borne out, and I think that women would have more influence actually if they did not vote, but, according to the advice of Augusta Evans Wilson, made their firesides seats of Delphic wisdom.

One word of advice must be given to workers for this new order. Considerations of strategy and tactics forbid the use of symbols of lost causes. There cannot be a return to the Mid-

dle Ages or the Old South under slogans identified with
them. The principles must be studied and used, but in such
presentation that mankind will feel the march is forward.
And so it will be, to all effects. It is a serious thing to take
from the average man, and perhaps from anyone, his belief in
progress. The average man's metaphysic is summed up by this
word; "progressive" is his token of approval. Therefore the
future will always be the future, and we need not lecture
tediously on the imperishability of principles. It is enough if
we let them inform the new order, while adorning them with
the attractions of the hour. "The river of knowledge often
turns back on itself," and there are progressive revolutions to
an earlier condition. As long as we keep our course clear by
acknowledging the primacy of knowledge and virtue and
avoid a surrender to suppositious "objective necessity," we
can still reconstruct our life on a humane basis.

There is a certain harrowing alternative to be pointed out
as a possibility of our inaction or our failure. It is undeniable
that there are numerous resemblances between the Southern
agrarian mind and the mind of modern fascism, and I would
affirm that fascism too in its ultimate character is a protest
against materialist theories of history and society. This is
certain despite the fact that fascism immersed itself in materialist techniques for its conquests, and thereby failed. This
other society too believes in holiness and heroism; but it is
humane, enlightened, and it insists on regard for personality
more than do modern forms of statism under liberal and
social-democratic banners. Above all, in meeting the problem
of motivation it does what social democracy has never been
able to do. Now that truth can once more be told, let us
admit that fascism had secret sympathizers in every corner
of the world and from every social level. It attracted by its
call to achievement, by its poetry, by its offer of a dramatic
life. It attracted even by its call to men to be hard on them-

selves. Social democracy will never be able to compete with this by promising to each a vine-covered cottage by the road and cradle-to-grave social security. People who are yet vital want a challenge in life; they want opportunity to win distinction, and even those societies which permit distinction solely through the accumulation of wealth and its ostentatious display, such as ours has been, are better than those that permit none. From the bleakness of a socialist bureaucracy men will sooner or later turn to something stirring; they will decide again to live strenuously, or romantically.

The Old South may indeed be a hall hung with splendid tapestries in which no one would care to live; but from them we can learn something of how to live.

Bibliography

Books and Articles

Alexander, E. Porter, *Military Memoirs of a Confederate*, New York: Charles Scribner's Sons, 1907.

Allen, James Lane, *Flute and Violin*, New York: The Macmillan Company, 1925.

——. *The Reign of Law*, New York: The Macmillan Company, 1900.

Andrews, Eliza Frances, *The War-time Journal of a Georgia Girl*, New York: D. Appleton and Company, 1908.

Avary, Myrta Lockett, *Dixie After the War*, New York: Doubleday, Page, and Company, 1906.

Avirett, James B., *The Memoirs of General Turner Ashby and His Compeers*, Baltimore: Shelby and Dulany, 1867.

——. *The Old Plantation*, New York: F. Tennyson Neely Company, 1901.

Aycock, Charles Brantley, *The Life and Speeches of Charles Brantley Aycock* (ed. R. D. W. Connor and Clarence Poe), Garden City: Doubleday, Page, and Company, 1912.

Baldwin, Joseph Glover, *The Flush Times of Alabama and Mississippi*, Americus, Ga.: American Book Company, 1853.

Bassett, John Spencer, *The Southern Plantation Overseer*, Northampton, Mass.: Printed for Smith College, 1925.

Beard, Charles A., *The Economic Origins of Jeffersonian Democracy*, New York: The Macmillan Company, 1927.

Beatty, R. C., *Colonel William Byrd of Westover*, Boston: Houghton, Mifflin Company, 1932.

Beaty, John Owen, *John Esten Cooke, Virginian*, New York: Columbia University Press, 1922.

Beauregard, P. G. T., *A Commentary on the Campaign and Battle of Manassas*, New York: G. P. Putnam's Sons, 1891.

Beveridge, Albert J., *Abraham Lincoln* (2 vols.), Boston: Houghton, Mifflin Company, 1928.

Beverley, Robert, *The History of Virginia*, Richmond: J. W. Randolph, 1855.

Bledsoe, Albert Taylor, *An Essay on Liberty and Slavery*, Philadelphia: J. B. Lippincott Company, 1856.

———. *An Examination of President Edwards' Inquiry into the Freedom of the Will*, Philadelphia: H. Hooker, 1845.

———. *Is Davis a Traitor?*, Baltimore: Innes and Company, 1866.

Brown, Samuel R., *The Western Gazetteer; or Emigrants' Directory*, Auburn, N.Y.: H. C. Southwick, 1817.

Brown, William Garrott, *A Gentleman of the South*, New York: The Macmillan Company, 1903.

———. "The Ku Klux Movement," *Atlantic Monthly*, LXXXVII (May, 1901), pp. 634-644.

Bruce, Philip A., *Institutional History of Virginia* (2 vols.), New York: G. P. Putnam's Sons, 1910.

———. *The Plantation Negro as a Freedman*, New York: G. P. Putnam's Sons, 1889.

Buck, Paul, *The Road to Reunion*, Boston: Little, Brown, and Company, 1937.

Buckingham, J. S., *The Slave States of America*, London and Paris: Fisher, Son and Company, 1842.

Busch, Moritz, *Bismarck: Some Secret Pages of His History* (2 vols.), New York: The Macmillan Company, 1898.

Cable, George W., *The Creoles of Louisiana*, New York: Charles Scribner's Sons, 1884.

———. *John March, Southerner*, New York: Grosset and Dunlap, Inc., 1894.

———. *The Negro Question*, New York: Charles Scribner's Sons, 1910.

———. *Old Creole Days*, New York: Charles Scribner's Sons, 1927.

———. *The Silent South*, New York: Charles Scribner's Sons, 1885.

Campbell, Lily B. (ed.), *Mirror for Magistrates*, Cambridge: The University Press, 1938.

Carpenter, Jesse Thomas, *The South as a Conscious Minority*, New York: New York University Press, 1930.

Cartwright, Peter, *Autobiography*, New York: Carlton and Porter, 1857.

Cary, Constance, *Recollections Grave and Gay*, New York: Charles Scribner's Sons, 1911.

Cash, W. J., *The Mind of the South*, New York: Alfred A. Knopf, Inc., 1941.

Chamberlain, Daniel H., "Reconstruction in South Carolina," *Atlantic Monthly*, LXXXVII (April, 1901), pp. 473-484.

Chesnut, Mary Boykin, *A Diary from Dixie*, New York: D. Appleton and Company, 1905.

Chevalier, Michael, *Society, Manners and Politics in the United States*, Boston: Weeks, Jordan, and Company, 1839.

Clark, Thomas D., *The Rampaging Frontier*, Indianapolis: The Bobbs-Merrill Company, 1939.

Clarke, James Freeman, *Autobiography, Diary and Correspondence*, Boston: Houghton, Mifflin Company, 1891.

Clay-Clopton, Virginia, *A Belle of the Fifties*, New York: Doubleday, Page, and Company, 1904.

Code of Honor, The. Its Rationale and Uses, By the Tests of Common Sense and Good Morals, with the Effects of its Preventive Remedies, New Orleans: E. A. Brandag and Company, 1883.

Cooke, John Esten, *Hammer and Rapier*, New York: G. W. Carleton and Company, 1870.

———. *The Heir of Gaymount*, New York: Van Evrie, Horton and Company, 1870.

———. *A Life of General Robert E. Lee*, New York: D. Appleton and Company, 1871.

———. *Mohun, or the Last Days of Lee and his Paladins*, New York: F. J. Huntington, 1869.

———. *Surry of Eagle's-Nest*, New York: G. W. Dillingham, 1894.

———. *Wearing of the Gray*, New York: E. B. Treat and Company, 1867.

Couch, W. T. (ed.), *Culture in the South*, Chapel Hill: The University of North Carolina Press, 1934.

Coulter, E. Merton, *College Life in the Old South*, New York: The Macmillan Company, 1928.

Craddock, Charles Egbert, *Where the Battle Was Fought*, Boston: Houghton, Mifflin Company, 1892.

Craven, Avery, *Edmund Ruffin, Southerner*, New York: D. Appleton and Company, 1932.

———. *The Repressible Conflict*, Baton Rouge, La.: The Louisiana State University Press, 1939.

Cumming, Kate, *A Journal of Hospital Life*, Louisville: John P. Morton and Company, 1866.

Curry, J. L. M., *The Southern States of the American Union*, Richmond: B. F. Johnson Publishing Company, 1895.

Cutting, Elizabeth, *Jefferson Davis*, New York: Dodd, Mead and Company, 1930.

Dabney, Charles W., *Universal Education in the South*, Chapel Hill: The University of North Carolina Press, 1936.

Dabney, Robert Lewis, *A Defence of Virginia and through Her of the South*, New York: E. J. Hale and Son, 1867.

Dabney, Virginius, *Liberalism in the South*, Chapel Hill: The University of North Carolina Press, 1932.

Daniel, F. E., *Recollections of a Rebel Surgeon*, Austin, Tex.: Von Boeckmann, Schutze and Company, 1899.

Davis, Jefferson, *The Rise and Fall of the Confederate Government* (2 vols.), New York: D. Appleton and Company, 1881.

Dawson, Sarah Morgan, *A Confederate Girl's Diary*, Boston: Houghton, Mifflin Company, 1913.

Dean, Henry Clay, *The Crimes of the Civil War*, Baltimore: printed for the publisher by Innes and Company, 1868.

De Leon, Thomas Cooper, *Belles, Beaux, and Brains of the 60's*, New York: G. W. Dillingham, 1909.

——. *Four Years in Rebel Capitals*, Mobile: Gossip Printing Company, 1890.

Dixon, Thomas, *The Clansman*, New York: Doubleday, Page, and Company, 1905.

——. *The Leopard's Spots: A Romance of the White Man's Burden*, New York: Doubleday, Page, and Company, 1902.

——. *The Traitor*, New York: Doubleday, Page, and Company, 1907.

Douglas, Henry Kyd, *I Rode with Stonewall*, Chapel Hill: The University of North Carolina Press, 1940.

Duke, Basil W., *History of Morgan's Cavalry*, Cincinnati: Miami Printing and Publishing Company, 1867.

——. *Reminiscences of General Basil W. Duke*, Garden City: Doubleday, Page, and Company, 1911.

Dunning, William A., *Essays on the Civil War and Reconstruction*, London: The Macmillan Company, 1898.

Early, Jubal Anderson, *A Memoir of the Last Year of the War for Independence*, Lynchburg, Va.: C. W. Britton, 1867.

Eaton, Clement, *Freedom of Thought in the Old South*, Durham: Duke University Press, 1940.

Eggleston, George Cary, *A Rebel's Recollections*, New York: G. P. Putnam's Sons, 1889.

Elliott, E. N. and others, *Cotton is King, and Pro-Slavery Arguments*, Augusta, Ga.: Pritchard, Abbott and Loomis, 1860.

Ferral, S. A., *A Ramble of Six Thousand Miles through the United States of America*, London: Effingham Wilson, 1832.

Fitsgerald, Virginia, "A Southern College Boy Eighty Years Ago," *South Atlantic Quarterly*, XX (July, 1921), pp. 236-246.

Fitzgerald, O. P., *Judge Longstreet*, Nashville: Publishing House of the Methodist Episcopal Church, South, 1891.

Fitzhugh, George, *Sociology for the South*, Richmond: A. Morris, 1854.

Flanders, Ralph Betts, *Plantation Slavery in Georgia*, Chapel Hill: University of North Carolina Press, 1933.

Fleming, Walter L., *Documentary History of Reconstruction* (2 vols.), Cleveland: Arthur H. Clark, 1906-7.

Fox, John, Jr., *The Little Shepherd of Kingdom Come*, New York: Charles Scribner's Sons, 1909.

Freeman, Douglas S., *R. E. Lee* (4 vols.), New York: Charles Scribner's Sons, 1934-5.

——. *The South to Posterity*, New York: Charles Scribner's Sons, 1939.

Fremantle, Arthur J. L., *Three Months in the Southern States*, New York: Bradburn, 1864.

Fulkerson, Horace, *Random Recollections of Early Days in Mississippi*, Vicksburg: Vicksburg Printing and Publishing Company, 1885.

Gaines, Francis Pendleton, *The Southern Plantation*, New York: Columbia University Press, 1924.

Gay, Mary A., *Life in Dixie During the War*, Atlanta: Foote and Davies, 1894.

Ghodes, Clarence, "Some Notes on the Unitarian Church in the Ante-bellum South," *American Studies in Honor of William K. Boyd*, Durham: Duke University Press, 1940, pp. 327-366.

Gildersleeve, Basil, "The Creed of the Old South," *Atlantic Monthly*, LXIX (January, 1892), pp. 75-87.

———. "A Southerner in the Peloponnesian War," *Atlantic Monthly*, LXXX (September, 1897), pp. 330-342.

Glasgow, Ellen, *The Battle-Ground*, Garden City: Doubleday, Page, and Company, 1922.

———. *The Descendant*, New York: Harper and Brothers, 1897.

———. *The Voice of the People*, New York: Doubleday, Doran and Company, 1936.

Gordon, John B., *Reminiscences of the Civil War*, New York: Charles Scribner's Sons, 1903.

Grady, Henry W., *The Complete Orations and Speeches of Henry W. Grady*, New York: Hinds, Noble, and Eldredge, 1910.

Grayson, William J., *The Hireling and the Slave*, Charleston: McCarter and Company, 1856.

Grund, Francis J., *The Americans in their Moral, Social, and Political Relations*, Boston: March, Capen and Lyon, 1837.

Hague, Parthenia Antoinette, *A Blockaded Family*, Boston: Houghton, Mifflin Company, 1888.

Hall, Basil, *Travels in North America in the Years 1827 and 1828* (2 vols.), Philadelphia: Carey, Lea, and Carey, 1829.

Hamilton, Thomas, *Men and Manners in America* (2 vols.), Edinburgh: W. Blackwood, 1833.

Harris, Joel Chandler, *Free Joe and Other Georgia Sketches*, New York: Charles Scribner's Sons, 1897.

———. *Gabriel Tolliver: A Story of Reconstruction*, New York: McClure, Phillips and Company, 1902.

———. *Mingo and Other Sketches in Black and White*, Boston: James R. Osgood, 1884.

———. *On the Wings of Occasions*, New York: Doubleday, Page, and Company, 1900.

Harris, Julia Collier (ed.), *Joel Chandler Harris, Editor and Essayist*, Chapel Hill: The University of North Carolina Press, 1931.

Haworth, Paul, *George Washington: Country Gentleman,* Indianapolis: The Bobbs-Merrill Company, 1925.

Hawthorne, Nathaniel, *The Works of Nathaniel Hawthorne* (Standard Library Edition, 15 vols.), Boston: Houghton, Mifflin Company, 1883.

Herbert, Hilary (ed.), *Why the Solid South? Or, Reconstruction and its Results,* Baltimore: R. H. Woodward and Company, 1890.

Hesseltine, W. B., *A History of the South,* New York: Prentice-Hall, Inc., 1941.

Hodgson, Joseph, *The Cradle of the Confederacy,* Mobile: Register Publishing Office, 1876.

Honeywell, Roy J., *The Educational Work of Thomas Jefferson,* Cambridge: Harvard University Press, 1931.

Hood, John B., *Advance and Retreat,* New Orleans: Published for the Hood Orphan Memorial Fund, 1880.

Hubbell, Jay B., *The Last Years of Henry Timrod,* Durham: The Duke University Press, 1941.

Ingraham, J. H., *The Sunny South,* Philadelphia: G. G. Evans, 1860.

James, G. P. R., *The History of Chivalry,* New York: Harper and Brothers, 1862.

Jefferson, Thomas, *Works* (Federal Edition 12 vols.), New York: G. P. Putnam's Sons, 1904-5.

Johnson, Thomas Cary, *Scientific Interests in the Old South,* New York: D. Appleton-Century Company, Inc., 1936.

Johnson, William B., *The Loves of Jonathan and Virginia,* Philadelphia (no publisher): 1873.

Johnston, Joseph E., *Narrative of Military Operations,* New York: D. Appleton Company, 1874.

Jones, Charles C., Jr., *Historical Sketch of the Chatham Artillery,* Albany: J. Munsell, 1867.

Jones, John Beauchamp, *A Rebel War Clerk's Diary* (2 vols.), Philadelphia: J. B. Lippincott Company, 1866.

Jones, J. William, *Life and Letters of Robert Edward Lee,* New York: The Neale Publishing Company, 1906.

Kell, John McIntosh, *Recollections of Naval Life,* Washington: The Neale Company, 1900.

Kemble, Frances Anne, *Journal of a Residence on a Georgian Plantation in 1838-39,* New York: Harper and Brothers, 1863.

Kennedy, John P., *Horse-Shoe Robinson,* New York: American Book Company, 1937.

——. *Swallow Barn,* New York: G. P. Putnam's Sons, 1906.

Kennedy, W. G., *Ichabod, or, The Glory of the South Has Departed, and Other Poems,* Sumter, S.C.: W. G. Kennedy, 1882.

King, Grace, *Balcony Stories,* New York: The Macmillan Company, 1925.

———. *Monsieur Motte*, New York: A. C. Armstrong, 1888.

———. *Tales of a Time and Place*, New York: Harper and Brothers, 1892.

Kirke, Edmund [James Roberts Gilmore], *Life in Dixie's Land*, London: Ward and Lock, 1863.

Le Conte, Joseph, *'Ware Sherman*, Berkeley: University of California Press, 1937.

Le Grand, Julia, *The Journal of Julia Le Grand*, Richmond: Everett, Waddey Company, 1911.

Leigh, Frances Butler, *Ten Years on a Georgia Plantation*, London: Richard Bentley, 1883.

Lloyd, Arthur Young, *The Slavery Controversy*, Chapel Hill: The University of North Carolina Press, 1939.

Longstreet, James, *From Manassas to Appomattox*, Philadelphia: J. B. Lippincott Company, 1896.

Lothian, Marquess of, *The Confederate Secession*, Edinburgh: William Blackwood and Sons, 1864.

Lunt, George, *The Origin of the Late War*, New York: D. Appleton Company, 1867.

Madison, James, *Papers of James Madison* (3 vols.), Washington: Langtree and O'Sullivan, 1840.

Magruder, Julia, *Across the Chasm*, New York: Charles Scribner's Sons, 1885.

———. *Miss Ayr of Virginia*, Chicago: A. S. Stone and Company, 1896.

Malone, Dumas, *Edwin A. Alderman*, New York: Doubleday, Doran and Company, Inc., 1940.

Marshall, Charles, *An Aide-de-Camp of Lee*, Boston: Little, Brown and Company, 1927.

Martineau, Harriet, *Society in America*, New York: Saunders and Otley, 1837.

Maury, Dabney H., *Reminiscences of a Virginian in the Mexican, Indian, and Civil Wars*, New York: Charles Scribner's Sons, 1894.

Miller, Stephen F., *Bench and Bar of Georgia*, Philadelphia: J. P. Lippincott Company, 1858.

Mims, Edwin, *Sidney Lanier*, Boston: Houghton Mifflin Company, 1905.

Monteiro, A., *War Reminiscences by the Surgeon of Mosby's Command*, Richmond: Everett Waddey Company, 1890.

Morgan, Mrs. Irby, *How It Was*, Nashville: Publishing House of the Methodist Episcopal Church, South, 1892.

Morton, Louis, *Robert Carter of Nomini Hall*, Williamsburg, Va.: Colonial Williamsburg, 1941.

Mosby, John Singleton, *Mosby's War Reminiscences and Stuart's Cavalry Campaigns*, New York: Dodd, Mead and Company, 1887.

Moses, Montrose J., *The Literature of the South*, New York: Thomas Y. Crowell Company, 1910.

Murphy, Edgar Gardner, *The Problems of the Present South*, New York: The Macmillan Company, 1904.

M'Caleb, Thomas (ed.), *The Louisiana Book*, New Orleans: B. F. Straughan, 1894.

McDonald, Mrs. Cornelia, *A Diary*, Nashville: Cullom and Ghertner, 1935.

McGuire, Hunter, and Christian, George L., *The Confederate Cause and Conduct in the War Between the States*, Richmond: L. H. Jenkins, 1907.

McGuire, Judith W., *Diary of a Southern Refugee*, Richmond: J. W. Randolph, 1889.

McIlwaine, Shields, *The Southern Poor-White from Lubberland to Tobacco Road*, Norman: University of Oklahoma Press, 1939.

North Carolina Normal and Industrial College, *Charles Duncan McIver*, Greensboro: J. J. Stone, 1907.

Olmsted, Frederick Law, *The Cotton Kingdom* (2 vols.), New York: Mason Brothers, 1861.

——. *A Journey in the Seaboard Slave States* (2 vols.), New York: Dix and Edwards, 1856.

Page, Thomas Nelson, *Bred in the Bone*, New York: Charles Scribner's Sons, 1912.

——. *The Burial of the Guns*, New York: Charles Scribner's Sons, 1910.

——. *Gordon Keith*, New York: Charles Scribner's Sons, 1912.

——. *John Marvel, Assistant*, New York: Charles Scribner's Sons, 1910.

——. *The Old Dominion*, New York: Charles Scribner's Sons, 1910.

——. *In Ole Virginia*, New York: Charles Scribner's Sons, 1926.

——. *Red Rock*, New York: Charles Scribner's Sons, 1925.

——. "The Southern People During Reconstruction," *Atlantic Monthly*, LXXXVII (September, 1901), pp. 289-304.

Page, Walter Hines, *The Rebuilding of Old Commonwealths*, New York: Doubleday, Page, and Company, 1905.

——. *The Southerner, A Novel; Being the Autobiography of Nicholas Worth*, New York: Doubleday, Page, and Company, 1909.

——. "Study of an Old Southern Borough," *Atlantic Monthly*, XLVII (May, 1881), pp. 648-658.

Parrington, Vernon L., *Main Currents in American Thoughts* (3 vols.), New York: Harcourt, Brace and Company, Inc., 1927-30.

Pember, Phoebe Yates, *A Southern Woman's Story*, New York: G. W. Carleton, 1879.

Phillips, U. B., *Life and Labor in the Old South*, Boston: Little, Brown and Company, 1929.

Pike, James S., *The Prostrate State*, New York: D. Appleton and Company, 1874.

Poe, Edgar Allan, *The Complete Works of Edgar Allan Poe* (17 vols.), New York: E. R. Dumont, 1902.

Plutarch, *Lives of Illustrious Men* (3 vols.), Chicago: S. A. Maxwell Company, n.d.

Pollard, Edward A., *Life of Jefferson Davis*, Philadelphia: National Publishing Company, 1869.

———. *The Lost Cause*, New York: E. B. Treat, 1866.

Power, Tyrone, *Impressions of America; During the Years 1833, 1834, and 1835* (2 vols.), Philadelphia: Carey, Lea, and Blanchard, 1836.

Pro-Slavery Argument, The, Charleston, S.C.: Walker, Richard, and Company, 1852.

Pryor, Mrs. Roger A., *Reminiscences of Peace and War*, New York: The Macmillan Company, 1905.

Putnam, Sallie A., *Richmond During the War*, New York: G. W. Carleton and Company, 1867.

Quintard, Charles Todd, *Doctor Quintard*, Sewanee, Tenn.: The University Press, 1905.

Ramsdell, Charles W., "Lincoln and Fort Sumter," *Journal of Southern History*, III (August, 1937), pp. 259-288.

Read, Opie, *The American Cavalier*, Chicago: Thompson and Thomas, 1904.

———. *A Kentucky Colonel*, Chicago: F. J. Schulte and Company, 1891.

———. *A Tennessee Judge*, Chicago: Laird and Lee, 1893.

Richardson, E. Ramsay, *Little Aleck*, Indianapolis: The Bobbs-Merrill Company, 1932.

Roman, Alfred, *Military Operations of General Beauregard*, New York: Harper and Brothers, 1884.

Ross, Fitzgerald, *A Visit to the Cities and Camps of the Confederate States*, London: William Blackwood and Sons, 1865.

Royall, William L., *Some Reminiscences*, New York: The Neale Publishing Company, 1909.

Sage, Bernard, *The Republic of Republics*, Boston: Little, Brown and Company, 1881.

Seitz, Don C., *Famous American Duels*, New York: Thomas Y. Crowell Company, 1929.

Semmes, Raphael, *A Memoir of Service Afloat*, Baltimore: Kelly, Piet, and Company, 1869.

Simms, William Gilmore, *Poems Descriptive, Dramatic, Legendary, and Contemplative*, New York: Redfield, 1853.

Sinclair, Arthur, *Two Years on the Alabama*, Boston: Lee and Shephard, 1896.

Smedes, Susan Dabney, *Memorials of a Southern Planter*, Baltimore: Cushings and Bailey, 1888.

Smith, F. Hopkinson, *Colonel Carter of Cartersville*, New York: Charles Scribner's Sons, 1908.

———. *Colonel Carter's Christmas*, New York: Charles Scribner's Sons, 1907.

Smith, John, *Travels and Works of Captain John Smith* (2 vols.), Edinburgh: John Grant, 1910.

Southwood, Marion, *Beauty and Booty,* New York: published for the author by M. Doolady, 1867.

Spencer, Cornelia Phillips, *The Last Ninety Days of the War in North Carolina,* New York: Watchman Publishing Company, 1866.

Spencer, Theodore, *Death and Elizabethan Tragedy,* Cambridge: Harvard University Press, 1936.

Stephens, Alexander H., *A Constitutional View of the Late War Between the States* (2 vols.), Philadelphia: National Publishing Company, 1868-70.

Stiles, Robert, *Four Years Under Marse Robert,* New York: Neale Publishing Company, 1903.

Sullivan, Edward, *Rambles and Scrambles in North and South America,* London: R. Bentley, 1852.

Sweet, W. W., *The Methodist Episcopal Church and the Civil War,* Cincinnati: W. K. Stewart, 1912.

Sydnor, Charles, "The Southerner and the Laws," *Journal of Southern History,* VI (February, 1940), pp. 3-23.

Tandy, Jeannette Reid, "Pro-Slavery Propaganda in American Fiction in the Fifties," *South Atlantic Quarterly,* XXI (January, 1922), pp. 41-52.

Tate, Allen, *Reactionary Essays on Poetry and Ideas,* New York: Charles Scribner's Sons, 1936.

Taylor, Richard, *Destruction and Reconstruction,* New York: D. Appleton Company, 1879.

Thomas, F. W., *John Randolph of Roanoke and Other Sketches of Characters, Including William Wirt,* Philadelphia: A. Hart, 1853.

Trent, William Peterfield, "Dominant Forces in Southern Life," *Atlantic Monthly,* LXXIX (January, 1897), pp. 42-53.

——. "Gleanings from an Old Southern Newspaper," *Atlantic Monthly,* LXXXV (September, 1900), pp. 356-364.

——. *Robert E. Lee,* Boston: Small, Maynard and Company, 1899.

——. *William Gilmore Simms,* Boston: Houghton, Mifflin Company, 1892.

Trollope, Frances, *Domestic Manners of the Americans,* London: Whittaker, Treacher, and Company, 1832.

Tucker, N. B., *The Cavaliers of Virginia,* London: A. K. Newman, 1837.

Twelve Southerners, *I'll Take My Stand,* New York: Harper and Brothers, 1930.

Wade, John Donald, *Augustus Baldwin Longstreet,* New York: The Macmillan Company, 1924.

——. "Profits and Losses in the Life of Joel Chandler Harris," *American Review,* I (April, 1933), pp. 17-35.

Warre-Cornish, F., *Chivalry,* London: The Macmillan Company, 1901.

Washington, George, *The Writings of George Washington from the Official Manuscript Sources* (37 vols.), Washington: United States Printing Office, 1931-40.

Watterson, Henry, *The Compromises of Life*, New York: Fox, Duffield and Company, 1903.

Wertenbaker, Thomas Jefferson, *The First Americans*, New York: The Macmillan Company, 1927.

———. *Patrician and Plebeian in Virginia*, Charlottesville, Va.: The Michie Company, 1910.

Whipple, Henry Benjamin, *Southern Diary*, Minneapolis: The University of Minnesota Press, 1937.

Wilkinson, J., *Narrative of a Blockade Runner*, New York: Sheldon and Company, 1877.

Williamson, James J., *Mosby's Rangers*, New York: R. B. Kenyon, 1896.

Wilson, Augusta Evans, *Devota*, New York: G. W. Dillingham, 1907.

———. *Macaria; or, Altars of Sacrifice*, Richmond: West and Johnston, 1864.

———. *St. Elmo*, Chicago: M. A. Donohue and Company, n.d.

———. *A Speckled Bird*, New York: G. W. Dillingham, 1902.

Wilson, John Lyde, *The Code of Honor; or Rules for the Government of Principals and Seconds in Duelling*, Charleston: James Phinney, 1858.

Wilson, Woodrow, *Division and Reunion*, New York: Longmans, Green and Company, 1893.

———. "The Reconstruction of the Southern States," *Atlantic Monthly*, LXXXVII (January, 1901), pp. 1-15.

Wirt, William, *Letters of a British Spy*, New York: Harper and Brothers, 1861.

Wise, John S., *The End of an Era*, Boston: Houghton, Mifflin Company, 1900.

Wright, Louis B., *The First Gentlemen of Virginia*, San Marino, Calif.: The Huntington Library, 1940.

Wright, Louise Wigfall, *A Southern Girl in '61*, New York: Doubleday, Page, and Company, 1905.

Yeats, W. B., *A Vision*, London: The Macmillan Company, 1937.

Contemporary Southern Periodicals

Bob Taylor's Magazine (Nashville, 1905-1906).

Confederate Veteran, The (Nashville, 1893-1932).

Danville Quarterly Review (Danville, Ky., 1861-1864).

De Bow's Review (New Orleans, 1846-1880).

Land We Love, The (Charlotte, 1866-1869).

New Eclectic, The (Baltimore, 1869-1870).

Our Living and Our Dead (Raleigh, 1874-1876).

Richmond Eclectic, The (Richmond, 1866-1868).

Russell's Magazine (Charleston, 1857-1860).

Scott's Monthly Magazine (Atlanta, 1865-1869).

Southern Bivouac, The (Louisville, 1885-1887).

Southern Historical Society Papers (Richmond, 1876-1909).

Southern Literary Messenger, The (Richmond, 1834-1864).

Southern Magazine, The (Baltimore, 1870-1875).

Southern Quarterly Review (Charleston, 1842-1855).

Southern Review, The (Charleston, 1828-1832).

Southern Review, The (Baltimore, 1867-1879).

Taylor-Trotwood Magazine, The (Nashville, 1907-1910).

Tom Watson's Jeffersonian Magazine (Atlanta, 1907-1915).

Trotwood's Monthly (Nashville, 1905-1906).

Pamphlets

Alderman, E. A., *Sectionalism and Nationality*, New York: The New England Society of the City of New York, 1902.

———. *The Spirit of the South*, Berkeley: The University of California Press, 1906.

Bagby, George W., *A Week in Hepsidam*, Richmond: Geo. W. Cary, 1879.

Bruns, J. Dickson, M.D., *Address to the White League of New Orleans*, New Orleans: A. H. Hyatt, 1875.

Campbell, James B., *Two Letters from the Hon. James B. Campbell, U.S. Senator from South Carolina, on Public Affairs, and our Duties to the Colored Race*, Charleston: Walker, Evans, and Cogswell, 1868.

Chamberlayne, John Hampden, *Why Despair?*, Richmond: James E. Goode, 1880.

"Civis" [B. Puryear], *The Public School in Its Relation to the Negro*, Richmond: Clemmitt and Jones, 1877.

Dabney, R. L., *The New South*, Raleigh: Edwards, Broughton, and Co., 1882.

Fuzzlebug, Fritz [pseud?], *Prison Life During the Rebellion; Being a Brief Narrative of the Miseries and Sufferings of Six Hundred Confederate Prisoners Sent from Fort Delaware to Morris' Island to be Punished*, Singer's Glen, Va.: Joseph Funk's Sons, 1869.

Gordon, John M., *Burial of a Confederate Soldier*, [no imprint], 1865?

———. *Southern Rights, and Northern Wrongs*, Norfolk: Hodges Printing Company, 1872.

Harris, Chas., *The State Sovereignty Record of Massachusetts. By a Son of Norfolk*, Norfolk: J. W. Fatherly, 1872.

Lawrence, Effingham, *Race Issue*, New Orleans: Jas. A. Gresham, 1874.

McKim, Rev. Randolph H., *Lee The Christian Hero*, Washington, D.C.: Brentano's, 1907.

Norwood, Thomas M., *Civil Rights*, Washington: U.S. Government Printing Office, 1874.

Palmer, B. M., *The Present Issue and Its Issues*, Baltimore: John Murphy, 1872.

Pickens, Hon. Francis W., *Letter of Hon. Francis W. Pickens. The Crops and Condition of the Country. Effects of Emancipation. The Different Races of Mankind*, Charleston: Courier Job Press, 1866.

Rhett, R. B., Jr., *A Farewell to Subscribers of the Charleston Mercury*, Charleston: Courier Job Press, 1868?

Ruffin, Frank G., *The Cost and Outcome of Negro Education in Virginia*, Richmond: Everett Waddey, 1889.

Rutledge, Col. B. H., *Address* (Memorial Day, May 10, 1875), Charleston [no imprint].

Stephens, Alexander H., *Address of Hon. Alexander H. Stephens Before the General Assembly of the State of Georgia, 22nd February, 1866*, Milledgeville, Ga.: Boughton, Nisbet, Barnes, and Moore, 1866.

United Confederate Veterans, *First Annual Convention*, Chattanooga: [no imprint] 1890.

Wardlaw, James B., *Southern Literature—Its Status and Outlook*, Macon: J. W. Burke, 1890.

General

Battles and Leaders of the Civil War (ed. R. U. Johnson and C. C. Buel), New York: The Century Company, 1887-88. 4 vols.

Confederate Military History (ed. Clement A. Evans), Atlanta: Confederate Publishing Company, 1899. 12 vols.

Congressional Globe (XVII), Washington: Blair and Rives, 1848.

Dictionary of American Biography (ed. Allen Johnson), New York: Charles Scribner's Sons, 1928-37. 20 vols.

Library of Southern Literature (ed. E. A. Alderman and Joel Chandler Harris), Atlanta: Martin and Hoyt Company, 1909. 16 vols.

Register of Debates (IV), Washington: Gales and Seaton, 1828.

South in the Building of the Nation, The, Richmond: The Southern Historical Publishing Society, 1909. 12 vols.

War of the Rebellion, Washington: Government Printing Office, 1880-1901. 70 vols.

THE PUBLISHED WRITINGS OF
RICHARD M. WEAVER

by Paul Varnell

The items in this bibliography are arranged chronologically, and within each year into categories of books, articles in books, major articles and review articles, and short reviews. The only omissions of which I am aware are any reviews, save one, which Weaver wrote for the Chicago *Tribune:* the *Tribune* keeps no records of who reviews what books for it.

It is my pleasure to thank the people who provided aid and advice: Mr. and Mrs. Louis T. Dehmlow, who provided a partial list they had compiled; Prof. Richard Johannesen; Mr. Ronald J. Reinoehl, who provided items from early volumes of the *National Review* at a time when they were unavailable to me; and Mr. John F. Lulves, Jr., who originally suggested and encouraged publication.

1943
"The Older Religiousness in the South," *Sewanee Review,* LI (April, 1943), 237-49.

1944
"Albert Taylor Bledsoe," *Sewanee Review,* LII (Jan., 1944), 34-45.
"The South and the Revolt of Nihilism," *South Atlantic Quarterly,* XLIII (April, 1944), 194-98.

1945
"Southern Chivalry and Total War," *Sewanee Review,* LIII (April, 1945), 267-78.
"Scholars or Gentlemen?", *College English,* VII (Nov., 1945-46), 72-77.

1947
Review of Leo Daeck, *The Pharisees and Other Essays, Commonweal,* XLVI 1947), 484.

Review of Robert Rylee, *The Ring and the Cross, Commonweal,* XLVII (1947-48), 46-48.

Review of Ward Moore, *Greener Than You Think, Commonweal,* XLVII (1947-48), 179-80.

Review of Hermann Broch, *The Sleepwalkers, Commonweal,* XLVII (1947-48), 620-22.

1948

Ideas Have Consequences. Chicago: University of Chicago Press. (Reprinted in paperback, 1960.)

Letter to *The New York Times Book Review,* March 21, 1948, p. 29. (Reply to Howard Mumford Jones's review of *Ideas Have Consequences.*)

"The Etiology of the Image," *Poetry,* LXXII (June, 1948), 156-61. (Review of Rosemond Tuve, *Elizabethan and Metaphysical Imagery.*)

"Orbis Americanum," *Sewanee Review,* LVI (1948), 319-23. (Review of Henry B. Parkes, *The American Experience* and Leo Gurko, *The Angry Decade.*)

"Lee the Philosopher," *Georgia Review,* II (Fall, 1948), 297-303.

"To Write the Truth," *College English,* X (Oct., 1948), 25-30.

Review of Beatrice Webb, *Our Partnership, Commonweal,* XLVIII, (1948), 166-67.

Review of Charles A. Lindbergh, *Of Flight and Life, Commonweal,* XLVIII (1948), 573.

Review of *The Diary of Pierce Loval, Commonweal,* XLIX (1948-49), 122.

1949

"Culture and Reconstruction," *Sewanee Review,* LVII (1949), 714-18. (Review of T. S. Eliot, *Notes Toward a Definition of Culture.*)

"The Rhetoric of Social Science," *Journal of General Education,* IV (1949-50), 189-201. (Reprinted in *The Ethics of Rhetoric.*)

Review of Samuel H. Beer, *The City of Reason, Commonweal,* L (1949), 73.

Review of Bertrand de Jouvenel, *On Power, Commonweal,* L (1949), 466-68.

1950

"Agrarianism in Exile," *Sewanee Review,* LVIII (Autumn, 1950), 586-606.

Review of Henry Steele Comager, *The American Mind, Commonweal,* LII (1950), 101-103.

Review of Herbert Feis, *The Road to Pearl Harbor, Commonweal,* LIII (1950-51), 20-22.

Review of George Orwell, *Shooting an Elephant, Commonweal,* LIII (1950-51), 283-84.

1951

"Nehru: Philosopher, Prophet, Politician," *Commonweal,* LIV (1951), 432-33. (Review of Jawaharlal Nehru and Norman Cousins, *Talks with Nehru.*)

Review of Ferdinand A. Hermeus, *Europe Between Democracy and Anarchy,*
Commonweal, LIV (1951), 266.
Review of Edward Crankshaw, *Cracks in the Kremlin Wall,* Commonweal,
LIV (1951), 582.

1952
"The Tennessee Agrarians," *Shenandoah,* III (1952), 3-10.
"Aspects of the Southern Philosophy," *Hopkins Review,* V (1952), 5-21. (Re-
printed in Rubin and Jacobs, *infra.*)
"Looking for an Argument," *College English,* XIV (1952-53), 210-16
(co-author).

1953
The Ethics of Rhetoric. Chicago: Henry Regnery Co. (Reprinted in paper-
back, 1965.)
"Aspects of the Southern Philosophy," in Louis D. Rubin, Jr., and Robert
D. Jacobs, eds., *Southern Renascence* (Baltimore, 1953), 14-30. (Reprinted
in paperback, 1966.)
"The Impact of Society on Mr. Russell," *Commonweal,* LVII (1953), 504.
(Review of Bertrand Russell, *The Impact of Science on Society.*)
"And for Yale," *Commonweal,* LVIII (1953), 31-32. (Review of Editors of
the *Yale Daily News, Seventy Five.*)

1954
"The Spoiled Child Psychology," from *Ideas Have Consequences,* reprinted
in T. A. Barnhart, W. A. Donnelly, and L. C. Smith, eds., *Viewpoints:
Readings for Analysis.* New York, 1954, 423-34.
"Liberalism with a Ballast," *Sewanee Review,* LXII (April, 1954), 334-41.
(Review of Lord Acton, *Essays on Church and State;* G. E. Fasnacht,
Acton's Political Philosophy; and Gertrude Himmelfarb, *Lord Acton.*)
Review of Russell Kirk, *A Program for Conservatives,* Chicago Sunday
Tribune Magazine of Books (Section IV), October 24, 1954, 3.

1955
"Ultimate Terms in Contemporary Rhetoric" from *The Ethics of Rhetoric,*
reprinted in *Perspectives, U.S.A.,* XI (1955), 122-41.
"History in a Dry Light," *Sewanee Review* LXIII (Spring, 1955), 280-86.
(Review of Clement Eaton, *A History of the Southern Confederacy* and
Thomas J. Pressley, *Americans Interpret Their Civil War.*)
"Who Are Today's Conservatives?", University of Chicago Round Table of
the Air (Broadcast No. 1092), February, 1955. (With Aaron Director and
S. G. Brown. Includes an excerpt from *The Ethics of Rhetoric.*)
"Easy Conclusion," *National Review,* I (Nov. 26, 1955), 29. (Review of Theo-
dore L. Lentz, *Towards a Science of Peace.*)

1956

"The Best of Everything," *National Review*, I (Feb. 1, 1956), 21-22. (Reprinted in *Life Without Prejudice*.)

"The Middle of the Road: Where It Leads," *Human Events*, March 24, 1956. (Reprinted as an American Conservative Union *Special Report*, January, 1966.)

"The Land and the Literature," *Sewanee Review*, LXIV (Summer, 1956), 485-98. (Review of Clifford Dowdey, *The Land They Fought For* and Willard Thorp, ed., *A Southern Reader*.)

"Misunderstood Man" *National Review*, I (Jan. 4, 1956), 30. (Review of Hudson Strode, *Jefferson Davis: American President, 1808-1861*.)

"From Poetry to Bitter Fruit," *National Review*, I (Jan. 25, 1956), 26-27. (Review of Joan Dunn, *Retreat from Learning*.)

"Mr. Hutchins as Prophet," *National Review*, I (Feb. 8, 1956), 26. (Review of R. M. Hutchins, *The Great Books: The Foundation of a Liberal Education*.)

"Language and the Crisis of Our Time," *National Review*, I (Feb. 15, 1956), 27. (Review of I. A. Richards, *Speculative Instruments*.)

"Cold Comfort," *National Review*, I (March 7, 1956), 29. (Review of R. M. MacIver, *The Pursuit of Happiness*.)

"Flesh for a Skeleton," *National Review*, I (March 28, 1956), 26. (Review of Tobias Dantzig, *Number: The Language of Science*.)

"Anybody's Guess," *National Review*, I (April 18, 1956), 20. (Review of P. M. Angle and E. S. Miers, eds., *The Living Lincoln*.)

"On Social Science," *National Review*, I (May 9, 1956), 20. (Review of Stuart Chase, *The Proper Study of Mankind*.)

"Safe for a While," *National Review*, II (June 20, 1956), 21. (Review of Lester Asheim, ed., *The Future of the Book*.)

"Informed and Urbane," *National Review*, II (June 27, 1956), 19. (Review of John P. Dyer, *Ivory Towers in the Market Place*.)

Review of S. F. Bemis, *John Quincy Adams and the Union*, *Freeman*, VI (June, 1956), 62-64.

"Which Ancestors?", *National Review*, II (July 25, 1956), 20-21. (Review of Russell Kirk, *Beyond the Dreams of Avarice*.)

"Inglorious Exit," *National Review*, II (August 18, 1956), 20-21. (Review of Charles P. Smith, *James Wilson: Founding Father*.)

"Social Science in Excelsis," *National Review*, II (Sept. 29, 1956), 18-19. (Review of Leonard White, ed., *The State of the Social Sciences*.)

"Education for What?", *National Review*, II (Nov. 24, 1956), 20-21. (Review of J. D. Redden and F. A. Ryan, *A Catholic Philosophy of Education*.)

Review of Arthur A. Ekirch, Jr., *The Decline of American Liberalism*, *Mississippi Valley Historical Review*, XLIII (1956-57), 469-70.

"Person and Journalist," *National Review*, II (Dec. 8, 1956), 19. (Review of Joseph F. Wall, *Henry Watterson, Reconstructed Rebel*.)

1957

Composition: A Course in Reading and Writing. New York: Holt, Rinehart, and Winston.

"The South and the American Union," in Louis D. Rubin and James J. Kilpatrick, eds., *The Lasting South* (Chicago, 1957), 46-68.

"Life Without Prejudice," *Modern Age,* I (Summer, 1957), 4-8. (Reprinted in *Life Without Prejudice*.)

"The Middle Way: A Political Meditation," *National Review,* III (Jan. 20, 1957), 63-64.

"The Roots of the Liberal Complacency," *National Review,* III (June 8, 1957), 541-43. (Reprinted in A. G. Heinsohn, *infra,* and in *Christian Economics.)*

"On Setting the Clock Right," *National Review,* IV (Oct. 13, 1957), 321-23.

"Cotton Culture," *National Review,* III (March, 16, 1957), 264. (Review of David L. Cohn, *The Life and Times of King Cotton.)*

"The Western Star," *National Review,* III (April 13, 1957), 358-59. (Review of Clement Eaton, *Henry Clay and the Art of American Politics.)*

"Proud 'City of God,'" *National Review,* III (June 15, 1957), 578. (Review of René Guerdan, *Byzantium: Its Triumphs and Tragedy.)*

"Integration is Communization," *National Review,* IV (July 13, 1957), 67-68. (Review of Hugh D. Price, *The Negro and Southern Politics;* Carl T. Rowan, *Go South to Sorrow;* and Leo Kuper, *Passive Resistance in South Africa.)*

Review of Amaury de Riencourt, *The Coming Caesars, Freeman,* VII (Oct., 1957), 61-63.

"Trumpet-Tongued Foe of Coercion," *National Review,* IV (Oct. 15, 1957), 307-308. (Review of R. D. Meade, *Patrick Henry: Patriot in the Making.)*

"Science and Sentimentalism," *National Review,* IV (Dec. 7, 1957), 524-25. (Review of André Missenard, *In Search of Man.)*

1958

"Individuality and Modernity," in Felix Morley, ed., *Essays on Individuality* (Princeton, 1958), 63-81.

"First in Peace," *National Review,* V (April 5, 1958), 329-30. (Review of Douglas S. Freeman, *George Washington: First in Peace.)*

"The Lincoln-Douglas Debates," *National Review,* VI (June 21, 1958), 18-19. (Review of P. M. Angle, ed., *Created Equal? The Complete Lincoln-Douglas Debates of 1858.)*

"Open All the Way," *National Review,* VI (Nov. 22, 1958), 339-40. (Review of D. J. Boorstin, *The Americans: The Colonial Experience.)*

1959

Education and the Individual. Philadelphia: Intercollegiate Society of Individualists. (Reprinted in the *Intercollegiate Review, infra,* and *Life Without Prejudice.)*

"Up From Liberalism," *Modern Age,* III (Winter, 1958-59), 21-32. (Reprinted in *Life Without Prejudice.)*

"The Regime of the South," *National Review,* VI (March 14, 1959), 587-89.

"Concealed Rhetoric in Scientistic Sociology," *Georgia Review,* XIII (Spring, 1959), 19-32. (Reprinted in Schoeck and Wiggins, *Scientism, infra.)*

"Contemporary Southern Literature," *Texas Quarterly,* II (Summer, 1959), 126-44.

"Reconstruction: Unhealed Wound," *National Review,* VI (Feb. 28, 1959), 559-60. (Review of Hodding Carter, *The Angry Scar.*)

Review of Forrest McDonald, *We The People, Freeman,* IX (May, 1959), 58-62.

"Christian Letters," *Modern Age,* III (Fall, 1959), 417-20. (Review of Randall Stewart, *American Literature and Christian Doctrine.*)

1960

"Concealed Rhetoric in Scientistic Sociology," in H. Schoeck and J. W. Wiggins, *Scientism and Values* (Princeton, 1960), 83-99.

"Conservatism and Libertarianism: The Common Ground," *The Individualist,* IV (old series, May, 1960), 4-8. (Reprinted in *Life Without Prejudice.*)

Mass Plutocracy," *National Review,* IX (Nov. 5, 1960), 273-75, 290. (Reprinted in *The Individualist,* V, October, 1960, 5-8.)

"Illusions of Illusion," *Modern Age,* IV (Summer, 1960), 316-20. (Review of M. Morton Auerbach, *The Conservative Illusion.*)

"Dilemma of the Intellectual," *National Review,* IX (Sept. 10, 1960), 153-54. (Review of G. B. de Huszar, ed., *The Intellectual: A Controversial Portrait.*)

1961

Relativism and the Crisis of Our Time. Philadelphia: Intercollegiate Society of Individualists.

"Relativism and the Use of Langauge," in H. Schoeck and J. W. Wiggins, *Relativism and the Study of Man* (Princeton, 1961), 236-54.

"Reflections of Modernity," in *Speeches of the Year,* Brigham Young University, 1961. (Reprinted in *Life Without Prejudice.*)

"History or Special Pleading?" *National Review,* X (Jan. 14, 1961), 21-22. (Review of Harvey Wish, *The American Historian.*)

"A Moral in a Word," *Modern Age,* V (Summer, 1961), 330-31. (Review of C. S. Lewis, *Studies in Words.*)

"The Altered Stand," *National Review,* X (June 17, 1961), 389-90. (Review of Robert Penn Warren, *The Legacy of the Civil War.*)

"Modern Letters Con and Pro," *Modern Age,* V (Fall, 1961), 426-27. (Review of Edward Dahlberg and Sir Herbert Read, *Truth Is More Sacred.*)

1962

"The Importance of Cultural Freedom," *Modern Age,* VI (Winter, 1961-62), 21-34. (Reprinted in Morley, *The Necessary Conditions, infra* and *Life Without Prejudice.*)

"The Roots of the Liberal Complacency," in A. G. Heinsohn, ed., *An Anthology of Conservative Writing in the U.S., 1932-1960* (Chicago, 1962), 54-58.

"A Hobble for Pegasus," *National Review,* XII (Jan. 16, 1962), 30-31. (Review of Robert E. Lane, *The Liberties of Wit.*)

"A Great Individualist," *Modern Age,* VI (Spring, 1962), 214-17. (Review of Guy J. Forgue, ed., *Letters of H. L. Mencken.*)

"Anatomy of Freedom," *National Review,* XIII (December 4, 1962), 443-44. (Review of Frank S. Meyer, *In Defense of Freedom.*)

1963

Academic Freedom: The Principle and the Problems. Philadelphia: Intercollegiate Society of Individualists.

"The Importance of Cultural Freedom," in Felix Morley, ed., *The Necessary Conditions for a Free Society* (Princeton, 1963), 142-60.

"Language Is Sermonic," in R. E. Nebergall, ed., *Dimensions of Rhetorical Scholarship* (Norman, Oklahoma, 1963), 49-63.

"The Power of the Word," from *Ideas Have Consequences,* reprinted in J. A. Rycenga and Joseph Schwartz, eds., *Perspectives on Language* (New York, 1963), 298-310.

"Two Types of American Individualism," *Modern Age,* VII (Spring, 1963), 119-34. (Reprinted in *Life Without Prejudice.*)

"The Southern Phoenix," *Georgia Review,* XVII (Spring, 1963), 6-17. (Review of paperback reissue of "Twelve Southerners," *I'll Take My Stand.*)

"A Further Testament," *Modern Age,* VII (Spring, 1963), 219-22. (Review of Joseph Wood Krutch, *More Lives Than One.*)

1964

Visions of Order. Baton Rouge: Louisiana State University Press.

"The Image of Culture," from *Visions of Order,* reprinted in *Modern Age,* VIII (Spring, 1964), 186-99.

"The Humanities in the Century of the Common Man," *New Individualist Review,* III, No. 3 (1964), 17-24.

"The Southern Tradition," *New Individualist Review,* III, No. 3 (1964), 7-16.

1965

Life Without Prejudice and Other Essays. Chicago: Henry Regnery Co.

"The Phaedrus and the Nature of Rhetoric," from *The Ethics of Rhetoric,* reprinted in M. A. Natanson and H. W. Johnstone, eds., *Philosophy, Rhetoric, and Argumentation* (Penn State, 1965), 63-79.

"The Spaciousness of the Old Rhetoric" and "The Phaedrus and the Nature of Rhetoric," from *The Ethics of Rhetoric,* reprinted in Joseph Schwartz and J. A. Rycenga, eds., *The Province of Rhetoric* (Ronald Press, 1965), 275-92, 311-29.

"Ultimate Terms in Contemporary Rhetoric," from *The Ethics of Rhetoric,* reprinted in Dudley Bailey, ed., *Essays on Rhetoric* (Oxford, 1965).

"Education and the Individual," reprinted in *Intercollegiate Review,* II (Sept., 1965), 68-76.

1967

Rhetoric and Composition, 2nd ed., revised with the assistance of Richard S. Beal. New York: Holt, Rinehart, and Winston.

1968

The Southern Tradition At Bay: A History of Postbellum Thought, edited by George Core and M. E. Bradford. New Rochelle, N.Y.: Arlington House. (Weaver's doctoral dissertation, originally titled "The Confederate South, 1865-1910: A Study in the Survival of a Mind and a Culture.")

"The American as a Regenerate Being," edited by George Core and M. E. Bradford, *Southern Review,* IV, n. s. (Summer, 1968), 633-46.

"Realism and the Local Color Interlude," edited by George Core, *Georgia Review,* XXII (Fall, 1968), 300-5.

Forthcoming

George Core and M. E. Bradford, eds., *Richard Weaver on Southern Life and Letters* (working title).

Ralph Eubanks, *et al.,* eds., an untitled collection of Weaver's articles on writing and rhetoric.

Some Articles about Weaver

Bryant, Don. C., review of *The Ethics of Rhetoric, Quarterly Journal of Speech,* LX (1954), 75-76.

Core, George, review of *Life Without Prejudice and Other Essays, Georgia Review,* XXI (Fall, 1967), 412-16.

Davidson, Donald, "The Inspired Amateur," *Modern Age,* X (Spring, 1966), 206-7. (Review of *Life Without Prejudice and Other Essays.*)

Davidson, Eugene, "Richard Malcolm Weaver—Conservative," *Modern Age,* VII (Summer, 1963), 226-30.

Ebbitt, Wilma R., "Richard M. Weaver, Teacher of Rhetoric," *Georgia Review,* XVII (Winter, 1963), 415-18.

Eubanks, Ralph T., "In Memoriam, Richard M. Weaver," *Georgia Review,* XVII (Winter, 1963), 412-15.

Geiger, George R., "We Note . . . the Consequences of Some Ideas," *Antioch Review,* VIII (June, 1948), 251-54. (Reprinted in Paul Bixler, ed., *The Antioch Review Anthology,* Cleveland, 1953, 411-15.)

"In Memoriam, Richard M. Weaver," *New Individualist Review,* II, No. 4 (Spring, 1963), 2.

Johannesen, Richard L., "Richard Weaver's View of Rhetoric and Criticism," *Southern Speech Journal,* XXXII (Winter, 1966), 133-45.

Kendall, Willmoore, "How to Read Richard Weaver," *Intercollegiate Review,* II (Sept., 1965), 77-86.

Kirk, Russell, "Richard M. Weaver, R.I.P.," *National Review,* XIV (April

23, 1963), 308. (Reprinted in *The Individualist*, II, new series, Sept., 1963, 2, and in *Confessions of a Bohemian Tory*, New York, 1963).

Kirk, Russell, "Ethical Labor," *Sewanee Review*, LXII (July, 1954), 485-503. (Review of *The Ethics of Rhetoric* with another book. Reprinted in *Beyond The Dreams of Avarice*, Chicago, 1956.)

Milione, E. Victor, "The Uniqueness of Richard M. Weaver," *Intercollegiate Review*, II (Sept., 1965), 67.

Muller, Herbert J., review of *Ideas Have Consequences*, *Antioch Review*, IX (March, 1949), 99-110.

Powell, James, "The Foundations of Weaver's Traditionalism," *New Individualist Review*, III, No. 3 (1964), 3-6.

Vivas, Eliseo, "The Mind of Richard Weaver," *Modern Age*, VIII (Summer, 1964), 307-10. (Review of *Visions of Order*.)

Wallraff, Charles F., review of *The Ethics of Rhetoric*, *Arizona Quarterly*, X (Summer, 1954), 183-85.

Index